307.1
T213 lem

1/2012

Empowerment on an Unstable Planet

EMPOWERMENT ON AN UNSTABLE PLANET

From Seeds of Human Energy to a Scale of Global Change

Daniel C. Taylor

Carl E. Taylor

Jesse O. Taylor

OXFORD
UNIVERSITY PRESS

Oxford University Press, Inc., publishes works that further
Oxford University's objective of excellence
in research, scholarship, and education.

Oxford   New York
Auckland   Cape Town   Dar es Salaam   Hong Kong   Karachi
Kuala Lumpur   Madrid   Melbourne   Mexico City   Nairobi
New Delhi   Shangha   Taipei   Toronto

With offices in
Argentina   Austria   Brazil   Chile   Czech Republic   France   Greece
Guatemala   Hungary   Italy   Japan   Poland   Portugal   Singapore
South Korea   Switzerland   Thailand   Turkey   Ukraine   Vietnam

Published by Oxford University Press, Inc.
198 Madison Avenue, New York, New York 10016
www.oup.com

Oxford is a registered trademark of Oxford University Press

Library of Congress Cataloging-in-Publication Data

Taylor, Daniel C.
Empowerment on an unstable planet : from seeds of human energy to a scale of global change / Daniel
C. Taylor, Carl E. Taylor, Jesse O. Taylor.
p. cm.
Includes bibliographical references and index.

ISBN 978-0-19-984296-4 (cloth : alk. paper)

1. Social change. 2. Social change—Case studies. 3. Economic development—Case studies.
4. Community action. 5. Social action. I. Taylor, Carl E. II. Taylor, Jesse O. III. Title.
HM831.T39 2012
307.1'401—dc23
2011026979

9 8 7 6 5 4 3 2 1

Typeset in Chaparral Pro
Printed on acid-free paper
Printed in United States of America

DEDICATION

In hope, for generations yet to come . . .

ACKNOWLEDGMENTS

We lead this list of thanks with a salute to Luke Taylor-Ide who worked at the center of the SEED-SCALE applications described in this book for both Afghanistan and Arunachal Pradesh, India, for five years. Luke is also the creator of a parallel to this book, an information-rich online platform for learning SEED-SCALE, to which we direct the reader's attention: www.seed-scale.org.

Also at the high table is our now-deceased colleague Jim Grant, who, as Executive Director of UNICEF, launched SEED-SCALE. Across the Atlantic is our longtime colleague Halfdan Mahler, who, as Director General of the World Health Organization, led fundamental work in community-based change for all. Singular mention is due Patricia Rosenfield, Chair of the Carnegie Scholars, a member of the original UNICEF task force, whose enthusiasm for this project has been balanced only by the rigor of her critique. Similarly, special thanks is due Betsy Taylor, who helped sort out dynamics within SEED; and also to Henry Taylor, who helped in the statistical analyses over the years. The original task-force members have been mentioned in our earlier volumes, and we remain profoundly grateful to each.

Teams of colleagues around the world have contributed as well. Some are named in the chapters, but many more are not:

In Arunachal Pradesh, first thanks goes to the women's action groups and farmers clubs that have for more than a decade implemented SEED-SCALE in their communities and daily lives. Among them we express individual appreciation to Gegong Apang, Tage Kanno, Omak Apang, Audrey Apang, Rima Langbia, Amko, Biri Mima, Byabang Rocket, Nani Sha, Pekyom Ringu, K. D. Singh, Oken Tayeng, and Nalong Mize, but there are many more than these, for such is the way with statewide social movements.

From the Afghanistan team, the wonderful women of Rostam and Saya Dara deserve special thanks, as do Shukria Hassan, Stan Becker, Besmillah Sakhizada, Mullah Azizi, Akbar, and others from Dehkudaidad: Said Arwal, Ajmal Shirzai, Rajpal Yadav, Ishfaq Hussain, Hamidullah Natiq, Seija Terry, and Chris Taylor. With great sadness, we also acknowledge our close friend and colleague Dan Terry, who lived and worked in Afghanistan for more than thirty years before being brutally murdered there months before this book was finished.

Many at Future Generations contributed, but needing individual mention are: Nawang Gurung, Traci Hickson, Laura Altobelli, Jason Calder, Flora MacDonald, Rebecca Vaus, LeeAnn Shreve, Peter Ide, Mike Stranahan, Henry Perry, Bob Fleming, Mike Rechlin, Dan Wessner, Deidre Heiner, Carol Mick, and Bruce Mukwatu. We are grateful also to the many students in the Future Generations Graduate School who contributed.

From the Tibet Autonomous Region and the Green Long March of China, first we thank the 1,000 *Pendebas* who in varying ways utilize the ideas herein. But without the extraordinary efforts of Chun-Wuei Su Chien, there would have been neither parks nor *Pendebas*. Many thanks also to Caroline Hsiao Van, Ding Zongyi, Tsering Norbu, Guangchun Lei, Cili Norbu, Robert Gibson, and Frances Fremont-Smith. A word of recognition, also, for certain concerned officials in the Communist Party in Tibet, where across three decades the lesson learned is that it is possible to deeply disagree, yet work in relationships that are highly productive for both sides. Bridging disagreement to create forward movement is one of the attributes of SEED-SCALE.

Over the decades, these ideas have evolved and been refined. Helpful critiques enriched our learning from a long list of people, of whom we single out a few: Abhay and Rani Bang; Raj, Mabelle, Shobha, and Ravi Arole; Sarah Werner, Kevin Starr, Nazo Kureshi. And specifically from Johns Hopkins: Tim Baker, Bill Reinke, Henry Mosley, Bob Lawrence, Bob Parker, Al Somer, Anbarasi Edward, Bob Black, Reds Wolman, Ben Lozare, Edyth Schoenrich, and Archie Golden. The more complete list of colleagues at the Johns Hopkins School of Public Health is long and was very helpful.

Across what now constitutes a century of engagement by four generations, this has also been a family dialogue. It began with John and Beth Taylor, who left the plains of Kansas for India in 1914, a place where they worked for thirty-three years under British rule and twenty-three years under Independent India. Other family members with critiques and experiences who contributed are Mary, Claire, Carter, Jennifer, Tara, and Herbert.

The following assisted in important ways with individual chapters or the production of this manuscript: Lee Stuart, George Stranahan, Andrew Mahlstedt, Ann Hawthorne. In addition, our team at Oxford University Press has truly been the best: Nicholas Liu, Stefano Imbert, Leslie Johnson, Anindita Sengupta, and, with special appreciation, the editor who kept pressing us on, the patient and undaunted Maura Roessner.

Understanding continues to evolve. While SEED-SCALE is developed enough so that we can use it, it is always developing. Shaping a better world on our insecure planet is a journey every person now engages in, and we look forward to sharing this with many more. Your suggestions and critiques are welcome. A discussion blog is found at www.seed-scale.org; specific comments can be sent to daniel@future.edu or to jotaylor@umd.edu. We cannot list you all, but we remain deeply grateful.

CONTENTS

Introduction: A Process for Change Available to All　　*xi*

1. What We Can Do With What We Have, Here, Today　　*3*
2. Connecting to the Larger Field of Development
   and Social Change　　*25*
3. If Traditional Development Practices Were Effective　　*45*
4. The Option Available to Everyone: Mobilizing
   Human Capacity　　*65*
5. To Grow Empowerment: Four Necessary Principles　　*87*
6. Maintaining Momentum: Seven Tasks　　*113*
7. Staying on Course: The Five Criteria of Evidence-Based
   Decisionmaking　　*137*
8. The Process of Going to Scale: Interaction Among
   Three Dynamics　　*157*
9. The Global Imperative of Going to Scale: Examples of
   Environmental Action in New York City and China　　*187*
10. Confronting Empire　　*211*

Notes　　*229*
About the Authors　　*261*
Glossary　　*264*
Index　　*267*

INTRODUCTION: A PROCESS FOR CHANGE AVAILABLE TO ALL

There is no wealth but life. Life, including all its powers of love, of joy, and of admira-
tion. That country is the richest which nourishes the greatest number of noble
and happy human beings; that man is richest who, having perfected the function of
his own life to the utmost, has also the widest helpful influence, both personal,
and by means of his possessions, over the lives of others.[1]
John Ruskin, *Unto This Last*

This book is about solutions for all: all people, across the entire planet.
When all are not advancing, humanity is dividing.[2] Recent global economic failures have not only increased the proportion of the disadvantaged,
but also made clear the tenuousness of current prosperity. Such vulnerability is echoed in the reality of major climate change and the probability of
pandemics. Denial is an option, as is living in hope of technological remedies,
or attempting to change regulatory systems. But such responses duck the
fact that until solutions start reaching all they limit the likelihood of truly solving the underlying conditions. We need a process that changes the fundamen-
tals of our response capacity, and we need to start using this process now.

The good news is that in pursuing opportunity for all those of us who have
achieved the good life do not need to give it up. Instead, we can continue
to improve—but to do so we need to more systematically use our most plentiful base of change: our human energy. We increasingly try to do everything
with money, which is a scarce commodity. Indeed, its efficacy is predicated
upon its scarcity. However, as this book will argue, a currency is available that
is underutilized and universally present: the energies of people. Simply put,
deep, fundamental change in our lives happens because of what people do,
people making use of what they have, where they are, today.

As our subtitle suggests, positive integration of community action has
the potential to scale up to global solutions by integrating with systems of

governance, technical expertise, and cultural expression, becoming, in short, the stuff of civilization. Most examples in this book show this process occurring in communities excluded by the systems of global development. For the marginalized, social mobilization is the only immediately available option. But as other examples show, social mobilization is also under way among the privileged, for example in New York City's parks and a China-wide youth environmental movement.

Once its potential is understood community-based growth can grow very quickly as people teach each other, hold each other accountable, and iteratively enact localized adaptive decisions to respond to opportunities. Such growth, unlike many other approaches, does not begin with policy reforms by national governments, nor does it depend on the commonly assumed infusions of financial support, nor does it depend on technological innovations.[3]

There is an urgency to put in place such solutions. Riots and terror cells anywhere call forth our armies because those riots can spread and terror's networks are as far-reaching as they are invisible. Epidemics today remind us that our children's health is vulnerable to viruses in a pig in Mexico or in a chicken in China tomorrow. World finances sit exposed to computer hackers anywhere from across the ocean to down the block. Global climate change, more serious and more certain every year, is producing natural systems that are less reliable and ever more prone to destructive extremes. Clearly, the traditional solutions—technological fixes, gated enclaves of privilege, vaccines, armies, and regulatory systems—are inadequate. Terrorism can appear anywhere, mutations can occur at any time among any population, and armies increasingly cause civilian casualties that transform military victories into quagmires in which soldiers come to fight not an enemy but a population. In the modern world, isolation behind gates, borders, or conference rooms is both ineffective and ethically bankrupt. All life rides into the future together on a planet increasingly defined by instability.

Since World War II, development projects have invested 2.3 trillion dollars to advance health, alleviate poverty, educate, and provide other services around the world.[4] Even more important than the money, tens of thousands of professionals have dedicated their careers to building schools and clinics, to establishing micro-credit schemes and agricultural projects, to controlling disease—and, in the notable case of smallpox, even eradicating it. As a result, five billion people's lives have improved.[5]

Despite such achievements, two billion people still live in grinding poverty, ill health, and illiteracy, and without constructive governance.[6] That so many have been excluded from advancement is a concern not simply for them, but for us all. Two billion is approximately the same number of individuals living in poverty, ill health, illiteracy, and repressive government or colonialism as when the modern global development project began. In other words, while percentages have changed, the absolute number of the absolute poor remains the same. Moreover, the natural environment, on which today's model of growing prosperity rests, is now in stark across-the-board decline as a direct result of the achievements that came for the five-billion-strong prosperous majority.

A dual-pronged challenge lies before us. Undeniably there has been progress—five out of seven humans have a better shot at life than did their grandparents. But the systems improving the conditions of human existence are working at only two-thirds capacity, as the numbers excluded grow and the gulf separating the prosperous from the destitute yawns ever wider. Furthermore, the vast experiment of industrial modernity that humanity has pursued since the late eighteenth century has wreaked havoc upon the ecosystems on which it depends, and now threatens to choke the planet itself with steadily rising effluence.[7] The processes for advancement in the twenty-first century need to evolve in such a way that they no longer contain within them inherent processes of planetary destruction and human destitution.

Many of the worsening conditions of people's lives today are the result of earlier well-intended actions. We live in a world of feedback loops. The predicament, as Michel Serres sums up: "What everyone does gives rise to harm inflicted on the world, and this damage, through an immediate or foreseeably deferred feedback loop, becomes the givens of everyone's work."[8] And this is true for even the most altruistic of enterprises. We can, and we must, act. But in doing so we need a process that takes such feedback loops into account, recognizes the inevitability of imperfection, and corrects itself when we make mistakes. One of the most important transformations wrought by the understanding that human energy is the currency of social change is the availability of starting points. It does not simply open the process of change to all; it also removes the prerequisites for action, meaning that productive social change can begin anywhere, at any time.

When John Ruskin penned the words at the head of this introduction in the mid–nineteenth century, he threw a challenge before a society plunging into what would later be called "development." The combined forces of industrialization, empire, and capitalism had enabled Victorian Britain to become the first industrial society to enjoy a standard of living that we now associate with middle-class existence, and which in many respects continues to serve as the paradigm for modernization around the globe.[9] In response, Ruskin contrasted true "wealth" with what he called "illth," or the version of material prosperity that destroy humanity and nature alike. Furthermore, Ruskin argued that modern political economy assumed that human beings were "all skeleton," and thus founded "an ossifant theory of progress on this negation of a soul."[10] While talk of the "soul" may strike the twenty-first-century ear as overly spiritual, Ruskin moves immediately to describe its reappearance in terms of workers' resistance to such dehumanizing mechanization.

Ruskin's "soul," in other words, can be taken to mean "will." And the undeniable existence and diversity of the human will have indeed long been a problem for economic models that treated human beings as rational, calculating machines. People cannot necessarily be counted on to act in their own "rational self-interest," may resist modernizing "improvements" that conflict with established cultural norms, and may generally want different things from those who are attempting to shape their actions and goals.

"Human energy," as we use the concept throughout this book has the potential to suggest connotations similar to the mysticism of Ruskin's "soul." However, our intention is not to conjure up auras or supernatural forces, but rather to consider the more prosaic product of human hands, hearts, and minds—essentially anything a human being does or can do through the combustion of calories, which are, after all, individual units of energy. In addition to capturing a more complete image of human endeavor, recasting social change in terms of human energy has the advantage over pure economics in that it does not depend on structural inequality. Whereas money functions, as Ruskin recognized, "only through inequalities or negations of itself," empowerment through human energy is an aggregating force.[11] Money is powerful because other people want it. Its power thus increases with degrees of inequality. This means, among other things, that if it is taken to be the central factor in social-change initiatives, those who do not have it are powerless. With nothing to invest, they have no basis on which to participate in the system.

It is thus fitting that one of the most potent instances of the power of human energy dramatizes the power of the poor. A quotation from Ruskin's essay "Unto This Last" was one of the few adornments of the room at Sevagram Ashram that was home to Mahatma Gandhi. Gandhi, as has no other, proved that this alternative currency of social change can transform life, pioneering a process of simple actions leading to transformative change. While Ruskin was a man of large ideas and grandiose abstractions, Gandhi's genius lay in simplicity, building on Ruskin's understanding—the symbolic centrality of salt, the value of homespun cloth, the act of nonviolent refusal—and in this process he gave people a means for societal transformation that not only scaled up to one-fifth of humanity but also established the assumptions of the great independence movements of the 1950s and 1960s. Today we more fully understand the process.

Gandhi's innovation in the management of human energy is arguably the equal of Einstein's $E = MC^2$ in transforming the understanding of physical energy. It unleashed a new way of engaging tyranny. Einstein's insight ultimately wrought destruction on two cities in Japan (and far more in places like the Marshall Islands where nuclear bombs of even greater magnitude have been dropped since). Gandhi's, on the other hand, helped dismantle the world's then most powerful empire, and did so relatively amicably.

Before Gandhi's time, freedom had been won in Haiti, America, France, Russia, and other places through violence. Gandhi utilized the genius of nonviolent empowerment. On a village spinning wheel, Gandhi wove the fabric of a new nation, a truth of community-based determination that was ensconced in the constitutional stipulation that the Indian flag be woven of *khadi* (home-spun cloth). The quest went beyond political independence, offering people the means to many freedoms: poverty, caste, gender discrimination, illness, and illiteracy. Gandhi showed his people not what they needed, but what they could do with what they already had. He showed how control could be broken through partnership with those who held the control.

Many development projects speak of "empowering the people" and "grow-ing capacity in communities," yet this well-intentioned language too often remains only that. Genuine human progress involves the use of human hands, hearts, and minds to do what we can with what we have, here, today. Every human being, even the most impoverished, has a portion of discretionary energy to direct. Begin with that, grow it. Impoverished Indian villagers could place one foot in front of the other to follow the Mahatma on the salt march to the sea; they could guide thread over a wooden spindle; they could refuse to eat. Such simple actions grew to overpower an empire, and once-marginalized people gained the freedom of aspirations for the future. The real meaning of freedom that Gandhi was pursuing has been lost in the histrionics of democ-racy, but Amartya Sen emphasizes precisely this liberating element of develop-ment to create economic opportunities, political liberties, social powers, good health, basic education, cultivation of initiative, and protective security.[12]

Using their own energies, people can overthrow their burdens and attain such multifaceted freedoms without consuming or selling off their scarcest resources. Working in partnership with their governments and the experts they can access, they can start to build on what they already have. Then, much as economic growth compounds profits, communities compound this resource so that benefits accrue to all. Economists term this "a process of increasing returns." In the process advocated here, the returns come in the form of com-pounding human energy rather than money. Examples in this book demon-strate increasing returns growing in very challenging places: among them saving thousands of children from dying in India, protecting six million acres around Mount Everest in China and also promoting peace in Afghanistan.

This alternative thesis runs counter to the dominant paradigm in which the foundation of societal advancement is seen to be economic growth—and the belief is that profits generated by economic growth provide the basis for improving health, education, physical security, and even the environment. There is no doubt that economic growth can generate surpluses that then allow society to invest in itself. However, this truth is not universal; economic growth does not benefit all people. It lifts some, at times lifts even most, but by its very nature it thrives on disparity; it benefits some more than others.

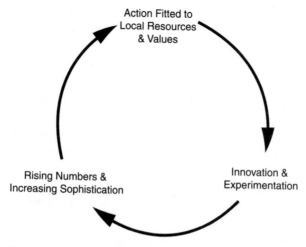

Figure. The Human Energy Engine: The revolution of rising aspirations creates a feedback loop between action, innovation, and expansion that operates like a flywheel, driving the process.

Those who already have get more, while those with nothing to invest are left behind. To make money you need money, natural resources, or other people's labor to exploit. This mode of advancement works for those who possess one of these resources—and it works best for those with all three. But it does not work for all.

The emphasis on economic growth has had a destructive dynamic for communities. As economist Stephen Marglin insightfully states, "Undermining community is the logical and practical consequence of promoting the market system."[13] The market system is based on the expectation that individuals will act in rationally calculating self-interest, but the consequence is competition that pulls communities apart. Communities are the organizational structure humans have worked within over millennia to channel and apply their energy. What is needed is a process of community-strengthening through which individuals are supported.

Community, as we use the term, is any group that has something in common and the potential for acting together. It is a three-way partnership of people with their governments and with those outside who have an interest in people's well-being. It is large enough to resist exploitation and small enough that each individual has a voice in shaping life's impact on him- or herself. This way of using the term *community* allows its extension across geographical locations, as occurs with professional or ethnic communities, and, increasingly, through the Internet. The word has linguistic roots in *communitas* (fellowship), deeper roots in *communis* (common), and parallel branches in *communio* (communion) and *communicatus* (shared). The human species has consistently advanced in collectives, whether clans, tribes, communities, or nations.[14] (We go to war and die for community; when we die for ourselves there is no future.) A sense of community turns members from behaving in only individual interest to putting in place networks of relationships that support all. *Homo sapiens* (man that is wise) is not *Homo economicus*; a great deal more than money makes the foundation of wise life. Defining "community" as "a group with something in common and the potential for acting together" is a functional description. Because of its emphasis on action, the definition reminds us what community really is: the mechanism that has evolved to channel the energy of individual people into powerful collectives.[15]

Two billion people have been excluded from the promises of development. They lack economic resources, have short life expectancies, and are unable to send their children to school.[16] And yet despite all that they lack, these two out of seven among us live. Returning to Ruskin, they have "no wealth but life." They adapt, they struggle, they survive. And that is a remarkable achievement. Progress can build on this form of wealth, but doing so involves a radical rethinking, not only of how the development project is to proceed, but also of its very premise. Traditional efforts at social change are limited because they operate within a paradigm of control, control achieved either by paying people (health services, schools, conservation projects), or control by coercion (ranging from mild regulations to totalitarianism). Disempowerment is not so much an obstacle for such initiatives to overcome, but a logical outcome of their existence.

As the Gandhian example makes apparent, empowerment can be used to confront empire and oppression, whether overt imperialism of the old school or the often more insidious and amorphous empires of corporate dominance and even well-intended philanthropy. But in order to realize its potential we must discard the idea that some communities are "developed" and others "undeveloped." Discussing global inequality in such linear terms masks the fact that wealth achieved by the "developed" world was in part extracted from the so-called developing world through a process of active "underdevelopment," first by colonial regimes and later through global markets.[17] Social change is deeply rooted and is always underway; there is no "ahead" or "behind." One type of root may be devastating life-giving resources, creating an unsustainable product; another type of root may have carried life across seemingly impossible circumstances for millennia; but the roots that all seek are those that produce fruit sustainably and for all. Few groups have such truly life sustaining roots, but all communities are seeking them. All communities are developed and are always developing in an ongoing, contextualized process. The opportunity before us now is the potential to develop change more effectively.

The argument of this book is this: Empowerment is what people can do. In practice, this differs from "grassroots" or "bottom-up" development efforts because it is not premised on communities' taking action alone. Instead, such an approach seeks to build a partnership with structures of authority, outsiders, and communities so that *all* are empowered by the process in ways that mutually reinforce each other. What this book will describe as "SEED-SCALE" is more a comprehensive theory of change than a methodology: a means to structure and channel individual actions toward context-specific solutions. Any given application will look different, and will indeed be different, but will nevertheless comprised the same set of functions. This functional approach helps communities, governments, and social-change agents (development professionals, NGO workers, academics) adapt to the ever-changing circumstances of our unstable planet because it means that one is never completely without options: there is always something to be done.

Social change operates in the complex intersection of economics, human social relations, and natural ecology (the socio-econo-biosphere). This is the most complex system humanity has ever tried to comprehend. Indeed, it will always remain beyond full comprehension, but not beyond effective action. We adapt within it every day, all of us. To be more effective we need to maximize our adaptive processes, while recognizing that we will never be able to comprehend, much less control, the whole. This is why the process begins with SEED, or "Self-Evaluation for Effective Decisionmaking," the means by which each individual, and each community, identifies the next effective action in the midst of changing circumstances. We are not controlling or leading the process; we are adapting to optimize our position, event by event. This is a process of enhancing relationships, not of controlling operations, for the socio-econo-biosphere is too complex to control.

Each participant's perspective on this process differs, but all are also participating in the same phenomena, particularly as social change goes to scale. To make that point, we use the acronym "SCALE," but with multiple meanings. Going to scale in numerical growth, SCALE One (Stimulating Community Awareness, Learning, and Energy) differs from improving quality of life, SCALE Squared (Self-help Centers for Action Learning and Experimentation), and both of these evolve within policies, finances, and knowledge: SCALE Cubed (Synthesis of Collaboration, Adaptive Learning, and Extension).

The primary engine that drives such change is learning: learning how to adapt behaviors and to use resources that are available. If new resources are introduced, people adapt to those, but new resources are not needed as people learn to work within their contexts. There are few true requirements for a better life, but learning most assuredly is one. Humanity uses learning to fantastic effect. The ability to learn, to adapt, and to innovate across the broad spectrum of human experience, might be the truest definition of "progress" one can posit.

This book is grounded in examples from real communities in which the process advocated was used. As father, son, and grandson, we have observed the lessons here across generations, decades, and disciplines. For Carl, whose childhood was spent in ox-cart clinics in the jungles of India early in the twentieth century and who continued on to field programs in Afghanistan (see Chapters 3 and 5) early in the twenty-first, the ideas presented here truly reflect a lifetime's work. For all three of us, the experiences that inform these pages began early in our childhoods and now include fieldwork in over seventy countries, as well as leadership in a variety of international forums. The SEED-SCALE terminology that describes this process via multilayered acronyms coalesced out of a dialogue from around the world that began in the years before the 1995 United Nations Social Summit, when two of us co-chaired two international task forces associated with UNICEF and the leadership of its then–executive director, James Grant, drawing on the literature of social change throughout the prior century. Two monographs were produced from those task forces and circulated at the 1995 Social Summit.[18]

Field activities followed throughout the 1990s to understand the approach further. A helpful critique of SEED-SCALE continued with colleagues around the world, and a subsequent volume was published in 2002.[19] But the most important conclusions about how to "grow" empowerment among peoples were learned sitting on the floors of village huts, from people who showed us how they were getting real results. Time and again, from their evidence it was clear that when effective social transformation occurred, the determinative component was the energies of people applied to their priorities, rather than the deliverables given or specified by outsiders. When people came together with a common vision, amazing things got done. Whether in palaces talking to kings or in mud homes talking to destitute widows, the bottom line remained much the same: change came when people had gotten to work using what they had. It seldom came from gifts or external prescriptions telling them what to do. These discussions refined the SEED-SCALE process: when people got to work effectively, building on their successes, strengthening partnerships, learning from evidence, and new behaviors were being adopted—empowerment happened. These were the features; with study the process to achieve them became clear.

The examples in the following chapters provide supporting evidence as well as illustrating the process. The accompanying photographs connect the theory of SEED-SCALE to the reality of its implementation. No case is "pure" SEED-SCALE, since the process is always being adapted. Nor are the cases intended as enduring examples. Change occurs through fits, starts, and transformations. In time, the communities whose dynamic movement is described here may stagnate, while others become more innovative. Any individual example is a manifestation of ongoing adaptation, an expression of the dynamics of the process rather than an edifice constructed by it. SEED-SCALE is not a formula to be followed but a mindset with which to bring forward energy that is latent, ready to grow from inside a situation, using the range of internal and external resources available. It is a process that tailors movement toward a richer life to the specifics of every community's ecology, economy, and values. Thus, although each example is situated in its own time and place, they all show the process being employed by communities working with what they have to build futures they wish to inhabit.

Précis *of Chapters*

Chapter 1 names empowerment as the foundation undergirding all social change, framing social change in terms of the concepts of the discipline of *emergence* and complex adaptive systems. The chapter presents a case from a valley in northeastern India in which people improved their health, supported each other as they learned skills, then produced economic wealth plus the wealth of life. The primary resource used was the energy of people working in new, more effective ways.

Chapter 2 reviews the literature of international social change, showing the progression in understanding from an initial view that economic growth was the engine of social change to the current nuanced understanding of the complex socio-econo-biosphere, and within that, the central role of the people themselves.

Chapter 3 uses the case of Nepal to show that traditional development frameworks are inadequate. In Nepal, half a century of work by the people, supported by abundant foreign aid and expert help, should have transformed the country. Yet both national and international assistance in major aspects failed, while the industry of the Nepali people did not.

Chapter 4 explores how human empowerment operates, drawing on physics for helpful parallels for growing human energy. The case used to demonstrate the role of human energy is that of modern Afghanistan, as it moved from a potential for peace in 2002 to a growing insurgency by the people. The Afghan instance is extreme, but it shows clearly that in complex systems, what works is not to view a project as autonomous and capable of operating according to its parameters, but to recognize that positive change is a constant strengthening of relationships among people and with power structures so that they become enabling.

Chapter 5 describes how empowerment in primary health care in northeast India sparked widespread progress using the SEED-SCALE principles. Four principles are necessary for empowerment: (1) Build from success; (2) create a three-way partnership: Bottom-up (citizens), Top-down (government), and Outside-in (change agents); (3) base decisionmaking on factual evidence rather than on opinions or politics; and (4) use behavior change, rather than provision of services, as the determinative outcome.

Chapter 6 uses an example from urban Afghanistan showing the creation of community-based schools, garbage cleanup, and remarkable cooperation among tribal groups. Empowerment grew and, from it, significant social improvement in this community through use of the seven SEED-SCALE tasks to: organize a local coordinating committee, identify successes already happening, learn from the experience of others, gather data about local resources, craft these into a work plan, hold partners accountable, and make corrections to strengthen the four principles.

Chapter 7 shows how momentum stays on track by using self-evaluation, a feedback loop of action and learning what worked, then acting in a more informed way and learning more, illustrated by a case of ecosystem monitoring in northeastern India. Five criteria are used in assessing the learning feedback: equity, sustainability, holism, interdependence, and iteration. These bring communities together, allow momentum to engage the needs of all, and guide social change to stay on course.

Chapter 8 addresses the challenge of going to scale, nurturing community-based potential by using top-down dynamics to structure policies and financing so that capacity grows. The illustrative case is establishing the nature preserve around Mount Everest where synergistic interaction between growth in numbers of people combined with growth in the quality of people's lives to form the then-largest nature preserve in Asia and the first major preserve in the developing world to integrate conservation with social and economic development.

Chapter 9 scales up from the Everest example to a global perspective in the wealth of life. Momentum for community-based change is underway worldwide, with many initiatives, but the challenge every place faces is how to make it more effective in a context of declining resources. The process has been until now hit-or-miss. Achieving its potential does not presume substantial new resources—but can it learn to bring parts and people already in place together in more effective ways? Two widely divergent success stories are presented that focus on environmental change: New York City and China's Green Long March.

Chapter 10, building from the teachings of Mahatma Gandhi, draws together the components of the SEED-SCALE process, as a means to overcome disempowerment. Empowerment can be taught. Doing so requires engaging the resource of people's energies, focusing on what is already working, and expanding in impact using partnerships of citizens, government, and change agents to realign action utilizing the resource available to all: human energy.

The distinction about social change made by this book is summed up by two verbs: "need" and "can do." Traditional development uses "need"—the people need *xyz*, donors need *abc*. By contrast, SEED-SCALE uses "can do." As a global human community we can do the job with what we have, beginning today, continuing into the future, and reaching everybody. People all over the world have heard promises of what will inevitably never come. It is time to get to work.

Empowerment on an Unstable Planet

CHAPTER 1

What We Can Do With What We Have, Here, Today

"Seriously," Elli says, "this whole district looks like it was flung up by an earthquake."
On hearing Elli speak this one word, *earthquake*, something weird and painful happens
in my head. Up to that moment this was Paradise Alley, the heart of the Nutcracker,
a place I'd known all my life. When Elli says *earthquake* suddenly I'm seeing it as she does.
Paradise Alley is a wreckage of baked earth mounds and piles of planks on which hang
gunny sacks, plastic sheets, dried palm leaves. Like drunks with arms round each other's
necks, the houses of the Nutcracker lurch along this lane which, now that I look, isn't
really even a road, just a long gap left by chance between the dwellings. Everywhere's
covered in shit and plastic. Truly I see how poor and disgusting are our lives.[1]

Indra Sinha, Animal's People

This book explains how to launch wide-reaching, community-based change
that grows to scale and is sustained over time. The process, which is
termed SEED-SCALE, differs from the normally promoted approach of change
agents and donors, which starts with a needs analysis, develops a plan with
concrete targets, then drives change with a funding stream. But there is a
deeper difference seldom outrightly talked about: control. While "empowerment" is now widely promoted, its deeper implications grounded in the
dynamics of power and control are often ignored.

Consider the epigraph above: *Animal's People* is set in the slums of a fiction-
alized version of Bhopal, India, where the Union Carbide plant exploded
in 1984, killing thousands in a dramatic industrial "disaster" that might be
more accurately dubbed negligent homicide. Even decades later, the American
corporation (since bought by Dow Chemical) ignores orders for its executives
to appear in Indian courts. Animal, the novel's narrator, is so deformed by
the poisons that he walks on all fours. Remarkably, he does not feel powerless until he sees his home through the eyes of an American doctor who has

come to open a clinic and is appalled by the sight of what Animal has just described as the "Champs-Élysées" of the neighborhood, its "boulevard of dreams." That dream is shattered by the way Elli sees it. Animal is disempowered not by the material conditions of the slum (known as the "Nutcracker") in which he lives, but by seeing his life through the aid worker's eyes. Rather than viewing the Nutcracker as a place the residents control, this new vision presents it as a product of an event utterly beyond human control, an earthquake. In that instant, Animal loses his knowledge that his people built it, using what they had, even when that was next to nothing. The feeling of achievement, which was so strong as to transform a neighborhood, was taken away by a change in vision.

How do we nurture empowerment? *Animal's People* is fiction, but the reality it models is one faced by communities around the globe. A continuum of efficacy and control spans our worldview; the actions of our days move within it. On one end, life is self-fashioned; on the other, we live as guests in the designs of others. We can create our world, building our relationships and shaping our realities or, we can be residents in a world that has been built for us. In practice, we will always be doing some of both. We move back and forth along this continuum, engaging constantly with what the world gives to us and what we make of it.

SEED-SCALE offers a process for each community to develop its own services and enhance its efficacy and control. The approach uses resources all communities have, and builds from actions that have already started. This is not what is normally termed "grassroots (or bottom-up) development" because the SEED-SCALE mode of development utilizes top-down resources. (Grass does not grow on its own.) SEED-SCALE also differs from the normal "partnership" based development of bottom-up and top-down because it is not premised on scarce resources of needing money. SEED-SCALE presents a process through which the bafflingly complex systems of economics, politics, even environmental change, can be engaged in constantly unfolding solutions that are fitted to specific local context. Answers are never perfect, only good enough, but they are always evolving. The result is that most todays are better than the days before.

Communities exist. Begin with this truth, and cultivate that real but elusive essence—that resilient engagement with life that made "Paradise Alley" out of a dusty street in a slum. SEED-SCALE offers communities a means to do that, bringing together groups of partners using already existing resources. SEED-SCALE is not a path to a utopian ideal. The examples in this book are neither dream towns nor perfect applications of the process—they are imperfect experiments in a better life. Nor does SEED-SCALE offer an escape from the forces of modernity or globalization. Instead, it offers a way to engage these macro forces on their own terms, rather than succumbing to external control. Communities need not wait, predicating action on some macro-decision in distant boardrooms or funding to enable "development." They can begin where they are, using what they have, as they have always done.

Around the world, realistically grounded, community-based change is underway. This book is an attempt to strengthen this movement by offering a process that explains how to do better this realistically grounded, community-based change. Life is what we who live it make of it. Society is comprised of what human beings do, and what SEED-SCALE does is to strengthen this reality of the ways communities work, opening wider doors already unlocked. Communities are not professional delivery systems; they are people going about their daily ways of life. The future lies in changing behaviors and relationships that are already around us, taking actions that are available to all, and utilizing the human energy that is the planet's most rapidly expanding resource base. The process does not happen on its own. Communities teach communities, and refine, innovate, and expand momentum. Movements already underway are made more effective through iterative, expansive, societal evolution. We begin with an example from fieldwork of the last two decades.[2]

In northeastern India, in a community seldom visited by outsiders, two newcomers crested a spiny ridge after a difficult climb. Rima Langbia and her husband walked on foot, the only way to reach Bameng. Houses and offices perched on the ridge like birds on a branch, looking out over valleys where about twenty distant clusters of houses were scattered. As Rima climbed, she had talked to women along the trail, asking questions, comparing the number of babies to the older children, whom the infants outnumbered roughly three to one. Using a simple formula, Rima ran the numbers and quickly recognized that a newborn in these villages was more likely to die than to live. No woman Rima had talked to as she climbed had been literate. The land had evident agricultural potential, but nevertheless much of the food was brought in from outside, and people reported scarcity, especially during the monsoon when roads were cut off by mudslides and flooding.

The government had programs to build roads, homes, clinics, schools, and in times of scarcity had sent in even more food. A government construction program had brought Rima's husband, an engineer, to Bameng. Entering the town, Rima noticed the free clinic was crowded. At its gate she learned that two nurses provided services while the doctor worked out of a private pharmacy so he could charge fees. Going through town she had seen water lines provided by the government, and how people had connected additional pipes to them so that the lines now spluttered from low pressure and did not provide water to the distant houses. She asked about the school and was told the teacher came on opening day to take enrollment, and then returned on the last day to get thumbprints in the register and "graduate" students to the next year. People eagerly shared one such tale and then another. Project after project had been started, but like the food that was handed out, there was never enough. Over the years, many projects had been abandoned in favor of new initiatives with the same results. She heard vivid stories of how Bameng was a community in great and urgent need.

Bameng is one of 6,000 such clusters of villages in Arunachal Pradesh, a state in the northeastern corner of India (about which more reports will be given in later chapters). This Himalayan state is one of the most beautiful, wildest places left on Earth, secluded between Bhutan to the west, Myanmar to the east, and the Tibet Autonomous Region of China to the north. Kept intentionally isolated as the "North East Frontier Agency" (NEFA) under the British, the state has remained demarcated from the rest of the country since Indian independence. Arunachal Pradesh is home to one of the most diverse populations of tribal people on the planet and one of the few remaining intact Asian subtropical jungles and "cloud forests." Isolation has maintained cultural integrity in these villages, but it has also left them in poverty, and ill-prepared to face rampant pressures to log the forests for timber, or harness the hydroelectric potential of Himalayan rivers to sate the ever-rising appetite for energy demanded by India's surging economic growth. Such potential for natural resource wealth inevitably leads to corruption and backroom deals far from the eyes and voices of the people. While the resource base differs, the core questions before the people of Bameng are similar with those before every community around the world: How do we improve our lives amid the dazzling complexities of the modern world? How do we take ownership of our futures without becoming victims of homogenizing globalization? How do we profit from yet sustain our local ecology?

Within a month of arriving in Bameng, Rima started a women's group: "Come learn how to keep children from dying, why boiling water is important, and how to read and write." Within three months, as women shared with their

Figure 1.1. A couple on the porch of their bamboo home looking over the Bameng valley at sunset. (*Photo credit: Daniel Taylor*)

neighbors, that first "Women's Action Group" had expanded to five. From the first day with the first group Rima kept a register of births and deaths, and asked the participants to recall those from the previous year. Her book showed that in the twelve months before the action groups, 23 children had died; the year following, this number was reduced to 13. The clinic had been trying to lower the deaths in Bameng for almost a decade. Nevertheless, the numbers from the Women's Action Groups, which now extended to about 30 clusters of houses throughout the valley, showed that at the time of Rima's arrival Bameng's mortality rate had not been appreciably lower than that of towns distant from the clinic.[3]

One year after starting the action groups, by working together, the women had mastered the home-based care that Rima had taught for diarrhea, pneumonia, and other diseases, and started preventative practices such as regularly boiling their drinking water. Almost no money had been spent. As a result, in one year the women had nearly halved mortality rates while spending essentially nothing in a context where the clinic had had virtually no impact on mortality despite many years of work. The women now used the clinic for conditions they could not care for, which in turn meant that it was less crowded and its services were more effective. Actions once isolated inside individual homes were now being collectively monitored and managed. Earlier isolation had been replaced by connection to a growing body of group knowledge, and this was coupled with more appropriate use of professional services. The Women's Action Groups were the focal points, but they did not do everything on their own. Much of their effectiveness came through transforming the relationship with government services to make them more effective and engaged. Change that had begun with health spawned other initiatives such as literacy classes. By the second year, women were planting vegetables, gathering firewood from the slopes to sell to shivering government servants on the windy ridgetop, and pooling firewood and vegetable earnings to leverage loans from the local bank. Women on the ridge now sat out in the sun practicing their lessons, and talking about new business opportunities.

By the third year, the number of action groups had increased to 17, and the activities were implementing health, income generation, gardening, and literacy programs. Initiatives that had begun with the women had expanded to involve the men, some of whom had started orchards of oranges, bananas, and pineapples, while others now grew bamboo commercially. Five years later, almost every home had vegetable fields and orchards, and sales often earned families over 10,000 rupees per year (ten times the annual cash many of these families had seen before). As organized groups, the villagers had pressured the absent schoolteachers to show up for classes, helping them arrange village-based housing. Some of the families started a private school and paid tuitions for more intensive education for their children. Seventy percent of children were attending one school or another, and 40 percent of women throughout the valley had learned to read and write. The action groups had connected to each other throughout the valley, and through group pressure the women had mandated that the former practice of child marriages be hereafter banned.

In this expansion in health, literacy, schooling, agriculture, and income-generation, not a rupee had been given to any of these "neediest" communities. The communities had learned to engage government services and staff already present, and these government services were more effective because people were seeking the services and doing so with knowledgeable questions, rather than the services seeking them as targets.

Bameng's transformation may sound much like an example of people helping themselves in the manner customarily cast as "grassroots" social change. However, that would be a misreading of the situation. This dramatic sequence of actions was not from the "bottom up" in isolation, but through growing utilization of "top-down" of government services augmented by stimulus from the "outside-in" of a change agent, Rima. Ineffective systems were not replaced but adapted. People were transforming their communities, using what was available to address local priorities, but they were not doing so alone. The bottom dramatically rose up, but in so doing helped the top-down become more effective.

Three points should be noted. Rima did not provide a service, nor did she spend any money, or introduce an incentive of any kind. Instead, through that initial women's group, she changed the *context* of village life by facilitating connections into new behaviors, both among people and between the village and government entities bringing knowledge and connectivity into the village. Relationships grew more effective. Second, what she taught caused women, then men, to recognize what they could do. People started working together, sharing techniques and expanding into new arenas and further innovations. This assumption of control is the true power of empowerment. Third, Rima was measuring the process as it happened. Beginning with a quick survey as she climbed the hill the first day, she kept records that guided decisionmaking like a scientific experiment: an idea was tried, tested, and, on the basis of the results, modified for increased success.[4] This process of *try-monitor-improve* was repeated with continual refinement, and continues even though Rima herself has now left Bameng.

The residents moved from waiting for government services, to pressing for them, and then finding ways to make them more effective. A conventional needs-analysis approach would have noted that "services exist, but they cannot get the last kilometer to the home" (a common problem with service-delivery models of all kinds). Now, people were stepping out of their homes and walking much more than one kilometer to get to, and even to help create, those services.

What happened in Bameng? As with almost every other state in India, the government had provided an array of programs that had been running for years.

These did not change until after the process of social change had begun. No new program was set up: the UN did not arrive, nor did USAID, the Gates Foundation, other nongovernmental organizations (NGOs), or church-based relief groups. Rima was not a charismatic leader or a social entrepreneur from whom action emanated, as evidenced by the fact that changes continued after she left the community. What grew in Bameng was internal capacity, and it occurred through a process that can be replicated. Growth was not overnight, but a steady evolution over five years. Throughout, change was maturing in the community, with one change prompting others, and in so doing it restructured community services. Such rapid-but-not-threatening change has long inspired, and usually eluded, development efforts. In what follows, we describe how this happened and why it fundamentally differs from other development approaches.

THE COMPLEX CONTEXT OF SOCIAL CHANGE

The contextual challenge Rima faced (as all efforts do) is that life operates within complex systems of economics, social issues, natural forces—random realities that are beyond our understanding, and variables which are beyond our control. To improve our lives, efforts must address unfathomable complexities while also being simple enough to act on immediately.

In seeking the needed simplicity, most programs ignore the complexity; meanwhile most theories that try to address the complexity are not simple enough to implement. While the interlocked aspects of economics, social issues, natural forces, and random realities are beyond control, it is possible to address their complexities by addressing the relationship defining dynamics between the parts instead of trying to alter the parts themselves. It was such a changing of relationships, rather than entities or components, that Rima started. She did not worry about inputs; she did not try to create specified outputs. She worked inside the system that she found and made relationships already there more effective.

A classic illustration of changing relationships in a complex system was given by the mathematician John Holland using the example of a standing wave in front of a rock in the river: it appears constant in shape, size, and location, yet everything inside it is adapting.[5] The wave, like a community, appears constant but that constancy is made up of always readjusting parts. If the wave is disturbed, it instantly repairs itself and goes on adapting to change, then readapting. Relationships among ever-changing drops are altered by the unchanging rock, whose effect is determined by many variables of the larger context of river, rate of flow, and riverbanks. In communities, balance among forces in always-changing process similarly creates a form that remains over time despite the changes in the lives of individual constituents.

Similarly, Rima was a new addition into the flow of community and also changed the relationships. Since complex *human* systems can learn, it was possible in time to take Rima out of the complex system and have the altered relationship mode continue.

The concept of "emergence" as articulated in complex adaptive systems provides a lens to understand how order emerges from complexity, and so we will return to it repeatedly throughout this book. John Holland, who brought forward the wave example above, is one of the key theorists of emergence, which he sums up with eight concepts, of which five are especially relevant to social systems: (a) "Systems are composed of copies of a relatively small number of components that obey simple laws"; (b) "Interactions between the parts are non-linear, so the overall behavior *cannot* be obtained by summing the behaviors of the isolated components"; (c) "Emergent phenomena in generated systems are, typically, persistent patterns with changing components . . . recall the standing wave in front of a rock in a fast-moving river where the water particles are constantly changing though the pattern persists"; (d) "The context in which a persistent emergent pattern is embedded determines its functions"; (e) "Interactions between persistent patterns add constraints and checks that provide increasing 'competence' as the number of patterns increases."[6] Each of these dynamics is evident in the Bameng example.

Rima was dropped into the flow of Bameng's life. She thus became a catalyst for the change without actually directing it. Instead, forces inside the complex system drove the change by adapting to the introduction. This is a huge point: certain people or actions may be the occasion for social events to occur, but they do not actually *cause* those events. Instead, the events are caused by energies inside the system. There was no "plan" to create health, literacy, and rising incomes. What changed were decisionmaking procedures among the people. Rima made relationships among the people more effective, then the women's action groups sorted through the specifics (call these "operating formulas" or "decision rules" if alternative terminology is preferred), and that readjusting of relationships created new shape to the constantly adapting lives. (Here, of course, the "standing wave" analogy breaks down because neither rocks nor rivers are conscious or capable of self-direction.)

Rima taught a simple-to-implement process of actions that reshaped complex life forces on that Himalayan ridge. In the process, she planted seeds that grew to larger, community scale. A crucial distinction is worth repeating: Rima was not telling people what to do; nor was she stipulating outcomes or even goals. Instead, she was teaching a process. Whereas traditional development starts with a plan and expects predetermined outcomes (and must therefore fund these external initiatives with external monies), Rima was letting the design evolve through adjusted relationships contextualized in dynamics and resources within the community.

GROWING THE SEED: STARTING SOCIAL CHANGE

Let us now focus on the salient features of the Bameng example that illustrate how to begin this growth. When the right pattern starts, founded in the principles that cause success to grow on itself, momentum grows reliably and exponentially. The principles, tasks, and criteria for these seeds growing to scale will be discussed later. However, three points in the Bameng story are key to starting the process:

- Work with what is there. Predicating action on scarce resources or things that are limited immediately creates a barrier to getting started.
- Use a method that grows a sense of community, rather than singling out individuals or small groups as either particularly needy or successful. (Yes, Rima began with a group of women, but it was open to all women, and moreover the starting point of preventing children's deaths had universal appeal.)
- Recognize people's risk-adverse nature. People are more comfortable seeking the sure, if small, successes and building on these rather than jeopardizing their scant resources.

For roughly a century, the major body of scholarship in social development (summarized in the next chapter) promoted economic growth as the foundation of social change. The expectation was that rising wealth could then be reinvested in social benefits such as roads, clinics, schools, libraries, and museums; in short, the infrastructure of modern life. Capital begets capital, both financial and cultural. First the currency is created, then it is spent on the people. The alternative, as developed in Bameng, is to begin with human behavior, focusing on growing locally elected social benefits as the goal. First, get people to come together because life is improving for all. Then, with a base of community cohesion engendered, move into income generation, which in turn stimulates the economic base to reinforce social growth and ensure that the evolution will be sustained into the future.

The monetary approach (preferred by those with capital because they get more capital) has led to a variety of approaches for international assistance, all predicated on spending money. Some such projects begin with direct infusions of funds as gifts or loans; others with targeted technology that requires external production; still others with expert, salaried help. Whatever the mix, these approaches share two guiding assumptions: first, the engine that must be fired is economic growth. Second, the spark that lights the fire and at least the first tank of fuel (if not the entire machine) must be brought in from elsewhere. External action must (to mix a metaphor) "prime the pump."

But the Bameng example does not fit this model:

- There were no "projects."
- No money was spent.
- Change in one life area did not stay in that sector but prompted change in others (health, education, poverty alleviation, agricultural production).
- Entrenched inequities (child marriage, disempowerment of women) were removed.
- Existing government services became more accountable and effective.
- Change continued after Rima departed. (The data above report five-year progress, and Rima left Bameng after three years.)

Even though the usual project inputs were not made, and no desired outcomes were specified up front, familiar development goals did result: raising income, lowering mortality, creating literacy, improving the status of women, and expanding food security. However, more important was a seldom articulated outcome: hope. What Rima brought was a process, and through the process the way people engaged with each other changed, and that engendered hope, not just for one action group, but hope that grew through the valleys. Hope—not money—became the driving force of change. The details of the process Rima brought, including where and how Rima learned it, will be explained in subsequent chapters. However, its essence is this: do what you can with what you have; then do it again, better.

Another example (which indicates the ways SEED-SCALE attempts to articulate an ancient process) is the Arunachali people's abilities to use bamboo. Arunachal Pradesh is locked off from the outside world by Earth's most rumpled geography (including the Brahmaputra Gorge, the deepest gorge on the planet). Additionally, it was isolated by endemic malaria coupled with hostile tribes. The British let few outsiders enter (including their own officers) for a hundred years after tribal warriors defeated their initial forays up the Brahmaputra. Since India's independence sixty years ago, Arunachal has remained politically isolated by the Indian government (which even today requires special permits even for Indian citizens). A lengthy list of what the people of Arunachal do not have (in development-speak, a "needs assessment") could be readily compiled. But they do have bamboo, and until about two decades ago, people in Arunachal used bamboo for almost everything. They ate its shoots as a food, cooked in it (fill the tube with rice or a fish and put the tube into the fire), wove split strands into walls of their homes, coupled curved tubing to make waterproof roofs (split bamboo, lay one set of halves upward, the other set down, creating interlocking channels), fashioned weaponry (spears, bows, and arrows), wove storage baskets, hats, backpacks, even clothing. Most remarkably, with bamboo alone, they strung some of the world's longest traditional suspension bridges across their deep mountain

Figure 1.2. A 400-foot-long locally made bamboo bridge of Arunachal Pradesh. *(Photo credit: Daniel Taylor)*

gorges (up to 500 feet in length). The people of Arunachal, like people everywhere, have used what they have and have displayed remarkable innovation in doing so. And when something better than bamboo came along, they adopted that. Corrugated tin went onto roofs. Machine-made clothes replaced homespun jungle fibers. Steel cables now hold up most of the suspension bridges. Arunachal is not unique in this. Self-reliant building with what is available is humanity's longest-running construction technique. But what is now becoming common is the belief that to develop assistance must come from outside.

It is difficult to look at some of the changes that happen in cultures that used to be self-reliant without a sense of aesthetic loss. Bamboo bridges display an artistry that those of concrete and steel cannot match. The technique of building with what you have, adapting objects to new purposes, and fashioning innovations out of the materials at hand is what anthropologist Claude Lévi-Strauss dubbed *bricolage*, a dynamic he located at the heart of culture itself. It is also a hallmark of aesthetic modernism, a connection which reminds us that culture consists of innovation as much as tradition, of adaptive engagement with new circumstances, as well as adherence to tradition and established values.[7] Rather than being an impediment to "progress," as it is often painted in development discourse, culture glimpsed as *process* provides the means by which communities fashion the future by appropriately connecting to the past.

The point is this: Arunachal people had a way of life using what they had, adding new things when they arrived, experimenting and making innovations. Then came the way of gifts and professionals, and the people took that as well. However, the new introductions created a sense of dependency, and with that the people lost the sense of their own capabilities. Bameng and other communities became so dependent on food from outside that when roads were cut during the monsoon, people who once knew how to live from the jungle began to starve. The appeal of outside goods is undeniable. People prefer well-designed items to makeshift, ease and durability to laborious construction. The rapidity with which rubber-soled flip-flops replaced traditional sandals around the world illustrates the point. At first it seems that benefits come, but something more than aesthetics is lost by these transactions: the locus of control. Such development grows dependency. Those who bring such items make profits (so gross national product rises), but the way the parts of life fit together changes with the danger that such change weakens the community instead of strengthening it. A challenge at the center of this book is how to retain the locus of control in the community yet also enable the community to profit by engagement with broader world systems. Furthermore, maintaining the integrity of local tradition is crucial, not simply out of motives of cultural preservation, but because not all new ideas are improvements. Many technological fixes have unintended consequences, especially in the form of environmental degradation. Successful future adaptation depends on being able to reach into the past.

It is in order to enable such dynamic adaptation, that SEED-SCALE focuses on human energy as the currency of change. The units are in calories, hopes, expectations of mutual obligation, and the like—the stuff of culture and of history rather than pure economics—items that adapt in life-context. Such units are very different from the currency of dollars, pounds, rupees, or other identical linear units. But possession of human energy is universal: every living person has it, and we use it to drive the currents of our forward progress. No other resource has zero "have-nots." While money has a universal transferability, its biggest weakness (and indeed the mechanism by which it functions) is its scarcity. By starting with an available-to-all base, social change can operate in a world of plenty instead of one of scarcity. With human energy there is no more "underclass"—those once living at or outside the economic margins can enter the social change process.

The slums of the world provide another example of people improving their lives through the driving force of human energy. Return to the epigraph above: the mere existence of "Paradise Alley" constructed out of the refuse of economic growth is a triumph of human energy in the face of the most life-denying oppressions that industrial modernity has on offer. Slums are a reality that those of us who do not live in them would do well not to wall off from consciousness. One-seventh of the people of the world, a billion human beings, live in urban slums, places where the services of development do not reach. This "planet of slums" continues to grow, both in raw numbers and percentage of the global population.[8] The usual perspective views these places purely as sites of squalor, but their residents display the ingenuity of people building with what they have.[9] Competition for material resources is fierce, yet in this life-or-death situation, where there is seldom a police force and never an effective service infrastructure, self-imposed norms of control exist. People's energies make slums work.[10] This is the fundamental blindness of Elli's well-intended indignation in the epigraph above delivered to a government doctor who responds, "It's not my department." In her certainty that cleaning up the slums "must be someone's department," Elli overlooks more powerful implications of the fact that it is Animal's home.[11] We, as authors, do not minimize the real suffering such existence entails. We have seen it. But we are also pointing out the real achievement such communities represent. In John Ruskin's terms, they have no wealth—but they do have life.

A notable instance of a slum-turned-prosperous-settlement is the case of Conjunto Palmeira in Brazil, on the outskirts of the city of Fortaleza. There, those who shared leadership learned to coordinate community energies, and with that coordination, the community pressed for electricity, bus service, a school, and sanitation. An event in the sanitation story indicates this energy-grounded way of working: when government did not provide garbage pickup, the people gathered a week's worth of stinking refuse, carted it to the city center, and dumped it in front of the municipal offices. Not surprisingly, the government changed its behavior. An example of how they moved from human energy to monetary is that, lacking financial resources, Conjunto Palmeira created its own currency,—a form of credit card that is used in local stores and promotes purchasing local products.[12] Such actions become possible when communities realize control is in their hands, enabling them to see an opportunity, grab it with collective ownership, and build forward momentum on it.[13] This ability to identify and act on a new opportunity, mobilizing change collaboratively, is a key characteristic of a successful adaptive social system.[14]

Human energy can be measured physically in time and calories and manifests itself in many forms: labor, ideas, emotions, and bonds among people. A portion is gathered from each person, and indeed only modest amounts are required from each to build significant social capital. (If everyone gives a few hours a week, then. . . .) At essentially no monetary cost, collected human energy can concentrate in a town square, or it can be distributed throughout the town according to need. It is very flexible and highly powerful. The community changes as a result. As action moves forward, energies compound and are not used up like financial assets or fossil fuels. Harlan Cleveland and Garry Jacobs have shown how the manner in which communities amass and allocate such reserves, applying them in knowledge, labor, money, art, and so on represents the true wealth of that society, in contrast to the pure economics.[15] As in rural Bameng and urban Conjunto Palmeira, this compounding energy creates a society shaped by the conditions that truly matter, one with strengthened connections both among the people and to government and non-government agencies.

Rima was expending energy as she counted children and noted ages, stopped and made conversations; but that was not the most significant energy. When climbing a steep Himalayan ridge it is easier to press on in measured steps, devoting attention to the trail and one's own breath. When arriving in a new community, it takes time, effort, and will to circulate the news that you are starting a women's group, to find a place to meet, and to make tea to lubricate discussion (especially if you talk others into making the tea so that from the outset the process is collectively owned). These investments cause society to grow. On one hand, such investments appear marginal—they cost nothing in the currency transfers of the world—but on the other hand they transform many lives, and create a change that continues to grow. Such investments are not the normal stuff of development and feel risky for an individual new to this process. The three points noted at the head of this section help lower the risk. With Rima's investment, her energy grew in combination with the energies of others, and as the process evolved more women were investing their hours in making changes. As other people invested more of themselves, fear of failure decreased, comfort levels grew, and people began to work more creatively. Social capital was compounding. An adaptive response had started to a complex set of forces involving 30 villages with the tug and pull of 2,000 people, in an ecosystem of unpredictabilities, now partnering with once-ineffective government programs.

SOCIAL CHANGE AS PART OF COMPLEX ADAPTIVE SYSTEMS

Society is a complex adaptive system comprised of human behaviors, a product of the interactions among all its parts. Most contemporary approaches, while recognizing society's complexities, do not utilize the central feature of complex systems: the interaction among the parts. Instead, they focus on the parts as discreet entities, perhaps adding new parts, upgrading old ones, or changing positions among them, but always with the view that it is the parts themselves that matter. Therefore, the results of most contemporary actions are partial and do not utilize the potential of the whole. It is not until the whole adapting system is engaged that empowered, sustained, holistic change can result. In complex adaptive systems, the whole is not the sum of the parts, but a different product determined by *how* the parts are relating to one another.

By changing only their relationships to each other, the same people with the same educations and financial resources can bring an epidemic under control or they can succumb to it. By changing only their relationships, the same people with the same educations and financial resources can take a peaceful community to war, or they can bring an end to violence. In complex adaptive systems, the whole changes when relationships among the parts regroup; something new is created out of the old whole. The parts are surely needed, but how they come together defines the product. As Ruskin argued, a human being is profoundly different from the sum of the nervous, circulatory, musculature, reproductive, and skeletal parts. So, too, are communities in the aggregation of people, each with their distinct identity, each adapted to time and place. The transformation into the whole results from changing relationships between the parts, and these adaptive reactions in turn transform the constituent parts themselves.[16]

While the above is almost self-evident, almost all contemporary approaches to creating societal change emphasize only the parts, and attempt to connect these in a linear manner. Plans are written out, budgets are tabulated; hierarchies are set up with lines of control from the leadership down.[17] Such approaches attempt to treat the complex world in linear terms, even though we know full well that it is not. A health program identifies needs, sets up services to address those needs, puts in place a funding stream, monitors results; the premise throughout is that health results from management of the parts. While there is validity to such linear thinking because it gives clarity, it is inherently limited because it is predicated upon the establishment of limits rather than embracing the dynamics. It is very different from what Rima did: strengthening the actions within which health operates—which is to say, the relationships among people's actions. In emergent solutions, processes internal to the system and resulting from how the parts are interacting direct the change.

What is it that directs this emergent ordering? In complex systems a set of procedures directs the interactions among the dynamics.[18] In an ant colony, where wonderful patterns of collective action and marvelously complex architecture emerge, it is not the "queen" that gives directions (functionally, she is essentially a set of reproductive organs). Rather, the ants, stupid and powerless as individuals, follow simple rules that tell each how to interrelate. What makes a city operate is how people relate on the street, how the government interacts with the citizenry, how businesses connect to the world beyond—all the quotidian actions of everyday life. Each interaction helps constitute the whole. These interactions are guided by both formal and informal procedures, comprised of laws, customs, and habits. Assuredly, it also matters that the city has its formal structures such as employees, streets, buildings, water and electrical services; but it is procedures that direct the functioning of all of these, and many of the most important procedures are often never written down.[19] Every complex system has its procedures, and these are what differentiate a successfully adapting complex system from chaos.

The Bameng example shows how teaching the procedures of social change instigated transformation in the villages. The villagers did not change; they were the same people living in the same place. Rima did not give directions. What happened was that Rima taught new procedures, and out of these people shaped new organization. The people grew that new organization interactively. Rima may have been the instigator, but she was not the cause—that was the people and their energies.

Within a complex adaptive social-systems approach, there are communities within communities, each following the procedural process: at the smallest level an action group, then the larger community coordinating group, regional representation, even the nation. These can be considered social *fractals*, building units of society nested one inside another; each a mirror of the organization above and below it, a complex system unto itself where the sum is greater than the parts, each sum then a part of a larger sum. In fractal geometry, a simple pattern repeats both outward and inward. This social nesting fractal process is analogous to physical-world nested fractals such as atom, molecule, cellular organism, complex organism, ecosystem.[20]

To grow social change, utilize this fractal structure with one social unit nesting within larger units. One or a few communities develop restructured community relationships (as the first Bameng action groups did) then with that as an example other communities adopt their model, then many communities learn from those, and eventually the growth expands region-wide. To borrow a metaphor from our Internet age: change goes viral, growing from multiple nodes. Growth occurs from processes inside each system, causing it to be sustainable, causing it also to adapt and be more in tune with local needs. No central command (or plan) is in control; there is no central line of reporting.

When the expansion is using parts and resources extant in communities, constantly adapting from internal learning, solutions grow from the inside out. This is social emergence. Emergence allows an understanding of relationships and their consequences that separately organized disciplines cannot: showing in the case of communities how social fractals nest one inside the other, how they connect laterally to other units, and then collectively create complexity. As will be explained, the SEED-SCALE process grows such change though four principles implemented by seven iterative tasks. While keeping straight multiple principles and tasks and then using these to figure out new solutions may seem daunting, such a process is easier to learn and manage than NGO or government regulations, which require handbooks, manuals, contracts, and reporting structures to spell out their lines of control. In this principle based approach radically different solutions emerge (a fitted-to-site logic) as different communities implement solutions fitted to what that community has and what it wants.[21] Implementation according to rules creates order out of complexity in a manner analogous to the way the winds of nature blow across a desert to pile once randomly distributed sands into systematic dunes, or the movements of ants to grow wonderfully complex anthills.[22]

The emergent products are results of thousands of adaptive actions fitting and refitting (*adaptare*, Latin "to fit"). The process through which such adaptive integration takes place defines such systems.[23] Every community is developed and always developing. It is not a matter of a community moving from "developing" to "developed," but rather of embarking on a never-ending process of "fitting," of always staying apace with the world.

In a world of adapting social change, sorting out often conflicting interactions and multilevel relationships becomes confusing. In that process, emergence provides clarity not through mapping out the complexities, but by giving ways to respond to the complexity. The complexity is accepted, even celebrated, because it can be dealt with rather than the approach that is in fact more complex (and in the specifics of time and place less accurate) of analyzing, designing, and implementing. Emergence goes directly to implementation, allowing design to unfold along the way, always readapting within an ongoing analysis of vast numbers of interactions to improve the design.[24]

To use emergence in this manner, where complexity is accepted as *the* defining feature of society, a shift in mindset is needed. Despite what bureaucrats and leaders like to think, social change is not, and cannot be, run by directives or according to plans. Orders can be given, people will work to budgets, but the result is people implementing projects, not social change from within. At best, such projects result in a collection of actions that bring about changes within the society; but such change stops at the boundary of control and expires with the budget. This is why so many "pilot projects" succeed as projects and fail as pilots. Social change that grows internally and is sustained is a product of decisions made in response to shifting contexts. Management in these situations occurs through creating more effective order each time. The process is always happening; now it is being better managed through the uniform application of principles.[25] Not understanding this internal potential, and relying instead on what they can control, is the great error of bureaucrats, academics, and professionals.[26]

As David Ekbladh argues in a compelling summation of American approaches to development in the twentieth century, both Western and socialist efforts were distinguished by "grand plans that endeavored to lay down great technological monuments, alter nature, and, most important, to transform human perceptions," particularly in order to counter each others' claims of competing ideological systems, all of which held the promise of "modernization" before the world.[27] David Korten articulates the result (and the alternative) when he argues: "When power resides with people and communities, life and innovation flourish. When power is centralized in distant government agencies or corporations, the life is sucked out of the community, and services are organized to serve the needs and convenience of the providers. Those who

Figure 1.3. Children of Bameng Valley making do—sliding downhill on homemade slab-of-wood sleds. *(Photo credit: Daniel Taylor)*

make the decisions prosper, and the local people bear the consequences."[28] In contrast to planned-out, externally driven models, social change that grows from internal strength depends on a process of constant adaptation to an ever-changing world in which conforming to the dictates of external plans or budgets is impossible. The stabilizing force comes from analyzing and applying the governing principles (though one can track the activities and in doing so see the procedures change). To return to the lesson from Bameng, such change consists of groups of women and men always working with the resources available, doing more when more is available, doing things differently as one person has shown another a better way. There was no plan. Nobody was in control. But procedures were being implemented.

THE THESIS

The understanding provided by emergence has been largely overlooked in international development.[29] Economic development tends to see change as a progression from poverty to wealth, and this linear transition as resulting from inputs and deterministic policies. Similarly, medicine sees change as a progression from sickness to health. Agriculture views the challenge to be toward assuring food security. Education sees a progression through sequenced grades in school. And while each may recognize that theirs is a slice across a complex system, none of these provides a framework for acting in the whole view that is the community's experience.

Emergence offers such a framework, a framework that encompasses everything from health, to education, to income, to governance, to disaster preparedness; it engages the complex system and it gathers together separated disciplines. Engagement is through decision rules, but throughout this book we will term them operating principles—the foundational dynamics by which the SEED-SCALE process functions. Those presented here are not the only possible operating principles. A variety of principles are possible. For example, a familiar package might be: People seek what is best for them individually, maximize safety in any event, and optimize short-term gain.

After two decades of evidence-review of what has worked over time to advance communities, coupled with following field applications to test these, the SEED-SCALE approach has determined that the following principles, when assessed according to the criteria of equitable, sustainable, holistic, interdependent, and iteratively maturing action, are consistently able to foment more effective and lasting change.

- First principle: Build on success. Continue to improve what is working in the context of the resource base and each moment in time.
- Second principle: A three-way partnership among the top-down (government, major corporate interests, organized religion, etc.), bottom-up (community with its varied segments), and outside-in (NGOs, experts, ex–community members now living elsewhere). The top-down is the environment that can be enabling or disabling. The bottom-up is the foundation of change. The outside provides catalytic training and other inputs. All three of these partners are needed.
- Third principle: Evidence-based decision-making. Ground decisions in a situation's reality: try an idea, see results, improve, see new results, try again—continually evaluate and adjust.
- Fourth principle: Behavior change. Societies are amalgams of people *doing* things; thus, societies change as people change their actions. Behavior change is, therefore the universal goal.

In traditional developmental approaches, where the outcomes sought are deliverables based on donor or government priorities, the determinative dynamic is resources provided coupled with control over those resources to assure achieving the outcomes. Development is something done to a population. By contrast, in the complex-adaptive framework offered by SEED-SCALE, direction comes from principles growing through internal action and constantly evolving decisions from local levels engaging both local and external determinants. No attempt is made to set goals or promise outcomes such as specific drops in mortality, illiteracy, or poverty. The distinguishing feature is people in applying the principles—their doing so gives expression to a range of priorities and it grounds action on their resources. Control is distributed. While some form of centralized control operates in nearly any scenario (a local chief, business, government, or international agency), the processes of people constantly maneuvering to expand their domains of influence puts checks on that control and opens spaces for action within it.

Illustration of people's constant maneuvering to optimize their circumstances is seen in cities, where (as in all social systems) the central driver of change is human aspiration. Cities are communities taken to the next scale up—a nearly totally human created world, created by bringing together aspirations and actions. Aspirations come in many forms: power, popularity, economic gain, security. Aspirations are a force that is inside people. They can be shared, rapidly aggregated, and can result in societies making great sacrifices to achieve them. In cities, these energies create new order at sometimes very significant scale (there are now 19 megacities of 20 million or more people). Where cities focus their aspirations defines the directions they will go.

The term *revolution of rising expectations* was coined in India during the 1950s following the giddy experience of independence from Britain. Living in India during those years, we watched that energy explode before our eyes. Out of political freedom unleashed aspirations that transformed life expectancy, agriculture, income, and education, as well as political autonomy. Individual aspirations coalesced into collective energy to drive this broad change. Expectations rose; then, in the 1960s, they plummeted. While "rising expectations" first encapsulated hope, the phrase took a cynical turn to convey disillusionment. As used then in India, it suggested that rising aspirations outpaced the delivery of results, meaning that the drive to "develop" could never sate demand and lost the key idea of hope that drives change. In contrast, we suggest an alternative, the *revolution of rising aspirations*, to foreground its positive aspect.[30]

Instead of seeing expectations as outpacing delivery of results, using the term "the revolution of rising aspirations" brings forward the positive dynamic: rising aspirations mobilize, refine, and expand action. Aspirations are the foundation of the resource stream rather than the cause of exceeding them, the foundation that brings together everything from creativity to cash. When economic growth (a scarce resource) is viewed as the foundational currency, the notion of rising aspirations launches a process of never-met satisfaction. The remedy is to couple aspirations to results so that a feedback loop is created that synergizes aspiration and action. Aspirations become the basis of development, rather than its nemesis.

Chapter 8 will present an extensive discussion of the revolution of rising aspirations as the engine of "going to scale." The point to emphasize here is that the revolution of rising aspirations drives not only the empowerment-based mode of development (as realized aspirations grow empowerment), but also its the potential to go to scale. If the driver is scarce (money, natural resources, and the like), then social change extends only to those limits. By focusing on human energy as the resource base for aspirations, the revolution of rising aspirations bypasses the "limits to growth problem" that comes from a growth strategy framed in terms of finite resources.[31] And if the resource base is no longer finite, there is an inexhaustible base on which to scale up. In altering the emphasis from material to human energies, expected outputs may expand from material products to those such as enhanced family and community relations, artistic expression, security, entertainment and sports, acquisition of knowledge, and on across the range of human experience. Furthermore, and not incidentally, such "growth" is not dependent on devastation of the natural world.

Important clarification is needed about the idea of "going to scale." Usually, when practitioners speak of "going to scale," they mean numerical extension: a project grows larger in size or coverage. This understanding speaks to only one dimension of a multidimensional process, however. It misses the feedback loop found in the revolution of rising aspirations, which causes a self-fueled process of change to emerge, where aspirations morph into other energy forms just as action spread across the multiple spheres of community life in Bameng. Going to scale, as SEED-SCALE uses the term, means quantitative growth in synergy with a rising quality of life. Relationships among the parts realign according to aspirations; this allows a whole new organization of priorities to emerge. People want more than just health or income or knowledge. A first advance in the good life calls people to want wider options, and achieving these leads to more innovations. The synergy becomes active between quality of life and quantity of people participating. Rising quality of life brings more people to participate, and this numerical expansion increases human resources. That larger base leads to next stages of quality, and the feedback loop generates true scale.

The feedback loop creates momentum toward the persistently receding horizon of development, the constantly rising, never-achieved aspirations. As policies, financing, and knowledge bases interact with aspirations and actions, they become the material and informational drivers for scaling up. The feedback loop presses on, connecting relationships between minds, muscles, and dreams. In this feedback growing out of the momentum of individual communities aggregating with others comes the dynamic with potential to benefit all people across time. This process is not new; it is what has propelled communities to prosper under widely divergent circumstances for millennia. Rising aspirations lead not to inevitable frustration, but are the way toward realizing hope.

CHAPTER 2

Connecting to the Larger Field of Development and Social Change

The day is not far off when the economic problem will take the back seat where it belongs, and the arena of the heart and the head will be occupied or reoccupied, by our real problems—the problems of life and human relations, or creation and behaviour and religion.[1]
John Maynard Keynes

The bulk of this book elaborates the SEED-SCALE process, its principles, tasks, and evaluation criteria, and the multiple dimensions of SCALE. These discussions are grounded in real-world examples, either from field work in which the process was intentionally applied (as in Afghanistan, India, China), or in which the principles can be observed despite the fact that they were not being intentionally applied (as in the New York City parks). In order to streamline these discussions for clarity and make them accessible to the widest possible audience, discussion of other development approaches and scholarship is kept to a relative minimum. However, this chapter will attempt to contextualize SEED-SCALE in relation to the broader field of development thinking and scholarship.

To understand how SEED-SCALE is distinguished from mainstream development approaches, the current global campaign by governments and international organizations for the Millennium Development Goals (MDGs) offers an instructive evidence base. The MDGs arguably constitute the greatest intentional effort in world history to reach the sector of humanity that has been excluded from global prosperity. The MDGs are receiving huge infusions of money, with the majority of international agencies trying to coordinate efforts in support of them. And yet, the success of even this massive coordinated effort is in serious jeopardy. Thus, the MDGs provide an apt means for considering the limitations of current approaches to development and international assistance.

The Millennium Declaration sets forward its vision as follows: "The MDGs are the world's time-bound and quantified targets for addressing extreme poverty in its many dimensions—income poverty, hunger, disease, lack of adequate shelter, and exclusion—while promoting gender equality, education, and environmental sustainability. They are also basic human rights—the rights of each person on the planet to health, education, shelter, and security."[2] This declaration was signed by 192 member states and twenty-three major international agencies, and constitutes nothing less than an effort to manage the socio-econo-biosphere. Much like a business seeking to deliver results, eight goals are projected, which are to be localized for each country. The plan to meet them uses proven interventions grounded in global best practice. Twenty-one targets were set for 2015, with a price tag attached to each.

The idea is for all signatory countries to make progress toward these goals, as each goal seeks percentage reductions based on starting levels in each country, with aggregated reductions reflecting global progress. In some countries, there has been success with specific goals, such as reducing maternal mortality. However, overall progress is bleak. The 2009 United Nations report states:

> Major advances in the first (goal) against extreme poverty from 1990 to 2005, for example, are likely to have stalled. . . . Likewise, the encouraging trend in the eradication of hunger since the early 1990s was reversed in 2008. . . . Meager progress on child nutrition from 1990 to 2007 is insufficient to meet the 2015 target . . . these ongoing crises may also hold back progress toward gender equality. . . . The ability of countries to mobilize domestic resources for development is also in jeopardy. . . . Debt service to exports ratios of developing countries are likely to deteriorate further.[3]

In other words, the MDGs are falling short of the mark on goal after goal.

The point to note in the above explanation is not to drill in goal-by-goal, but to note the unquestioned assumption that achieving the MDGs rests on the ability to mobilize resources. The world's largest development initiative was designed on the basis of raising money and applying it to the task at hand. This was done in an era of global financial pressure and declining international donations, and in this highly constrained financial climate depended on mobilizing *domestic* resources. Where are the poorest countries in the world going to get those resources? Are they to take on crushing debt? Are they to exploit the natural resources that remain unpillaged? Neither is an acceptable or viable option. Many poor countries already devote a significant portion of their gross domestic product to servicing their extensive debts. Natural resources are often more of a curse than a boon, first drawing colonial regimes, and later corporate exploitation, leaving the country itself ecologically stripped and (aside from a few corrupt officials) largely without economic benefit.

Moreover, according to the former Director of Development Research at the World Bank, there is no fallback proposition: the well-being of five billion people depends on this program.[4] If the MDGs are not achieved, blame will be on parsimonious donors: "If the global community responds constructively to the crisis, the goals can still be achieved. Honouring the commitment to increase aid is critical."[5] Despite such resonant pleas, why risk the fate of billions people of people on an assumption of generosity when there is no evidence the affluent are going to share their wealth at requested levels with the distant poor? A few years earlier, in the 1990s, when the world was afloat in money, perhaps there was a plausible hope that a new age of generosity might dawn. But now, when that flotation device has been revealed to be a bubble, when wars and rising climate catastrophe exacerbate pressures on countries attempting to recover from economic collapse, we cannot rationally assume such generosity.

However, the MDGs need not stall. The delivery model on which the program was founded is flawed, but by turning to a complementary model it is possible to achieve the goals. Instead of trying to send services to the "unreached," we can help them create their own services and reach back to engage with the services that the world is able to provide: do what the people of Bameng did on a global scale. Today, there are top-down enabling facilities for the MDGs in every country. They may be inadequate, they may be scant, but they are not nonexistent. Rather than lamenting their weaknesses, we can build on what is there.

What is weakest, weaker than any of the service agencies or funding streams, is adequate engagement by the target populations in the process. What is costing so much money is *paying* for services that a great portion of which people could do for themselves with their energies. People do not know how to use what little is there, how to do what the people of Bameng did and close the "last kilometer to the home" by leaving their homes and walking to the services. *The most important service is the one not being utilized: what the people can do themselves.* Like the people of Bameng before they mobilized, the people of the world have now been taught to expect government to come to them. They have lost the sense of what is possible with the resources that they already have. A great deal of culpability in this loss lies with the international community, which has spread the assumption of disempowerment as a baseline for development. However, this is not a call for go-it-alone grassroots mobilization: once people have taken the first crucial step of retaking control, the next step is to engage with services. Engaging local services, especially if inadequate and few, will not simply occur willy nilly. Just as occurred in Bameng, people need to learn how to utilize services and adapt their application to the needs of the local context. Learning how to engage what is there is not simply telling government and experts to get out of the way, as in libertarian calls for abolishing "big government." Learning how requires learning on both sides: the community learning and government and experts learning to work in true partnership. Such learning occurs iteratively, event upon event, interaction upon interaction, until real partnership is built.

As is so clear with the MDGs, the assumption that the aid model should be delivering services to the people, driving initiatives with money, is unquestioned. Transforming an approach so ensconced is difficult. Many vested interests profit from it, whether monetarily or in terms of professional promotion and prestige. Thus, attempting to broaden awareness will be particularly hard at the macro-level of international policy. By contrast, the vested interests of communities lie in their own immediate futures. If action begins with community mobilization where ready allies are eager for strategy, the process can begin and grow.

One of this book's authors personally saw an earlier global initiative to mobilize communities from the top-down be derailed. In 1978, the International Conference on Primary Health Care in Alma-Ata, Kazakhstan, was the first modern global forum to put forward a global development agenda. Carl co-wrote the background papers and designed the global strategy for the Alma-Ata conference. The pronounced strategy was community-based and placed a premium on equity: "Health for All by the Year 2000." This was to be achieved by international support for scaling up already functioning projects around the world, many of which Carl had been involved with as the founding chairman of the Department of International Health at Johns Hopkins University. While doing research for this book, Carl pulled a volume off his shelf, and sheets of yellow paper slipped out, notes scrawled while sitting on the dais at Alma-Ata in 1978. The paper tallied differences in inflection in how speakers spoke the conference's theme: Health for All. "Some people," he wrote in his notes, are saying "'*health* for all' and others are saying 'health for *all*.'" When Carl tallied up the inflection differences in the 147 speeches, his conclusion was that those who said '*health* for all' came predominately from the First or Second Worlds, while those who said 'health for *all*' came primarily from what was then being called the Third World.

As Carl worked in many of these countries over the next thirty years, it became evident to him that the "*health* for all" people had won. The business and the profession of health were in control. Under the banner of getting health to all, they won funds to evolve more technologies, strengthen their delivery systems, and build the apparatus of international health assistance. Approaches of health delivery that had real potential to reach all, using existing technologies, extant systems, and above all, centered on using people rather than professionals, were ignored.[6] Halfdan Mahler, the Director General of the World Health Organization who oversaw the 1978 Alma-Ata conference, also followed the efforts over the thirty years. Like Carl, Mahler did not believe that the goal was unattainable. A passionate leader with a distinctive ability to focus on those most in need, Mahler had driven the original bold vision, but in 2009 he said: "We had it wrong in 1978. What came about was 'Hell for all' as the business of health stole the idea."[7]

Today, in a similar manner, to improve the MDGs, the professionals suck up money doing technology evolution and delivery analysis. Doing so, they keep themselves in business.[8] The global business of "helping the poor" thrives on the argument of needing to improve delivery before actually doing it, developing technologies that support labs and offices rather than people, and in being so focused on themselves, overlooking capacity already there among communities and their existing partnerships. All speak of *community*, but what has happened is that communities have become viewed as targets, rather than as agents to be empowered.

Conference speakers at Alma-Ata who emphasized *for all* had the right understanding. When diseases disappear from a community, all benefit. But to achieve that, it is most effective to focus on the areas where the most impact can be seen with the least effort. Focus on the most common sources of illness, rather than the rarest. Above all, focus on what can be done with what is already available. (For a person hurt by the roadside, there is much that skill can do with few resources, even though if that person were in a hospital there would assuredly be more—when life and death are in balance, as with development, a lot can be done with a little.) By contrast, the speakers who emphasized *health* gave priority to finding more sophisticated responses, eradicating individual diseases, developing and distributing new technologies. While a worthy goal, what happened was that the majority of resources disappeared into searching for health improvements, while delivery to all never happened. William Easterly identifies this process of development's serving itself rather than its intended recipients as resulting from "Planners" who live in their universes of organizations, meetings, and documents, as opposed to "Searchers" who are out in local contexts assembling answers.[9]

Jeffrey Sachs, director of the Millennium Project, which set up showcase villages around the world demonstrating technologies to achieve the MDGs, embodies this approach of perfecting best practices.[10] Early in his career, Sachs addressed the challenges of poverty by large macroeconomic analyses focused on governmental policy adjustments.[11] Experiencing the challenge we all encounter of getting "macro" ideas only partly right and missing the method of growing large-scale policy through iterative evolution (the approach China used splendidly to grow its transformative economic advancement), Sachs nevertheless did come to see that locale-specific solutions were needed. The MDG approach was designed under a commission that he chaired with specific foci on the roles of poverty, gender, and human capacity, with specific technologies identified that could address these.[12] Then, as director of the Millennium Project, Sachs led the team proposing that change could be scaled up from the model villages that were showing these breakthroughs. The glaring problem for this extension is that the model villages themselves are heavily funded projects. Few other villages are following them, and those that are, do so mostly because external incentives have been provided. They are thus "models" in the true sense of the word, bearing some correspondence to the real world but essentially different from it. It is a mistake to confuse the fact that such models can teach us things about the real world (which they assuredly can) with thinking that they can *become* real—much like mistaking an architect's scale model of a building for the bricks of a foundation.

In this respect, the Millennium Villages (and indeed the MDGs more broadly) risk repeating some of the central problems that James C. Scott identifies for why "certain schemes to improve the human condition have failed." Taking a broad historical and geographical scope, Scott examines what he calls "high-modernist ideology," which he describes as "a strong, one might even say muscle-bound, version of the self-confidence about scientific and technical progress, the expansion of production, the growing satisfaction of human needs, the mastery of nature (including human nature), and, above all, the rational design of the social order commensurate with the scientific understanding of natural laws."[13] Tracing the workings of this ideology through such disparate instances as Napoleon's France, Lenin's Russia, Nehru's India, and World Bank "villagization" initiatives in Tanzania, Scott identifies a common thread of denying complexity in exchange for simplified models, coupled with the attempt, through money or (often) coercion, to force reality to conform to the plan. In contrast, Scott points to the ways communities have consistently resisted such command-and-control schemes through the application of local solutions and practical, adaptive knowledge.

While development thinking has largely shed the excesses of high-modernist ideology, with its taste for big dams, planned cities, and (most importantly) authoritarian control, the error of trying to ship in solutions derived from experience from other places, often relying on outside financing and technology, remains evident in the MDGs. The solution lies in iteratively learning from local experience and *adapting* new ideas and technologies from outside in accordance with it. It is almost impossible to get the design for a complex system right by borrowing from another site. Even when the design is right, skills to implement it typically are not present. Thus, the other aspect of the send-the-solution-in approach involves placing action in the hands of outside experts—especially when doing so makes money for those involved in the sending. What this approach has right is that standardization must occur in order to go to scale. (This is the problem with purely local, "grassroots" or "bottom-up" development schemes.) What is wrong is to think that standardized *solutions* can be applied in multiple contexts. As an alternative to the standardization of solutions, SEED-SCALE standardizes the *process* for *evolving*, locally specific solutions.

MDG global extension has treated development like a problem in the experimental sciences: discover the answers in a laboratory against benchmarks of scientific rigor, and then assume these have universal applicability.[14] Thus, Sachs and colleagues kept working on getting the formulae right, setting up model villages, and as it became clear that there were other variables beyond those initially programmed, they expanded the model to include in the eight MDGs the dimensions of population growth and environmental degradation. They then attempted to coordinate government and nongovernmental engagement along the lines of four principles: clear objectives, effective and scalable technology, clear implementation strategy, and adequate sources of financing. However, what was not done was to expand the partnership, most particularly in letting go of control—it is, after all, imperative that a researcher maintain control of the laboratory. In sum, it is clear that the larger MDG mental model is flawed in a number of aspects, all of which are explained by the fact that the people whose destiny is most at stake are left out of true partnership.

Partnership cannot flourish until control is relinquished,. Development is not achieved by discovery in the abstract, and then delivered like a prescription. The central, continually overlooked dynamic is what people can do with what they have; how they can be actors rather than gift-receivers.[15] Can there be a system of interconnections more complex than our planet? Control over a complex system is not possible. Mobilizing a few billion more dollars in support will not do the trick; nor will calling in celebrities and scholars to advocate on behalf of the MDGs. If either of those approaches would work that would be apparent by now, even if it had not expanded to scale. The process is not profile-driven, just as it is not resource-driven. Change is a process that the people lead in their communities, in conjunction with external partners. It grows in iterative steps of feedback from what they have, rather than trying to fill in what they lack, no matter how well-intended such gifts and initiatives may be.

Poised against such established approaches is a mounting critique, although so far the criticism focuses primarily on inefficiencies in developmental assistance, rather than recognizing that the premise of giving services to people misses the first need, which is their self-mobilization. This is not a situation where the engine needs to run more efficiently (and hence simply needs new spark plugs, a better distributor, or simply an oil-and-filter change) but rather that two engines exist: One is designed to run on money delivered through top-down frameworks, while the other runs on human energy delivered from the bottom-up. Perhaps more accurately, we could say that these two engines have been running side by side, the former driving formal development programs, and the other people's efforts betwixt, between (and in times in spite of) them. What we need is not so much to choose one over the other, but to build a hybrid integrating the two so that they feed off of and support each other.

Easterly's critique has already been mentioned: despite $2.3 trillion invested in aid, results have not appreciably helped those most in need, who continue to live shortened, illiterate lives, plagued with ill-health and few options.[16] Dambisa Moyo focuses on the region many consider to be the area of highest need, Africa, where $1 trillion in aid has not lowered poverty. Moya shows that the countries that actually rejected aid prospered, while those that accepted aid saw poverty increase; her point is that the provision of aid typically undermines effective government capacity.[17] That countries were able to develop by rejecting aid confirms that capacity exists in these countries, ready to be scaled up: what works is not aid, but growing successes and partnerships. In this, communities are not developing on their own, devoid of top-down support, but governments are not letting aid skew their extant, and perhaps fragile, top-down systems by introducing a massive program (such as HIV/AIDS treatment without community health services, or micro-credit without transparent governance) that throws off the balance of maturing balanced, locally mobilized momentum.

Political economist Dani Rodrik, whose perspective was shaped growing up in Turkey, which over his lifetime has undergone a near population-wide enabling of internal development, makes a similar argument: Economic growth that mobilizes a nation is a consequence of local growth that occurs within larger frameworks, not just economic stimulus of aid, and the extent to which these larger frameworks are adapted in ongoing iteration to nurture bottom-up growth.[18] Economist Gregory Clark in his review of world economic history shows a rather startling conclusion that the pre-1800 world had better standards of living than the poor of today. Clark says, "Countries such as Malawi or Tanzania would be better off in material terms had they never had contact with the industrialized world. . . . Modern medicine, airplanes, gasoline, computers—the whole technological cornucopia of the past two hundred years—have succeeded there in producing among the lowest living standards ever produced."[19] Clark's conclusions (which are strikingly similar to our experience in Nepal, where the bottom quintile there did not benefit from development; discussed in the next chapter) bears repeating for emphasis: Those excluded from the benefits of global modernity are not simply less well-off than those who have profited from it, *they are living in material conditions less conducive to life than those of pre-industrial society.* Thomas Dichter and Paul Polak in their separate work agree that exploitation might be the result, but suggest this is not the intent, and offer modest ways around the problem.[20] John Perkins not only luridly describes corruption and incompetence, but asserts that it is intentional, outlining development as business's first seeking profits, and to achieve these, creating false datasets and false successes.[21]

Under the banner of ultimate good, assistance for the poor, sick, uneducated, and homeless is indeed now big business. Promoting the need for vast monetary sums to do unquestioned good, what has become unquestioned is the premise of funneling money. The model has a flaw in its design, where actions are performed in one country and accounts submitted in another, with monitoring focused on the accounts in the donor country, not on the results intended in the recipient country. Majid Rahema and Victoria Bawtree respond to such exploitation of the poor, characterizing the process as: "a tiny minority of local profiteers, supported by their 'patrons,' set out to devastate the foundations of social life in countries. A merciless war wages [sic] against the age-old traditions of communal solidarity."[22] Paul Collier, whose job at the World Bank was to study development assistance, sums up the challenge this way: "With some exceptions, aid does not work so well in these environments, at least as it has been provided in the past." (And then he gives his conclusion for how to fix the problem, which is precisely our point: internal mobilization.) "Change in the societies at the very bottom must come predominantly from within."[23] Aside from the fact that money is a scarce resource, particularly unavailable to those who need it most, aside from money's tendency to create cultures of corruption, the biggest flaw in the monetary development model is this shift in focus from internal community mobilization to external manipulative control.

THE GREAT CONFUSION

How, then, can assistance proceed? A different model must be used, one that grows internally, directly connecting to the people so that it stays targeted to their priorities and engages their energies and local resources in the process. Furthermore (it sadly cannot go without saying), the first beneficiaries should not be the intermediaries. However, as noted above, what we are arguing for is not either internal capacity *or* external assistance, but rather a hybrid. Both are needed to address the massive forces and interconnections of today's world. Our primary objection to present actions is that the balance is lost due to international assistance's built-in self-serving purpose of achieving predetermined ends through external manipulations, which ensure that control will be retained through budgets on which people become dependent. Those involved work for a project—toward its specified plans, outcomes, and budgetary guidelines—rather than for improving the collective quality of life. They are well intentioned, to be sure, earnestly hoping and believing that their initiatives will help, but they remain accountable to accounts first, communities second.

What is immediately lost in this approach is an ability to recognize all the successes and resources inside the community. More important, this process does not recognize that a society is not a mechanical system but rather an adaptive system of responses. Let us make the distinction clearly, because the pages that follow concentrate on explaining the internal mobilization that is so often ignored in the present model: service delivery and budgets are essential. We are not arguing against them *tout court*, though in pointing out their flaws it may seem that an argument of their irrelevance is being made. Advanced alone, they are like extending a hand for a handshake with no reciprocal hand coming back, or to use the earlier metaphor, running the process with only one engine when a second, even more powerful, is idling. To make services and budgets maximally effective, the capacity and resources of people must be nurtured—indeed, they are the foundation on which economic growth is built. Moreover, if the people-based response is nurtured, then the range of added available resources expands greatly.

Furthermore, with true community engagement, accountability rises and accuracy of action sharpens. The interacting bottom-up and top-down and outside-in teach each other how to be more effective. That is how adaptive systems work; improving the interactions makes the whole system work better.

International action after World War II in what might be termed "the John Maynard Keynes era" whose far-reaching theories solidified the position that economic policy was determinative, adopted the control-the-system model. W. W. Rostow's influential work from the postwar period spoke of the "take-off" when social capital, technology, and investments caused wealth to accumulate, and society to start rising through five stages of growth.[24] This assumption was politely challenged by W. Arthur Lewis, who was himself from the developing world and pointed out how economic growth first takes labor from the subsistence sectors, then as the supply of cheap labor tapers off, causing wages to rise and wealth to accumulate, turns to other cheap sources of labor.[25] In 1979, Lewis was awarded the Nobel Prize in Economics in conjunction with Theodore Shultz, who had highlighted the critical role of "human capital" as the base on which financial capital grew.[26] Why had Japan and Germany recovered so dramatically after World War II? Shultz's part of the answer was that they had an educated workforce that knew *how to work within the system*. Lewis recognized the role of internal agents learning to adapt, but still came forward with a linear prescription that social change is a rising curve defined by the dynamic of growing economic prosperity. Yes, people were key players with their labor and skills, but those people were considered fundamentally economic agents.

Amid the growing complexity of the economic argument, a simple answer was wanted, and the complexity kept being overlooked. Gross national product (GNP) came to be synonymous with the way to measure an advancing society. The debate was occurring in a world of marvelous technological growth, and the larger mental models of inputs and outputs, of machines making change, of ever faster-paced life, all combined to create a wider belief that life could be controlled and that what controlled everything was economics.

Nascent sensitivity to the complexity of the process started during the 1950s, following the realization that Marshall Plan–type economic reconstruction could not replicate its success in the global South. However, this broadening awareness became politicized as development assistance turned into a battlefield of the Cold War. The dialogue that then played out held that the South had to choose between the differing economic structures of East and West, with Western free-market capitalism contending that wealth would create a better world, while the Communist East argued that the state was needed to allocate the returns of wealth in a just manner. Despite this polarization, both approaches were consistent in applying a linear, process-of-control argument based on economic growth: adopt free-market capitalism (or centrally managed socialism) and the good life will result.

There is, of course, no such clear line, either from capitalism or socialism. But when the Berlin Wall fell in 1989, capitalism's triumph was held to be self-evident, even the "end of history."[27] Oversimplification of the contributing role of the marketplace then took global dominance, even inside Central Asia, as the former Soviet republics moved pell-mell to the marketplace. Expecting almost magical global growth, a chorus rose for further loosening the shackles holding back the planet's economic engine. Moves for economic globalization followed, with the dominant themes articulated as the "Washington Consensus," a package of ten policies to stabilize, privatize, and liberalize economies. This economic-turned-political momentum ignored the fact that the wider scholarship not part of the Washington Consensus was determining a more nuanced explanation. This did not matter to the politicians and press who were oversimplifying economics (see discussion below) in the continuing belief that economic growth was determinative. Nor was it publicly noted that the Washington Consensus had adopted the central-planning mentality of the failed communist system. Complicating arguments that tried to draw out the nuances, such as that by the World Bank's vice-president, Gobin Nankani, were ignored: "There is no unique universal set of rules . . . we need to get away from formulae."[28]

During the 1990s, a number of countries' economies were surging—Brazil, South Korea, Thailand, Malta, Indonesia, Oman, Botswana, Japan, and China, along with the countries of North America and Europe. Because the metric used to measure national change was the GNP, this surge appeared unidirectional and unequivocal, with an increasingly complex nexus of social dynamics and internal inequalities obscured from view (a measurement limitation, as measuring social dynamics is almost assuredly a function of technical limitations in measurement ability). Other indicators such as the Human Development Index and the Gini Coefficient were developed in order to address this inadequacy. However, these remained inadequate to deal with societal complexity because they failed to shift attention to the *relationships* among factors rather than simply recognizing multiple contributing parts. Furthermore, despite their superiority, these more relevant indicators have typically continued to be ignored in favor of the single, familiar, simple number reflected in the GNP.

Discussion seeks a causal connection with some magical economic stimulus factor, and regularly misses the functional connections of a complex adaptive system. For example, Brazil and Oman are rising almost in parallel in economic measures, but they should not even be measured against each other since their growth comes from very different sources (a diversified economy in the former instance; the single commodity of oil extraction in the second). Botswana has a very high Gini Coefficient (measure of internal inequality) at 63, compared to South Korea at 32, but the internal complexities of the two are so radically different that any attempt to draw inferences from this comparison is questionable. Selecting the right principles of measurement makes all the difference, and is more important than which specific factors are being measured.

There is progress, however. Attempts to understand these dynamics have been increasingly embracing aspects of complexity. The role of information technology in communicating the complexities and the role of knowledge in its management has become almost universally recognized, as has the problem of the "digital divide" in opening access to it. Amartya Sen's contributions highlight, first, the role of equity, and in subsequent work, the need to expand people's options and freedoms.[29] Benjamin Friedman placed economic policies within political and social histories, emphasizing the extent to which economic growth must be considered within the complexities of social and even individual ethical life.[30] Vijayendra Rao and Michael Walton placed economic growth within cultures and relations among people, analyzing the process as "a set of contested attributes, constantly in flux, both shaping and being shaped by social and economic aspects of human interaction."[31]

In 1987, the Brundtland Commission presented what may be the pivotal statement of the wholeness of the human endeavor: "In the middle of the twentieth century, we saw our planet from space for the first time. Historians may eventually find that this vision had a greater impact on thought than did the Copernican revolution." The commission attempted to turn action from economic growth alone to "sustainable development," connecting economic growth with the three unraveling dynamics of environment, population growth, and human security. "Sustainable development is development that meets the needs of the present without compromising the ability of future generations to meet their own needs."[32] The environmental lens kept being reground through the 1990s as mounting environmental evidence was showing that human actions were disrupting essential natural balances. The United Nations panel on climate change began projections that turned earlier awareness-opening postulates of the change into hard-to-refute global fact.[33]

Since then, the macro-picture of a planetary whole comprising a complex socioeconomic biosphere of morphing values and awareness has been growing clearer, even in the context of a society almost single-minded in its pursuit of wealth. Regrettably, this was a largely Western discourse, which frustrated many in the global South as they were under pressure to deliver results to their people, whose aspirations were rising even faster than their population numbers. In 1999, these leaders, calling themselves the South Commission, spoke with rare unity, calling for expanded South-to-South cooperation and proposing a crucial paradigm shift: outside money was not enough. Development would come from mobilization of their unity, and Southern economies must be self-fueling and ground their growth in their own resources.[34]

Across the decades, the notable voice missing in this discussion at the high tables of global policy-making was the voice of the people. In the 1960s, Paulo Freire had been at the forefront of that movement, especially in advocating for the oppressed: "Knowledge emerges only through invention and re-invention, through the restless, impatient, continuing, hopeful inquiry human beings pursue in the world, with the world, and with each other."[35] Freire sought participation of the people in change. In his only academic year, trying to train others in his methods, he spoke of how he would "using literacy training, mobilize a village in a few days against the oppressors, then get out before they arrested me."[36] Mobilizing people for confrontation, while the in-your-face aspect of it appeals to the justice-minded and activists, is not a mentality that appeals to people who are daily making hard life choices; most such necessity-focused people are reluctant to risk their family welfare to confront oppression.

In a line-of-control world, confrontation makes sense, and when oppression goes on long enough, rebellion is likely to erupt. But in a complex adaptive world, people innately understand that confrontation pulls social systems apart—in complex always-adapting social systems there are ways of channeling the adaptation. Structural barriers that get in the way are real, but the need is not just to remove them but also to replace them with enabling systems. The answer here is adaptation that takes apart the unjust at the same time that it builds the new—and to achieve this evolution, build from successes, strengthen three-way partnerships, promote decisions based on evidence, and focus on changing behaviors. Toward this end, the adaptive response of iteratively improving not only takes down but also builds up. That momentum must have the participation of the people.

From the 1970s on, many policy shapers such as Peter Evans, Fernando Cardoso (after an earlier Marxist stance), and others realized this point; namely, that confrontation was unlikely to succeed; they argued that the poor should join the system, even if it meant doing so in dependent relationships, and within that context accumulate wealth.[37] This position of engagement with people and building process grew. By the 1990s, traditionally top-down organizations as the World Bank were actively seeking to engage people, arguing for dependent relationships and saying that through such could grow ultimate economic independence as they accumulated wealth.[38] A substantial evidence base is coming together that shows that people who have stable incomes learn how to grow that base into one of rising empowerment.[39]

The issue is not one of the value of empowerment, as in the growing global understanding there is almost universal agreement that empowered people are essential. Rather, the yet-to-be-agreed answer is how to get to empowerment. Is it a requirement that people go through a dependency phase? Is there a direct approach by which people can move to empowerment? What the evidence from the SEED-SCALE applications described in the following chapters shows is that the answer to the first question is "no," and the answer to the second question is "yes."

Mobilization of people using what they have has been the enduring mode of human advancement. Before people had agricultural surpluses, before trade, before monetary profit, social conditions improved by transforming calories into the other energies of hope, trust, and solidarity, and lives got better. Admittedly, in the two centuries of industrial modernity, the rate of advancement surged—but what is cause and what is effect? It is unlikely that in the complex human condition the progress came from a single cause, and perhaps the change was consequential, not causal. Factors such as passing and storing information, first on paper and now in electrons, or leadership, or participatory governance, or technology, each appear to have had roles in the complex adaptive social dynamics, economic factors, and ecosystem influences in play.

Moses Coady, a pioneer in growing empowerment, succinctly stated the reality of the process as being how the poor "will use what they have to secure what they have not."[40] This statement was made in 1939 from the windswept land of Nova Scotia in the years of the Great Depression, when there was little money but abundant evidence of social good coming from the actions of people. Empowerment grows from inside communities. This recognition is not new: its powerful role in North America goes back at least to the time of Alexis de Tocqueville, who in the second volume of *Democracy in America* speaks of America's distinctive abilities to engage its citizens in social change. Though the devastating westward expansion in search of land and resources must not be discounted, much of the rise in the quality of life in America during the nineteenth century can also be attributed to participatory mobilization through a wide range of neighborly helping, democratic processes, people-based cooperatives, the Grange, and religious units.[41]

Abraham Lincoln's role in providing such enabling structures in this period is often overlooked despite the reams of scholarship attending to his achievements. With Lincoln's great contribution of holding the nation together and emancipating the slaves, his many innovations to empower rural America are seldom noted. By introducing three classes of mail service (including the postcard for quick, cheap, and brief communiqués), setting up mail-sorting on moving railroad trains, and supporting expansion of the telegraph for nearly instantaneous communication (superseding the Pony Express) he advanced the nineteenth-century equivalent of the Internet. Lincoln was personally fascinated by the telegraph and the idea of instantaneous communications, and each day he crossed the White House lawn and go and sit by the equipment.[42] To be effective in the modern world, people require more than information. Lincoln understood that modern life came from what Andrew Carnegie would aptly term "the advancement and diffusion of knowledge," and he used essentially free federal lands to establish land-grant colleges in every state, thereby making access to higher education no longer an option for just the Eastern elite. But Lincoln also recognized the connection between people-based developments and economic ones. The energies of an awakened people had to help awaken the postwar economy. To expand the use of money, he turned the dollar into a standard national currency and set up a national banking system, and to allow money to go places where there were no banks, he restructured the postal service so it could issue money orders, thereby setting in motion small monetary sums moving back and forth across rural America.[43]

Bottom-up growth does not happen on its own. If people were able to advance on their own, they would have long ago. Bottom-up growth occurs through partnerships. One of the most articulate statements of how partnership with people can be created comes from another pioneer in social change, Jimmy Yen, speaking from China in the 1930s:

Go to the People.
Live with the People,
Learn from the People.
Plan with the People,
Work with the People.
Start with what they know,
Build on what they have.
Teach by showing, learn by doing.
Not a showcase, but a pattern.
Not piecemeal, but integrated.
Not odds and ends, but a system.
Not to conform, but to transform.
Not relief, but release.[44]

The two recurrent words through the above injunction are "with people"— not "for people" or "from people"—which is to say, in partnership. In Bameng, Rima was growing empowerment with the people. Money joined the process from what they did together, but what she was using to generate that money was management of the resource all the people in the Bameng area had. For development to reach all, it must be driven by a resource available to all, not the scarce resource of which they have the least. Following chapters describe the details of the method she used, but before turning to these, it is helpful to outline the scholarly discourse on empowerment.

The articulation of "empowerment" as the currency of change has been led by Robert Chambers, who emphasizes the importance of participatory methods for evidence collection, analysis, and decisionmaking. Chambers has professed himself "astonished by the analytical abilities of poor people. Whether literate or not, whether children, women, or men, they showed that they could map, list, rank, score, and diagram better than professionals."[45] Experiments with a family of participatory approaches have followed from his advocacy: Rapid Assessment Procedures (RAP), Participatory Rural Appraisals (PRA), and Rapid Rural Appraisals (RRA). These are methods for people to become involved not just in analysis and decisionmaking, but also in action.[46] Such methods introduced the concept of *objective assessment* to refute the belief that subjective accumulation of anecdotes is the only realm open to the community, while genuine data belongs to the professionals. As their effectiveness grows clearer with continuing work, the meaning of the PRA acronym has evolved to Participatory Reflection and Action, since the methods are no longer applied exclusively in rural settings. Using PRAs, community people segue from anecdote to objectivity, bringing in evidence as a meeting ground for differences in earlier perceptions.

Further methodologies to engage people are becoming available. One of the best known is Asset Based Community Development (ABCD), which took form in the late 1980s and works with communities to discover their strengths; that is, what they already have.[47] ABCD informed the SEED-SCALE synthesis during the UNICEF-sponsored global review in the 1990s, giving form to Principle 1: Build from success. ABCD is now being used globally with support from the Ford Foundation and instructional methods from Jody Kretzmann and John McKnight. Case evidence shows that the approach, applied in an iterative cycle, produces real and lasting community-based change.[48] Similar to ABCD is Positive Deviance, which seeks the examples in a community that are unusual but working well—the deviants. Determine why these deviants are working, then scale those up within the resource and personnel streams of the society. Carl worked with Gretchen Berggren when the approach was first evolving in the early 1980s; now it is being promoted through the Positive Deviance Program at Tufts University.[49] An important note of clarification: positive deviance, like ABCD and PRAs, focuses on one principle. These methods are powerful entry points for empowerment and lead to social change, and SEED-SCALE embraces their methodologies. Where SEED-SCALE differs is that it represents a whole theory of change, which also includes an evaluative feedback loop and a means for scaling up, not just an entry point that grows seeds of empowerment grounded in participatory values.

A global effort to understand empowerment was made by the World Bank, resulting in the *World Development Report 2000/2001*, which identified empowerment, opportunity, and security as the three critical components of development.[50] This World Bank study defined empowerment, not as political uprising or community participation, but rather as the collection of internal societal dynamics central to economic growth: "A growing body of evidence points to the linkages between empowerment and development effectiveness both at the society-wide level and at the grassroots level."[51] The World Bank study concluded that four elements produced empowerment: (1) Access to information (two-way information flows from government to citizens and from citizens to government); (2) Inclusion and participation (treating poor people as co-producers); (3) Accountability (political accountability, administrative accountability, social accountability); and (4) Local organizational capacity (the ability of people to work together, organize themselves, and mobilize resources).[52] In subsequent work, Deepa Narayan, the editor of the earlier sourcebook, brought together a team to measure empowerment, and as a result, many more factors than these four were identified. The study struggled to determine which were most important, whether qualitative or quantitative approaches should be used for measurement, whether the assessments should be self-administered or external. Their conclusion was that empowerment is context-specific, and that for each site, appropriate indicators must be developed.[53] Other attempts to measure empowerment have been equally challenging.[54] As further work adds layers and traces additional connections, what is clear is that empowerment connects to almost every aspect of human well-being. And those linkages, reaching into the complexity of human experience, are exactly why it is so powerful.

An empowered populace is an immediately identifiable reality—you know it when you see it—but it is also an ornately complex phenomenon. It is sort of like a person: immediately recognizable, easily named but difficult to adequately define, the product of very complex, separate physical and psychological dynamics. Thus, attempts to foster empowerment (and descriptions of those attempts such as this book) are almost by definition chasing the ineffable. The task is closer to that of a craftsman who learns the "touch" of a tool or material than to that of one who masters a mechanical task by rote. It is inevitably grounded in the messiness, the stickiness, of on-the-ground realities.

Empowerment is the nexus of the relationships in the complexities of human well-being. It is not a sector-specific dynamic like economic growth, or health, or education. It is not the parts, but rather that which comes about from the sum of all the parts. Because empowerment is a product of interactions within complex adaptive systems, its measurement will be difficult (as is true for measuring a standing wave in a river, the wholeness of a person, or the dedication to religion, country, and homeland that inspire dramatic courage). It is for this reason that the true evidence of empowerment is often manifest in literature and art, which embrace its complexities, rather than in metrics, which reduce them. Not yet having standardized measurement techniques hardly invalidates the dynamic, however. Difficulty in measurement does not diminish empowerment's importance, *or that of the attempt to represent it.*

BRINGING THE PARTS TOGETHER

Table 2.1 below summarizes the difference between SEED-SCALE and its orientation toward change through empowerment, and the operational framework of traditional development that drives change through money and exercises control through budgets. It is easy (and incorrect) to see the approaches as being in contradiction. There are, as the above makes clear, core differences between the two approaches, and it is important to note the differences. For example, does a partnership begin with a budget or by determining the agenda? In executing a project, is the emphasis on getting the work done and then improving the next time, or on getting the work done right and with excellence? However, it is also vital to recognize that these approaches are not mutually exclusive. Rather, one must find a productive, mutually reinforcing balance between them. The answer is always "both."

The approaches listed in the table below complement each other; they are not mutually exclusive. The difference between empowerment and traditional development is not so much that they seek different objectives but that they have different emphases. Empowerment seeks to mobilize the community. Traditional development seeks objectives that are known ahead of

Table 2.1 OPERATIONAL DIFFERENCES BETWEEN SEED-SCALE
AND TRADITIONAL DEVELOPMENT

	SEED-SCALE	Traditional Development
Key Resource	Human Energy	Financing
Planning Mindset	Evolutionary Growth	Construction Engineering
Planning Process	Agenda=>Plan=>Budget	Budget=>Agenda=>Plan
Who Does the Work	Three-way Partnership	Professionals
Implementation Structure	Local Institutions	Consultants/Project Units
Ultimate Accountability	Community	Donor
Approach	Build on Successes	Fix Problems/Answer Needs
Criteria for Decisions	Evidence	Power, Opinions & Habits
Major Desired Outcome	Behavior Change	Measurable Results
Criteria for Evaluation	Strengthening 4 Principles	Budget Compliance
Learning Mode	Iterative, Experimental	Get it right the first time
Management Mode	Mentoring	Control
Commitment Horizon	Depends on Utility of Partnership	Depends on Donor's Budget Cycle

the project, usually objectives held by a donor, a government, or a community that has figured out its priorities. Until now, what has been absent is the awareness that there are two approaches. SEED-SCALE is a means of engaging the complex dynamics of social, economic, and natural worlds, the socio-econo-biosphere. It does not seek to control them, but rather guides adaptation by communities as each of these influences people's lives and as those lives (together with larger political, cultural, and ecological factors) influence one another.

In this sphere, options are infinite and layered one on top of another with interactions that are even more infinitely complex. The socio-econo-biosphere that is planet Earth represents the largest and most complex of systems. To shape a future within this world, utilization of the dynamic of the revolution of rising aspirations is essential. It is sustainable, aspirations are one resource of which we have an inexhaustible supply. Because the dynamics empowerment engages are hyper-complex, ways must be found, not to clear a path through the complex forces, but to find it. The whole route does not need to be mapped, just the next steps (indeed, mapping the whole would be futile because those next steps change the whole anyway). This is true not only for villagers, but also for all involved, as politicians and donors need matters simplified just as much as villagers do. Who (except possibly academics) really wants more complexity?

Empowerment emerges through the interaction of the bottom-up energies of people with the top-down and outside-in factors of governments, religion, nonprofits, media, and business. The top-down and outside-in are part of community reality—the wish that they will simply go away and leave communities alone is untenable in an age of global connection—but they are not factors over which there is easy community control. On the contrary, they often attempt to exert their own control over the community, and have the financial and political means to do so. SEED-SCALE provides a process to engage these factors within the context of the broader global complexity. Ordered according to functions, SEED-SCALE shows what needs to be done by all parties around a community focus. It is a way of thinking and planning about complex adaptive social systems that top and outside perspectives can use so they can engage that bottom-up action.

From the bottom-up, using SEED-SCALE, the people of the world, particularly those on the margins, have an alternative. People who were earlier left out now can come into the process. They can engage the complex modern world that is coming upon them whether they like it or not. They need not wait while linear plans come forward, while the money to drive those plans gets used before results reach them. With a process easily taught and immediately implementable (as the cases show, the process can be taught amid war zones and to the illiterate). Experience is affirming what Barbara Ward, an economist who was seminal in shaping the approach of empowered peoples leading their own change, asked decades ago: What can people who lack access to the economic growth engine or are excluded for some other reason do to participate in the benefits of modernity?[55] The answer she gave is that they can either wait for help to come to them, or they can go out and help themselves. SEED-SCALE gives them a way to go out and help themselves.

Many people are moving in this way. This book describes achievements by the poor, by women long held back, by immigrants who came into cities searching for a better future. These examples are not unique but part of growing global momentum. As Robert Chambers notes, there is "a growing family of approaches and methods to enable local people to share, enhance, and analyze their knowledge of life and conditions, to plan and to act."[56] Paul Hawken sees in the mobilization of people working in the rapidly growing organizations of civil society the "great hope" for the future, and he estimates two million such groups are at work around the world.[57]

In this larger context, SEED-SCALE brings together a way to operationalize people-based action. It is distinctive in that it comes from a complex systems approach. In applying SEED-SCALE success often comes when women, or historically excluded groups, begin the process. Doing so engages their energies, which until then have been outside the process, in the larger societal momentum. But the most important feature of this process is that it is available to all. The primary costs are the costs of learning, then going forward using the resources at hand.

CHAPTER 3

If Traditional Development Practices Were Effective

Your Majesty, our research shows that eighty percent of your people are healthier today than they were fifty years ago. However, for twenty percent of your people health did not improve. Moving into the modern age split your country. While many would argue that advancing four-fifths is progress, the fact that one-fifth of your people are worse off shows that fundamental problems have not been solved . . . perhaps this is the root reason for your country's growing civil unrest.

Daniel Taylor, Report to His Majesty Birendra Shah,[1] *(Fall 2000)*

Having examined the social changes at the scale of Bameng Village, and then reviewing the frame of global discourse, this chapter moves to social change within a nation: the Himalayan kingdom of Nepal. The Nepali case shows that effective, positive social change is the consequence of how local, community-based actions grow, first within local realities and then according to how external supports are utilized. The process is driven first and foremost by aspirations that transform a community's reality by engaging the world's complexity. This process moves forward inexorably. People's lives, and the lives of those whom they love, literally depend on it. People will overcome tremendous barriers to achieve this end. If government and donors do not join this driving force, the people do it on their own, ignoring government and the funded agencies. If the incompetence of those in power goes on too long, people turn to revolution and violence.[2]

If the best current development practices were effective, then they should have worked in Nepal. Six decades, several billion dollars, and the careers of some of the world's finest development professionals were invested in the kingdom to reduce poverty, illiteracy, and illness. Yet today, 30 percent of Nepal's population remains below the poverty line, with one-fifth of the country living on less than a dollar a day; half the population is illiterate, and mortality for children under age five is sixty per thousand live births.[3] Furthermore, Nepal is no longer a kingdom, the monarchy having been deposed because of its inability to deliver the promises of modernity. That fact might have been a positive change had effective democracy followed the monarchy's dissolution, but ethnic and geographic divisions are driving a once-national vision toward a breakup into a to-be-determined federalized provinces, with the likelihood that many of these will be drawn into varying degrees of subservience to India over coming decades. Nepal approaches, in other words, the brink of failure as a state. The external advice and aid, rather than helping the people and reforming the monarchy, enabled the monarchy to remain closed and ultimately to collapse.

There were plenty of good intentions in all the right places. Economic growth was to reduce poverty. Education and elections were to build accountable government. Health services were to double life expectancy. For each, targets were set, and programs generously funded (throughout the 1960s and 1970s, USAID funding was particularly generous).[4] But, while there was progress in many measurable program indicators, in each sector dysfunction grew in terms of how system relationships were functioning. Programs that were started fell apart when funding was diverted to other programs that interested donors. Newly built school buildings and schools a few years after being built by donors looked abandoned.

The problem in Nepal is not lack of resources. Financial resources have almost always been adequate, especially foreign aid and subsidized low-interest loans, and they were used with program planning documents that should have promoted wider social change. Nor was there a lack of natural resources. Nepal's spectacular scenery, extending from lush, animal-rich lowland jungles to the summits of the Himalaya, joined with immemorial traditions of pilgrimages, made the country a premier eco-tourist destination. There was not just potential, but actual profits, as diversifying businesses in whitewater rafting, mountaineering, tiger-watching, and Tibetan carpets brought in tourist dollars. Moreover, enormous hydroelectric resources pointed toward even greater income—India was ready to take as much electricity as Nepal could send (though there was always friction over the payment rates). In addition, innovations were launched in appropriate technology, mountain agriculture, microcredit, poverty reduction, and the advancement of women. To preserve the land, a network of national parks was created, and environmentally sensitive agricultural practices were promoted. All these good initiatives occurred in a country that had no history of colonial occupation or ethnic or religious violence to recover from. In short, except for the major barrier of being landlocked, with one country, India, effectively able to control its trade, and the fact that it remained a monarchy in the late twentieth century, Nepal met the commonly considered conditions and received the believed-to-be-necessary inputs for successful development.

And yet, as encapsulated in this chapter's epigraph, our comparison of social and ecological change in Nepal, based on in-depth study of the country from 1949 to 1999, showed that after this half-century, the bottom fifth of the population was further behind than when development efforts started. Simple indicators made this point as in 1999 we repeated the first health survey ever done in Nepal in 1949.[5] Malnutrition was higher among the poor, in a nation where food productivity had gone up, yet for the poor there was less food. The core reason why the quality of life had gone down for the bottom quintile was that the currency of change had shifted. In 1949, a barter economy based on human energies gave employment options to poor people, but by 1999 the monetary economy had removed labor-based options; money was now required to participate in the modern world.

The Nepal experience is unique in many respects. But, it also offers an historical and geographic microcosm of the "great divergence" since the Industrial Revolution, in which development tends to benefit roughly the top three-quarters of a population as measured by indicators such as life expectancy, food security, and leisure. For the bottom quarter, things get worse. According to Gregory Clark, who examines the issue at the scale of global economic history, this means that the living conditions for that bottom quarter are actually lower than they had been over the thousands of years of human existence prior to industrial modernity.[6] Economic development benefits those with access to financial or natural resources; its competitive dynamic thrives on disparity. To those without wealth it denies the very basis of life.

Figure 3.1. Carl examining a district official while doing the health survey in 1949 on the first scientific expedition into Nepal. *(Photo credit: Robert L. Fleming, Sr.)*

When modern development began in Nepal in 1950, the Rana family had ruled the kingdom tightly for a century. Successive kings were held prisoner inside the palace while the Rana oligarchy ruled. The country was closed to the outside world. Citizens were blocked from access to change (children often had to escape to India to go to school). The Ranas amused themselves by imitating European royalty with an array of dalliances, tiger hunts, and intrafamily power jousting. They had kept the British Empire at bay by providing the services of the legendary Gurkha regiments during the so-called Indian "mutiny" of 1857 (a mercenary service to the world that continues today, with Britain, India, Brunei, the United Nations, and private corporations still bringing in significant income into the country) and thus retained the independence of isolation.[7]

In 1950, with backing from India, King Tribhuvan broke from his palace arrest and joined a democratic movement that ousted the Ranas. India then pushed the now-open Nepal to adopt a democracy similar to its own. After Tribhuvan died, his son, King Mahendra, worried about India's growing influence over Nepali politics and wary of the single-party rule in Communist China to the north, modified multiparty democracy to a "no party" democracy, one in which each candidate stood on his or her own reputation. Without a party to connect them, candidates could not gain a significant following, allowing the monarchy to consolidate its authority. During the 1960s, as monarchies lost credibility around the world, in Nepal the monarchy was viewed as progressive. It had freed the country from the Ranas and opened it to the world. The authority of the king was further solidified by belief that he was a reincarnation of the god Vishnu. In a global era of shifting leaders, Nepal seemed blessed with stability and promise. The country had a strong leader who spoke of movement toward democracy, secure in his position as both potentate and pope.

The decades that followed were an era of grand works masking an erosion of national sovereignty. India took control over Nepal's trade, timber resources, and hydroelectric power. The Chinese literally moved some of the greatest mountains in the world to link Nepal to their country by road. From the mid-1960s to the 1970s, the United States and Soviet Union jockeyed, offering competing munificence for symbolic alliances on the world stage. In public gestures of reform, King Mahendra offered changes in health care, education, technocrat leaders, and land tenure without loosening control of the political process and caste structures.

Meanwhile, outsiders flocked to Nepal, enraptured with its beauty and eager to help. Trekking vacations turned into careers; Peace Corps volunteers came and never left. By King Mahendra's death in 1972, two dozen countries were giving aid, virtually every United Nations organization had programs in Nepal, and international banks, public and private, were offering development loans. Almost every offer was accepted, even when they operated under contradictory philosophies. There was no lack of resources, but there was a flagrant lack of coordination among increasingly complex systems, with little effort at adapting. In 1972, King Birendra, educated at Eton, the University of Tokyo, and Harvard University, assumed the throne, age twenty-seven, remarkably well prepared.[8] He surrounded himself with some of Nepal's best-trained people, made education a priority, pressed for effective financial institutions, promoted agricultural expansion, initiated what would grow into a network of nature preserves, and used the authority of the monarchy to focus a development agenda. Contradictions were dealt with by assigning donors different valleys.

Donors stepped forward, and rivalry between them enabled the tiny kingdom to manipulate powerful countries. King Birendra was a member of the Nonaligned Nations movement. Like many leaders in this group, he believed the need was to balance powers, and he argued that this required strong leadership. In the era of Indira Gandhi's India and Mao Zedong's China, in the global business world of corporations that had expanding balance sheets, his argument for strong leadership was accepted. The term "people's participation," increasingly popular in the global lexicon during the 1970s, became "people's manipulation." The process of development by the well-intended appeared to be working; it felt good to be members of the well-intended power elite, and it was also a very good life in idyllic Nepal.

The highest mountains in the world had until then also been its highest fences, but even they were being conquered by a network of roads. The USAID program had, as noted, generous unrestricted money from the sale of American wheat in India plus imaginative leaders and technical staff. Other countries were also bringing in their best staff and ample funding. Across the rugged Himalaya, primary schools were built, and many children hiked for days out of the valleys to go to secondary school and college. The economy was diversifying. Ideas inundated the country through movies, media, and Nepalis migrating in and out of the country to work in India and elsewhere.

But while much seemed to be changing, the extended royal and Rana families were supported by wealthy émigrés from India and old caste structures and held onto power in the palace, army, and commerce. Despite trappings of modernization, caste-based rule remained. A vital feature of modernization was absent: political dissent. Those who disagreed with the reigning order were forced to go to India. Meanwhile, wily merchants operated outside legal restrictions, creating a separate economy, and the royal, Rana, and émigré structures profited, now isolating all in the inner decisionmaking clique.

In this increasingly complex world, the people's aspirations continued to rise. Their progress ran squarely into the still-entrenched, increasingly wealthy factions. During the decade of its existence, not one major recommendation of national reform from the inside-the-palace think tank was approved. Then, in 1977, a signal was sent to the rising tide of progressivism when four ministers and two senior bureaucrats were accused of profiteering from trade in handmade carpets. Falsified invoices for carpets they never saw were cited as evidence and led to their being thrown out of office. While all four were ultimately cleared in the courts, the implications were clear: the old order retained control; the cart that carried old privileges was not to be upset. The international community agonized for a few months because they had lost four fun-loving and candid minister friends, but those throughout the Nepali leadership got the message and pulled back on participatory agendas.

On the streets, the rejection of openness was not so readily apparent. Kathmandu overflowed with hundreds of thousands of tourists, and a growing number of hotels, restaurants, and privately owned banks. All that engagement was allowed, for it made money for the privileged. Throughout the 1980s, peaceful lawlessness rose. Nepalis raced to grab a share. In the health sector, care shifted from free government health centers that gave preventive as well as curative services, to private clinics with pharmacies that were owned by doctors and adjacent to the government clinics. In the education sector, schools stood in the villages, but there were few teachers. For foreigners, the sublime Himalayan world plus the charm of the people deflected attention from systemic weaknesses.

The international community acquiesced in maintaining old-order structures. For example, during these decades not one embassy or aid agency had more than a handful of token low-caste employees in managerial positions or engaged in systematic affirmative-action hiring. Development was growing into a world of appearances: outputs were measured and contracts fulfilled, but connections between programs tended to be ignored. The never-articulated but everywhere-enacted developmental mantra of the 1980s might be summed up as, "Deal with the pieces, but don't challenge the whole." There was little sustained effort to challenge the trappings of development to address the core issues, which were both much deeper and more systemic than the increasingly blamed misrule by the monarchy. It was the whole, not any one part, that was at fault; societies are complex adapting systems, and their advancement matures through changing the relationships among the relationships.

By the mid-1990s, a growing portion of the country was in revolt. In the decade of ensuing Maoist revolution, the government turned to brutality. But in 2006, a people's movement rose up and threw out the monarchy. This popular uprising spanned the nation; every town, it seemed, had protestors on the streets. Surprised by the people's energies, political parties agreed to cooperate. Even the Maoist rebels came out of the jungle and joined the political process. An effort began to rewrite the country's constitution, but after four years that became mired in debate. The people had spoken and forced the change, but they did not know how to govern. Those entrusted with governance remained dysfunctional, consumed by infighting, with the external actors of major business interests and international governments persisting in manipulating events.

By 2010, a once-expanding infrastructure built by foreign assistance was crumbling: roads, government offices, clinics, schools, postal services, agriculture extension services, even tax collection. An increasingly corrupt government system could not maintain infrastructure that aid had built. Ancient divisions of caste and tribe persisted, crippling social advancement as half of the national population, women, still were only symbolically included in decision making.[9] Corruption still persists and probably grows, with national progress weighed down by decades of debt as officials have signed loans that those who follow have obligations to repay. Of the thousands of people trained to lead the country, great numbers of the most gifted have left.

A characteristic we have seen in many developing situations is at work in Nepal. Development is a topic led by professionals: whether donors, government agencies, or expert advisors, they come to it with a private language that communicates with similar parties around the world, and this language works through formulaic structures. In such a context, there is little effort to change dynamics among the relationships. National officers who work with international advisors know that, if they act properly they, too, will become international advisors. What is created is a complex, global adaptive system of "development business." By not reshaping the interplay of forces in the local, complex adaptive system, the global business goes on, maintaining the conditions on which its existence depends. Shakeups to reassemble a local system are feared for what they might mean to the whole.

The monarchical rigidities in Nepal presented many problems, but the role of the donors in remaining focused on their sectors and valleys was complicit in the monarchy's world of appearances. Donor nations could have pressed for change, but they were focused on the pieces. In most cases, pressing for change would have required only adhering to the norms of their own standards of financial accountability, governance, and equity. But though they mentioned such issues with officials, they never pressed for reform on the ground.

Only in the final years of massive incompetence did abolishing the monarchy become necessary, for the monarch was until then the essential glue holding together the country's ethnic and geographical diversity. It took the Maoists, who got thoroughly frustrated that the complex system was not adapting, to push for revolution. Birendra as an individual was a man who had the interests of his people as his priority; this was a belief held by many who otherwise disagreed with him.[10] However, lack of change in the monarchy and caste system, lack of transparent financial policy or an effective judiciary, and lack of action by the international community blocked reforms, ultimately making each group weaker.

Reticence to challenge entrenched structures degenerated into lawlessness. Corruption had long been decried, with blame conveniently placed on merchants and royalty. But, as often happens in such situations (the present situation in Afghanistan being a case in point), the role played by the international community was seldom acknowledged. The evidence that the internationals were using Nepal for their own goals reads almost like fiction. In the 1960s and 1970s, the United States supported clandestine military operations based out of Nepal to spawn rebellion in Tibet against the Chinese Communist Party, training Tibetans in terrorist tactics with the blessing of the Dalai Lama. In the 1980s, India sent photo-reconnaissance aircraft across Nepal without asking permission. China responded by offering Nepal anti-aircraft guns. The Soviet Union set up complex informant-monitoring systems, watching the United States, India, and China. By allowing all of these often-conflicting enterprises to go on in secret, this small country was holding world powers hostage.

Fault lines grew deeper as time passed. The pervasive corruption supported a bureaucracy filled with more qualified-on-paper people than there were socially useful tasks for them to perform. Even trade in ancient (stolen) idols and endangered wildlife by members of the old aristocracy was no longer unnoticed, only unreported. Foreigners and national leaders seemed to think the momentum of growth would eventually resolve these issues. (That economic growth will promote accountability is a commonly made assertion with no robust evidence base.) In Nepal, the growth that was occurring was based on bending or breaking laws rather than strengthening them. Tourism, carpet weaving, thousands of urbane Nepalis giving a modern face to the nation, the huge potential (though never responsibly developed) for hydro-electricity, the majestic mountains—all these provided a reassuring curtain hiding the underlying issues.

There was no lack of evidence of the problems, either about what was going on at the highest levels or about what was not going on in the villages. Hundreds of international scholars and thousands of educated Nepalis were doing research. The authors of this book are securely on this list of culprits, having run annual medical expeditions from the mid-1970s to 1990 in valley after valley with our survey in 1949 being the country's first scientific health survey. Like most well-intentioned researchers, before going to the field we asked the government what information would be helpful, and on returning, made the data available. We had access to the health ministry, the planning commission, even the palace itself, but though they were always appreciated, in no instance can we point to how our findings informed actions. The focus of our evidence-gathering, as is often the case, was to advance our research priorities. Simply publishing about communities did not connect our findings to the people. (Peer-reviewed journal publication with supporting statistical tests causes the findings to become even harder to understand.)

It took years for us to wake up to the fact that for research to be truly helpful, different questions must be asked, and, without exception, the results must be presented differently.

THE COLLAPSE OF GOVERNANCE AND AID EFFECTIVENESS

The once-loyal populace did not need scientific data. When murmurs of trouble arose, it was customary to blame outside interference, usually India. And there was indeed cause for blaming India, as in the flashpoint over the Chinese anti-aircraft guns, which Indian spies had seen crossing the border from China, led to a temporary freeze in trade. Another was Nepal's refusal to continue hydroelectric development favorable for India, following the pattern established by the Kosi and Gandaki river projects, about which we heard a great deal of grumbling inside the palace. The profoundest concern was India's systematic pressure to bring Nepal within the orbit of "Greater India," a concern that had the concrete evidence just next door in India's annexation of the once-independent Sikkim. In the late 1980s, India pushed for Nepal to accept a political status similar to that of Bhutan, a country that lacks full bilateral relations with countries other than India. This demand by the Indian ambassador was coupled with fomented protests on Kathmandu's streets. As protests grew in 1990, King Birendra surprised everyone with a high-minded decision. Rather than accepting India's offer under the Bhutan model in exchange for protecting his personal position, he opted for a multiparty democracy. For several years, the country was giddy with the prospect of multiparty participation.

The people, however, had no experience with parties jousting for power. They had been voting in a partyless system. There was no structure for fair elections. Thus, during the 1990s, whatever candidate had the money, thugs, or access to ballot boxes during the night "won" the elections. Elation with democracy plummeted. Where there had been a court system (of sorts) to appeal to and, *in extremis*, a monarch, an increasingly disaffected king saw that he had little option but to let the multiparty system work through its learning curve.

Practice is needed to learn the roles each participant must play in complex systems to make them effective. It is an ongoing adaptive process as new procedures form, hence the value of an approach such as SEED-SCALE that starts adaptation at the manageable, comprehensible, community level. In a control-based structure it is hard to gain that practice. Complex adaptive systems, when recognized as such, allow graduated training. (This is the value of India's extraordinary 73rd amendment to its constitution, which codifies a participatory approach from the community level upward, an amendment with roots in Gandhian practice, and about which more will be discussed.)

When systems are set at the community level, they can scale up in fractal units to the national, creating both structures and processes for the adaptive learning context.

Meanwhile, with the government pretending to change even without seeing aspirations reliably move to actions, increasingly frustrated people gathered in the isolated western hills. They designated themselves "Maoists," although their doctrine was not that of Mao Zedong. More accurately they were desperados, intent on the violent overthrow of the entire order. The Maoists correctly discerned that the system had decayed. We knew some of these people before the rebellion began. Most had started out proud of their small achievements, dedicated to positive change, hopeful that their school, clinic, or marginalized ethnic group could build a better future. But time and again, those hopes had been dashed. The redoubt they created in the western forests was a perfect place to nurse anger. Surrounding them were people of low caste and from ethnic minorities passed over by change, villagers who had been deprived of economic options two decades earlier, when their primary export crop (hashish) was outlawed.

Interestingly, these far western hills were where the United States had made a multimillion-dollar attempt at integrated development in the 1980s. The idea was the right one, bringing all the linear programs together into synergy. American officials had used their influence to get permission for a model program. In this region, mostly free from the residue of previous failed efforts, excellent Nepali staff were recruited and lived side by side with well-trained, Nepali-speaking American advisors. After two cycles over ten years, the project was closed. Washington's funding priorities had changed. From this project no clear metrics of rising prosperity were coming from the field to show a success. If a traditional multi-sector approach could ever work with money, good ideas, and staff sensitive to the people, this USAID project should have done so.

On a national scale, this program was similar to the MDG program presented in the previous chapter, of setting model assistance in place. We walked through some of the villages after the program people left. The people had been talked to, but not listened to in a manner that then let their actions take over. They had been asked for input, not given control. Behind that explanation, we recognized that the explanation for the lack of letting go was that the USAID budget had to be reported to U.S. financial auditors. Multi-sector work, engaging people, was being attempted, but it was driven by a tight line of monetary control connected more to Washington policies than to village-by-village conditions in the hills of Nepal. A budget-driven project is a process of service delivery, and that focus makes it easy to overlook the lead that must be taken by people's aspirations and energies. Things were being given to communities, rather than a process being developed by them. Into the vacuum of a departed project, the Maoist movement spread. The rebels pointed out that American development workers and educated Nepalis had profited handsomely, but that villagers had little to show for it. Whether that statement was true or not did not matter; the people knew they had never "owned" the process being delivered to them.

As the challenge from the Maoists spread out of the western hills, Nepal's government retaliated, using police with inadequate training. From the initial Robin Hood posture that had given them safe haven in villages, the Maoists turned to terrorism. The government responded with punitive destruction in the villages. Villagers, asked if they supported the Maoists, knew that a "yes" meant, jail (or worse) today, while a "no" would be turned against them by the rebels tomorrow. Periodically, we shared our ideas about the forces that were growing with the king. But he felt the only way to deal with dissent was to crush it. (From his viewpoint it was a threat to him; he did not see how it represented energy that he might harness.) Meanwhile, across Nepal, intellectuals who had first welcomed the uprising became disillusioned. The international community was just baffled. Why was this happening in idyllic Nepal? Had the growing rebellions been seen as pressures within a complex system resisting strictures stifling adaptation, the international community could have used the rebellion as an opportunity to press for change. The government had grown scared, and in this opportunity the internationals, had they been tough, could have exerted pressure. However, to do so effectively they would have had to come together, an unlikely coordination among the United Nations, the Europeans, and the United States, along with the distinctly vested interests of India and China, a collective in which all desired control.

Then everything did change. It was not revolution, not international pressure, not a force that had Nepal's interests at stake. Crown Prince Dipendra fell in love with a woman from the wrong branch of the Rana family.[11] Negotiations between prince and parents degenerated into fights. The king and queen insisted that if the prince wanted to marry this woman, he must abdicate his claim to the throne. The prince, used to having his every wish granted, found himself inside high palace fences through which there appeared to be no exit. There was, however, access to drugs and an arsenal of weapons. He spoke to his closest friends about his lack of options. One night, following an explosive afternoon session when his parents again told him he would have to abdicate, drugged and dressed in combat fatigues, this man, one of the few who could have changed the national direction, walked into a family dinner in the palace and opened fire with automatic weapons.[12] When he finally turned a gun on himself, he had killed the king, queen, and five other members of his family. For many of its citizens, the regicide/matricide/fratricide/ homicide/suicide was nothing less than the death of the nation.

The aftermath of the tragedy could have transformed the disillusionment into forward-looking social action. However, the newly crowned King Gyanendra (brother of late King Birendra) was more interested in asserting his position (and his compulsion to hold control) than in seizing the opportunity for social advancement for his country. It was one of those moments of crisis (such as America had on September 12, 2001) when taking the high road and pointing to a collective positive future could have turned all factions forward, but taking the path of control made all sides harden.

Protests started. The king felt challenged and attempted to solidify his position rather than using it to take action against the corrupt systems that were larger than him individually. Then, to a nationwide extent beyond all imagination, in the spring of 2006, across the nation in virtually every village, the people said "Enough! The monarchy is the problem and must go." After the devastating regicide, civil war, and somewhat fair elections, with a totally unexpected voice of the people, came expulsion of the king in 2008.

Today, Nepal may be poised for real change. The question is whether competing factions in the leadership will continue to fight over control or whether they will engage in partnership with the rising aspirations of the people. The people have shown that they have the will. The concept of governance has embedded in it an assumption of central control, but this need not be the case. Governance happens when the people support it. The concept of development similarly has the concept of giving to people, but as this book argues, for such giving of services to be effective, the mobilization of the people is required. What is profoundly clear is that people are capable of making the systems work, as long as a framework is in place for their rising aspirations to be accommodated.

THE POWER OF PEOPLE'S ASPIRATIONS

An example of what is possible when government and assistance let people have control is the story of Omkar Prasad Gautam, a leader for Baglung District in central Nepal in the mid-1980s. Omkar learned that foreign assistance had paid 700,000 rupees to build three suspension bridges in his district. But rather than either simply being grateful for what seemed to be an extravagant gift or complaining about wasteful government spending, he prevailed on the government to give him an equivalent sum. With citizens as engineers, and local purchases, the community constructed *sixty-two* suspension bridges for the same 700,000-rupee sum.[13] The National Planning Commission called for an international assessment of these bridges, and the verdict was that all were as strong as the first three. Three years later, a follow-up assessment found that, as communities were maintaining the sixty-two bridges, they were in better repair than the bridges that had been given, which people assumed the donors would maintain.

Nepal is filled with such examples: community-based clinics and schools, forests, microcredit schemes, and water supply systems. Even more persuasive proof of people's energies are the thousands of trails, temples, village

Figure 3.2. Lendoop, a villager who helped build this suspension bridge, spontaneously performs repairs as he crosses it. *(Photo credit: Daniel Taylor)*

waterspouts, and herculean terraces built without any external assistance. (The terraces have literally leveled the mighty Himalaya.) These constructions of the people's energies have lasted for centuries and are the true national developmental infrastructure on which the country's prosperity depends. They are particularly evident in communities where former Gurkha soldiers brought in ideas acquired while serving outside the country. Nepal has, in recent years, come precariously close to being a "failed state." But the Nepali people have not failed; rather, their support structures have failed the people.

Another example of the diffuse, emergent manner in which the people pulled themselves forward lies in Nepal's ecotourism industry. If ever a country was endowed with ecotourism potential it is Nepal, and the Nepali people did not let this potential slip into the hands of outside corporations. (In fact, credit for keeping corporations out might lie with the government incompetence that frightened away American Express, the Sheraton Corporation, and their ilk). Along the splendid hiking trails, families who had sold rice and lentils to traders for generations took notice of possible profits as trekkers started walking by in the 1970s. Tea stalls started packing in cases of beer and Coca-Cola, installed black tanks on the roof where the sun heated the water and a hose ran to a shower, and added spaghetti and apple pie to the menu alongside rice and lentils. One family saw what another was doing, then tried to do them one better. Learning that sleeping space on the floor did not bring much money, hostel owners packed in beds and mattresses, then partitioned space into small rooms. A family home expanded to become an inn. Nearby farmers began growing a wider variety of vegetables and selling them to innkeepers; then chickens and their eggs, fruit, and orchards that even grew into distilleries. Citizens bound for centuries by caste and food taboos welcomed tourists to rituals, rebuilt their houses, and learned English, German, and Japanese. Sherpas started taking tourists on organized treks. The Nepalis noted that Westerners had ridden some of the rivers, and they started guided rafting, then bungee-jumping off the high suspension bridges, hang gliding, hot-air ballooning, jungle rides on elephants, even elephant polo. Himalayan summits became points of income generation as Sherpas changed mountain climbing from an avocation to a profession, taking clients on ascents of Everest for as much as $70,000.[14] This is a supreme example of a system learning to adapt. There was no central plan, but there was constant experimentation and learning. It would have been impossible to figure out global tourism patterns and their possible impact on Nepal—but it was possible to figure out year-by-year how to adapt a great view from a bend in the trail into a point where tourists injected international funds into the local economy.

What is interesting about this ecotourism growth is the mode of partnerships by which it evolved; there was the aforementioned learning by one family or shopkeeper from another. But there was also important adaptive learning prompted by some international agencies and by individual foreigners who fell in love with a village or a particular family. In certain instances, small financial capital was provided, but usually what made the biggest difference was coaching individual Nepalis through a business plan, helping them learn process of trying, adapting, and trying again.

While the hills were self-assembling this potpourri of ecotourism, the cities of Kathmandu and Pokhara witnessed an equally diverse tourist growth. Much of this took the form of hotel alternatives, restful gardens, and fusion cuisine. With distinctive decors from hippy to Himalayan, then adding in specialized personal service, the growing ecotourism business was always adapting. No Kathmandu tourism development plan was being followed. Street vendors sold necklaces, Khukri knives, custom-embroidered T-shirts, religious statues, and any other artifact imaginable. Expansion grew on the backs of any business that seemed to be working. Most famously, the Kathmandu Guest House, in a once-hidden part of Kathmandu City, spawned today's colorful and imaginative Thamel district with its hundreds of shops and restaurants.[15] Nor is this form of "development" distinctive to Nepal. On the contrary, it is precisely this kind of emergent intelligence that lies at the heart of the world's great cities.[16]

A

B

Figure 3.3. A. Photograph from 1949 is the Kagbeni Caravanserai where traders stopped en route from Tibet to India. *(Photo credit: Carl Taylor)* B. Photograph from 1999: the Bob Marley Hotel in Muktinath where trekkers now stop, a 20-minute bus ride from the old Kagbeni Caravanserai. *(Photo credit: Jesse Taylor)*

Tourism persisted in adapting even when the Maoist rebellion was at its peak. Though in radically reduced numbers, people kept coming to see the mountains, wildlife, and people: hang out in Thamel, visit the ancient sites of Kathmandu Valley and Pokhara Valley, trek the Annapurna Circuit to Everest, or the Langtang Valley, ride elephants in the Chitwan jungle, and maybe cross the Nepal-Tibet border. As virtually all such business was locally owned, it was capable of flexing and adapting to the downturns. Rather than leaving the country when troubles hit, such local ownership adapted, and continued the critically important function of recycling the money through the population and giving hope and cash to the people.

What has worked in Nepal? What has worked is what has always worked: the Nepali people, and they have worked hard. They historically leveled the Himalaya to make their fields and carved engineering marvels through precipitous cliffs, and channeled irrigation ditches around mighty mountains. They continued to apply their energies, first in intelligent creativity, next in communal solidarity, and then in backbreaking labor to build a world-class tourism industry, a new network of community-owned roads; and community forestry took over land conservation with a nationwide growth of trees on once-denuded hills.

Nepal is not a failed state, as the more recent political uprising of the people to push King Gyanendra aside clearly demonstrated. The people are trying to own their future, but the systems intended to enable that desire, both national and international, have impeded the people's efforts. Nepal is an example of what happens when process is not attended to and instead the inputs and outputs only of giving aid are deemed to be sufficient. Despite the failures of both those in an official capacity and those who funded them, the Nepali people persevered.

When our Nepal research began in 1949, the bottom quintile was better off than they were half a century later. In an economy based on barter, everyone had access; every person had his or her quotient of human energy that made him or her a player in the economy. But as the country moved to a monetary economy, those who had no entry capital were denied access. If you cannot even afford flip-flop shoes, you are passed over for jobs even as a porter. If your children cannot purchase schoolbooks, they cannot go to school, even if fees are waived. Once a barter economy is gone, you can no longer pay for health care by giving the doctor a chicken. (Maybe the health care then was not modern medicine, but it was far better, than modern medicine that cannot be afforded.)

Six decades of development have interceded, decades in which the bottom quintile did not benefit. And yet, despite the absence of enabling opportunities for the poor, the people of Nepal have shown their perseverance. Just as they built the millions of terraces up the slopes of the Himalaya, they can build bridges, not just real bridges but also metaphorical ones.

They can build their future. They can grow an ecotourism economy. The people of Nepal have demonstrated their capacity by massive investments of human energy. The fundamental process of doing development for people at best works only as long as the money is flowing. The alternative approach is development done by people, which lasts, and costs much less (up to 80 percent less), but this does not mean the community will be going it alone. For a community-based approach, the people need support. If communities could have "pulled themselves up by the bootstraps" they would have, long ago. The distinction between being "done to" and "done by" is critical; in the first the people are targets, receptacles, even consumers. In the second they are citizens and agents of change who are building on success, employing three-way partnerships, making evidence-based decisions, and focusing on the universally available outcome of behavior change.

There are four distinct ways to engage communities. Is the community the physical place or setting for action? Is it the target to which a service is delivered? Is it a resource, a source of labor that is being paid or pushed to do work? Or, is the community the agent by which planning and work is done? Each of these ways might be said to be "community-based," but it is important not to confuse them. Empowerment results only when people are the agents of change. In each of the others, where the community is a setting, a target, or a resource, community-based work can be under way, and people may be using their energy, but for energy to grow into empowerment, people need to have agency. What is important in achieving that is sharing control.[17]

A HOPEFUL EXAMPLE OF GROWING SUCCESS

Arguably, no service of development is more unquestioned than the assumption that it is a government's duty to build and maintain a national road system. Health services, schools, or communications can be private, but around-the-world a road network free and open to all is viewed as a public right. Nepal is challenging this assumption. Nepal's community–government partnership in road-building points to the direction that national social change must go. Partnership-based road-building started small, learned from its successes as evidence came in, and is now changing national road-building behavior. Across the country such community roads are being built, one of Nepal's helicopter pilots reported in June 2010: "Each month I see approximately a dozen new roads; they are all being built by the people. Usually there are about one hundred people at work, and once I saw three hundred. When I fly over such roads that were started five years ago, I am surprised to see most being maintained and improved."[18]

Nepal's national road network began in the 1960s and 70s with major aid from China, India, the United States, and the World and Asian Development

Banks to surmount the mighty Himalaya. Then in the 1980s the national road system began to fall apart, victims of dysfunctional government and corrupt contractors. But in the late 1970s a seed of government–people partnership was started under King Birendra with small block grants to communities; several communities built roads, adding to the grants their own funds and labor. Experiments by the government and the Netherlands Development Organization were sustained throughout the 1980s, experimenting not only with whether to build by shovel and pick or by bulldozer, but also with levels of grant money and levels of community funding. Some roads started charging tolls to pay for maintenance and recover investment costs.

However, it was in 1994, during the nine-month reign of the United Marxist Leninist government, that a major expansion occurred. "Community development councils" were offered block grants of 300,000 rupees. While a variety of project options were possible, many undertook road-building. It is impossible to determine in the ten years how many roads were built and how many were under construction. An informal Rural Roads Forum was created in which communities and government and donors discussed options and shared experiences. The Rural Roads Forum had records of six hundred kilometers being built by November, 2009,[19] but estimates are that the number is five times higher, as indicated by the observations of the helicopter pilot quoted above.

A systematic study of this explosive road growth, interviewing government officials, examining available records, and visiting roads under construction, has arrived at the following conclusions. When communities contract to bulldozer operators rather than using local crews, construction is more rapid (typically by a factor of five), but the roads wash out sooner in the monsoon, are more likely to prompt landslides, and the costs paid to the bulldozer leave their valleys (one month of bulldozer use equals roughly 120,000 people-days of income). On the other hand, the local labor crews promote cooperation and pool investments among "village development councils." The locally run, pick and shovel approach typically starts with a meter-wide track that is motorcycle passable the first year, adjusts its alignment over the next couple of years, and uses land and rock cut from the slope as road fill rather than pushing this over the hill, with the result that a more stable road is created. Road-building is an effective way to get women into the labor force, because when a work crew is needed, the labor demand is high. Road construction has also proven a powerful means of educating people about the value of trees and grasses for soil stabilization, masonry skills, and foundation-wall construction. Of course there are problems, the dominant one being absence of road engineering: professionally laid-out community roads have fewer costly errors and have been substantially easier to maintain. (The government, in addition to seed money, should ideally provide technical design assistance. If this were done as a practicum for engineering students, it would have the added benefit of allowing them to apply and refine their skills, while keeping costs lower than would be the case with a fully-professional team.) Intra-community struggles have also sometimes been a problem as old grudges have reignited.[20]

In terms of larger impact, the hundreds of scars across the Nepali landscape bring surprising benefits. For example, a wider range of income-generating production is possible as a result, with the option of sending vegetables and fruit to market. (Altitude variation up and down slopes allows production in one season low on the slope, then of the same crop higher up, later in the year (particularly useful for high-in-demand vegetables.) Children have access to school, sick people can get to medical care, government officials can visit, and tourists can more quickly reach the places they want to go. But the most important benefit, it seems, is community mobilization, lines of local pride; roads are tangible evidence of what they did to change their circumstances. They did not do this themselves; they built in partnership with government, connecting their villages to the broader networks of the nation and the world.

Bringing people together in interdependency is centrally important in the modern age; strengthening the bonds of complexity promotes the synergy

Figure 3.4. Flattening the Himalayas through human energy. The terraced fields of Nepal provided the basis for their food security for centuries. *(Photo credit: Daniel Taylor)*

and the cost-efficiencies that are fundamental for effectiveness in our present, fast-moving global age. By strengthening the net of complexity, with a system that engages participation by all, those on the margin have new opportunities. Thus, the story of development in Nepal is for half a century one in which many of the complex pieces were put in place, but the whole did not come together—the sum was a series of linear initiatives and not a complex adaptive system working together. And yet, for the future, as seen in the roads, bridges, and ecotourism lodges, and even more clearly in the eons-old trails and terraces, Nepal is also an example of the triumph of the networks of human energy.

CHAPTER 4

The Option Available to Everyone

Mobilizing Human Capacity

Seeds still fascinate us. Somehow these small capsules enclose specifications that produce structures as complicated and distinctive as a giant redwood, the common day's-eye (daisy), and a beanstalk. They are the very embodiment of emergence—much coming from little. . . . We will not understand life and living organisms until we understand emergence.

John Holland[1]

THE IDEA THAT ORDER CAN EMERGE

When development practitioners speak of empowerment, it is often as a quasi-mythical phenomenon, easy to recognize but nearly impossible to define. Thus, while its potential is recognized, the dynamic is often largely dismissed because it is so difficult to measure and even harder to predict. However, empowerment is real, and as the near-consensus regarding its importance as summarized in Chapter 3 suggests, it is increasingly recognized as fundamental to social change, especially given the increasingly recognized limits to the sustainability of current economic models. In such a context, "you know it when you see it" is hardly an adequate understanding.

Do we humans ride into the future lacking a reliable process for managing the quality of our lives, just waiting for the fundamental dynamic or the magic solution that will shape our futures to emerge? Can the processes whereby the people take ownership of the future be sparked, guided, and replicated in the myriad contexts and conditions under which communities attempt to adapt to the turmoil of the modern world?

Empowerment is human energy. In previous chapters, we have described its functioning in Rima's actions on a Himalayan ridgetop, traced its success and failures in Nepal, and pointed to the ways this understanding differs from the dominant literature on development and social change. In this chapter, we will draw on parallels from physics to understand it as energy. The discipline of physics is, after all, the study of energy, and while human energy lies outside its purview, there are parallels. Drawing on concepts elucidated in physical energy helps us crack open the "black box" of how empowerment works, and thus how it can be proactively used. In so doing, let us be clear that we use the parallels from classical physics metaphorically; actual correlations of physical energy phenomena to those of human energy are not direct. Furthermore, while such a comparison does give us concrete ways to analyze this difficult topic, the linear models of classical Newtonian physics are inadequate for an understanding of the complex context of social change.[2] Thus, throughout this chapter the use of classical physics is balanced by continued incorporation of the concept of *emergence*, another construct physics uses to elucidate energy.

THE CHALLENGE OF MEASUREMENT

One of the key difficulties in defining empowerment is its measurement. To engage empowerment in a scientific manner requires a method of measuring it other than the (frustratingly apt) "you know it when you see it." However, direct measurement of the always-adapting interrelationships through which empowerment is generated is impossible. Empowerment is not stable enough or discrete enough to be measured directly. Instead, measurement must depend on proxies that show the consequences of empowerment. Over the years, we have experimented with a range of metrics, perhaps the most comprehensive compendium of which has been gathered by the World Bank.[3] Chapter 7 has a more thorough discussion of monitoring and measurement, but among the proxy indicators we have used, several have proven both informative and easily measurable: increased mobility, influence in decisionmaking, readiness to seek help, and expanding education.

Whereas empowerment itself may be hard to measure, its consequences are not. Table 4.1 presents an example of the use of these proxy indicators in an application in the highlands of Afghanistan.[4, 5]

Empowerment blossomed in the Rostam and Saya Dara valleys in the Bamyan Province of Afghanistan when the community was organized through women's action groups (similar to the ones Rima organized in Bameng), about which more details will be provided below. In this application in Afghanistan, training began in "Women's Only Workshops," and was then structured through women's action groups where the women applied the principles and tasks that caused empowerment to emerge. What confirms that this was a process of emergence from community energies rather than traditional

Table 4.1 RESULTS FROM EMPOWERMENT TRAINING OF ROSTAM
AND SAYA DARA WOMEN*

	Before Training	After	Statistical Significance
Can you now travel to attend training?	39.7%	76.3%	.001
Can you influence decisions in family and village?	67.0%	77.5%	.05
Does education improve family and village?	87.3%	99.4%	.001
Will you help a woman having a difficult delivery?	36.8%	88.4%	.001

*To access the simple but full survey used: http://www.seed-scale.org/multi-media/resource-tools/afghan-empowerment-survey

services is that only training was provided in Rostam and Saya Dara, after which the staff departed. No new service was introduced. The intervention was solely one of improving actions by the women: first in terms of what they did by themselves, then by what they did connected to each other, and then in connecting to existing services.

Over the next two years, not only did the women's action groups continue, but change also radiated from health improvements to wider civic actions. These changes resulted in a number of tangible health behavior improvements (see Table 4.2 for representative changes), which collectively caused under-age-five child mortality to decline by 46 percent (see Figure 4.1). Health was being transformed by the community, not by outside services coming into the community.

Major life changes emerged because of the new ways communities were applying their energies. They were changing because they wanted to, and knew how; they were not being forced or incentivized. Complex social dynamics of rural Afghanistan, specifically as related to the behaviors of women, had been fundamentally altered. The intervention that caused this had lasted only a couple of weeks, conducted by trainers with modest ongoing supervision led by the remarkable Dr. Shukria Hassan. By contrast, a service-delivery program would have stalled when external inputs stopped.

Table 4.2 HEALTH BEHAVIOR CHANGE FOLLOWING TRAINING
OF ROSTAM AND SAYA DARA WOMEN

	Before Training	After Training
Using clean spring water for drinking	45%	74%
Using surface water for drinking	46%	22%
Getting skilled help for birth delivery	37%	98%

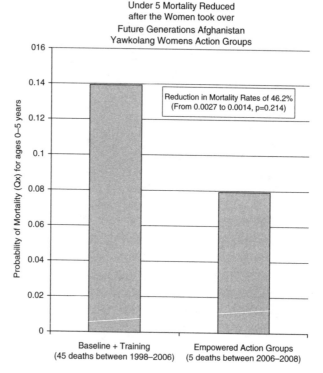

Figure 4.1. Reduction in under age-five child mortality before and after empowerment training.

Furthermore, the achievements of this program compared to those from the best such programs in the country (with whole health centers and professional staff in support) achieved reductions in child mortality of 20 to 23 percent during this same period, whereas reductions seen here were 46 percent.

Doubling the best of what traditional service delivery could achieve for a fraction of the cost (10 percent) is powerful. To understand better what happened, in 2008 a team returned to these valleys. To conduct their assessment, the lot quality assurance sampling assessment method used two years before was strengthened by employing a retrospective pregnancy history methodology developed by Professor Stan Becker at Johns Hopkins University.[6] Careful retrospective pregnancy histories were conducted for all the women in the two valleys, even tracking down women in the high pastures so that a full population census was done of all women. How had women equipped with only two weeks education nearly halved the child mortality rate in their villages? It was not professional services being delivered to them, but rather their changing the actions in their homes. Because of what they now knew the women now only took their children to the nearest clinic for complex problems requiring advanced medical knowledge, while childbirth and the majority of illnesses were treated in the home. Three dynamics comprised the intervention in Rostam and Saya Dara: gathering the women into reinforcing units, providing education so they learned more effective behaviors, and ongoing supervision by a local facilitator (a local mullah). The impact from these three caused subdued and scattered women's energy levels to be amplified into empowerment.

As with Rima in Bameng, change happened quickly: in this case with modest financial cost given that the change agents (Rima's earlier role) were paid for their teaching. What was innovative about the monitoring of this project in Rostam and Saya Dara was its ability to separate out attributes of empowerment and measure them. This is important because it meant not just that change occurred among the women who were organized and trained (i.e., the women's action groups), but also that measurement was population-wide through a full population census. Getting to 100 percent of a population in war-riven Afghanistan required perseverance, but exceptional cooperation was achieved because the women, who knew everyone in the region, were conducting the survey themselves (with parallel spot checking by our external team for accuracy). Thus, the process of conducting the survey itself became the locus of further empowerment. The mobilization introduced through the action groups radiated out through all the women, even those off at considerable distance tending flocks in the high pastures.

Figure 4.2. Women surveyors conducting the census of households in the Rostam and Saya Dara Valleys. One hundred percent of the households were contacted over three visits. *(Photo credit: Besmillah Sakhizada)*

Drawing on concepts of energy as developed in physics, it becomes possible to frame the dynamics of human energy. In its physical form, human energy might be measured in calories, but such a literal yardstick is insufficient to explain how humans create society.[7] Society is, after all, much more than the sum of labor-producing machines. We have proposed already that human energy is driven by aspiration, an aspect as difficult to measure as it is real. Aspirations can be harnessed into actions in the revolution of rising aspirations, or frustrated until exploding into armed revolution—the former seen in Bameng, the latter in Nepal. Human energy unfolds in mutating forms: aspirations, actions, affection, aesthetics, anger, to name a few, all of which have changed society for better and for worse, and all of which, though distinct, can flow one into another.

BACKGROUND ON EMPOWERMENT IN AFGHANISTAN

Some background on empowerment in Afghanistan is helpful. Across the centuries, the Afghan people have humbled empires, from Alexander, to Genghis Khan, to Britain, to the Soviet Union. This ability to humble empires in the past was no more rebellion than it is insurgency today, for the Afghan people were never subjects. It is people insisting on controlling their own lives.

Following the overthrow of the Taliban in 2002, massive shipments of tents, wheat, clinics, schools, roads, telecommunications, and even bottled water came into the country. With these commodities also came an invasion of accounting ledgers and donor stipulations as to what must be done. Despite careful receipts and notations in the ledgers, the gifts reached the people in only limited amounts. The elections, carefully monitored for fairness, put in place leaders who were not monitored once they took office and perpetrated fraud. The mandates imposed to protect and advance their women ended up making them vulnerable to terrorism. In such contexts, when actions to do good all seem to go wrong, the explanation does not lie in the specifics, but with the application of a wrong action model. In this case, the wrong model was the mindset of the West, that of control: control of terrorists, control of local populations, control in creating the new government. A resource stream implemented each of these goals, with accounting back to the donor. In these efforts, recognition that the people themselves wanted control over the processes of change was lost. The following encapsulates one way the story can be told, summed up in the flowering of poppies.

In the summer of 2003, in fields that the year before had grown wheat, poppies grew through the highlands now freed of the Taliban and the ban they had imposed. A record crop was harvested, the elixir sent for processing. The next summer more fields were planted in poppies. Harvests increased so much that by 2007, three-quarters of world opium production came from Afghanistan's fields, and by 2009, 90 percent. Promoting this growth was a resurgence of the defeated Taliban, Al-Qaeda, and warlords who, as news reports make clear, created a partnership of convenience.

Colleagues who had been working in the highlands building partnerships (partnerships that had adapted across ten years of Soviet occupation, seven years of civil war, and five years of Taliban) reported that on various occasions when the Taliban and Al-Qaeda dispersed, commanders gave out poppy seeds, saying, "Go home, plant these. They will produce many times the profits you can get from wheat. First our *jihad* struck America from the sky. Now we will enter America through her blood veins." With that, the fighters scattered by pickup truck, donkey, and motorbike. The insurgency's efforts at partnership had begun with sequence of actions that farming people knew how to do: plant seeds, harvest, send off processing, and reap the profits.

In the meantime, a downward spiral of misguided international action had begun. Afghanistan had just experienced four years of near–biblical-proportion drought, so foreigners started bringing bags of wheat to halt an impending famine. The wheat was given away, and while it did ameliorate the famine, it also glutted the market, causing wheat prices to tumble. People then asked, Why grow wheat? Practically, they turned to the alternative in the little black seeds. At first poppies were planted in hidden valleys, then as harvests proved the way to acquire the modern commodities that had now burst onto the local market, soon all but the most public wheat fields were transferred to poppies. On some level, the people were aware that those who had so recently oppressed them were being helped to return. But against the

Figure 4.3. Community meeting: The crowd is skeptical of promises being made. (*Photo credit: Daniel Taylor*)

backdrop of recent famine and austerity juxtaposed with the hope of a better life after war, the seeds provided entrée into the now-tantalizing world of the cash economy. Pragmatic farmers turned their attention to tomorrow rather than the day after.

For the donors meanwhile, the more wheat and assistance they could give away, the more "management overhead" money they made. Moving money was their incentive, not building positive feedback loops of rising energy.[8] Partnerships were being built, but they were for profiteering. Accounting ledgers confirmed the bags of wheat delivered, wells drilled, immunizations given, miles of new roads built. But all these are measures of contractor performance, not growth of local capacity. Indeed, former Afghan finance minister Ashraf Ghani has estimated that 90 percent of the millions of foreign aid invested in his country was wasted, channeled into overhead and contracts by international agencies.[9]

The Afghan people wanted much of what came from the donors (schools, clinics, water wells). After twenty-three years of conflict they knew how to survive a war, but what were the skills to survive a peace when it comes bearing gifts from outside rather than readjusting the relationships among people? Officials came to communities, then drove away in Land Cruisers after making their offers with paperwork the people could not read, wrapped in further paper layers requiring steps they did not know how to take. While donors must attend to their sources of money, contracts are not effective if not also expressed in a way the people understand. School buildings were put up where one school must serve a certain population number, causing schools to be built between three villages . . . and then vandalized. Similarly, clinics had equipment that contractors thought was necessary but local health providers could not use—or clinics were built with only one door, making it impossible for conservative Muslim women to enter. Yet with free things on offer, Afghans filled out the forms. A new world had burst into their lives as though jumping out from the pictures on their new televisions. The common requirement of contributing some labor, as almost all projects expect, is not a foundation for partnership when directions are coming from outside. There had never been a true national government, and the new one in Kabul grabbed at the opportunity to use international support to establish itself. The internationals were trying to control the insurgents, but the model of attempting to buy participation through giving was a model not of partnership but of vassalage and control.

Meanwhile, the group that had been militarily trounced managed to partner with people who, by and large, did not want to be partners with them by utilizing a commodity that the people knew was bad. Why did the international community that was itself now risking domestic political capital, spending billions of dollars, and sending its young people to die, lose the partnership potential that had been in their hands? While there was no doubt much corruption in the process, the answer does not rest in blaming corruption (and certainly not when that corruption is left abstract and unattributed as if often the case in international reporting on the subject), just as it does not lie in blaming the Afghan people, who obviously will take free gifts if offered. Nor does this represent a lack of sincerity from the internationals, who were giving not only their funds but their lives in a well-intentioned effort to help. The answer lies in the wrong mental model being used in this process, a model of external design, a model of external control, a model centered around a scarce commodity that caused people to compete for it rather than for the objectives for which it was being generously allocated. The Afghan people were victims of good intentions, ignored as partners, victims of the wrong operational model.

People in mud-brick villages, where one-quarter of the children die before age five, kept signing papers, but the papers providing accountability back in other countries were disconnected from local reality. And, when coupled with a whole sequence of actions that sought to take control from the people (including exploitive, corrupt local leaders), that disconnection created the context for inflaming a push-back that was being encouraged by a recovering insurgency that was now able to regroup because it had money. Well-digging stopped at the depths specified in the contracts, whether or not they had

Figure 4.4. Afghan elder instructing youth in farming techniques. *(Photo credit: Daniel Taylor)*

reached water. Children were not going to school because the new building had no teacher. Apricot and mulberry orchards were still denuded because, while the mandated saplings had been planted and counted, soon thereafter they were eaten by roving donkeys. Contract terms in all the above instances were met. But the energy that was growing in people was anger.

GETTING THE MODEL RIGHT

As social change goes forward, if progress is apparent, it is easy to forget the imperative of not being content and of continually refining the ideas. Getting the process as effective as possible at the beginning is key to initiating empowerment in which an idea advances the quality of life and that feeds back to build the sense of community ownership that calls more people to participate. First iterations at the beginning, even when they seem to be working well, can improve. As with a mathematical curve in which the trajectory is established in the first iterations of a formula's application, it is the beginning of social change that initiates the cycles that accelerate rising capacity inside the community, or start tugging that community apart. Growing community energies right from the beginning is what Rima did so splendidly. Getting the ideas right at the beginning makes it easier to get them to grow later. In the Afghanistan instance, the international model of complicated service-delivery set in motion aspirations that were antithetical to engaging local actions, whereas the poppy-growing engaged local capacity. What the international actions started was exploitation, condoned by both international and national interests. In 2005, to remove at least a level of contractor and international NGO meddling, one Afghan ministry told half of the foreign organizations to leave the country. Instead, the international organizations forced the Afghan minister who was trying to clean up the system out of his job. As with the faked carpet scandal in Nepal, the message got through. No one else tried to change the system, which by then was being exploited at the highest levels of government.

Because flawed beginnings were allowed to grow, the Afghan people were alienated. One unintended consequence became the fact that the Afghan people were missing in action when it came to the war effort. Whereas at first just Al-Qaeda was the foe, following a flawed beginning as the years passed, despite elections, the Afghan people were excluded from the nation-building process. (In a policy-level correlate to the poppy seeds, the exclusion of the Taliban from the negotiation process at the critical nation-building Bonn Conference forced them into a militant position rather than offering them the role of democratic opposition which would have engaged them in governance rather than war.) While many Afghans were (and remain) deeply opposed to the Taliban, they were disallowed a way to work with (or publicly argue with) their fellow citizens. To build a nation, partnerships must be built across differences with people and government working together, and the government that had been imposed in Afghanistan did not engage the people across the breadth of the social, political, and (most important) ethnic spectrum.

The alienation that unfolded is a tragedy because there was ready engagement of the people at the beginning. The year 2002 was one of hope; conditions for partnership were ripe. Afghanistan in 2002 was in that golden space of apparently endless possibilities that can emerge in the aftermath of crisis described by William Wordsworth at the end of the French Revolution as, "thrilled with joy, . . . standing on top of golden hours, human nature seeming born again."[10] Such times are special. Empowerment is poised, indeed pregnant, ready to give birth to a new life for people. But in Afghanistan, with the people ready, the positive momentum slipped away. What had been a war to "smoke out" one man, Osama bin Laden, became a war against millions of people. The energy of the people turned. If ever there was a case study in how to turn off human energies, that example is found in recent international assistance in Afghanistan. The Afghan example is extreme; it is at least hopeful that international action will never repeat these errors.

Figure 4.5. This Hazara (most discriminated-against ethnic group) woman understands the dynamics of the Afghanistan struggle. She wears three coins, one from the United States, one from Pakistan, one from Iran. *(Photo credit: Daniel Taylor)*

FEEDBACK LOOPS TO CAUSE ENERGY TO GROW

Emergence demonstrates how order emerges from the process inside constantly adapting complex systems.[11] Growth that occurs is often not like a plant steadily growing from a seed, but like in Afghanistan, where it is a product of sudden swings: first in a positive way, with "the golden hour" of optimism and joy, then in a negative way, with the turn to a rising insurgency. Energy feedback loops—times when energy cycles back on itself and causes energies to rise or fall dramatically—prompt these leaps one way or the other.

The creation of a hurricane provides an illustration. In keeping with the Second Law of Thermodynamics, heat disperses. However, at times over the oceans, rising energy causes other energy, not to disperse, but to gather, as rising water vapor condenses; the low-pressure zone beneath causes more warm, moist air to be pulled in, which rises, releases its energy above, and more energy below is pulled in. This is a positive feedback loop. So long as a negative feedback loop does not interfere (typically cold drawn up from ocean waters), then as the cycle goes around again and again, hurricanes and typhoons self-assemble. This energy-gathering, drawing in more, and that drawing in still more, is a concept that transfers to social situations, like the nation of Nepal when it said "Enough!" to the monarchy. When applied to human energy, this positive feedback loop is what we are calling *empowerment*.[12]

In Afghanistan, first a positive feedback loop was operating, then a negative one.[13] It was similar to the emergent patterns seen in a flock of birds suddenly changing direction, or a colony of ants working, or sand particles swirling across the ground gradually forming ordered dunes , or the adaptive growth of city slums and shantytowns.[14] In places where there is no controlling force, order comes from one event feeding into other events at a self-exacerbating pace. In trying to spark such change intentionally, the key is iterative action. Make one trial; if it works, repeat it. More likely, that first trial does not work, and the next trial needs to learn from the first. This is followed by an informed second trial, leading over time to an aggregated growth of knowledge and skills. Such feedback loops of learning-through-doing are very different from action that follows a predesigned plan like a blueprint.

The theory of emergence presents no omniscient godlike decider who tells the sands to form into dunes. No linear command and control process or bureaucracy determines outlays in accordance with goals and reports outcomes. Patterns emerge from procedures. Systems find their resulting reconfiguration because all parts depend on each other, and that dependence incorporates the feedback cycle. In social systems, the environment of culture, economics, and ecosystem cause local communities to adapt and react. An evolving adaptation is underway. If an action does not work better than it did yesterday, one can go back to yesterday to find a better answer for tomorrow, but fundamentally, momentum keeps going forward. Simple responses grow complex solutions. The key to the process is iteration: progression does not seek to be ideal, just better than yesterday.

Such systems become more resilient the more their participants are involved in these constantly adapting units. Rather than being managed from outside, control arises from the processes inside each unit, which are nested inside each other. The basic idea is that each is a basic building block defined for its scale, but also a model for the next. In SEED-SCALE, these units of assembly are individual communities, which may include only a few individuals at the smallest level, but can also branch out through ever-expanding webs of connection to encompass an entire species riding a shared planet into a common future.

When such ideas are applied in the social sphere, people want predictability. Humans do not want to be randomly blown around like grains of sand, gradually shaped into an ordered dune by the whims of the wind. People have instinctively tried to shape such order since time immemorial. Rules fall into place to hold each other accountable—not formal laws, but the more basic (and fluid) cultural codes that condition not only what we do, but what we want and how we think. These are agreements sealed by handshakes, not contracts bound by law. Such informal ordering may be all that is available, as in frontier outposts or ungoverned-by-law slums, but because of the dynamics of emergence, this structuring order is enough. Such order self-assembles; it is not assembled by external forces. Through this process, disparate actions become social movements; those slums become settlements. In the context of what might be seen as a negative enabling environment in which forces are pulling structures apart, such order arises through a positive feedback loop that channels human energy into pattern and structure.

Such emergent change depends on how knowledge, technology, and resources come together. At times, the pace moves rapidly, other times slowly. In the current age, with its ever-accelerating march of knowledge, technology, and resource-consumption, the challenge before communities is how to adapt quickly enough to not become victimized or simply bypassed by the rapidity of global change.

SEED-SCALE gives a design to that feedback process. By giving a design (based on analytical evaluation of earlier experience) the probability rises that the acts of each day will fall into optimal order for tomorrow, lowering the tendency toward randomness. The structure of this feedback is guided by the four principles already mentioned, and operationalized by seven iteratively-performed tasks that will be discussed in Chapter 6: organize a coordinating committee, identify local successes, learn from related successes, gather evidence at the locale, put together a plan, implement that plan, make corrections according to the guiding four principles. In each case, the goal is not perfection, but rather simply performing each task as effectively as possible at that time and place, recognizing that action can always be improved in the next round.

Order is produced by community members acting in collectives rather than as individuals. This internal ordering disperses control in favor of cooperation.[15] As communication increases, so does specialization and organization. The more this occurs, interactions that are unpredictable become legible as patterns, to which action that protects the interests of community members can respond. Where social entropy would have pushed the emerging order apart, such iterative performance of set tasks focuses energies so that a new threshold of stability can be achieved.[16] How to take such action through an iterated cycle of tasks will be described in subsequent chapters, but for the moment the operative point is this: small recurrent actions have the power to be far more transformative than major plans or initiatives, in part because they can change and respond to evolving circumstances, also partly because smaller actions have lower barriers to execution. In this book we are obviously advocating that such focusing of energy arise out of social empowerment, but it should be noted that a variety of forces could be (and have been) used to focus order, from the iron fist of totalitarianism to the "invisible hand" of the marketplace. Indeed, any instance of social organization could be understood via the model of a complex system self-assembling so that the growth continues.

Figure 4.6. These girls walking through the snow to literacy classes being held at the local mosque are able to create and attend these locally run classes only because of strong community support. *(Photo credit: Katrina Aitken)*

Communities, as defined throughout this book, are groups of people with something in common and the potential to act together. This means that communities are essentially bundles of human energy. If a community exists, then it has energy in its people that can be mobilized in the direction of their aspirations. It is important to realize that energy is not being "created." Instead, it is always already present in the lives of people, scattering as they go their daily ways but always with the potential to be brought together and transformed. Indeed, it is precisely the extent to which that energy is already running along common channels that determines whether the group of people can be called a community. No community is so depleted that it utterly lacks internal energy.

Consider the parallel to a landslide: latent energy is poised like rocks resting on a hill. The hill appears stable, and may have been so for hundreds or even thousands of years. Then some act causes a single rock to shift, or a rivulet of water to pour into a new channel underground, and suddenly the entire hillside gives way. Some very small energy of activation catalyzes this latent energy just as one rock rolling can precipitate a landslide. (Social analogues abound: we know them as revolutions, in which the initial "spark" is a crucial part of the historical narrative—"the shot heard round the world.") In such moments, continuing with the landslide parallel, the transformation wrought entails not only the mobilization of many rolling rocks, but also a transformation of latent energy into kinetic energy, with sound, smells, and heat. All this is in keeping with the First Law of Thermodynamics, which states that energy cannot be created or destroyed, but it *can* change from one form to another. With a landslide, no new energy is created; all that energy was already latent in the conglomeration of boulders, mud, trees, and roots that was the hillside. In a similar manner, those latent energies are already extant in every community, and can be brought forward through small catalytic actions.

Returning to the challenge of dissipating energies in Afghanistan, an approach grounded in complexity is the only option with a hope of transforming the present quagmire in accordance with the aspirations of the Afghan people. This is not a process of trying "to fix" the situation. Afghanistan is simply too complex for the internationals to try to fix it: thirty million people with ancient animosities, external governments on all sides jockeying for leverage, near-total breakdown of physical, financial, and educational structures, all coupled with the internationals' disinclination to use the one strong structure that was in place, Islam. But, this complexity has within it the potential of readjusted relationships that can be used *by the people* for rebuilding.

The Afghan instance is helpful because it is so extreme. It shows how far the "we can fix your country (whether you like it or not)" mentality undergirds the actions of world leaders. The international community sends its sons and daughters to die and spends billions of their currencies to compound errors in an unremitting negative feedback loop, or more accurately, a positive feedback loop of unremittingly negative results. The Afghan experience is an evidence base almost everyone in the world is familiar with that renders the reality of complexity comprehensible. To better understand the forces at work, let us turn in greater detail to concepts from physics. The extent to which principles from physics transfer to human energy is unclear, but there are helpful parallels. A substantial literature exists on the role of human energy in improving people's lives.[17]

INSIGHTS FROM CLASSICAL PHYSICS

As emergence brings from physics relevant constructs with which to understand human energy, classical physics is also helpful. The first relevant feature is the concept of *conservation of energy*. Energy cannot be created or destroyed. Joule, Helmholtz, Kelvin, and others have shown that energy, when it transitions from one form to another, is not lost but transformed. It remains energy in the same quantity, when transition occurs from electricity to motion, heat, sound, or light.

Energy in humans is also transformed.[18] In the case of Afghanistan, the hope that came with freedom in 2001, and saw the country "standing on top of golden hours, human nature seeming born again" was real energy. Empowered expectations like that were not going to just disappear. That energy was inevitably going to find outlets. This constancy is crucial for understanding the dynamics of social change. A resource more powerful than arriving armies was already there. It could be engaged, or it could be ignored, and allowed to switch to self-survival, the planting of poppies, and roadside bombs. While the potential labor of the people was lost to the country as it turned to selfish ends, a more important energy was also lost, their aspirations: hope, anger, collective knowledge, a compound force that could have fed back into itself to build a nation or one that could turn outward aggressively on nations trying to help.

In his 1687 *Principia Mathematica*, Isaac Newton advanced *mass*, *momentum*, and *force* to define energy. In physics, mass is volume multiplied by density; in social dynamics, the social mass parallel would be the number of people relative to the density in which they cluster. Thus, mass in a city is greater than that of the same number of people in a rural setting thanks to the greater density of people in a city. As a consequence, as physical energy flows better through denser substance (metal versus air), social energy viewed according to densities explains why urban energies spread more quickly than rural. (An increasing concern, both in Afghanistan and worldwide, as millions yearly migrate into the cities—see the case in Chapter 6.) But the fundamental point in the Afghan context is that social mass was not mobilizing in a positive way as a result of international action. Instead, positive feedback was dispersing, undermining the cohesion required to form a functioning nation.[19]

Newton's First Law, concerning inertia, sheds light on how social mass changes direction. (In this respect, we might say that the insurgency's great achievement lay in transforming social mass, sowing the seeds of its resurgence as it dispersed.) With physical forces, momentum continues in the same direction until acted on by another force. Similarly, societies follow traditional ways until some force changes their direction. The separate tribes in Afghanistan with warring feudal histories were easy prey for the Soviet invasion, but when their scattered energies became coordinated, they toppled the Soviet force. When coordination stopped during the civil war, the scattered factions returned, then became focused again by the Taliban arriving from Pakistan. To again bring together the scattering of energies will be a challenge, because of the extent to which the aid-giving process has promoted individualistic behaviors.

However, the resurgent Taliban achieved collective energies using the force of religion to unite a people otherwise ethnically, geographically, and linguistically separated—a unification that they had not been able to achieve earlier despite their own zealotry. Earlier, their zeal had been characterized as Sunni, and thus created a barrier with the Shia Hazara. But now, in the second coming of the Taliban, they were able to craft a clearer Islamic identity in contrast to the perceived (and often genuine) anti-Islamic attitudes of the international community and are bringing Shias into their alliance. Religious zeal is one of humanity's most powerful energies of mobilization; it costs little and sustains itself with scant support (especially when mosque/mullah or church/priest infrastructures are in place). Billions of aid dollars could not create the desired forward momentum, while the energy of religion mobilized a people even though they well knew the oppressive excesses of the group using this force.

According to Newton's Second Law, the acceleration of an object is proportional to the force acting on it and inversely proportional to its mass. This explains why a small group of people accelerating their momentum (such as a few hardcore Taliban or a fast-moving Arunachal women's group) can redirect a larger social process. A few people moving strongly draw in followers, and the now-increased mass adds more changes, further redirecting momentum. As the process builds, the whole population turns. In other words, a slow-moving society can be viewed as rigid and unable to change, or it can be an opportunity if acceleration enters, gets ahead with a small force the larger group identifies with and shows new direction. This is what the defeated Taliban did: they moved quickly with the poppy seeds, positioning themselves to fulfill rising aspirations, a way-of-life improvement that was available to all. The influx of free wheat, free schools, free clinics, and free wells, did not create a pull because it confounded possible emergent energies with paperwork and restrictions. One resource was available to all; the other, even though free, became a scarce resource because only a few had the ability to put it to use.

Such understandings can be put together using a Newtonian force analysis. Social mass was dissipated by the internationals into individualistic behavior. Inertia was ceded to the one unifying force in the country, allowing an energized Taliban to accelerate out in front of the social mass with a new vision of how to unify this disaggregated context of human energies. Of course, more is involved in such transformations than acceleration of social mass. As noted, empowerment is a positive feedback loop of accelerating human energies. As the process moves forward, the nature of energy among people changes, becoming stimulated, amplified, and focused as a laser does with light.[20] Such activation happened with the poppy seeds. The seeds were tiny black things that suggested people could make money—but when connected to people's energies in their natural environment, the seeds started producing empowerment along with the opium. Such growth toward rising aspirations did not happen with the paperwork that created barriers between the people and blocked the creation of a feedback loop. Managed differently, outside engagement through education could have led to people to reinforcing actions such as creating the women's action groups mentioned earlier, or the mosque-based schools that will be described in Chapter 7. The mental model of development for the people (rather than development by the people) blocked the growing of people energies.

CONSEQUENCES OF HUMAN ENERGY

The relationship between matter and energy famously asserted by Einstein is direct ($E = MC^2$), and the formula indicates that huge amounts of energy can come from a small amount of matter. No suggestion is made here that this formula applies directly to social change, but the analogue is an important one: a major energy source can be tapped by utilizing relatively small amounts of our material selves. Human energies are magnificently expansive and varied. They are the substance of our happiness, health, and homes, in addition to being the intangible substance of our knowledge and our relationships. The value of these is vastly more than that of material and monetary commodities so frequently confused with happiness, health, and home. Moreover, energies can radiate out into the infrastructures of communities, and loop back to further enrich life.

Let us return to the Rostam and Saya Dara valleys and their remarkable growth of energy. How did that occur, and with virtually no money spent? The women's groups reduced the mortality of children under five by nearly one-half, twice what the best national programs had been able to achieve. (Table 4.1 showed how the dynamics of education, mobility, and readiness assist one another to empower these communities.) The social mass of Afghan women came together, and that mass was combined with knowledge and supervision. It should be no surprise that mobilized and educated women working in groups were able to double the impact of "best-practice" formal health services. Furthermore, if mobilization and education could halve disease death rates, might similar action do the same for death rates by bullets? After all, even the most ardent human enemy is more easily reasoned with than a microbe. Mobilized and coordinated people are fully capable of denying safe haven to terrorists. Once again, the mindset brought to the task is critical: is ending war really a confrontation between armies or is it mobilizing the energies of peace? If the later, peace then is the product of adaptations in complex systems.

Empowerment grows out of strengthening community bonds coupled with expanding knowledge. As bonds in physics are the forces holding physical objects together, and as more complex bonds occur, more complex atoms and molecules result, so the parallel extends to social bonds as the myriad forms of human connection give rise to social forms that are both more complex and more resilient. Effective interaction, both in complex interdependent economics but even more in complex interdependent social relations, is the dynamic that carries communities forward, putting collective interests ahead of the individual.[21]

Economist Gary Becker makes a helpful and related clarification about family investment, noting that when families move from investing in many children to fewer, then those fewer receive more education and health, and the societal result is development.[22] This investment grows a resource in society different from what was presumed by simple economic production. The distinction is that children are valued now not for labor but as building capital in all the human aspirations. Growing such bonds over time produces civilization, shown in the real wealth of societies (art, literature, values) that create social depth rather than pure, striving materialism.[23]

Empowerment can happen instantaneously when a group is under threat and people rapidly strengthen their bonds for protection. Usually, the process is grown through cycles of positive feedback that lead to ever-increasing acceleration, like a flywheel. In Bameng, initial action was a small push—Rima sitting on the floor in a bamboo house discussing a simple but important technique (the medical journal *The Lancet* said oral rehydration therapy "may be the most important medical discovery of the twentieth century"[24]). But the larger impact for the Bameng women was awareness that improving their families' health was in their own hands. That *Eureka* of new awareness changed their inertia from being stalled to adding firewood-collecting and vegetables for sale, and learning how to read and write; and once underway, the cycles kept growing. Many development programs would have been pleased just to bring down child mortality. But what happened in Bameng was that momentum took off, and, more important, that transforming energies were internalized, leading to sustained action. It was both outward-radiating, in that one type of activity started another, and longitudinal, in that it was sustainable over time. This is profoundly different from the model of service delivery, where the process is driven by outsiders and change stops when the money stops. Today, in Bameng women and their husbands walk around in nice clothes, know how to read and write, and have bank accounts, while vegetable gardens, bamboo orchards, and cardamom and ginger grow beside their homes. Meanwhile, they are turning to the next innovation.

This discussion of growing human energies to create larger impact has been illustrated with examples in Bameng as well as Rostam and Saya Dara valleys where seeds of women learning to take action grew to the scale-level impacts of their valleys, but much larger impact is really required. In Chapters 8 and 9 the process will be outlined of how localized demonstrations can grow to significant scale. However, it is useful to note here how the women's action groups of Rostam and Saya Dara did have significant impact. The projects themselves did not scale up, but their data did. Rostam and Saya Dara are distant from Kabul, and with the war under way, the two valleys saw few visitors. However, their statistics could come out, and what made a difference in this instance was that their statistics were not compromised because of the war. Most notably, from these distant valleys to influence larger policy a full population census was achieved—all 1,060 women in the population. Being a census there was no sampling concerns, the data truly reflected what had occurred. These two distant valleys became a national demonstration. Adhering to rigorous scientific methodology is difficult for community-based projects—but when it is achieved small community-based projects can become national trend-setters. Further, to get the empowerment dynamic mobilized, it is necessary participants believe the project is under their control, not that of scientists. It is impossible to overstate the need for data people can use— and trust. We repeatedly have made the error in our field work of not getting a baseline of evidence against which later progress can be compared. Having the Lot Quality Assurance Sampling (LQAS) baseline for this project was much better than the usual nothing, but the more rigorous pregnancy-history method allowed collection of truly accurate retrospective data.

The national health system, extending from the health minister to ten thousand health posts, had experienced a persistent gap in service delivery: the "last kilometer to the home" problem. Now, with the women's action groups, the national program had a new structure, proven with solid data, that covered that last kilometer, mobilizing women so they did what they could in inside-the-family health care and then accessed the health system for what they could not. Women's action groups offer a method to gather, train, support, and supervise women to do two-thirds of basic health care, then refer into the health system the one-third that cannot be done in the homes. The statistics from this demonstration showed that this approach doubled the prior best project effectiveness. In Afghanistan, awhirl in opinions and power struggles, this project offered scientific evidence of high quality. Because of it, international contractors joined with the government and advanced action to replicate the women's action groups. (In order to avoid the politicization of this becoming a women's-rights project, the name was changed to "Family Health Action Groups.") Regrettably, what was copied was the structure rather than the process. Communities were mandated to create the action groups rather than growing them from internal energies. Recognizing that this is less than ideal because it again misses the central insight that relationships, procedures, and process are what matters in complex adaptive systems rather than the entities themselves; it is still major progress.

Empowerment stimulates and accelerates energies already inside communities. It cannot be sparked by telling communities what to do, for then action will be driven by external resources and directives. Energy needs to grow from within the communities (energy-growing principles, tasks, and monitoring criteria can help systematize this process). Then, community momentum can engage services waiting outside. The diagnosis by Albert Einstein remains as true today as it did when he said it: "The world will not evolve past its current state of crisis by using the same thinking that created the crisis." Each crisis contains energy that can be turned to create opportunity. To break free, thinking must break from old routines. Crises are occurring within complex systems that have, for varying reasons, gotten out of hand. Bringing in added control, trying to make them work by driving them with more technology or money, is "using the same thinking that created the crisis." An approach is needed that readjusts the system. As a foundation for this process, the next chapter offers four principles.

Figure 4.7. This circle of women (from one of the rapidly expanding women's action groups) is learning how to safely cut an umbilical cord to prevent tetanus. *(Photo credit: Gladys T. McGarey)*

CHAPTER 5

To Grow Empowerment

Four Necessary Principles

Emergent complexity without adaptation is like the intricate crystals formed by a snowflake: it's a beautiful pattern, but it has no function.
Steven Johnson[1]

In 1998, the government of Arunachal Pradesh invited Future Generations to start SEED-SCALE applications.[2] Our team arrived in Palin on the heels of a cholera outbreak. An epidemiological survey conducted by the state health department had the month before recorded thirty cases of cholera and eight deaths in the main village. With the trauma of the outbreak still on everyone's minds, the Future Generations team asked the forty-plus women who had assembled to describe their experiences. All began to talk at once, each trying to get her story heard. To systematize data gathering, we divided the group into neighborhood clusters, then each group was asked to detail who had gotten sick; their family, date, location, age, gender; who had survived. Memories were vivid, and the women not only documented 345 cases and thirty-eight deaths, but for each case gave name, symptoms, age, family, and so on. The data were more dire, and accurate, than the official numbers we had been given.

After congratulating the women on surviving as well as their data, we told them they could have prevented almost all the deaths. Rather than going for intravenous rehydration at the hospital, or packets of oral rehydration salts from the pharmacy, they could have made rehydration therapy in their homes that would have been more effective because it could be given immediately when vomiting and diarrhea started. By that afternoon, the forty women were expert at making the solution using rice flour and salt they had in their homes. The remainder of the day we discussed similar remedies for other common diseases, also using materials available in their homes, emphasizing that the control was in their hands for their families' lives. Cholera was not the focus of this discussion, nor was any other illness or technical health issue. The message was: the lives in your homes are yours—take control of them. Use what you have to make your lives better.

The following morning more women joined, and doubts and questions of the previous day were replaced by palpable hope as discussion continued. The women gave us a tour through the village. This was their village; they were proud of it. Rather than pointing to mud streets, roofs askew, or an absence of indoor plumbing, the women were showing us their homes. A water system had been installed several years earlier. Pipes to the homes that had been laid exposed on rocky ground leaked profusely and ran with mud and sewage from nearby gutters, but still the women were proud. Spider webs of jury-rigged pipes interwove haphazardly, replacing leaking fixtures and connecting additional houses. The day before, the women had listed the homes where infections had occurred, so as we walked, those cases were mapped, noting also on the maps where pipes were particularly damaged. Like light bulbs going on, the women saw how cholera cases were connected to where breaks in the pipes were. As women realized the pipes were to blame, they pointed to the maps, referring to dead children whom all the women knew.

A month later, a delegation of women, armed with maps and data, made the daylong drive to the capital, walking into the state's health and public works departments. As they had planned this trip, the women, who were rarely allowed to speak in public in their own village, knew it would be hard to walk into government offices. Officials had always barked at them, telling them to be mindful of their inferior positions. So, to prepare for this trip, each woman each morning practiced looking into a mirror, looking straight into her own eyes, saying her name, speaking of her accomplishments. After each woman felt comfortable speaking into the mirror, she gave her speech in front of her group. A collective decision was made, and the five women the group felt would best speak for them went to the city. While demands by illiterate women are easy for officials to ignore, this group could back up their requests: with their maps and numbers, a robust ability to articulate their claims, and the conviction that they represented village-wide solidarity. Repairs to the water system soon followed.

Government health services had made efforts to reach the people. Health staff resided in the village, but neither services nor staff had engaged the people's life situations. They were not connecting to the situations beyond sickness. The Palin experience crystallizes the trouble with the services-only approach to development around the world. However, it should be emphasized that the choice between services to the people and mobilization by the people is not either/or—both are needed. The problem is that currently the services approach is being pursued exclusively. Yes, when trouble or disaster

Figure 5.1. A member of one of the Palin women's action groups taking her turn teaching their group, explaining results from their recent household survey. (*Photo credit: Daniel Taylor*)

strikes, it is great to get help. Yes, certain diseases and challenges require specialized attention and technology to address. But before that, there is a lot you and your community can do. Most of the world's challenges are not in the disaster category. Most of the world's untimely deaths are not from cancer or heart disease, but from diarrhea. Nor does this only apply to poor countries. Many of the diseases of affluence, notably heart disease and diabetes, can be addressed far more effectively through prevention via such simple, do-it-at-home solutions as diet and exercise rather than the cumbersome healthcare business.

If this message is beginning to sound familiar, that is because it is. Rima Langbia, whose impact was described in organizing the women's groups of Bameng in Chapter 1 was one of these original forty women from Palin. The remarkable developments in Bameng were extensions of the initiative that began in Palin with mapping the cholera outbreak and then creating Palin-based women's action groups. When Rima's husband was transferred, she took the SEED-SCALE process with her, thereby extending the service of women empowering other women, using what they had. This sort of community-based action is already happening in communities around the world. The difficulty is that most site-specific events do not ripple outward to other communities. They are events emerging within the particularities of local stimulus. What SEED-SCALE offers is an easily transferable method to extend what is already happening from one community to another.

In this chapter, we will describe how such systemic change occurs based on the four principles of SEED-SCALE:

1) Build from success.
2) Form a three-way partnership among Top-down, Bottom-up, and Outside-in parties.
3) Make decisions based on evidence rather than anecdotes, opinions, or ideology.
4) Focus on behavior change.

As the case of Palin and the resulting expansion in Bameng illustrate, use of these four principles can spark empowerment, even in dire circumstances. The energy thus mobilized can allow people to transform their lives and press government to work more effectively. The people have restructured their actions, and so have government services. Going to scale occurs as people restructure the complex system of their world from the midst of local dynamics.

Before moving to the four principles, let us consider the situation in Palin in the words of one of its women—Amko, a woman who joined the movement

Figure 5.2. Four Principles to Keep Community Going Forward.

a couple of weeks after the impact of the women's groups had begun. (In other words, after the outsiders had left.)

> I was 18 when my parents sold me to be the third wife of one of the most famous Nishi hunters. It is more accurate to call me his slave. He would get drunk and beat me. But I ran to the deep forest and lived on herbs as my mother had showed me. My husband tracked me down, brought me back, tied me to our bed. I ran away again, but now he chained me to a log that I had to drag around. He threatened me with the sword, but I realized when he hit me with it, it was with the flat side. I understood he wouldn't kill me, so I would always scream so the whole village would know when he beat me. Soon his other wives grew scared, but I was learning how to make everyone just as unhappy as I was. Then I had a baby. Suddenly, I didn't want this for her.[3]

Women like Amko are familiar figures in development discourse—*New York Times* columnist Nick Kristoff has made a career championing their cause.[4] But Kristoff and others miss the critical dynamic—it is not championing their cause or their possibilities. Nor is confrontation with oppression the only answer, but rather enabling the oppressed to learn how to work safely as change agents within the systems that is the universal (and the major) part of the answer. Making progress is more important than acquiring "freedom" as defined from afar. Under the label of the "Third World woman," such women are often the target of programs with smiling faces gracing fundraising brochures arguing that a critical intervention will release them from bondage. As Chandra Mohanty argues, such women are assumed to lead "an essentially truncated life based on her feminine gender (read: sexually constrained) and being 'third-world' (read: ignorant, poor, uneducated, tradition-bound, religious, domesticated, family-oriented, victimized, etc.)"[5] As with the *burqa*-clad women featured in many depictions of the Islamic world, it is easy to typify such women as powerless and to propose intervention programs to liberate them.

Leaving aside the rhetorical partiality for targeting specific outrageous conditions (whether gender or poverty or race-bound), skipping all the analyses of cause, and instead turning to remedies, such approaches do not recognize the most important reality: those women are far from powerless. They can build from their strength, recognizing that it arises in part from the fact that that they know how to work within the system in which they live. These women are embedded in complex social systems (as are the absolute poor, or the ethnically discriminated against, or any other group subject to the outrages of disempowerment). To remedy the outrage, action must change the system rather than simply taking the victim out of the system. What is needed is not direct confrontation, but rather adjusting relationships. Make no mistake: injustices should be righted. But to do so, build on the remarkable strength evident in what these women have achieved in making homes, in raising children who smile, in cultivating life amidst the direst of circumstances. Help them grow within their system. Their real potential is to build on that which they have achieved so that their futures are ensured.

Communities can be gripped by pernicious exploitation, but they are exploited (as Mahatma Gandhi said repeatedly) only when they choose to go along with this exploitation. Action is needed (indeed, Gandhi was no passivist). But in a context where failed action may lead to greater travails, the answer is to find effective action. Development is creating freedoms, as Amartya Sen has rightly stated.[6] The task is not to liberate the victimized, nor is it a kind of heroic call for unrealistic self-liberation. Instead, the task is to have people who are trapped by whatever oppression take ownership of their futures and grow the capacity for developing their futures from inside, step by step. Often, as in Palin, the momentum brings along the oppressors. Amko did not polarize her relationship with her abusive husband, but worked from principles that changed their marital dynamics, causing the whole to evolve in partnership rather than opposition. Amko was not alone; many women of Palin were doing so, their group actions breaking the earlier each-woman-alone order and creating new social order, with the result that gender relations through the Palin valleys began evolving. What was underway was not women's liberation but whole societal growth.

Amko began attending meetings because she heard she would learn skills that would improve her daughter's life. As she gained inner strength she approached her husband: "You be nice to me, and I will be nice to you . . . and you have to wash your feet before getting into bed with me." The courage such action represents should not be underestimated—this was deal-making, not a threat. Strength inside Amko allowed her to work with her husband where both were changing, the process emergence terms "relationships among relationships." That depth of transformation is shown by the fact that ten years after being chained each night to a log, Amko won the prize as top female vocalist in the state, had a number of recordings that were making good sales, and was a partner with her now very proud husband. (One common consequence of such empowerment by women in action groups is the rapidity by which they adopt make-up; this simple action is visible sign to them and each other that they are taking on a new persona.)

Such inside-out transformation is diametrically counter to the outside experts going in and solving problems "for" the people. Growing from the inside-out is a learned skill for the inside. But it is important to realize that this is also a learned skill for the outside helpers. The dominant momentum of development runs counter to enabling change from the bottom up, as demonstrated by the example of the MDGs summarized earlier. If working from the inside out and helping complex systems to adapt happened naturally, it would have occurred long ago given the now half-century of abundant attempts. The process runs afoul of structural impediments, chief among them being that helping people is good business for the helpers.[7]

Despite the obstacles, the Palin women moved; they made a centuries-old, very complex (and deeply entrenched) system adapt, and did so spending only modest sums of money. What was spent was mostly for training in process implementation. A beginning in cholera treatment started a whole reorientation; it was step by step, building inner capacities so that women who had just months before been afraid to speak in their husbands' presence traveled to the capital city to negotiate with government officials. The cholera epidemic that had first traumatized them with death became an opportunity for new life.

Arunachal Pradesh, in the eastern Himalaya, is home to the second-densest population of tribal groups in the world after New Guinea. Each tribe lives in its own valley. The state also has one of the most extensive subtropical jungles remaining on Earth. For more than a century, these tribes resisted occupation by the British, who eventually gave up trying to conquer the area and separated it from outside contact as the North East Frontier Agency, or NEFA. Developmental policies from the late 1800s to the 1980s were to protect these "special" tribal people, keeping them beyond destructive influences of modernization and working to grow their autonomy.[8] A debilitating feature of this protectionism was the practice of the government taking care of people. In some cases, food has been literally delivered to villages by helicopters, and the state's budget is subsidized by the central government to allow uncommonly generous aid for people's needs. But, as has been shown in the United States in programs of trying to support Native American communities, budgets and services do not transform the conditions in which people live. As shown by the situation Rima found on arriving in Bameng, services were not engaging the deeper conditions encumbering the people. By 1998, some in the Arunachal state leadership realized that the approach they had been following was not sustainable, nor did it truly help. No matter how much was given to the people, their desires were never satisfied.

A decade later, it should be noted, under a new state government and with support from the central national government, a give-to-the-people approach has returned. Gifts are offered, but they are ruled by ulterior motives, ranging from national security (Arunachal sits on a disputed border between India and China, and both countries have troops massed in the area) to simple greed, as outside business interests eye the timber reserves and potential for massive hydroelectric installations and lucrative potential from support contracts to the military. Under such circumstances, the dependency fostered by gift giving threatens to take the locus of control away from the communities—which is, of course, precisely the point. However, against such seemingly mammoth forces, local mobilization using SEED-SCALE continues in Arunachal Pradesh.

While communities have the potential to learn, impinging external forces are learning also, developing a wider base of incentives and controls over the rising empowerment of communities. Still, all communities are developed and always developing, and this is an inexorable dynamic that can be utilized. The task is to move toward a future of communities' imagining and creating within resources of their control. Understood in these functional terms, development becomes a journey for which a map is needed both to point the way and to find the available range of resources. Learning how to use the map of the socio-econo-biosphere is more important than finding a vehicle or fuel. With a map, people can go forward using their resources, whether these be bicycles, ox-carts, sailboats, or that most ancient means, putting one foot in front of another. The need is to keep developing in some manner.

With the intention of helping his people engage the journey, the then–chief minister of Arunachal Pradesh invited Future Generations to begin SEED-SCALE applications in his state at three locations, nodes from which scaling up could grow: Sille, among the Adi tribe; Ziro, among the Apatani tribe; and Palin, among the Nishi tribe.[9] People familiar with the state expected the Adi and Apatani to be more responsive, as the Adi (the chief minister's own tribe) were powerful, the Apatani more educated. The Nishi (the communities of Bameng and Palin are Nishi) were included because they are the largest tribe, and in many of their villages the needs were greatest. However, many felt that the combination of poverty and reactionary attitudes revealed in Amko's story above would make significant results among the Nishi unlikely. What unfolded was the exact opposite: action in Sille and Ziro began slowly, while change took off in Palin.

Following the cholera epidemic, a traditional NGO approach would have been to fix the water pipes, maybe even attempt to address the gender disparities with education or confrontation with the headmen. But SEED-SCALE did not tell them what to do; it provided a structure for them to select priorities. As actions went forward they began to shift from technical solutions such as health care and water-pipes to the application of the Four Principles, Seven Tasks, and Five Criteria. The process became codified in workplans that told each person what he or she must do.[10] Women went off teaching in other villages, linked with *panchayats* (village councils), and accessed services.[11] As the Bameng example showed, men became interested and started Farmers' Clubs. With gardens, reliance on foraging in the jungle was reduced, and in two years the action groups were growing enough vegetables to meet family needs. The people, now discussing and planning in a structured manner, had noted buses bringing vegetables into Palin and that buses in the opposite direction carried only people. By 2004, production from the kitchen gardens had increased so that buses going away from Palin to distant towns were laden with Palin vegetables, while new savings accounts began to sprout in the local bank.

The workplans focused on what the people could do (rather than the conventional development plans that begin with needs, state the resources available, and specify outcomes delivered by those resources). Emphasis in the communities' workplans was placed on specific behaviors that could be changed. The women simply went forward. The improvements they brought home benefited the men, and as a result they got interested. Advancement of women became an incentive for men, rather than a threat. This momentum created partnerships, not only with the men but also with the top-down forces of government and religious institutions. These growing successes in turn built trust.

Such transformations in a population are neither uniform nor perfect, and this lack of perfection is not a problem. The direction of movement is what matters. As empowerment of women started to grow, even though the men were experiencing benefits such as children surviving and greater variety in foods, some men still locked up their women; others waved their swords and threatened dismemberment of Future Generations staff, and others drunkenly withdrew and mocked the process. The whole community of Palin, even after a decade, has not changed, and it is unlikely total change will ever occur, but the center of social gravity has shifted. As time moves on and benefits continue to accrue, reactionary voices diminish. The complex system is adapting.

In advancing the status of women the role of engaging men with positive opportunities is an often overlooked component. Empowerment is not a zero-sum game. Empowering one group does not need to mean taking power from another. In Palin, one man went so far as to change his name from "Charcoal" to "Rocket" in order to reflect his new outlook on life. Rocket entered civic life and has risen to be a major community leader, pressing for social reforms, and standing for and winning a number of civic offices from which he presses for systemic changes.

These shifts would not have occurred without stimulus. Bottom-up change seldom will sprout from grassroots without top-down and/or outside-in support. To give the Palin people as well as those from Sille and Ziro concepts and models to adapt, women and men were taken across India to the Comprehensive Rural Health Project in Jamkhed, Maharashtra, one of the most successful and systemic community-based development initiatives in the world.[12] There they learned skills in health, literacy classes, alcohol abuse programs, raising medicinal plants, spices, and tree plantations. Taking the ideas home, the people experimented with them. This process of action learning and experimentation (to be further discussed in future chapters) is central to SEED-SCALE.

At first, the women's action groups in Sille and Ziro did not mobilize with energy equivalent to Palin. And yet, they, too, had gone on the trips to Jamkhed and had had training and workshops. The difference in the groups lies in aspiration. People must desire change. The women of Palin wanted their world to change with an urgency not shared by people in Sille and Ziro. However, as Sille and Ziro women saw Palin's successes, they stepped up momentum. Meanwhile, the proud Palin groups started quarreling, and their collective energy weakened. Rifts grew, such as when one of their leaders faked a bank check and stole organizational money. Members started to take care of their own vegetable gardens and bank accounts, and promote their own family interests.

But then the Palin communities bounced back. The centrifugal forces of self-serving behaviors in the Palin communities could have broken the group's momentum, but several factors intervened. The first was international recognition: groups from around the world had started coming to Palin to study the success story. The people of Palin liked telling their story, even putting on skits to act out the bad old days (Amko's story related above was told in one such gathering), and through telling their story while educating outsiders they continued educating themselves. Second, the Palin communities saw other tribal groups starting to move. Particularly irksome was when the Apatani tribe started to make major progress. The Palin Nishi had once captured the neighboring Apatani for slaves, so tribal pride inspired them to outpace the Apatani. Third, consistent educational training was provided to the Nishi, Apatani, Adi, and to other tribes by the statewide organization of Future Generations Arunachal. An outside enabling environment gave constant reeducation. As a result, growth in numbers continued—the Palin action groups

Figure 5.3. Members of the Palin Women's Action Group and Farmer's Club performing a skit, enacting with humor the change in their interactions from the bad old days. *(Photo credit: Nalong Mize)*

grew to twenty-six, the Apatani groups to seventeen, and what was most significant in this was their cross-fertilization and intra-group competition.

THE FOUR NECESSARY PRINCIPLES

To grow empowerment, requires a framework that optimizes the self-assembly of behaviors. As previously stated, energies are always already present; the framework needs to direct them. In order to do so effectively, the framework needs to be perceived as beneficial by those participating, so that it draws in involvement, rather than appearing restrictive or confining. In such scenarios, where empowerment is the objective, the draw is rising quality of life for all participating, rather than offering incentives for conforming with outside directives. The reason to participate is thus fundamentally different than in control-based programs that seek goals determined from afar. Empowerment grows through the self-assembly of human energies. SEED-SCALE identifies four core principles to spark, guide, and sustain this process:

1) Build from success. This is not simple optimism, but growth from real achievements the communities have themselves done to keep momentum moving.
2) Form a three-way partnership between the Bottom-up, the Top-down, and the Outside-in. From now on in this book we shall capitalize Bottom-up, Top-down, and Outside-in to indicate that these are named functional forces—and each has multiple constituents. For example, the Top-down may include government, but in many situations may also be religion, international organizations (IMF, WTO, etc.), or big business.
3) Make decisions based upon locally specific evidence (rather than opinions, power, or ideology). In order to prevent power and ideology from influencing the process, such data should be gathered collaboratively, with all partners participating, rather than leaving evidence-collection up to experts or officials.
4) Focus on behavior change rather than target outcomes. Society is made up of what individual people do. Thus, all social change is behavior change.

Putting the four principles into action does not guarantee success (they are necessary but not sufficient), but absence of the four does seem to guarantee failure.[13] The four are not states that can be achieved in an absolute sense. Each has an idea contained in it that social change should aspire to, an end never to be fully reached but a goal toward which work should focus. The process describes a condition in which the change that is underway is "developed and always developing." The objective is to constantly try to achieve positive *movement* on all four.

Build From Success ←————→ Do Not Try to Fix Failures or Satisfy Needs

Three-Way Partnerships ←——→ Don't Direct from One (or even two) Directions

Decide from Evidence ←——→ Power, Money, Opinions, Dogma do Not Give Reliable Answers

Behavior Change is the Goal ←——→ Most Traditional Prescribed Outputs can be Faked

Figure 5.4. The Four Principles of SEED-SCALE and their opposites.

Building from successes does not preclude the fact that failures have to be dealt with. It also does not deny that there are needs. Instead, building from successes gives the starting points to grow solutions for the failures and the needs. Successes point the way forward. The second principle of engaging all the partners brings together potential energies. If partners are excluded, then not only are resources of energy left out, thus losing the potential for synergy, but denying them participation may also make these left-out partners antagonistic to the process. Remaining open to partners' joining can be difficult where deep ideological divisions exist—recall the exclusion of the Taliban from the Bonn Conference that enflamed the insurgency by excluding the possibility of dialogue and caused the subsequent military quagmire; or in more commonplace occurrence for hard workers who say, "Why should you join now when you were not active before?" The third principle, deciding based on evidence, counters the externally pulling forces of money, opinions, power, and dogma by introducing concrete evidence from that locale-specific reality to help build a shared vision of the situation. The fourth principle emphasizes what the participants can actually do. Behavior change is available to all, and as behaviors change they push the larger system to adapt. When behaviors change in response to realities, systems tend to adjust toward greater sustainability.

FIRST PRINCIPLE: BUILD FROM SUCCESS

Building from success (similar to the approaches of Positive Deviance and Asset-Based Community Development mentioned in Chapters 1 and 2) is perhaps the most frequently ignored principle. Taking what is working in the system and doing more of that accelerates the good already underway and promotes adaptation of the complex system to be more positively enabling. When a community so positions its future, the probability of achieving what the community wants is much higher than if it focuses on failures. Put simply, building on success identifies what works and promotes more of that—which is, incidentally, precisely how the wondrous complexity of the biosphere has evolved.

Despite the forward-looking tenor of the word "development," building on achievements is rare in the business. Professionals, officials, and even communities compulsively focus on problems: poverty, corruption, bad roads, poor schools, ineffective politicians, ethnic or religious factions. Ask people, "What should we do?" and the list will probably include everything that the community does not want to do or what it does not have. Every community, even the wealthiest, can produce a long list of needs and problems in short order. Doing so accentuates that the community is a place of deficiencies; it promotes despair rather than hope, and reveals, not an adapting system, but one becoming self-entangled.

Noting success rather than failure may be simply changing how a situation is viewed. The people of Palin worried about a resurgence of cholera, for outbreaks were periodic. (Prior to this episode, the last outbreak had been four years earlier, before the piped water system was installed.) Rather than holding the fear of cholera's return in front of them and pointing out the ways they were still vulnerable, the training emphasized the success shown by the people who had survived. Pointing out their continued vulnerability would have made them relinquish control to government or aid agencies. But emphasizing their survival started them on knowing how to respond when cholera came again, and it started actions that moved beyond cholera prevention and changed their fundamental condition.

An initial success is a first step toward continuing, which in turn sparks further resourcefulness. Action then builds from assets rather than harping on what is absent. People are jaded by promises—from donors, officials, and politicians—promises that replace real products. They know well what is absent. Building from success turns their focus to what they possess. This is like a business identifying its best-selling product then focusing on selling more of that rather than trying to cut into markets where they are less effective.

The Palin experience grew from perhaps the most powerful success in any community—its children. Focusing on children reliably starts forward-moving change. Children are not only a community's most valued possession, they are also a symbol of that community's future. View the children as their parents do, not as a conglomeration of shabby clothes, weak educations, illnesses, or, worst of all, evidence of the "population problem," but rather as the laughing lifeblood of the present.[14] Children have something their parents may have lost, the ability to find fun in even worst situations. As you read this sentence, in urban slums and tiny villages, every place there are people, there are barefoot children playing, pushing old bicycle wheels with sticks, playing soccer with a rusty tin can; they make do with what they have to make their worlds happier places and point to a community's happy future. Contrast that with professional services driving up in a Land Cruiser, people getting out with clothes and expectations that the community cannot realize (but which if asked of course the community will say it wants). While both ultimately are needed, which is the platform that will grow the energies of people?

Children are the growing self-portraits of their mothers and fathers, and in most cultures having children signifies personal achievement more than anything else. To the women of Palin, the power to prevent their children from dying sparked empowerment, and advancing the interests of their children led the fathers to accept new roles from the women. Health is often a pressing concern, but many other initiatives are cost-effective to build around children: a sporting event, a festival, a drama, or an environmental initiative arising from children's near-universal delight in animals.

As successes accumulate, people hold each other accountable. In Palin this was shown by the women's expecting that when their children went to another house they would be given boiled water to drink. Indeed, the women established fines for any family that gave another's child unboiled water. (Children tell others whether their mothers are boiling water; there are no secrets once community standards start to shift.) Holding activities accountable keeps momentum on track. Each mother's watchfulness for her child brought together shared concern—and hence shared action.

SECOND PRINCIPLE: FORM A THREE-WAY PARTNERSHIP—BOTTOM-UP, TOP-DOWN, AND OUTSIDE-IN

The term *community*, as commonly used, is a group of people who share a geographic location, such as a town or village. But this view does not include partners who have a vested interest in the community but do not live there, nor does it reflect the term's newest valence in the myriad "communities" that have formed on the Internet. The definition of *community* used by SEED-SCALE gathers all with a vested interest: *a group of people with something in common and the potential for acting together*. This definition opens the option that the group taking initial action, "the potential for acting together," may be only a sector of the community. The initial Palin group who started to act together about cholera contrasted with what would be defined as "the community" months later: the entire valley, "a group of people with something in common."

The community grew because the quality of life improved for the first few, which in turn attracted larger numbers of participants. The revolution of rising aspirations built cohesiveness as well as changing lives. As this revolution was becoming more effective, it was also becoming a more complex system. As social change grows more effective, it expands community, including those who do not live in the geographical area but relate to it, members who have moved away, government agents, commercial connections, and religious and civic affiliations. It also expands the possibilities in people's lives. As with the Palin example, the revolution of rising aspirations leads to more than increasing numbers of physical partners, expanding economic activity and interactions throughout the community.

The key to understanding the principle of the three-way partnership is remembering that it is a functional definition: "Bottom-up," "Outside-in," and "Top-down" are functions that are being fulfilled in some capacity in every situation. Inside, the key is transforming that the interaction among those forces from being one of dysfunction (confrontation or disconnection) to active partnership.[15]

The Bottom-up is made up of citizens who will do much of the work and reap most of the benefits. This includes infants to elderly; all genders, races, and ethnicities; rich to poor; those with physical prowess and the disabled. Those in the Bottom-up group often view themselves more as members of these subgroups than of the larger community, except when some event or outside presence in contrast forces community identification. And indeed, any of these subgroups may themselves constitute "communities," as in the instances where women's groups initiated action.

The Top-down are all the groups shaping policies, infrastructure, and financing. Government is the paradigmatic example, but international institutions (World Bank, the UN agencies, etc.), large NGOs, and major corporations are also part of this role, as well as major media and institutionalized religions. In the present era of globalization, when major corporations may be better-heeled, more powerful, and even better-armed than the local or national government, it is crucial to recognize the range of actors often taking on the Top-down role. As discussed in the Afghan example in the previous chapter, the role of institutional religion can be hugely powerful in mobilizing human energies.

The Outside-in brings in ideas and training, the change agents. These include not only NGOs, academics, researchers, activists, donors, and businesses, but also community members who moved away, and simply visitors. (Recall the role of individual tourists sharing ideas for hot showers, recipes, or a few words of a new language in Nepal's ecotourism success.) These are the partners who bring in ideas, technologies, and new perspectives, just as they have since the days of Marco Polo. It is no accident that throughout history, eras of technical, aesthetic, and philosophical innovation have been linked to increases in travel, exchange, and intercultural contact.

As suggested earlier in this chapter, these three functions of Top, Bottom, and Outside are proper names specifying roles. Thus, we assign a capital letter to the functional terms when used in this manner. However, actual identities are not fixed: any given individual may at different times function in a different role. A village headman, for instance, is part of the Top-down in a village meeting, part of the Bottom-up when talking with representatives of an NGO,

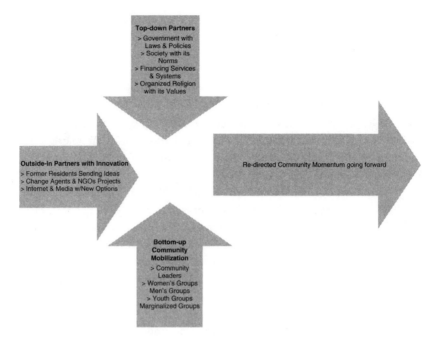

Figure 5.5. Operations of a three-way partnership.

and the Outside-in when he goes to another community to share ideas. People change roles. In a framework concerned with relationships, clarification about what function is underway is more crucial than what position is being filled. When Rima left Palin and went to Bameng, she shifted from being a member of the Bottom-up and became an Outside-in change agent. Recognizing the fluidity of roles opens entry into the sectors of a community, and it gives alternatives when one leader proves difficult or is incompetent. Perhaps most important, by introducing the role of innovation from the Outside-in, the three-way partnership diffuses the binary stand-off between Top-down and Bottom-up often found in control-oriented paradigms.[16]

When a three-way partnership is functioning, a dialectic may emerge. The thesis-antithesis-synthesis (which in turn produces a new antithesis) also offers a model adapting system. Work in Palin began by engaging women. Decisions had until then been made by a council of *gaonburas* (male village elders). Thus, at the beginning they functioned as the Top-down and the women as the Bottom-up. But the men's role changed as the women's movement marginalized them, and to catch up the men ended up as the Bottom-up while the women set the agenda. Shifted roles further solidified when women were elected to village councils under the 73rd amendment to India's constitution, which mandates political seats for women, and the women became formally part of the Top-down. Individuals in such partnerships are fluid, becoming active and withdrawing as demands press on them.

Partnerships in social change are not like job descriptions where people show up each day and perform within a certain set of parameters, rather they are an ebb and flow of people in structural tension, people in disagreement, people not doing what they promised and others picking up the slack. The fluidity of the process allows roles to morph in order to find new resolution.

THIRD PRINCIPLE: USE EVIDENCE FROM THE LOCAL SITUATION FOR DECISIONS AND AVOID DECIDING BASED ON MONEY, POWER, OPINIONS, OR DOGMA

Decisions in development are frequently made at a great distance from where they will be implemented by people who do not know that locale. They are then implemented through budget control. Contrast that process with decisions made inside the system by people who know the circumstances intimately and will have responsibility when something goes wrong. In this difference rests the reason for the failure of many international efforts to help other people. It matters little that the intention was to help when decisionmaking neither addresses the complexity of the conditions nor adapts to changing realities. More important, much lower accountability results when decisionmakers do not have to live with the negative consequences.

Making decisions that are on time, realistic, and appropriate requires both local input and deciding as close as possible to where it will be implemented. While few people would argue against the value of locally inspired evidence, what many would also say is: "Be practical: you know powerful people get their way; money and power drive decisions." These points may be true, but this does not mean that the resulting application of money, power, and opinions can change wrong decisions to well-advised ones. Moreover, it is unnecessary to make the issue a stark alternative, because in complex adapting systems there are options. Always. The decisionmaking system needs to adapt to money, power, and opinions, but also be able to act according to local reality. Decisionmaking has to engage an array of features: engage the whole network, recognize that control is dispersed, assess the many levels of organization, accommodate to the fact that systems are constantly revising, and understand that decisionmaking direction needs to anticipate the future so as to adapt to niches the system occupies.[17] Locally grown decisions are capable of precisely such inclusiveness. Furthermore, by including input diversity they advance the disorder within a system toward greater stability, achieve greater accuracy, and are less susceptible to the manipulations of power and ideology.

When objective accuracy is desired, it is customary to think of the scientific method, in which a measurement done by one person can be replicated by another, and indeed *must* be replicated in order to determine its validity. However, in the messy, rough-and-tumble immediacy of real life, there is a variety of ways to get accurate measurements, and a complex system uses all of them. Complex systems are opportunistic and varied: scientifically collected surveys, photographs, government records, input/output measures, or key indicators. Moreover, such approaches also need to be able to accommodate differing definitions of accuracy. For example, is the new store in town improving life, or is it not? The answer depends on who you are in the town.

Communities are always monitoring themselves. They do so through stories, gossip, and the everyday exchanges whereby everyone knows everyone else's business. Increasingly, they may do so through status updates and Twitter feeds. But it is important to note that accumulating evidence does not simply mean accumulating stories. Communities tend to enjoy anecdotes, and while funny stories may be true, good stories are usually good because they are exceptional. While a community's stories paint an important picture of it (and above all of how it sees itself), that image is often composed of exceptions rather than averages. Thus, it is vital to distinguish between anecdotes and data (the plural of anecdote is not data).

Evidence-based decisionmaking is also not the same as conducting research. The established paradigms of scientific research seek to understand truth posited as universal, taken to extend beyond a given community and be contingent neither on time nor place nor context. In furthering such projects, researchers tend to demand a level of replicable rigor necessary to the formation of theories. Most communities, though, do not care much about things beyond the purview of their own lives, which explains in part the derisive opinions many local people have of researchers (to local people researchers talk in a manner that appears calculated to make the local feel stupid.) Evidence-based decisionmaking, on the other hand, is not about ultimate truth but about guiding local action. Hence it needs to be sophisticated enough only to bring forward evidence relevant to the decisions at hand.

Community-led evidence-gathering stimulates local energy. Moreover, adapted in method, it can cross the spectrum of community issues (ecology, health, education, agriculture, religion, economics, culture). Palin is again illustrative. Epidemiologists from the state health department had done a survey. These numbers supposedly told what happened, and government health officers were trying to get the community to respond. But participatory assessment provided information that was more accurate, achieved coverage of the whole area (which is key to accuracy), but more important, the process got action underway.[18] Engaging the people in evidence-gathering was more powerful in directing action than the customary actions following research of trying to mobilize the community based on data in which the community was not invested.

Professionals with years of training in which they are told a particular method is "the right way" have difficulty not stepping into the evidence-gathering process to ensure that proper methodology is being followed.

Moreover, prestige in their peer-reviewed world is based on taking credit, not giving it to communities; they need to be able to claim, "This is my project." As a result, NGOs and scientists want evidence that has a different focus from that which a community would find helpful (for example the health surveys we conducted over the decades in Nepal). This element of researchers needing data for their purposes cannot be entirely dismissed. If the NGOs and researchers are not able to use the data as well, they will not be able to secure funding and continue as active partners. Again, the answer is both: the point is simply to be explicit about the range of needs and goals, rather than pretending that the ends most beneficial to the researchers will also benefit the community.

Beyond the above, possibly the greatest benefit of evidence-based decision-making is its ability to solve arguments within the community or between the community and outside partners. Evidence is, especially in contexts of power imbalance, the only reliable way to challenge opinion- or dogma-based views, and it is possibly the best way to neutralize embedded animosities. The more evidence is brought in, the more it can be shown to be accurate, the more likely that the strength of the power, money, or opinions diminish. In three words: facts diminish factionalism. However, as will be discussed further in Chapter 7, it is essential that such facts be produced through a collaborative process of *self*-evaluation. Those who own the process by which data are gathered own the data, and there are few rhetorical positions stronger than the claim to objectivity. Thus, in order to create a genuine meeting ground, facts must be established through collaborative processes and shared vision.

Figure 5.6. Seeking community evidence through house-to-house surveys in Arunachal Pradesh. *(Photo credit: Daniel Taylor)*

FOURTH PRINCIPLE: BEHAVIOR CHANGE, ACHIEVED THROUGH WORK PLANS

In a global mentality that views progress as measured in project outputs—the number of girls going to school, children immunized, income in people's bank accounts, higher speed Internet connectivity—it is a leap to accept the primacy of behavior change as the key result of social change. But the concept is not difficult. Intuitively, we all know that behavior change is central: nothing happens unless someone does it. Is health among people the product of clinics and doctors, or the result of behaviors people practice? The answer, of course, is both. But the first investment to achieve a healthy society that creates the largest impact with the least cost is to emphasize behavior changes. The argument is similar with school attendance, positive bank balances, and food security. All are important outputs to a stable complex society, and the behavior-change route is always available, always costs less, and once underway sets the stage for optimal utilization of services. Societies are grand conglomerations of behaviors; thus social change is first and foremost behavior change.

Rima achieved profound behavior changes achieving extraordinary reach: child marriage, status of women, home sanitation, domestic violence, school attendance, farming practices, and trade. As a result, the Bameng community became substantially more secure, and also more free. Development that increased their interdependency led to many freedoms. Projects often try to replace deep-outcome change with input tallies—opening an office, hiring staff, building buildings, writing reports, sending people for training—the reason is that they are accounting for money spent, thereby protecting their actions, but they are not proving results in people's lives. What is shown in the Bameng and Palin experiences is the potential for life transformation as one behavior trips others, causing change that is collective and multidimensional. Gains may be small at first. Then, as behaviors add, whether in number of people who join or as quality of life rises, a tipping point is reached and a new social norm stands. The community really is a different place. Bameng and Palin are at the smallest of scales, but similar phenomena will be described at much larger scale in China in subsequent chapters.

There will be big problems for communities as this progress goes forward. But if design direction is not coming from central authority while the scale-level growth is being encouraged, then typically the ineffective behavior changes will be localized. The Palin women's action groups achieved dramatic profits from their kitchens gardens one year by growing ginger. Women's groups in the not-too-distant Sangram valley decided to plant ginger in all their fields. At harvest, they joyfully stacked up mountains of the root. But the local merchant offered them virtually nothing. With their husbands laughing at them and no idea how to take the ginger to markets where their product scale could sell, the mountains rotted.

Behavior change is not just one change—such as learning how to treat diarrhea—but as local action engages, the behavior changes are progressive, occurring in outwardly radiating contact with the world. Action must change not just in specific actions, but also in more global awareness. Outsiders may help, but they should not be counted on. When local behavior changes have begun, it is imperative that systems planning also come with these. This sounds technical—complexity theory, emergence, and so on. But in reality, as is the hallmark of emergence, it is adaptive response. To do this, context is needed, and for that, local action groups. Complex world-adaptive planning will grow if there is context for it. What will occur is growth inside the group to allow it to engage outside forces with intentionality and with strength.

The business interests that live off social change do not get enthusiastic about behavior change: in contrast with promoting change by overhead-producing new technologies or building infrastructure. For example, the rehydration solution the Palin women made with rice and salt did not help any pharmacy or clinic, whereas both pharmacy and clinic profit from the sale of rehydration packets. And the profit priorities are global; for example, the World Health Organization, after two decades of evidence showing home-based rehydration efficacy, still promotes commercially sold rehydration packets because pharmaceutical interests push this onto a public-interest UN organization. But business interests, organized religion, and professional associations have another reason not to support local empowerment: local empowerment pushes back.

Conflicts frequently emerge as behavior change grows. For example, in Palin the women's meetings were being held on Sunday mornings. As the length of their meetings increased, with women wanting to learn more and adding an hour of literacy training after the meeting, suddenly there was a conflict with the Catholic mass. The priest instructed them to stop the literacy training, emphasizing the importance of mass. But the women countered by withdrawing from church services. After weeks of lowered attendance, the priest pushed back the time mass began. The women then made a point of attending.

A further tale from Palin illustrates behaviors adjusting with rising empowerment. Health lessons provided by Future Generations Arunachal with its offices in the state capitol of Itanagar addressed only a limited number of issues (sanitation, immunizations, oral rehydration, nutrition, pregnancy care). But the women had expanding questions, and to answer these they invited the physician from the government clinic. When first asked, the high-caste doctor from the State of Bihar said that he was too busy, and in addition, he added, he did not want to come to their crude bamboo hut. The women replied that, speaking of *crude*, his clinic was filthy. The doctor protested that cleaning the clinic was beneath his caste. One of the women suggested an exchange: if they cleaned his clinic, would he teach them? He agreed, and until the doctor was transferred, he regularly taught about reproductive health, the physiology of child development and human growth, starting classes in general science, and even general education. In return, his clinic was always clean.

GLOBAL APPLICABILITY

It may be tempting to view the principles of SEED-SCALE as relevant only for poor and isolated communities because the examples used are primarily from the margins (Arunachal, Afghanistan, and, in subsequent chapters, Tibet). But while the focus of the argument here presses action out to such unreached populations, SEED-SCALE is not so limited. SEED-SCALE offers a universal process to grow site-specific solutions of more affordable society-wide change.

Holding to the example in this chapter of health as the entry point to starting society-wide change, in the affluent world, health can play a similar role. In the United States, contrary to the mindset that health is produced by state-of-art high technology, implemented by skilled doctors, and so expensive it requires high-priced insurance, the error of this mindset is shown by the nation's rapidly rising health challenges: obesity, heart conditions, diabetes, mental illness, violence, and substance-abuse, including alcohol, tobacco, and drugs. These conditions all are addressed by a triple-domain health solution—a combination of technical, behavioral, and relational domains—and achieving effective interplay among these domains is precisely the strength of a complex systems approach.

However, the public discussion of society's solutions is often dominated by the technical domain: presuming illness results from infection, the answers are assumed to be state-of-art technology, skilled doctors, and financing accelerated by feedback loops of insurance. Solutions in this domain make money. Thus, there are always those with a vested interest in avoiding the human-energy-based solutions that not only are essential but that also do not make money. The frontier of health care lies in engaging the behavior and relational domains. Focused only on the money-making technical aspect, the health care system itself in the United States is sick. There is movement, though, in the United States with the diseases of affluence that technology cannot cure, to a patient-centered home, a mentality similar to the home-based, behavior changing, community-relations-enabling approaches that have been described for Bameng and Palin. The similarities are not in the structures of women's action groups but in the application of both prevention and cure coming from a feedback loop in which energies both change the individual behaviors and alter relations among people so collective empowerment grows. Empowerment-based health is not just for the poor.

Empowering people to take ownership of their health by creating the structures of healthy behaviors and societal relationships establishes a parallel currency of change in directed energies that seek not to take down the dysfunctional health system, but to build up a patient-centered, healthy home. Homes in the United States with a very different health needs profile caused by affluence can become health-nurturing as were the homes of Bameng and Palin, where the profile resulted from isolation and poverty. It is the system for solutions that is analogous, not the structure.

Understood in this manner, the four principles are as relevant in contexts like the United States as they are in Arunachal, Afghanistan, and Tibet: success-based orientation, a three-way partnership, evidence-based decision making, and outcomes focused on behavior change. The universality of these principles (they are not proprietary to SEED-SCALE but operate in any given scenario) is relevant not just at the local level, but also at regional and national levels, as will be further developed in Chapters 8 and 9 with examples from across China and New York City. (In those instances, conservation provides the case examples, rather than health.) Complex systems operate according to principles that define relationships, which work in the midst of both poverty and affluence. They apply across technical, behavioral, and relational domains. We need to expand our actions into the complex totality, to go beyond just the technical or the finance-driven domains. Moreover, when behavioral and relational domain-based actions occur, impacts move out of tight sectoral results and set in motion ongoing adaptations of an iteratively improving complex system. This is social change.

CREATING EMERGING SOCIAL STABILITY AND MOMENTUM

Riding a bicycle involves making adapting responses as it moves down the road: wiggle the handlebars, shift your weight, pedal harder. Riding with greater speed and skill causes increasingly stable momentum. None of these actions can be predicted from any distance by an onlooker, or even a minute before by the rider. Each action responds to the context that both bicycle and rider are in at each moment. Each action is an adaptive response, driven by principles that guide the bicycle forward.

The four principles of social change operate in a more complex context than riding a bicycle, but the idea is much the same: applied in combination, with greater speed and skill, momentum accelerates and stabilizes. What is important to note about the four principles, like the actions on the bicycle, is that they give a process that leads to momentum, momentum along an arrow of time appropriate to each moment at each locale. Seeing how the principles worked in Palin to move those communities forward is evident now in hindsight, but that potential was not obvious in 1998. On that day it was tempting to identify the problem as "cholera and the water supply," view deeper issues of gender and poverty as unsolvable, and depart from the village congratulating ourselves.

The four principles are not new. In the military, from ancient times commanders: (1) built campaigns upon successes, using strategy and tactics that worked; (2) created alliances with outsiders, other Top-down partners, and Bottom-up people support; (3) acquired intelligence to base field decisions on; and (4) while seeking technology and financing, knowing that most important for success was adjusting battle behaviors.

In the business world also, the principles operate: (1) corporations make profits from selling successful products and ending failures; (2) attention focuses on partnerships with the Bottom-up consumer, the Top-down policies of government and financing, and addressing Outside-in competition; (3) financial reports govern decisions (with few businesses surviving when decisions are made using opinions contrary to the data); (4) as new realities unfold, the businesses change behaviors with remarkable speed.

Parallels exist to the four principles in social change. In impact, the most significant was the work by Mahatma Gandhi changing the lives of one-fifth of humanity (described in Chapter 10). (In our repeated use of Gandhi in this book as an example, we are not lifting up the man, or his particular, often curious, beliefs, but his yet-to-be-equaled mobilization of human energy.) Building that empire-removing momentum surprisingly devoid of animosity took time, applying the principles as the cycles of his spinning pulled out threads of adapting understanding and effective participation. We have already noted asset-based community development; and participatory research and action (PRA) that emphasizes community teamwork, flexibility to fit local situations, finding the information needed, and gathering qualitative data from at least three sources.[19] Another process headed in the same direction is *appreciative inquiry* focusing on finding resources from field experience, then using them to continue positive change.[20] From the business world a parallel philosophy is *total quality management*, centering obviously on quality (building on success), participation (three-way partnership), emphasis on continual growth (iterative change), and seeking broader benefits (parallel to going to scale).[21]

In our work around the world, when we encountered effective social change, we almost always found the four principles were operating.[22] Usually they were not part of the formal methodology (for example, the case of New York City described in Chapter 9), but the four principles were being used because they made sense—just like they made sense to military commanders and corporate managers. In our experience, the four principles are least-common in programs that are well-funded. Calls for money replace building on successes. Hiring employees takes the place of building partnerships. Budgets rule rather than participatory decision making. And ultimate project success is determined by the congruence of budgets with project deliverables, not assessing behaviors changed. What drives such projects is control. Results often last only as long as the money. To continue the bicycle analogy, these projects operate like a bicycle with the pedals fixed directly to the wheel (as in a child's tricycle). The bike moves as long as you turn the pedals, but energy is not carried forward, meaning you get only as much energy out as you put in, and are unable to coast even when riding downhill.

How can projects go forward grounded in the four principles when the world of social change runs by donor priorities and government demands? One way is to create contracts—the community says to the donor: If you want that priority (for example, special health services like participating in global immunization campaigns, different accounting, or conservation), then this is what *we* want. In such instances, the strategy is not to deny the demand of the outside but strike a deal with it. Perhaps the outside will respond with: "We don't like what you propose, change to do it our way." Acquiescing to that demand may be necessary, but more likely the result will be that a dialogue is started that can grow into partnership. A community may have difficulty negotiating contracts with enough strength to truly push back, but by implementing all four principles, polarization is reduced and options are opened. The more such negotiation happens, skill levels rise, and like riding a bicycle, stability and momentum increase.

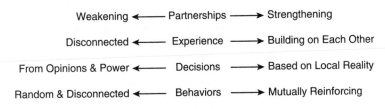

Figure 5.7. Directions of the Four Principles.

If communities are to move forward, as Palin shows, the key is involving people. As the numbers of women involved rose and the speed of their change did also, the product was so significant that it overcame entrenched patriarchal dominance in which women were chained and beaten, to improving family health, education, and safe housing. Momentum began with a small cluster of forty women. Then the momentum grew, not in opposition but as a forward-moving energy that gathered in the men. Forces that had paralyzed both women and men were transformed.

More recent changes have occurred as momentum kept going forward: the Palin action groups (there were twenty-six of them at that time) decided to stand on their own. As mentioned, there had been organizational tensions with the larger structure of Future Generations Arunachal from which they had been started. So, the twenty-six groups created themselves as a legally separate society, taking over property that the outside organization had paid for. They started training courses and special events where they did not invite their state, national, or international affiliates. Using money raised by their own efforts, they took a trip to Nepal to instigate their own learning experience, returned and created training manuals and videos, starting a newsletter and an annual report.

Such actions could have been viewed as a hostile breakaway, as the Palin group did not adopt the name of the parent organization, let alone ask its permission. Fortunately, their learning curve of empowerment was recognized by the larger group, as was their intent to own their own direction and decisionmaking. Rather than forcing its control over this self-initiation, the original organization continued to pay certain salaries within the Palin group. They even elected a Palin person (Rocket) to chair the state organization, turning the issue of control upside down.

Done adroitly, working from principles shows results and stimulates others to catch up, opening opportunities for all, getting out in front and bringing along the powerful. In Palin, a small number of women started to move, and as their momentum went forward it was far from a straight-line process, yet, erratic though it was, it was net-forward. This caused others to join, and that enticed the men. The principles were held to—that was what was key, not holding to the structures. Ultimately what resulted was a new organization with new governance, and that new organization prompted new legal organizations to start in Sangram, then in Ziro with the Apatani, other sites, and the breaking up of the larger as they grew into smaller units, each of which then continued to grow.

Growth in such instances of complex systems has been described with the specially coined word *chaordic*, a hybrid of chaos and order, a word initially describing the way the VISA credit card company grew from multiple banks, extending its model by principles causing each site to be better fitted to its situation. The process proved more adaptable and rapid than the centrally controlled expansion model being pursued by MasterCard and American Express.[23] With VISA, as with expansion of new community action structures in Arunachal Pradesh, the chaordic growth happened in such a way that the sites were benefiting *because principles were driving the growth*, and this caused confrontation with central management to be minimized. Chaos and order operating in cross-corrective tension is an energy-generating engine.

Progress will generally be imperfect. A "beginning" is just that, not the whole journey. The beginning is kept growing by all four principles' being fostered. What is important is adhering to all four principles. Assist a critical mass to grow through internal energies; that is the way of atomic reactions, started by outside stimulus and grown to great force by restructuring internal bonds and mass.

A member of our family brought back a helpful adage from the Cameroon seventy years ago, following a decade of patient work there: "Don't mistake going slow for being stopped." When going slowly and following the effective principles, suddenly the momentum engendered can position you far out ahead.

CHAPTER 6
Maintaining Momentum

Seven Tasks

An Afghan boy called to a man working in the field, "Your wife fell into the river!" The farmer raced to where she'd gone to fill her water jug—then started running up the bank. "No!" shouted the boy. "The current carried her downriver!" The frantic farmer turned, "Boy, you don't know Afghan women. Always, they must swim against the stream."
Modern Afghan joke

Consider a modern city: a person wants a dozen oranges and takes a taxi to a store where a dozen oranges wait—a simple human desire satisfied by a global supply chain. No mayor or central office gave a directive that people should eat oranges or put in place a funding stream to have oranges or taxi positioned. The shopkeeper did not know who would come looking for oranges but assumed that someone would; the taxi driver guessed his probabilities and went down a certain street. A city in which oranges from South America and taxis built in Japan spontaneously show up, where children go to school with a high likelihood of surviving because they are getting adequate vitamins, is considered "developed."

Now consider another city, one where the shop shelves are sparsely laden, where travel is by foot, where only rich children go to school and a third of all children die—such a city is considered "undeveloped." Both cities are evolving an emerging order out of seemingly chaotic movements, and both are operating the best that each can using what they have. The parts of these two cities are very different, but the process by which order emerges out of the relationships among those parts is almost identical. Both cities are developed and always developing. SEED-SCALE guides that process more effectively. It is equally applicable in both situations, but in the "developed" city with all its wealth the necessity of utilizing the alternative currency of human energy is less immediately apparent, but can still be beneficial for social goals like lowering crime or raising community cohesion.

Pondering the complexities of nature two and a half millennia ago, Heraclitus gave the following aphorism: "You cannot step twice into the same river, for other waters are flowing onto you."[1] As Heraclitus observed, rivers are not simple lines of repeating drops. Time may move with ticks, money may flow dollar-after-dollar, but with rivers, as with life, there is constant change: step in one time and be enveloped in water, step in again, and other waters are flowing onto you. The processes of life that we step into are always changing. The imperative for successful crossings is learning how to adapt to the flows that come: not control them, but adapt to them. Successful engagement with the always-changing parts coming at one is a process of readjusting relationships to the parts.

This is the reality of complex systems. The reality of actions by development experts is strikingly different. That is control-based, even in a context where control is difficult and where resources are inadequate to satisfy rising aspirations. For a city to move out of inefficiency and absence of safety and toward the ends it seeks, it must learn to use the operating procedures it has more effectively. These have emerged sporadically over time, but they can also be intentionally shaped. Communities need not wait. Many actors are ready.

Three dynamics operate to shape complex systems: *principles, tasks,* and *criteria.* Principles establish the values, the tasks set out what to do, and the criteria provide a way to monitor progress. In the prior chapter, four principles

Figure 6.1. On the streets of an Afghan settlement, a boy adapts by setting up his cigarette and egg business. *(Photo credit: Daniel Taylor)*

were presented (build from success, three-way partnerships, evidence-based decisionmaking, and focusing on behavior change). These principles guide community members in how to interact with each other and how to respond to forces acting on their system. This chapter outlines seven tasks to operationalize the four principles. The next chapter presents five criteria by which social change can be monitored. What results is a structure for actions wherein each action fits other actions, adapting into new relationships among the constituents. This approach, where order emerges from the inside, based on principles, tasks, and criteria, contrasts with social change where order is prescribed from the outside and actions follow in a linear direction.[2] Here is an example of how such emerging order occurred through application of the seven SEED-SCALE tasks in the rubble of Kabul, Afghanistan.[3]

One night in the spring of 2002, Abdullah Barat sat by the samovar with a group of hardened ex-combatants, veterans of wars and a variety of armies, drinking tea, eating flatbread and kabobs, telling war stories. As the night wore on, the talk turned to the gifts flowing in, and how long and to whom the flow of good would last. Some of the men, worried that nothing was coming to them, turned to the option of poppies. This was the moment for which Abdullah had been waiting.

"I am part of a new movement," he said. "We call ourselves the *Pagals.*" (*Pagal* is the Persian word for "mad"—not merely loopy, but full-throated mad, as with rabies.) "I've heard enough now to know I am sitting around this samovar with more *Pagals.* Our purpose is simple: If you are crazy enough to believe a better world is possible, join the *Pagals.* Membership dues are two hundred handmade bricks." Soon those ex-combatants were making bricks. Like Gandhi's homespun cloth, their mud bricks, made through their own energy, symbolized self-reliance and brought people together. Perhaps most importantly, 200 sun-dried bricks by themselves have little value; value is gained only when combined with the bricks of others. So, this group joined the *Pagals,* made their bricks, and joining with others they rebuilt the village mosque, then they rebuilt the school. Winter was approaching, so the *Pagals,* a group now organized and starting to set a new type of target to aim at, got permission to use a coal mine, and with their donkeys transported the coal back to the villages. While much of Afghanistan waited for gifts from outside, here, a day's walk from the valleys of Rostam and Saya Dara mentioned earlier, the empowerment process had also begun, this time among the men.

The joke in the epigraph, popular in post-Taliban Kabul, reveals a strikingly different view of Afghan women from the image in popular media, the powerless figures behind *burqas.*[4] Afghan men are not blind to their women's burdens. As life's currents push on families, both men and women struggle to swim against victimization. The people seek to advance in an Afghan way, growing the aspirations and values inside—this internal energy is what waits to move and can connect with the energies of others so hopes that might have seemed impossible assemble into mosques, schools, a way of life put together despite life's vicissitudes, despite the burdens they carry.

Abdullah's mobilization did not stop with the Pagal Party in the remote province of Bamyan. He taught the process wherever he went. Prior to September 11, 2001, two decades of war following four years of crushing drought had taken away the traditional uses of land. People cut fruit trees for fuel and killed their sheep for food. With liberation from the Taliban, refugees from the countryside walked or rode on trucks into Kabul by the hundreds of thousands for new opportunities. But the Kabul they came to had been destroyed. Still, believing that a better life was possible, the migrants packed into rubbled buildings and put up shelters with scavenged materials. Settlements grew without plan or services.

Abdullah regularly came from Bamyan (where the famous Buddha statues had been destroyed by the Taliban) to Kabul for staff meetings as part of his job for Future Generations Afghanistan. On these visits he often stayed with relatives. One such community had been started a decade earlier by prior refugees during the Afghan civil war; it was to this community that Abdullah came. They asked what he did back home, and he explained that every person has a few extra calories of energy, and that while most people invest most of their energy holding their place in life, there is a margin of energy that can be redirected. This can be used to drink tea and talk—or people can move from talk to actions that change lives. Indeed, he said, it does not require much energy to create change if one person joins his or her contribution with those from others.

Those gathered around nodded. Life had always been this way: Allah willing, life was shaped by what you did, here also in this war-scarred settlement. Abdullah said people working together could overcome most problems, as they had done in ousting the Soviet Union, Allah willing. Usually, though, individuals worked alone, seizing opportunities that benefited only them; then the industrious ones moved on, leaving the rest where they were. With this point Abdullah made clear a problem of many entrepreneurship models. There are among the poor, individuals eager to help themselves (microcredit, education, or other ways), but if they rise, how will those who lack the entrepreneurial drive fare? Advancement has come for some, but those left behind, they have lost the leaders they need who can help advance the whole group. What transforms the community is the whole moving forward, a point that is particularly telling in contexts such as Afghanistan, fraught with ethnic tensions and histories of violence.

"Who among us Hazaras really trusts the Pushtun, or the Tajiks?" Abdullah asked. The group was silent—then descriptions followed of outrages other groups had done to their group in the civil war, or even a century before to their people. "But now we're together in the city we must trust them," Abdullah went on. "Do you want to walk down the streets worried, as you were before, that with every step you may be attacked? We need to bring together our energies instead of having them isolated in fear." The people nodded; that day there had been a theft in their community, and all had been certain it had been by a Tajik, they had gone to the Tajiks and made the accusation, but then a Hazara boy had been found with the stolen item.

Long speeches followed as each affirmed his intent. "We need to learn more." So, without investing a dollar, without setting up a program, without staff, Abdullah taught SEED-SCALE. "Imagine a donkey," he explained, "a willful, stubborn beast as everyone knows. As donkeys you can continue to be ridden with a steel bit in your teeth with government or some warlord directing you. Or, you can stop being so stubborn and learn how to care for yourselves." The first task, he said, was that "you must learn to work with your neighbors, create shared leadership."

"Not so fast," all around him said; "we're not going share leadership with the Pushtun," and a familiar lament started. "We've been discriminated against for centuries; they made us slaves." Abdullah listened, but then repeated, "You must learn to share leadership. The Pushtun will never follow your leadership, you cannot conquer them, but for at least this community where we've been packed together you must create a committee amid this rubble, and share leadership."

Outrage was again the reaction. "After centuries of oppression, we deserve now compensation. We deserve. . . ." Drought these last years had taken what little they had, forced them to Kabul; they were not about to forget who had oppressed them. Rather than asking them to work with such oppressors, Abdullah should use his foreign contacts, forget the Pushtun, and get them resources. They had already made it clear in their earlier speeches that they would work hard, but to ask that they work with those whom they could not trust, who he had just admitted would try to control them, that was asking too much!

Abdullah repeated the positive point, that security would grow in their jammed-together cluster of makeshift homes only if they learned to work from collective resources. They had to learn to shape the new community they were now a part of, and within which their neighbors were their most important resource. There was no way international resources would help them— what might come today would not be there tomorrow. To create a future, the people must work together, there was no alternative: talking would get them nowhere; fighting, they would lose. If they wanted a voice in decisionmaking, they had to cooperate in leadership. Seven tasks could guide their actions.

Rather than figure out who would be the leader among them, an action that would immediately create competition, Abdullah advised a different approach. There were many groups in their neighborhood, they could select a couple of leaders from each. In this way they could move together; indeed, they would create a community by doing so, gathering the strength of all groups. The first task was to create a local coordinating committee.

The second task was to build from what they had. "We have nothing," the people replied. "We're poor—so if we do create a committee, your job is to go out and get international help; the international people bombed us, they are giving away wheat and even bottled water." But Abdullah answered, "You have survived—that's a major success. What are your other successes? Treat each as a seed that you can grow. Don't expect gifts of outside resources because, unless you start killing each other and bring the 'war on terror' here, the outside resources will not come here."

"Conducting our first survey," the committee secretary, Akbar, later informed us, "showed strength we never imagined. That task of learning about ourselves, how many had survived, what had happened to each of us, brought stories between ethnic groups that were much the same, with more in common than we had differences. We had known we were from four ethnic groups, but we had no idea we were 41,000 people."

The community undertook the third task: determining what successes had they seen in other places; then bringing those in, adeptly adapting them to adopt them. The local coordinating committee sent out the word: Keep your eyes and ideas open when you travel. Each person must be learning good ideas. The committee gathered funds and sent a group to Bamyan to see the work with the *Pagals*. Returning, they told everyone that their first survey had been only a head-count. Instead of just asking people with generalizations who they were and how many, whether literate or illiterate, or with adequate housing, a real survey would provide specifics.

So they engaged in the fourth task: gathering data about their community. Geographic boundaries were established for their community, using features such as hill slopes and ponds, and within these they gave a name to each winding, dusty alley. On each home they painted a number. What had seemed to be chaos began to be ordered.[5] Volunteers went house-to-house with a better-designed questionnaire; Abdullah had trained them how to ask their questions more objectively. It turned out the people crowded into these alleyways had come from eleven provinces and totaled 65,000, not 41,000 people.

With their data, the fifth task was to make more effective decisions. Wards were created, groups held meetings, designated buildings became neighborhood centers, and in three of them classes started (one was a mosque). Dialogue began among the wards, and an overall plan was drawn up. The first plan was basic, a few objectives and who would lead. Abdullah stressed the importance of plans that they could implement; a plan that required resources they did not have was a wish list, not a plan.

The sixth task was to implement the plans. One objective they had identified was getting out the vote in the upcoming elections, and on voting day, 90 percent of the community turned out behind their agreed-to agenda. Their candidates won and were told what they were now expected to deliver. A further objective was latrine building, because in studying other successes they

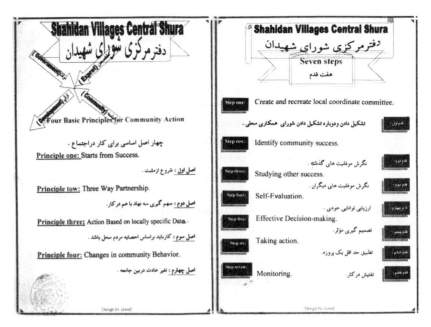

Figure 6.2. SEED-SCALE posters at the community center in Shaidan, Bamyan Province, Afghanistan. *(Photo credit: Daniel Taylor)*

had learned how street filth, particularly human feces, was causing many illnesses. A third objective was to add more classes beyond the reading and writing at their three learning centers, and in a matter of months, 150 students of both genders, mostly adults, were studying photography, computers, art, poetry, and Islam.

The seventh and final task was mid-course corrections—adjusting their actions should strengthen the four principles: Building from success, engaging a three-way partnership, deciding using evidence, and focusing on behavior changes they could accomplish. When one cycle of the seven tasks was completed, it started over. To this meeting more people came, speeches started, and members felt compelled to catalogue their problems, but the committee cajoled the group to focus on what could they strengthen. A breakthrough was identifying individuals who in the first round had shown leadership and inviting them to lead the group, and as a result sixty people were identified. Clearly, sixty was too many for one local coordinating committee, so rather than sending people away, subcommittees formed in the ten wards of their settlement.[6] As skill levels rose and people brought back ideas, more sophisticated workplans resulted. Diversification unfolded in the ten wards.

Progress was palpable in the dusty streets. Learning centers added more subjects: Dari and Pushtun language classes, English classes, more computers came as gifts (at times five people on a computer, coaching each other), instruction in calligraphy, residents lent personal cameras to support the photography classes, a youth theater led to drama performances. One center tried an idea, and if it was popular, another adapted it. As people learned to read, the community wanted a library. With no budget for books, requests went to all households; people searched their homes, then the city. A borrowing rotation was set up. More books came in. With prescience for their future, priority in borrowing books was given to children.

The political clout during the election started to produce results. At first, elected officials had done little, but the community did not let them forget who had put them into office. Soon, electrification partially lighted once-dark streets, and waste-collection began. With aspirations rising, the people started exploring ways to go back and forth to the city. A member was identified with a car, and he began episodic taxi service for a fee. The learning centers started jobs-training programs. With more people going out for jobs, more paychecks started coming in. Awareness grew, and they contacted a French NGO to open a clinic. Health worker training started so each neighborhood had basic skills, and a focus began on educating mothers and placing emphasis on health habits in homes.

Though they had extraordinary initial successes, their organization was still informal, so the coordinating committee formalized into a *shura* (governing council) and registered themselves with the government. Now they were legally authorized, but to give voice to both halves of their community, they registered a separate *shura* for women. (It was in this discussion that we first heard the joke at the top of this chapter about women swimming upstream.) What was important to them? What did they stand for? New questions were coming forward. A community-wide meeting was called. Afghans love grand speeches; rhetoric soars. They wanted a symbol of their achievements. After more meetings it was decided their symbol should be an eagle, wings outstretched. While eagles are symbols in many places across Afghanistan, almost always they are sitting, wings folded. The eagle chosen by the community that named itself *DehKudaidad* (place that is a gift from God) is flying directly at anyone looking at it, wings spread wide. DehKudaidad was a people on the move.

People who seek to help others are fond of Lao Tzu's parable, "give a man a fish and you feed him for a day—teach a man to fish and you feed him for life." And yet the do-gooders often seem to feel the need to hand out a few fish to whet the appetite, and then, when learning lags or action veers, they give a few more bites to help nourish the process. Such feeding has long been used to train wild animals (including eagles), but the core intention in that process is to take control over the life of another by making the individual dependent. Furthermore, even when they get around to the lessons, they are likely to import the proverbial hook, line, and sinker from abroad. The parable is easy to misread as being about fish—teach a man to fish and he gets more fish.

But that might not be the case: anyone who has spent an afternoon by a stream with a fishing pole knows that knowing how to fish does not guarantee a meal. The real point is that if you teach a man to fish, you have given him a series of actions he can perform to give himself a better shot at catching something to eat. This means that not only are any fish he catches *his* fish, but he has something to teach his sons and daughters.

Two years were required to accomplish the tasks described above, linking together unconnected individuals living in what had been a slum that changed into a vibrant community. An army could not have done that, nor a million dollars. Progress continued in the five years that followed. Visits today to DehKudaidad show statistics on the walls with charts of rising health, economic growth, community literacy, and pictures of government officials visiting and seeking community support. But, more powerfully, the results are visible in the homes. DehKudaidad is far from the hypothetical "developed" city suggested at the beginning of this chapter, but neither is it the slum. In a context of war, with no donated material assistance except discarded computers and books, using primarily learning that they accessed, in an insecure situation where everyone had good reason to remain in their homes, the people went out to their neighbors, applied the seven tasks, and created community. Ordered settlement emerged from a slum.

Following is a more specific discussion of the cycle of seven tasks DehKudaidad started.

A CYCLE OF TASKS FOR SOCIAL CHANGE

The seven tasks of SEED-SCALE are a cycle of growth. An analogy is found in one of the most universal human activities, the cycle of agriculture. In agriculture, the cycle is: clear fields, plow, plant, water, fertilize, weed, protect, and harvest. Each task is integral to the whole. If these tasks are separated, they do not grow a crop. What brings shoots out and takes them to harvest is doing *all* of them. Certain activities dominate at specific times, and they are completed in many different ways around the world, but ultimately, some version of each must be performed.

Not only is that which is produced far more than the sum of the parts—when done, the procedure self-replicates, and through mutation it can even improve in each cycle. Crops and technology differ around the world, but the basic activities do not. That is, the tasks are invariant, but what comes out of them changes according to system. What is operating is a huge nested system: one field, a unit unto itself, but also production within other fields around the world, creating an adapting global food system, each autonomous but also each connected, the global food supply—and each following the identical cycle of process regardless of ecology and regardless of financial capacity. The seven SEED-SCALE tasks advance an analogous cycle to grow social energy.[7]

Table 6.1 SEVEN TASKS OF SEED-SCALE (OBJECTIVES AND PROCESS)

Task	Objective	How
#1	Develop leadership	Create a Local Coordinating Committee
#2	Find a Starting Point & Resources	Identify Successes in the Committee
#3	Obtain a Relevant Education	Visit Other Successes Elsewhere
#4	Fit situation-ecol, econ, values	Conduct Self Evaluation Survey
#5	Determine direction & partners	Make Effective Decisions=>Create Plans
#6	Coordinate people, resources & time	Implement Plans, Gathering the Community
#7	Keep momentum on track	Correct to strengthen four principles

In earlier writing, we called the tasks "steps," but that implied sequential steps that needed to be completed in the specified order. Each task should done when appropriate, at its time, and each task must adapt to the conditions of that moment as a farmer adjusts to drought, locusts, or broken equipment. Giving to people a process they could do that advanced their lives (rather than a product to take) is what the Taliban and Al-Qaeda did; a cycle of tasks each year grew stronger as people became addicted to the profits from poppy crops. When people invest their energies, they are investing part of themselves; it is much more substantial than stepping forward to take something. *It is essential to complete the full cycle—do not fret about the quality of the cycle just completed, for the next cycle tasks can be improved.* Focusing on excellence in one task is like a farmer who spends too much time plowing and so will not reap a harvest. This does not mean excellence is unimportant, but what defines excellence is doing the full cycle and then repeating it.

Before presenting the specific tasks, it is useful to turn again to emergence. As is true with procedures in an emergent system, the procedures of social change do not resemble the larger system. Procedures must be simple or their application will not come spontaneously in order to address the larger complexity. Applying these procedures not only executes, but also anticipates and predicts, changes in the evolving larger complex system.

The business of international development has encumbered what is actually simple. In the wonderfully diverse nexus of people, place, and time, the contributing dynamics of world economics are complex—it is hard to get more complex—but in fact, actions do not need to engage such massive interactions. Build from the fact that all actions are site- and time-specific. The advantage of using a complex adaptive system mode, rather than the command-control (or multilinear) mode, is that actions to resolve the complexity can be simple procedures: a nested set of principles, tasks, and values that tell people how to adapt. From their implementation, complex answers come out of simple process.

TASK: CREATE (OR RESHAPE) A LOCAL COORDINATING COMMITTEE

Social change is best managed by a team representing all groups. Note the cohesion in DehKudaidad when leadership expanded to include wider circles among those who had worked in earlier cycles. To achieve effective leadership in a complex system, it is important to include as many factions as possible. Doing so coordinates the complexity. But if people are not working, they need to be pushed to the periphery of leadership, as leadership is a privilege that is earned by work.

Unfortunately, it is customary to look for the strong leader. Moreover, usually a charismatic leader is sought. We say "unfortunately" because such leaders are rare, difficult to keep, too busy to train, almost impossible to replace, and seldom inclined to be inclusive of others. For short periods, though, such charismatic leaders can make dramatic forward progress, and sometimes (Gandhi being a preeminent example) they can be wonderfully participatory. When a charismatic leader is in place, the person's first responsibility is to build a team confident and strong enough to be constantly challenging that strong leadership. Communities are likely to find such people too rarely for action to be predicated upon them. It is more reliable to start from the outset to create a collective. Size and composition of the committee will differ depending on local traditions and the stage of the project. However, it is hard to imagine a coordinating committee with fewer than seven members, perhaps four from the community, two officials, and one change agent. The committee can be larger, but efficient functioning requires preventing the committee from growing so large that it behaves like a congress. And, as was done in DehKudaidad, creating subcommittees starts the process of scaling up and also the activities of action learning and experimentation of SCALE Squared (discussed in Chapter 8).

The first coordinating group can be self-selected. As the cycle of tasks repeats, membership should bring in the marginalized, especially women. A term often used to identify the pioneers who start such change is *social entrepreneurs*. Our experience shows it is better when such pioneers motivate others in committee; to create community-wide energy, it is important that the community see itself as leading. Top-down or Outside-in partners may not join at first. For example, Abdullah's *Pagals* had to struggle until they involved the warlord of a local militia, Abdul Rahman. First, the general came as an observer. As he saw the group's effectiveness, his participation increased. Ultimately, he ran for district office, worked hard, and rose to be a deputy provincial governor, moving into being an even more helpful Top-down partner. The general's shift was mostly due to his motivation; however, such individuals join coordinating committees because they see such committees as giving them community bases.

TASK: IDENTIFY LOCAL SUCCESSES IN THE COMMUNITY

Stories in the war-torn land of Afghanistan are powerful; the tales bring laughter to lift burdens of the moment, and the memories often make people feel strong again or give them focus. A winning football team, a son or daughter who has become famous, how Afghanistan defeated the mighty Soviet Empire, or empires before—stories are the day-to-day ways of passing on the skills, resourcefulness, and determination needed to survive. Stories are the capsules of a past memory line that points to what the people can do in the future. Every community, even the most destitute, has its stories that trumpet its successes. These successes are part of their evidence to build with, just like bricks can be used to build.

The challenge is deciding what successes to select as social building blocks. Change agents are helpful in this, accenting successes that are especially relevant because they know what other communities are doing and they may see innovations in a community. Care must be taken to identify successes actually done by the community and not successes brought in by outsiders. In a culture that values politeness, a frequent tendency is to ascribe a community success to a leader or a donor (often with the hope of getting something). And equally frequently, if a donor has paid for a building or something else now in the community, that object that came in from outside can be incorrectly seen as a community success (unless it was community initiative that brought the outside object in). Revisit the experience of the Palin women: their success was *lobbying* to repair the broken waterlines; the waterlines themselves were a success brought in by the government. Politeness or pragmatics aside, for community energy to grow, the people must take credit: that is what grows their empowerment

The experience of Mahmood Jaghori, in central Afghanistan, illustrates how when people own a success it can grow to scale. In one village, Mahmood identified a woman with an eighth-grade education who wanted to contribute to her community, and using the local mosque as a place to meet, he helped her start a literacy class for women and girls. Men came to a parallel class run for a while by his cousin, but the men dropped out. The women's class continued, and news of it spread to nearby villages. A second group started in another mosque. News spread that it was now possible for women to learn to read and write, and that they could do so in the cultural safety of their mosques. Other communities offered their mosques, buildings that were empty except on Fridays and holy days. Mahmood's cousin Hashim started going from village to village to train and supervise the volunteer women in each site. Twelve mosque-based schools became eighty-four, within a year expanding to more than 200, then 260.

The idea was self-assembling as it went from village to village. While the concept was self-assembling by communities who acted, what kept it relevant to each locale was each community's owning the process with their energies and resources; it did not happen on its own, a team worked with the communities, helping them fit the concept to their situations. Action learning and experimentation creates the adaptation in a complex system. Procedures were being taught to assemble the mosque-based schools, similar to procedures when people lay bricks; the procedures are the same but the product differs. The differences in design that emerge come out of the community and outside.

Such going to scale seldom replicates first trials—adaptation is essential, a standard blueprint will probably not fit all situations. Modifications are needed, and with the mosque-based schools sometimes that meant moving the site to someone's house when a conservative mullah did not want to open the mosque doors, but the community wanted a school. More complicated modifications were needed when the volunteer schoolteacher wanted to use a different set of curricula, as the government now had its expectations. But what brought the women to class was their hunger to learn—responding to that brought more women. Classes soon had women who asked for manuals on mothers' and children's health, financial management, and even family planning. From the district of Jaghori, mosque-based schools spread to neighboring Malistan District, then jumped the mountain ranges to Dai Kundi Province. Within two years there were 438 mosque-based schools. Often classes covered in one year the two years of standard school instruction.

During the same time, in many parts of Afghanistan, other organizations were starting literacy programs, but in these programs after an equivalent two

Figure 6.3. Women meeting for a literacy class in a mosque. *(Photo credit: Daniel Taylor)*

years of work, the best of these, with roughly parallel investments, had only a dozen or so programs going. Why did the mosque-based initiative take off? The reason is partly that it was in the culturally acceptable, community-owned mosques, but even more it was that Mahmood and Hashim were not starting schools. Local groups in each instance were starting their own schools; communities that when they heard the concept then owned the concept and implemented it. Outsiders did not try to control the extension but focused on enabling local ownership. For example, they did not pick target villages and go to these. Rather, they waited; communities came to them, at which time they helped them through the process.

Meanwhile, across Afghanistan a variety of government agencies and nongovernmental organizations were pouring in resources: sending books, training teachers, paying salaries, offering supplies, and very often building the buildings. These programs were spending in some cases millions of dollars. In some instances they got villagers to contribute their labors to the building, but in trying to help, they were taking away ownership, for these outsiders owned the curricula, owned the teachers, owned the buildings—even if they were technically giving these to the communities. Mahmood and Hashim, always emphasizing the local engagement, spent a total of half a million dollars over three years in salaries, transport, and schoolbooks while enabling the creation of 438 schools.

Every momentum has points of vulnerability. To promote building from successes to be a sustained process it is useful to strengthen it with a *vulnerability assessment*. This differs from a "needs assessment," which makes communities feel incapable. For example, in the above program, one vulnerability was to mullahs who felt threatened by the literacy and empowerment of women. Another was to the growth causing too rapid a demand for simple commodities such as textbooks and leaving communities frustrated rather than empowered. A third was ineffective teaching. An additional vulnerability not worried about was whether the Taliban were coming to class; on the contrary, this was desired as a chance to build partnership. Continuing vulnerability assessment connects to the functional analysis, causal analysis, and role reallocation that are part of the Task of Effective Decision Making (or creating a plan) described two tasks later.

TASK: ADAPT SUCCESSES FROM ELSEWHERE

Mahmood's experience transferring success was not his success—although that is what many in the NGO world would claim—the success was adaptive growth, one community learning from another. People adapt ideas in order to adopt them; this simple step is at the core of ownership. When it occurs through formal extension by government or NGOs, the program is typically led by the external group and is standardized. But what happened in this project was enabling community adaptation. This promoted both ownership and a steadily better product. As will be discussed in Chapter 8, the process has two aspects and is termed *action learning and experimentation*.

Today, with the Internet, news, and trade, people constantly extend good ideas, everywhere. Global scanning is underway even in Afghanistan—the process can be termed "Surveillance for Success" if a formal term is wanted—it is the constant taking of ideas and trying them. It is a step in appreciative inquiry (part of asset-based community development) and also the positive-deviance approach, but what SEED-SCALE does is link this step to a larger process. The task of *studying successes elsewhere* formalizes this learning; it is most effective when hands-on and not taught theoretically. To promote it, sometimes what might seem expensive becomes cost-effective. For example, in 2004 forty-five leaders from Mahmood's schools and Abdullah's *Pagal* group made a month-long trip to India. At Jamkhed in Maharashtra State[8] and also the State of Uttaranchal, they saw projects of community governance developed in compliance with the 73rd Amendment to India's Constitution, which mandates participation by women and all caste groups. As a result of the trip, all forty-five leaders became more effective; it was this exposure visit that made General Abdul Rahman understand the process.

TASK: GATHER LOCAL EVIDENCE (SELF-EVALUATION)

An early project of the *Pagal* movement was planting trees, for much of Afghanistan had been deforested. After two and a half decades of war, communities were desperate for wood, so the *Pagals* decided to plant trees. They knew it would take years for the trees to grow; nevertheless, they traveled a day's distance leading a long donkey train to acquire saplings. As people on the route saw the loaded donkeys returning, interest rose. That group of madmen planted 150,000 poplar and willow trees; a few months later the *Pagals* surveyed them. Roughly one-half had been eaten by wandering donkeys.

The survey launched a hot debate, one that this time differed from earlier ones. In the oratory that followed in which the straying donkeys and their errant owners (who were often conflated) were called many colorful names, the *shura* took a decision that would earlier have been unlikely but was supported by the organized body of *Pagal* men: all donkeys in the valley should be confined, and any donkey found loose would be tied up until a fine was paid. Amusing scenes then unfolded of donkeys running across the land, pursued from one direction by a *Pagal* member with a rope so he could tie it up and by the frantic donkey owner from the other direction. Building on this success, the *shura* passed a regulation that *any* animal wandering into fields would result in its owner's being fined. In addition to protecting saplings, getting vagrant animals under control reduced a cause of violence in a violent society.

Another example of evidence's leading to action comes from Dr. Shukria, who led the project in Rostam and Saya Dara Valleys summarized in Chapter 4 that produced the dramatic reduction of child mortality by empowered women. In a five-day workshop, women shared their pregnancy histories with Dr. Shukria. Tabulation of each pregnancy (miscarriages, deaths of infants, children killed in war, and so on) provided not just the baseline numbers already mentioned but more important, narratives in the lives of women of the causes of child mortality. Using their narratives, Dr. Shukria in turn explained to the women how they could prevent most of these deaths (through preventive and home care as did the women of Bameng and those of Palin). A new form of health education had been stumbled upon—instead of teaching health science through all the body systems, this education occurred through explaining the life narratives of the women. Ownership of their family health was given to them through new knowledge that came from their own lives. With this understanding, the women could bring improved health into their homes; they understood health based on their narratives of children who had died, events of violence, and fears they had heard. Chapter 7 details how to conduct such community-based assessments. As with the *Pagals* measuring their tree loss, women's having evidence about their child loss made a foundation for behavior changes. Important in both examples is that the evidence was brought forward either by the people on their own, or, when professional help was needed, in a manner that was in a local (contrasted to scientific) narrative, leading to the same end of local ownership.

TASK: CREATE NEXT-ACTION PLAN (EFFECTIVE DECISIONMAKING)

Even when conditions are difficult, surveys can be conducted—having evidence makes tough decisions easier to make. The decision to fine owners of loose donkeys was possible because of a survey. This fact-based process led to greater participation in the community process. The next year, knowing how to keep saplings from being eaten, more than seventy village *shuras* surrounding the first site planted half a million trees, and the survival rate, which now they carefully tabulated, was 70 percent. Similarly, the pregnancy histories of women, with data of lives, births, and deaths, allowed Dr. Shukria to discover what was causing children and women to die, and this evidence base grew into the larger national program described in Chapter 4.

Good local data helps project work scale up. Such action grows through starting a systematic process fitted to people's objectives, fitted to their resources, and focused on a pragmatic future; that is, building on the Task of Identifying Local Successes, the Task of Adapting Successes from Elsewhere, the Task of

Table 6.2 SAMPLE OF WORKPLAN FRAMEWORK.

Objective	What to do	Where to do	When to start	When to finish	Who inside	Who outside	How to do	Needed training	Needed supplies	Remarks
#1										
#2										
2.a										
2.b										
2.c										
#3										

Gathering Local Evidence (Self-Evaluation), and the Task of Creating Next-Action Plan (Evidence-Based Decision Making.)

Making the connections is not difficult. A logical framework can put this together, one that gathers all the "W's": Who will do what, when, where, and with what. Table 6.2 provides such a planning matrix, a single page that gives the whole action plan. This simple workplan sometimes is usefully painted on the side of a house or put up as a community signboard to inform all in the community what needs to be done and who is supposed to be doing it. As skill levels rise or complex tasks are taken on, further pages of details need to be added to give schedules for each of the W's. Plans should be simple so they can be read by community members in a hurry, the marginally literate, or the politicians who make promises but "forget" to act.

Such a simple plan sets targets and outlines the process to achieve them. With momentum established, it is then helpful for the community to connect these to long-term goals, but the workplan is not the long-term plan. But as skill levels rise and long-term, realistic goals are in place, then better-thought-out goals will be put into place in the above plan. Time and again, people propose objectives for which they do not begin to have the training or resources to accomplish. *A workplan is not a wish list; rather, it outlines what is achievable with the resources that are available.* (In Palin, after their huge initial successes from 1997 to 2001, five of the seven items on the 2003 to 2007 workplans remained unaltered and unachieved throughout these five years.) With iterative growth, plans can grow sophisticated, as indicated above, but the plan should not begin as a complex one. It is not the product of a technical expert, but rather of the local coordinating committee, on which the expert might be a representative. The plans can start in different ways with simple life-changing actions as the women in Bameng did, or with a community census as DehKudaidad did. As people realize the results that are possible, they bring forward the deeper goals. Complex planning involves three functions: causal analysis, functional analysis, and role reallocation, and these can indeed become quite sophisticated.

Causal analysis focuses on the transition from defining priorities to determining next steps. A range of techniques is available: nominal group methods, participatory research and action (PRAs); situational analyses; planning, learning, action (PLAs); positive deviance, and asset mapping. All begin with agreement on priorities, and, with expert facilitation, community members engage to understand causes. Participatory dialogue moves from blaming outside forces to changes people can do themselves.[9] The causal analysis that then follows helps Outside-in and Top-down partners share ownership. A structured process is needed that includes local people, utilizes data, and focuses on behavior change, otherwise dialogue will be random and will not consistently lead to plans that move the community forward.[10]

Functional analysis helps communities identify better ways to get a job done. It looks at essential functions to achieve the agreed-to objectives, then tests alternatives. The iterative criterion that is discussed in the next chapter says: Next time do it better, don't just do it the same way again. Improving an aspect with each iterative cycle stops the common practice of letting past practices continue when still only partly working. Catch issues before they are broken; it is not necessary that they be totally fixed in any cycle, just improved.

If babies are dying, for example, a common response has been to improve the clinic or seek a better doctor. Such actions would certainly be improving the situation, but a functional analysis casts the search net wider—for example, finding out whether deaths can be prevented by care outside the clinic in the community. Functional analysis does not just try to fix the immediate problem, but steps back to see if functions can be more effective with less waste. It starts with focusing on the goal, then looks at all options to get to that goal.[11] Getting people to see functions in a new way is hard; it may be especially hard for professionals who realize that the changes will cause them to lose recognition or income.

Role reallocation identifies new ways to fulfill a function by focusing on who can best and most reliably do the job. It avoids traumatic change by promoting incremental identification of actions, then assigns to each partner more effective roles.[12] With evidence gathered, options identified, community priorities agreed to, causal and functional analyses completed, and role reallocation done, it is possible for communities to take on sophisticated objectives.

Monitoring the workplan is as crucial as bookkeeping is in financial management. Workplans monitor community energy the way a budget assigns money or an audit assesses whether a budget was followed. It is a good practice for communities to keep past workplans for evidence of progress—they become a community's self-portrait of their progress, with each plan like a dot on a graph, and collectively they chart the curve of change the community has experienced. Because they show results achieved, these can be used as a base of advocacy to government and agencies to bring outside resources.

TASK: PARTNERS EACH IMPLEMENT ACTIONS

Mobilizing action around the workplan does two things: it accomplishes priorities that were identified, but more important, implementation reshapes the community around this forward-looking, *always adapting* workplan,. This is why the committee is termed a "coordinating committee," for it is not a "controlling committee." The distinction is central; coordination engages people rather than directing them. Indeed, control is impossible in any sustainable manner in a complex system—various parties, both external and internal, will inevitably attempt to control the process, but the goal must always be to create balance. To nurture the growth of empowerment, the objective that is more important than any listed target is growing local ownership. This increases when members together learn how to complete their duties.

As many people as possible should be involved. To start, a few achievable tasks should be attempted. Emphasis must be on getting every cycle completed so that for the next cycle of tasks, understanding and skill levels are greater; the partnership strengthens. As energy increases, attention also needs to paid to shifting the roles of professionals. They tend to seek to keep themselves in leadership roles for a process that should be devolving them of leadership and turning them to teaching and coaching. They tend to be looking from external perspectives (and biases) while the vectors of determinative pressure in complex systems are mostly internal. When the roles of professionals can be altered toward internal control with professionals as partners (not excluded), then momentum becomes more rapid and comprehensive. In our efforts over the years, the most frequent obstacle to community work (more significant than any lack of money) has been some professional group who uses their power position to take control from that of partnership. Coordinating committees must be able to lead. Differences in social stratification, education, wealth, and opportunities for mobility will of course vary, but within the context of the committee itself, outsiders and officials must not outrank community members.

Politicians talk about partnership during election cycles, then between elections, this group seldom supports actions. Similarly, donors and NGOs talk—indeed they now require themselves to engage in the talk of community participation—but what they mean is community as the *setting* for work, or as the *free labor* for their priorities, or a *target group* to which to deliver their services.[13] What the SEED-SCALE partnership action task seeks is a fourth role, to have the *community as the agent of change*. To achieve this, the solution is muscular community committees.

TASK: MIDCOURSE CORRECTIONS TO STRENGTHEN THE FOUR PRINCIPLES

As the momentum of change grows, obstacles will emerge that no plan can prepare for. Midcourse corrections redirect the momentum. *Effectiveness in SEED-SCALE is the degree to which action strengthens the four principles, not the degree to which workplan objectives are met.* Midcourse corrections are times for learning as much as redirecting. The mindset of improvement, the recognition that there is always the next time, so this time does not need to be perfect, creates cohesion and creativity; it differs from the mindset of following orders. Robert Chambers uses the phrase of "embracing error" to reflect the needed open attitude. A simple way to frame this is that *effective social change avoids big mistakes; little mistakes are no problem if momentum is going forward and learning is taking place.*

Complex systems can adapt in a manner with a high probability of emergent success only when they have reasonably detected impacting forces. For this to occur, it is essential to have both sensitivity and scope in the detection process—all such detection requires a standard of values against which to measure. Hence, as those values, the primacy of making midcourse corrections against the four principles, not against workplans.

When people know midcourse corrections are part of the process, planning does not need many details. A process-driven mode is simple, guided by the principles: Start; then as momentum builds, make corrections according to those principles. The workplan is organic, not a fixed blueprint. Changes to the plan, though, must be recorded and paid attention to for learning to occur; in that way a chart of direction is created that is both evidence of the past and points the way forward.

THE TASKS OF COMMUNITY CHANGE AS A CYCLE

The process of moving gives stability in social change, like a bicycle gains stability as it gathers momentum, wobbly when first ridden, falling over a couple

Figure 6.4. Cycle of seven tasks.

times perhaps, but when the locus of control is with those riding it, then it is easily picked up, handlebars straightened, and the way forward continued. Critical to note here is that the point of control is within the community. When control is distant, a message needs to be sent outside, the corrective directions waited for; but by the time they come back, probably the situation has changed. (Bicycles are not ridden by someone running alongside and shouting what to do next —if the rider is truly unskilled, hold onto the seat, but let the rider learn.) In social change, keep momentum going, and, like riding a bicycle, when momentum is going, skill levels are growing. With steady movement, hope rises, confidence increases, and as speed increases, further stability is gained.

Mahmood's older brother, Ahmad, took the momentum started with women to engage their husbands in the 438 mosques. Under his guidance, with the now-moving momentum, the seven tasks fed community workplans. In one place, rammed-earth brick-making was started, greenhouses in another. Check dams were put across low places to hold water to promote seepage back into the ground that allowed fruit trees to come again to denuded fields. Classes were started to teach canning and fruit preservation. A room was rented in town and a line of sewing machines installed for sewing classes; in the room next-door a parallel training course began in computer skills using discarded computers from the American military. To extend the lessons, a community radio station opened. Noteworthy about each initiative is that five years after external funding ended, each of the above programs was still running (in 2010). While each of these initiatives has its specific value, what is more important is their diversity, and that they created a sense of comprehensive change within the complex system—and for Afghanistan comprehensive change creates the vital feature of stability. Their community was not moving forward in a wobbly manner, but had hope rising, confidence increasing—and those energies prompting further momentum.

The Seven Tasks stated in another way are: *Develop leadership* (reshape a local coordinating committee), *find a starting point and resources* (identify local successes), *obtain a relevant education* (adapt successes from elsewhere), *fit your economic, environmental, and cultural situation* (conduct self-evaluation), *determine direction and partners,* (make effective decisions), *coordinate people, resources and time* (partners each implementing actions), and *keep momentum on track* (make midcourse corrections to strengthen the four principles).

This cycle is effective for two reasons. Focused on local realities, it avoids impractical levels of expectation and flexes as each step is completed, with results improving each cycle. Success comes, not from getting the process "right" at the beginning, but from making things better as they go along. The second reason is that each cycle is defined by functions, not by outcomes. Like the agricultural cycle, this process can be applied anywhere. It becomes a universal process for site-specific solutions. A cycle composed of functions emphasizes the processes that need to be done, not the outcomes; this is why it can evolve local solutions fitted to time, place, and culture.

Return to the DehKudaidad case. Repeating the seven tasks caused a community whose homes appeared dilapidated and people inside to be fearful seemingly to self-assemble. Visibly, as the process went forward the community looked different, not only naming streets, collecting garbage, and installing water and electricity, but also in the sense of community as well as hope. People were talking to and working with each other in new ways. These are actions that take follow-through to grow. They are not ends but a process. And on a larger level, the process shaped a vision, catalyzed under a symbol they created for themselves with outstretched wings. Such momentum draws in outside assistance that otherwise would not come. The DehKudaidad people wanted help from outside—every community wants external help, SEED-SCALE does not deny that. But it is a question of what comes first: local energy or outside resources. When the local energy was created, then the outside resources came.

The experience of DehKudaidad is important: once momentum became established where the people started helping themselves, then external help started to come to them. Donors want to be part of ongoing success, they look for communities taking initiative; these are the conditions that suggest to donors their assistance will be a beneficial contribution. Today, many children of DehKudaidad know how to read, and they go to their local library. People go into Kabul for employment. It is the people who brought about the changes; they know that, and the fact that they know that is very important.

In Bamyan Province where Abdullah started his *Pagal* movement, several hundred women walked to a meeting where a large international contractor was talking of this meeting being their chance for "people's participation." The women were upset because assistance from a variety of donor groups had started projects but not finished them. The women had done a quick survey—the contractor had not come expecting to be confronted with data. (Afghan village women doing a survey, putting the numbers forward?) The data showed wells were built, but had not gone down deep enough to reach water, yet the well casings had nice contract-mandated cement tops. The new schools and health centers had passed the bookkeeping exam of the NGO that had built them with paper receipts, but the women's pictures showed cracks in the buildings' walls and detailed reports reflecting how much of the funds reflected in those receipts had actually reached the community. Other survey data showed high mortality among the children whom other NGOs had received funds to come to help.

Afghan women were putting pressure on one of the most powerful foreign aid contractors. The response from that contractor was "All those projects are of other NGOs, not ours." The new contractor had planned a routine "community participation" meeting, then going forward with the project they had received funding for under the donor's terms. But suddenly their paperwork had a crack running through it. Women who had been presumed illiterate came forward with a written letter of objection to their assumption of the new contract. Empowerment had grown. The contractor had to go back to the donor to renegotiate—and in that instance the contractor never came back.

CHAPTER 7
Staying on Course

The Five Criteria of Evidence-Based Decisionmaking

Any large social process or event will inevitably be far more complex than the schemata we can devise, prospectively or retrospectively, to map it.

James C. Scott[1]

Using precise senses of assessment each living being constantly monitors the change around it to improve its life: sight, sound, smell, taste, touch. Input is instantaneous and precision gradates to fine detail. Constant monitoring is a defining feature of sentient life. At national levels, monitoring again occurs with precision. It may take months, but national collections of evidence abound with thousands of people measuring nearly every imaginable aspect of society, from disease rates, to levels of voter satisfaction, to the gross national product.[2] But monitoring at the community level is often crude, falling between the macro-perspective of the state and the immediate sensory perception of the individual. Yet community-scale dynamics are crucial to our daily lives, we need both instruments to assess them and skill in their application. Does the average community know how its mortality rates compare to regional or national averages?— its rate of job creation?—the health of the local ecosystem? The difficulties of answering such questions are compounded in the less-tangible realm of attitudes, aspirations, equity, and empowerment that are crucial to a community's ability to take ownership of its trajectory into the future.

Modestly accurate monitoring on a timely basis is very valuable; it is better, as Carl Patton succinctly states, to be "roughly right rather than being precisely wrong." Patton's point is that quick and clean strategies can avoid the pitfalls of "the vast majority of today's planning decisions [which are] based on quick, seat-of-the-pants analyses."[3] He summarizes a number of quantitative approaches, as does Shahidur Khandker's handbook from the World Bank.[4]

Somesh Kumar's technique-filled book focuses on the scope of PRA applications as easy-to-do community tools and brings forward the qualitative set of options.[5] Being roughly right helps us avoid big mistakes, and big mistakes are what take the momentum out of communities; whereas small mistakes are relatively easy to adapt to and treat as learning opportunities.[6]

Communities monitor themselves through the stories they tell—from creation myths (both religious and national) to gossip about what happened to so-and-so's cousin last week. Stories should not be overlooked, as they contribute powerfully to a community's sense of itself, to its values, and to the cohesion that makes it a viable, adapting system over time. As philosopher Kwame Anthony Appiah argues, "Evaluating stories together is one of the central human ways of learning to align our responses to the world."[7] The trouble is that such stories, while valuable in establishing a shared vision, are unreliable as evidence of actual events. As evidence, stories become anecdotes ("Did you hear. . . . I saw. . . ."), which, while they may be true enough, are often unrepresentative of larger norms. Indeed, it is often the *abnormality* of an event that makes it an amusing anecdote. The problem is how to take a sample size of one (the anecdote) and scale that up to create a viable evidence base. Sampling and survey methods that have been developed to assess large populations lose precision when scaled down to the community level, and require extensive technical expertise. The need is for methodologies to scale up or speed up that are precise and instantaneous at the individual level. These may be not achieving the rigor demanded of peer-reviewed scientific data, but still they are providing solid, concrete evidence that will ground decisionmaking in the reality of time and place.

The focus of this chapter is how to guide effective action using evidence at the community level. Self-Evaluation, the first two letters in the SEED acronym, ensures that action is appropriate and helps create a shared vision rather than allowing one of the partners to determine the reality of a situation. In Self-Evaluation, progress is charted through adjusting workplans to discover gaps between plans and the unfolding process.

Self-Evaluation monitoring differs from basic research, whose purpose is to test truths or fundamental relationships. For instance, a scientific experiment might set out to test whether the oral rehydration therapy used in Bameng and Palin is an effective cure for diarrhea, with the aim of applying that knowledge elsewhere, while Self-Evaluation would concern itself only the impact oral rehydration is having on children's lives in that particular community.

The methods of scientific research are well established, and thus not discussed in this book, but one facet of them is worthy of note: their reliance on *process*. The scientific method is a series of actions, performed in the prescribed order. Furthermore, this sequence of actions must be staged before an audience—once a literal audience of credible witnesses observing the experiment, and now a virtual one created through peer review—who attest that proper protocols have been followed and the result is as reported.[8] The facts so established, in other words, are not *self*-evident but rather produced through the workings of the process. We raise this point to point out that the workings of this process accord the participants in it a great deal of power to decide what is relevant and true in a given situation. The remarkable discoveries of various scientific disciplines have led to an ever-increasing level of specialized technical knowledge demanded of those who would serve as the participants and witnesses in this process. And it almost goes without saying, yet in fact needs emphasis, that communities are thereby excluded. This means, on one hand, that the results of research can be both rigorously true and largely irrelevant to the immediate needs of the community, and, on the other, that such research methods serve to disempower community members by excluding them from the process of establishing the "reality" of the situation at hand.[9] Self-Evaluation seeks to overcome both of these problems.

Perhaps the greatest strength of the scientific method is its reliance on experimentation. Ideas are not simply propagated and argued for, they must be tested to see how they accord with external reality. Such experiments inevitably give rise to surprises and, most important, more experiments. A similar process of experimentation is built into SEED-SCALE (the "ALE" stands for "Active Learning and Experimentation"). Experimentation enables the iterative growth and refinement of the process by conducting trials for how programs can be improved. An idea is introduced in a community, and then experimented with systematically to adapt it to local effectiveness.[10] Thus, while the Self-Evaluation gathers information to improve a process, Experimentation allows communities to adjust their responses to improve the feedback, which in turn points out where further Experimentation is needed. The next chapter develops this role of Experimentation, while this chapter addresses Self-Evaluation as a way to determine how to keep community-based programs on course. Both Self-Evaluation and Experimentation operationalize Principle Three (use evidence-based decision making).

The case in this chapter comes from engaging people of the Apatani tribe in Arunachal Pradesh to monitor the ecosystem's health in some of the densest remaining subtropical jungles on Earth.[11] The conservation sector illustrates more starkly the challenge of involving people than do actions in sectors such as health or poverty, where people clearly have a direct stake. Involving local people as partners in conservation is unusual. Historically, conservation projects have been planned hundreds of miles from the site, perhaps even on a different continent.[12] People are usually seen as a problem that must be stopped from using the resource, often kept out entirely, even from ancestral lands. In contrast, this project combined local knowledge with infrared motion-sensing camera traps as a means to document wildlife in these remote, difficult jungles. In particular, it sought to capture on film the elusive *Neofelis nebulosa*, the clouded leopard, which had not been photographed in the wild on mainland

Figure 7.1. Conducting house-to-house surveys in Arunachal Pradesh. *(Photo credit: Daniel Taylor)*

Asia but which local hunters claimed lived in their jungles. If the cat could be captured on film, it would attest to both the health and the value of the jungles.

Arunachal has among the most pristine subtropical jungles left on Earth. We were invited in during a period of rampant timber-cutting. Rising population pressure altered ancient patterns of shifting cultivation (pejoratively called "slash and burn"), shortening the cycles during which previously cleared plots were allowed to regrow. A land-use system that had worked for centuries when the shifting occurred on fifteen-to-twenty year cycles was now causing serious soil erosion when reduced to a five-to-seven year cycle. To understand what was happening to the jungle as it related to social shifts and the actions of people seeking to improve their lives, we adopted a strategy that engaged local people in monitoring the health of the jungles.

Involving people in monitoring their actions and environment might be taken as introducing bias. Because those doing the assessment have an interest in the outcome, they are assumed to be likely to skew the results. Moreover, the scientific techniques of sampling, classification systems, use of instrumentation, and the like are skills unfamiliar to them and beyond their skill levels, especially in a context where many locals are illiterate. But these concerns miss the key point. Evolving workable methods to involve people in monitoring is justified on the basis of improving community life, guiding action, and, in the end, producing more accurate and useful evidence. Rather than viewing as a barrier the obvious lack of objectivity involved in people studying themselves, this involvement can be an asset: in studying themselves, people have a vested interest in getting the data right.

At the end of the nineteenth century, John Neville Keynes (father of John Maynard Keynes) distinguished three now widely recognized analytical frameworks: *normative* (analyzing the underlying values), *positive* (what are the facts from the past, what has been proven or shown), and *predictive* (what can be reasonably projected to occur). Accurate monitoring must consider all three. A recent review from Canada's International Development Research Centre took the needed first step in the application to social change or developmental assessment: "Before describing the severity of poverty in a country, one needs a normative framework to define what poverty is—to choose its variables and measures. That is, before analysing poverty positively, one needs to make a value judgment about how poverty should be conceptualized"[13] Similarly, monitoring methods also need to be first conceptualized based on the value of including people.

The monitoring system for the Apatani jungles had to have both broad scope and simple technique. Ecosystems are constantly changing: weather patterns shift, animals are killed, trees are cut. Small deviations can compound beyond control. Hence it is important for local people to have a way to monitor their ecology, especially in a world in which populations are expanding, expectations are rising, and past practices are rapidly disappearing under the pressures of modernity and globalization. Can this be done? As noted, a tenet of science is to create distance between researcher and subject (even the passive voice in which researchers report their experiments serves to syntactically remove them from the experiment). Subjects evaluating themselves make impossible such purported objectivity, and risk uncritical celebrations of local perspectives and traditional ecological knowledge, which may abandon rigor and accountability altogether. Moving to verifiable evidence and data calls for effective methodology. But with methodologies developed, the subjective participant brings site-specific knowledge of local realities and outlier conditions, coupled with greater engagement because the project directly affects his or her life, which enables greater accuracy.[14]

Self-Evaluation starts with minimal technical skill levels and grows in complexity as capacity develops. As skill levels increase with each application, accuracy grows to be as sophisticated as members desire and challenges require. In contrast with other field-based research approaches that also start simply (most widely used being the PRA methods[15]), these other field-based research approaches tend not to be as able to rise in sophistication as capacity increases.

For the jungles of Arunachal, the challenge was how to monitor the complex ecosystem of plants, animals, weather, and soils, coupled with all the uses people were making of the jungle, that included shifting cultivation, gathering medicinal plants, rat hunting, and allowing semi-feral animals to wander about in the jungle. Monitoring had to occur rapidly, accurately, and using local skill levels. To address these needs, SEED-SCALE relies on the concept of *key indicators*—assessing one variable that brings together other variables, rendering a complex situation more legible.[16] This approach of using an indicator that brings together many avoids the more challenging task of gathering evidence on a multitude of variables. It allows more rapid data-collection and simplifies sorting out interrelationships among multiple data sets. Monitoring focuses the direction of change in improvement (or decline) in relation to the community itself rather than against some external reference point.[17] The process assesses change across time instead of focusing on measurement at a single point. Conclusions of this kind of self-assessment tend not to be transferable out of that local context, but, for the purposes of understanding what to do next in the local condition, understanding quickly and accurately the direction of local change is what is useful.[18]

KEY INDICATORS

Key indicators assess relationships, as opposed to methods that seek extensive primary data and then statistically correlate it with other data sets so that the relationships are externally determined. Each key indicator attests to the existence of a certain set of relationships that has been verified as a valid assessment by an expert in the field. The community person who, because an expert has identified the site-accurate variable, then counts key indicators at points of time and notes the change, vastly simplifying the analytical challenges that would be beyond the skill levels of communities following customary survey procedures.

A common application of the key indicator concept in environmental science is the use of *umbrella species*.[19] Every ecosystem has certain species living at the top of the food chain. For that species to be plentiful and healthy, the systems that support the plants and animals must be intact on which the umbrella species depends. A biologist expert in the natural history of Arunachal Pradesh suggested that the presence of the very rare, little-known clouded leopard would indicate ecosystem health for these jungles.[20] Several options were available to determine whether or not clouded leopards were present, but we selected motion-sensing camera traps because actual photographs would provide concrete evidence that would easily "translate" into a variety of contexts.

If it were possible to show that clouded leopards lived in jungle that was near settlements, that would indicate that the whole unpopulated Talle Valley ecosystem was healthy. These top-of-the-food-chain carnivores analyze the habitat twenty-four hours a day using instruments far more refined than any infrared camera. Every day of the year, they scan the sights, sounds, smells (and tastes) of a complex ecology of animals, each of which requires a food chain that include grasses and insects as well as a dense jungle in which to hide from poachers. The success of this one species in surviving indicates the success of the entire ecosystem, however painful its dominance might be for the individual pheasant caught within the leopard's outsized canines (proportionally the longest of any cat since the sabre-tooth tiger). Monitoring of the whole complex system could be achieved by tracking this one indicator—in essence recruiting the leopard itself into the collaborative process of monitoring the jungle's health.

A team of biologists could have carried out such a task, but in that instance the data would have belonged to the outsiders. The use of motion-sensing camera traps provided a means for villagers familiar with the animals, jungles, and setting traps within them to be active participants in the monitoring process. They simply had to be trained in the use of the equipment, and one of us (Jesse Oak), a young American expert in simple electronics, undertook that task. The cameras gathered counts of the animals, then the investigators counted the pictures. Suddenly the finest-tuned means of monitoring the jungle, those employed by the clouded leopard itself, could be incorporated into the process of understanding the ecosystem. Photographs were a particularly good technique, for they allowed the team to determine whether multiple individuals were present, as each animal would have distinct patterns in the cloudlike spots on its coat. (Distinguishing between individuals would have been more difficult if animal scat or pugmarks were used for identification.) Photographing two individuals in one locale on the periphery of the ecosystem, as this project subsequently did, suggested that there was a strong population of these solitary animals in the ecosystem. Moreover, beyond the scientific information captured, the photographs of this rarest of all leopards (and its publication in *National Geographic Magazine*, September 2000) provided a rallying point, strengthening the partnership of conservation and bringing money to the project on a scale that a scientific report alone would never have achieved.

There are a variety of key indicator options. Some species, such as the clouded leopard, are effective indicators because they are at the top of a food chain and depend on a system in balance. Other indicator options, such as certain birds or butterflies, can be used because they depend on niches in the ecosystem, and to use this approach particularly vulnerable niches would be selected for monitoring. To determine the right key indicator, a choice must be made either of one that brings everything together or of indicators that identify niches of vulnerability. An expert who knows both locale and need should make this determination and select the indicators. (Again, the "Self" in Self-Evaluation refers to the three-way partnership as a partnership, rather than any one partner, i.e., the Outside-in or Bottom-up, acting alone.) Integrating the key indicator with associated evidence, using mapping technologies and basic demography, will help dramatize the range of connections, allowing options for increasing sophistication as the process moves forward

Figure 7.2. The presence of the Clouded Leopard indicates a healthy jungle habitat. *(Photo credit: Nani Sha and Jesse Taylor)*

and an increasing range of indicators are being tracked. Additionally, finding the right indicator allows an inclusive, empowerment-growing community mobilization that bridges entrenched differences as occurred with the women of Palin with the maps of their water pipes; or as the people of Kabul did in naming their streets, numbering their houses, and counting residents; or as the village hunters and a seventeen-year-old American boy did with the cameras in the jungle.

Use can start very simply (counting several types of birds or mapping a village by using an image from Google Earth). Then, as the partners learn how to conduct surveys and as community support grows, indicators and layers of monitoring can grow more complex. Another way simplicity enters this type of monitoring is to remember in Self-Evaluation that measurement is against the self—not against some external standard. Thus, in the clouded leopard example, it was not necessary to place the cameras in grid-based coordinates to achieve representational coverage of the study area, as scientific practice would have suggested. For this project, camera sites were selected in consultation with local hunters and based on tribal knowledge—examining pugmarks, sniffing scat, and even smelling the branches of trees—to determine where the leopards were most likely to pass. This raised the probability of getting leopard sightings, yet still achieved a reliable assessment technique. The results speak for themselves: the first photographs of a wild clouded leopard in mainland Asia, captured using only eighteen camera-traps, no high-paid expert staff, in just half a year. Most important, it engaged the community in the project—hunters who might once have been viewed with suspicion as potential poachers came forward to volunteer their expertise.

KEY INDICATORS FOR FIVE CRITERIA

Self-Evaluation in SEED-SCALE uses five perspectives to give a balanced, multidimensional perspective.[21] Very different aspects are being assessed. Whereas measurement seeks an objective standard and assesses objects in relation to the objective standard, *perspective*, as we use the term, assesses objects in relation to one another. What is important about perspective is that it is specific to each observer. The perspective is a variable in the manner of an expanding lens—where detail is high close up and breadth of information is maximized when the focal point is farther away.

The five perspectives used are:

- Equity
- Sustainability
- Interdependence
- Holism
- Iteration.

Conventional metrics for each of these would be very complicated. However, employing key indicators enables each to be captured as a recording captures the sound of a symphony (whereas measurement of that music would break the sound into its component instruments and write down in notation the score of each). Or, to give another example, a meal takes on its character because of the interplay of ingredients in the food, its pairing with the drink, the music in the background and smells in the air—that is the menu that the waiter hands the client (with the embossed cover telling the nature of the ambience and the list of foods inside the nature of the food) is the key indicator of the meal. The outcome in music, recipes, and perfumes (that formulate smells) is the relationships among the parts, not the parts themselves. Because of how those relationships come together, the nature of the whole changes. This is analogous to the balance found in life in a community that comes from its levels of equity, sustainability, interdependence, holistic change, and the iterative assessments among all of these.

Descriptions deriving from these five criteria may not publishable in academic journals, but they are accurate, and (more importantly) relevant to the

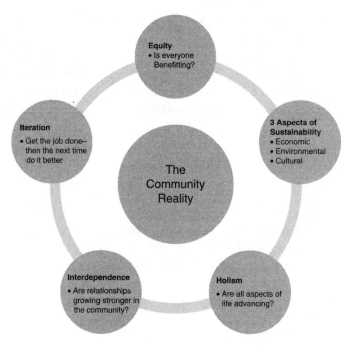

Figure 7.3. Five criteria to assess community reality.

community's scenario. They can be published in local newspapers and cited among partners. Thus, they can inform community-level dialogue and decisionmaking. With tangible indicators, the members of a community often find themselves in hot debates. Citizens and leaders (using indicators more understandable to them than scientific data) engage in arguments like scientists debating each other's methods. As with science, once the evidence gathering starts, participants push to be more precise as each side grasps that having evidence makes it more likely to prevail in an argument. Factions that otherwise would shout opinions at each other come into dialogue using facts. This does not mean that the factions will disappear, rather that the evidence helps to ground a shared vision in tangible, locally specific reality.

The following amplifies the five SEED-SCALE perspectives. As communities grow in sophistication for how to engage the complex world, they will add further perspectives.

Equity assesses the extent to which a community opens access and opportunity to all its members. This criterion is difficult, because partners often have a hard time being honest. (Communities frequently have developed complex ways of not seeing the inequities in their midst, or justifying it to themselves when such willed blindness fails.) The issue of concern is not so much whether there is equity or inequity, but the direction of change. When equity is perceived to be narrowing, members come together with extraordinary energy.

Given this potential to drive empowerment, equity needs to be assessed against local norms, not international norms. An example is the issue of gender equity. In some communities, equity would expect men and women to be treated equally. But in Palin, recognizing that the women were highly discriminated against, what was helpful was showing that discrimination was diminishing, rather than pointing out that there was still a long way to go. Then, both sides saw ways to go the next steps. Or, an example for economic equity: Scandinavian or Japanese equity standards in America would immediately be rejected as "socialism."

Equity measures the community coming together—out of that cohesion comes empowerment. Hence it also needs to be assessed vis-à-vis the partnership as a whole: how do the Top-down and Outside-in affect equity in the community? If some boats are not rising with the tide of social change, the tide will tear these from their moorings, making them sink or float away, as shown in the Nepal case. Letting the poor sink is not only a morally bankrupt response; it is also not a community-building one.[22] In Nepal, when perception shifted toward the possibility of participatory democracy, this alone caused the terrorists to shift their tactics in a way that the military's physical onslaught was unable to achieve. But when inequity registers in people's consciousness, it rots societies from within and exposes them to shame from without.[23] On the contrary, when equity awareness is going up, it creates both hope and pride very quickly.

Among the twenty-one countries in a study by Tim Jackson, a correlation shows that high levels of financial inequity (the United States had the worst, Japan, Norway, Finland the best) correlate with high levels of physical illness and social problems (again, the United States had the worst, now Japan, Norway, Sweden the best).[24] Regarding mental health, among the twelve countries compared against equity by Richard Wilkenson, the United States once again had the worst level of inequity and highest incidence of mental health problems, with Italy, Japan, Germany, and Spain having the lowest levels of mental health problems.[25] Such data show that communities value different equities (or at least allow different levels)— for empowerment to rise tracking of culturally relevant measures of equity will expand the community's energies.

Key indicators that assess equity can be glaringly simple, such as comparing the proportion of girls in the first and final years of school. A similar indicator could be comparing the proportion of an ethnic or caste group in a poor neighborhood with the proportion of the same group in a wealthy neighborhood. An indicator often valid in poor communities is child nutrition, which can be assessed in impoverished populations by simply measuring the circumference of the upper arm.[26] Our colleague in Nepal, Rita Thapa, asked villagers how to identify those in a community who are on the margin. "We always know those among us who are poor at any particular moment," they said. "In the evenings, look for smoke coming out the chimneys; the poor will have no fires because they have no food that day to cook."[27] This is a community undertaking; a day-by-day monitoring of equity.

Once equity is assessed, the partnership has to decide how to narrow the gap between those with power, property, or privilege, and those without. Assessment without action will only track a disempowering change, exacerbating it in the process by sapping community energy. A process of "surveillance for equity" makes transparent information available to the whole community in terms of who gets what.[28] Daily surveillance for equity is what the villagers whom Rita Thapa talked to in Nepal were doing. Assistance could then be targeted to those farthest behind, and care could be taken to examine how initiatives might be opened to them, giving attention to embedded prejudices and discriminations that could be addressed.

Sustainability has three aspects: environmental, cultural, and financial. Unless people's lives are sustainable in all three dimensions, the foundation for livelihood in a community is diminishing. All aspects of sustainability are threatened by the rapidly accelerating dynamics of climate change and its consequences. While global discourse on this topic argues for large-scale intervention and major funding[29], and international forums such as the 2009 Copenhagen Conference on Climate Change were stymied without consensus, community level action is possible immediately. Communities can protect their potential for sustainable livelihood. The first step is monitoring.

The natural environment is a community's physical foundation. Water, soil, energy, and genetic diversity bond a community to where it is located the way a building's foundation connects it to its site. Cultural sustainability through shared values and traditions protects people from the unfamiliar, and can be viewed as the walls within which a community lives and the windows and doors through which it perceives and engages with the world. Financial sustainability is like a roof that gives protection from life's travails and allows movement into life's pleasures.

Environmental change is most noticed when resources are gone. In the Arunachal jungles, the people realized they were losing thousands of trees to short-term economic profits, and that crops were not as productive on soils where the shifting cultivation cycle had shortened. Cut trees and less-fertile soil are one type of indicator of declining life; the clouded leopard was more complex, showing status of a whole ecosystem. Cultural loss is often commented on, with years in talk, then it is noticed that a societal treasure is gone. Such voids create aimlessness, and, when severe, become ideas for promoting the rise of fundamentalisms that preach a return to an idealized past. Systematic monitoring allows a culture to watch and adapt to change, protecting the parts that are cherished without clinging to archaic aspects. With financial sustainability, a distinction needs to be made between the sustainability of finances and "sustainable development," which is a well-intended but increasingly meaningless chimera. Modern development necessarily consumes resources;

it cannot morph into a perpetual motion machine. But technology and training can make development more efficient, and action can be taken to replenish and restore resources consumed. However, the goal is one of adaptation, rather than achieving an impossible equilibrium.

As with all aspects of social change, we do not know the endpoint. We do know the process—that of always developing while realizing that the destination is never reached. The challenge with regard to all three aspects of sustainability will be making the process, with each application, more sustainable. Otherwise, by definition, the process is killing itself and those dependent on it.

One key indicator for environmental sustainability is the distance a community transports its energy, building materials, and food supply compared with the distance transported in previous generations. Increasing distance often points to practices that have used up nearby supplies. For financial sustainability, an indicator is whether savings or debt loads are rising. For cultural sustainability, a possible indicator is the balance between tradition and modernity in community festivals (and, indeed, the existence of such festivals at all); the change in music from traditional to global pop; and perhaps most important, the extent to which events, aesthetics, food, and the practices of daily life manifest a sense of local identity. Particularly in the cultural realm, change and innovation are the stuff of life. The question is whether traditions are evolving in keeping with a living cultural scene or being subsumed in the homogeneity of globalized corporate pap. For all three types of sustainability, a community needs to ask as change goes forward, "Are the gains worth the costs?"

Interdependence: Communities connect with other communities, and such lines are vital to both community and planetary survival. The need is to watch whether these connections strengthen or weaken each side. Rising dependence restricts options. Dependent people do not own their futures; they become owned and must do as they are told.[30] In today's world of increasing connections, complete independence is impossible; even political independence, as connections to other political entities remain. The idea of independence is as impossible as the idea of sustainable development. Interdependency is a process of mutual give and take, whereas dependency is one of taking.

Interdependence is not only possible; it is key to development. The *1999 Human Development Report* by the United Nations showed how the shrinking aspects of space (as people move to urban lifestyles), shrinking time (putting pressure on labor), and shrinking borders (with economic globalization) are causing profound dislocation and making it increasingly difficult to govern at previously expected national and market levels.[31] In practical ways, there is little communities can do to change these dynamics, except learn to respond more effectively, and that comes about by strengthening their community in which the relationship lines are going both ways. For that to grow, accurate community monitoring is needed.

As interdependency rises, a community becomes increasingly able to survive a loss, just as a jungle with a diversity of species is more resilient to environmental change. A savvy community can even use offers that might otherwise lead to dependency to foster interdependence. Doing so takes conscious effort, because donors seeking fast results, politicians seeking reelection, and corporations seeking footholds advance attractive agendas that entice communities into dependent relationships. Relationships that have taken years for communities to evolve can quickly crumble.

A key indicator of interdependence is the relationship between imports and exports. Classically, exploitation occurs when exports are of natural resources and imports are of manufactured goods; and this balance can be measured. Furthermore, this can be assessed not only in terms of goods, but also in terms of less-tangible "import/exports," such as ideas, education, and even people, as in the much-lamented "brain-drain" experienced in many countries as their best and brightest leave to pursue wealth and status abroad.

Holism: The present development world is structured in what are often called *developmental silos.* Health works in its sector, education in its, and as these top-to-bottom delivery services are created, each goes about believing its service is the objective, each competing against the other for resources. The model, while good at delivering specialized services, is incomplete— because what gets lost is the horizontal strength that grows from synergy between sectors. In holistic action health makes a populace better workers and their growing labor capacity calls for higher educations and that connects to transportation and communications. Such balanced readjustment is less likely when each silo is effectively functioning unto itself. A holistic approach is designed to generate growth energy across the sectors, so that the most important growth is in the relationships among them.

Comprehensive, cross-sector action is too complex to initiate, but it is straightforward to grow such complexity, with one action inside others, by starting with small actions and focusing on the relationships between them. At present, common practice (following, say, the official policy of both the United Nations and World Bank) is that holistic development grows best outward from poverty alleviation, and from that will come rises in health, security, social openness, and improved governance. Over the years, not only income but many such "leverage points" have been proposed: for example, the idea that good health can improve the labor force, or that education can open a cascade effect to technology and governance. What is true is that all are effective; a variety can start the process, which is best depends on the situation. One is not better than another; the decision on the entry point depends on opportunities in each community. The key lies in then moving from that starting point with the energy that generates to other sectors. Continuing in one sector quickly raises both financial cost and implementation barriers of rising sophistication. Move out of the vertical silo and as quickly as possible into holistic action so synergies start. The sense of a rising overall prosperity draws communities together, as it did in Bameng, DehKudaidad, and Palin; success in one area opened opportunity in another, and human agency grew into these spaces. This momentum caused a self-assembling of resources and also engagement with the existing service silos.

In recent years, talk about holism has increased, but holistic action has been scant as specializations grew in its stead. Health projects focused on AIDS or polio, education on classes for girls, income generation on microcredit, and agriculture on plant genetics. So while talk about holism grew, programs overlooked the whole. For example, HIV/AIDS action caused public health systems to collapse, as personnel took better-paying HIV/AIDS jobs and stopped regular immunizations. If there is one pivotal need in order to move toward holism it is surveillance—assessing successes to build on and accompanying points of vulnerability, and noting points of intersection among initiatives.

A practical way for communities to achieve holistic programs is to act from localized, constantly updated, workplans, described in the previous chapter. The community can compare this year's plan to those from prior years. Are actions crossing into an increasing number of sectors—education, health, agriculture, and cultural heritage? In Palin, teaching mothers to stop the spread of cholera led to repairing the town water supply, which led to kitchen gardens, which led to income from vegetables, bamboo, and medicinal plants; and those actions led to a rise in income for women and men. With the clouded leopard camera-trapping, success in finding the leopard answered the question about ecosystem health, leading to the September 2000 *National Geographic* article that helped launch a nascent ecotourism industry: the Talle Valley now has a trekking route, a local guide service, and small huts where visitors can stay.

Iteration: iterative action, as distinguished from repetitive action, is change that incrementally *improves* as one cycle refines and builds on the one before. The two verbs here are important: "refine" and "build." An iterative process constantly adjusts assessment and action to solutions that more appropriately fit evolving needs. Failures should be viewed not as problems, but as opportunities for refinement. The point was made earlier about little mistakes being learning opportunities wherein each mistake gives those making the next attempt a better understanding of how to get better results. This cycling of iterative steps, each a lesson, decreases the chance of major mistakes. Solutions seldom burst forth fully formed. Rather, solutions mature out of sequential learning, growing out of actions in which people pay attention to what happened and what can be improved. Solutions evolve that address complex needs.

Learning inside the system, shaped by the principles and tasks, is what guides the process, not preconceived long-term plans. For this iterative process to work, the systems need information feedback. Iteration is the fundamental procedure (and the related areas of chaos and complexity theory), in which simple calculations are repeated, with each feeding into the next to reveal complex answers. Such iteration is how both ecological and cultural evolution occur when left to their own devices. SEED-SCALE simply instrumentalizes it. Iteration fosters momentum in a way that making plans and promising deliveries does not. Analysis feeds action, followed by further analysis feeding more action. Each time what is delivered is a step closer to the ideal, with the understanding that while this is happening the quality of life is rising without having established fixed goals, outcomes, or endpoints.

Nonetheless, iteration runs counter to one of the most foundational premises of development: the plan. While the days of high-modernist development schemes and Soviet-style Five-Year Plans may be behind us, development continues to be premised on plans that promise big deliverables. The Millennium Development Goals being the highest-profile contemporary example. That approach would be acceptable if the whole linear delivery system is in place with a resource base and a knowledge base. Few economies and few governments are so robust in the current age, for the world economy stumbles and worldwide governments become internally more combative. Lacking such a stream, iteration is another way that sets in motion a process that will last beyond the targets delivered.

And at the community level, communities have few funds and fewer technically skilled, available people. Within such a reality, the response available is to do the best you can; next time you will be able to do a little better because you learned from the prior attempt. Balance, adjustment, and congruence come closer each time between design and action. Every so often, all pieces come together, paradigm shifts occur, and the massive change is astonishing. But even in those instances, that apparently sudden transformation is an aggregation of small actions that have suddenly hit a tipping point.

Perhaps the best key indicator to track iterative process is the record of the iterations the community has tried: the community workplans. Keep past workplans: they show evidence, and comparisons between them are the best way of monitoring the growth of the process itself. The community can use such a record of performance, not only to guide its continuing action, but also to request resources from outside. With such a record of their growth history it is likelier that they will get outside resources. Furthermore, as with so many elements of the SEED-SCALE process, documenting iteration itself becomes a source of empowerment, as transformations and improvements that may have been difficult to see in individual cycles are thrown into relief when viewed in the aggregate. This then becomes a visible major success, fomenting further action.

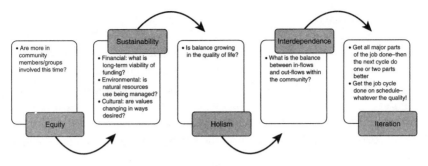

Figure 7.4. The recursive process of using the five criteria.

USING THE CRITERIA AS A MATRIX FOR SELF-EVALUATION

The five SEED-SCALE criteria provide a framework for a community's self-evaluation, allowing local definition and flexibility for expansion. They provide an organizational context for measuring and guiding progress against the past (iteration); where change can be environmentally, economically, and culturally sustainable (the three faces of sustainability); where it reaches all (equity); creates overall quality of life (holism); and provides a durable and resilient society (interdependence).

Picture the cloud forest where the camera traps were set. Plants and small animals are everywhere; each seeking to optimize its life within its niche. What makes the whole jungle prosper is that each beetle and bird is constantly assessing variables and adjusting actions accordingly. Each living organism circles between assessment and adaptive behavior, from the most small-minded worm to the clouded leopard. The assessments take but moments and give immediate answers: where to get more sun, how to avoid being eaten. But each answer, though simple, is of utmost importance; that one step is advancing the whole. Each answer, though just an individual life that is advancing, endures because it has come upon an open niche in the larger system.

As the crises before collective human life rise, an imperative is imposed on each of us to find the way to move our communities forward. Community-level action offers all of us the capacity to act. For this to be optimized, a process is needed that guides those actions so one person's actions contribute in the maximal way possible to the whole, keeping assessment simple and leading to feasible solutions. How does a community perform such ongoing monitoring? It would overwhelm most communities to start the whole five-criteria process at once.

Monitoring capacity grows in iterative stages. The first phase should involve a group interested in reaching out into the community and coordinating others. Create a map of the community so actors and boundaries are known; list the major successes for this community. This creates a basis on which successes can be augmented, as in the initial map of cholera cases in Palin. The second phase might add demographic detail to the map and break out functions that can be strengthened. Do not try to monitor all five criteria right away. To begin, select one or two of the five criteria of particular importance, and seek expert advice on a key indicator. To reiterate, this is one arena where outside expertise is particularly helpful, but if no expert is available, a community itself might well be able to come up with indicators on their own, as in the smoke from cooking fires mentioned above indicating poverty. However, over time expert assistance is required. One thing nearly all researchers love is to be asked about their research, and the greater connectivity of the Internet can open access to distant experts even when a face to face meeting is impossible. For each criterion, all that is needed is one indicator to give a beginning. The third phase might focus on effective decisionmaking, beginning with the components of causal analysis, functional analysis, and role reallocation. By this time, relatively sophisticated decisions are being made using a systematic process. Such a progression might require several years. While several years is longer than many would desire, in this several-year-period will be a progression that produces results, and results that keep improving. Small actions are infinitely preferable to over-extension.

This process is analogous to an animal in the jungle using its five senses, lifting its head, listening, smelling, looking, always repeating a simple and practical assessment. On the basis of that measured feedback, the animal goes on balancing health, food supply, climate, and threats. As information comes in, the animal runs for protection or chooses an afternoon nap. These are not foggy or idle judgments. Life grows from them, and has done so through innumerable iterations over the millennia of evolution. Skill in judgment increases with each application. Residents of the jungle survive based on the dynamics of interaction among the five criteria.

Let us return to the camera trap. The camera itself is sophisticated— precisely cut lenses, high-speed film (now gone digital), computerized software, and an infrared trigger—but this technology was simplified so its application could be managed by local people who do not read or write. A partnership was required—the expert to select an appropriate key indicator, an instructor to teach how to use the technology, and the community to know where to use the tool. From this came understanding of a complex adapting ecosystem, one that involved a host of species themselves interacting and being acted on by macro forces. Monitoring of extraordinary complexity was made possible and delivered solid scientific data.

One vital feature for such effective monitoring is proximity: to come all the way to the community level. Almost every potential for error is reduced when analysis moves closer to action. The shorter the distance between the group that decides and the group that does, the higher the likelihood that action will

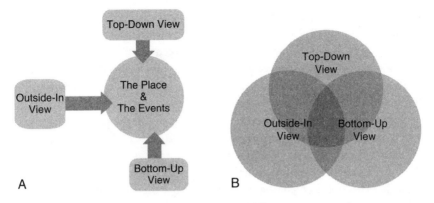

Figure 7.5. A. Whose view of community is true? B. Whose view is true—later.

be taken and be on target. Centralized planning, while sometimes very sophisticated, fails most often because of the spatial and temporal distance between information, decision, and action. Robert Chambers describes this close-to-community advantage as "appropriate imprecision." Imprecision becomes appropriate because the lag between assessment and action is short. In addition, self-evaluation, using simple metrics, achieves accuracy because the evaluator knows his or her situation, a great deal of knowledge is being brought to the situation that make simple tools more precise.

The mobilizing factor in the above process is empowerment. As half a century of demand on donors' financial resources increasingly demonstrated, providing money, even billions of dollars of it, was not enough. The World Bank commissioned a comprehensive review of empowerment, for even this explicitly financial body recognized its importance. Conclusions showed that measurement in conventional linear frameworks becomes complex (in our judgment to the point of being virtually unusable).[32] A parallel bank team approached the process using case-studies in five specific countries and developed a diverse set of indicators.[33] However, none of these is universally applicable. Empowerment, the collective of human energy that is so important to social change, remains at the end of their analysis community and time-specific. It remains "a you know it when you see it" process.

Rather than developing ever more sophisticated measurement techniques and complex rubrics of comparison, it is more helpful to recall that, as the epigraph of this chapter suggests, social phenomena will always be more complex than those techniques can account for. Communities exist in a world of signification; they react, respond, and adapt through stories, sensory experiences, and numerous other, immediately rendered quick judgments about the world as it comes upon them. Monitoring techniques have been evolved over centuries, *and they can continue to evolve.* They will most effectively do so by responding to concrete details and evidence, like a hunter examining pug-marks in the mud. To move prudently down the trail of life, way is found not by a map but by examining the most recent, immediately proximate, signs along the way. The trail of life is not a line known ahead, or well-marked like a road. Each community's lifeline is evolved as it goes through adjusting to the constantly changing socio-econo-biosphere.

Self-Evaluation in SEED instrumentalizes this basic insight by integrating four strands of research—participatory, operations, multidisciplinary, and information technologies—within the field of formative or action research. Equity, sustainability, holism, interdependence, and iteration, collectively look at the five challenges of whether the social-change process is bringing the society together. They allow momentum to be ongoing, engage all the community's needs, create a mutually supportive web of relationships, and assure that whatever happens today, tomorrow will be a step better. The process opens options for all members to participate. They can observe operations as they are occurring and make adjustments. This assess, act, reassess, new action, new assessment is so simple that what would have required complex statistics in standard research practices can now often be done with the click of a computer mouse—counting the species of birds in a community, or seeing who has smoke coming out of their chimney.

CHAPTER 8

The Process of Going to Scale

Interaction Among Three Dynamics

The Tibet Autonomous Region has achieved major conservation success over the last two decades. Starting from a situation of very little nature protection and environmental decline, today in Tibet:

- 40 percent of the land area is protected under conservation management.
- Wild animal population numbers are increasing for endangered species, including the snow leopard, Tibetan antelope, red ghoral, and argali sheep.
- Deforestation rates have decreased by over 80 percent, and large-scale tree plantations are being started in fragile river drainages.
- The use of environmentally friendly solar, geothermal, and hydroelectric-generated energy is expanding across Tibet.
- A new conservation-management approach is being developed in which local people work in cooperation with government and scientists to create an effective conservation partnership.

    Robert L. Fleming, Jr., et al.[1]

In 1992, Jim Grant, Executive Director of UNICEF, commissioned the task forces that led to the initial formulation of the SEED-SCALE theory of social change with one primary goal: taking community-based development initiatives to scale. All manner of successful initiatives were failing in this crucial regard of scale, and it is to the crucial question of *why* projects could not then, and they now can, scale up that we now turn.

The examples given previously from Arunachal Pradesh and Afghanistan do show "scaling up," whether in the large urban settlement in DehKudaidad, or the valley systems of Bameng and Palin. That level of scaling up is an accomplishment, but even larger impact is needed to address the challenges before an unstable world. This chapter describes processes for achieving region-wide scale. Few arenas display the need to rapidly go to scale like nature conservation, a realm in which depressing statistics are far more common than the positive, and dramatic success is revealed in the epigraph to this chapter.

The original UNICEF task force conclusion was that to grow scale-level impact required participation with communities, not control. Or, in the words of the monograph: "Experience shows that sustainable human development is achieved within a culture of partnerships. . . . Community members often need guidance from public and private officials who control resources and regulations. Sustainable human development is pro-poor, pro-nature, pro-democracy, pro-women, and pro-children."[2] People's participation in this brings in their wisdom, energies, and resources thus lowering the barriers of procedure, personnel, and resources. Up to that point, going to scale according to UNICEF strategies (like the Millennium Development Goals discussed in Chapter 1 and almost all efforts of the last generation) meant coverage of larger population numbers. To achieve larger numbers required services and staff, and that required money. An article on scaling up in *The Lancet* is an example of this assumption: "The main obstacles to the expansion of care are the dire scarcity of skilled providers and health system infrastructure."[3] Another recent review of scaling up methods concluded that successful scaling up required six factors: "attributes of the tool or service being scaled up conducive to scaling, attributes of the implementers, the chosen delivery strategy, attributes of the 'adopting' community, socio-political context, and research context."[4] The first review concluded that scaling up was driven by human and financial resource capacities; the second that the process is determined by the compatibility between the specific tool/service and the population targeted. Both analyses (and virtually all analyses over the last half-century) make it clear that scaling is *of an outside determined intervention done to communities* rather than *done by communities of their priorities and hence the scaling occurs because of externalites.*

Thus, conventional scaling approaches do not see growth capacity or the core growth engine as inherent in a community, and so seek to drive the process by their methods and resources. In that difference of *done to* versus *done by* lies the difference between traditional thought and SEED-SCALE which achieves scaling up through mobilizing populations via the revolution of rising aspirations. This occurs in several stages:

- First, scaling up occurs by communities' owning the process and engaging it by synergizing the resources they already possess and to which they already have access.
- Then, as scaling up starts to grow, the communities involved adapt the process to improve its effectiveness, thereby drawing in more participants.

- Next, communities seek out help to address the aspects that they cannot do alone, learning how to use outside services and resources and build networks with other communities, experts, and authorities.
- Finally, the increasing numbers and rising quality of life fundamentally alter community life, internally restructuring dynamics to be more enabling of growth and ongoing adaptation.
- At work in all these steps is the accelerating feedback loop of people's aspirations for a better life driving their actions, then the realization of the possibility of a better life drawing in more people, and the larger body of experimentation causing more innovation and expansion: the revolution of rising aspirations.

In an earlier volume, we outlined four scaling-up approaches: *Blueprint*, where an outside design is introduced that people adopt and may adapt; *explosion*, with a standardized design pressed upon people; *additive*, which evolves solutions community-by-community; and *biological*, wherein designs in one place spawn evolved designs in other places.[5] Each approach has merit, and which among them to use depends on the scaling-up objective desired. Applying the helpful clarification factors suggested by Merzel and D'Afflitti (community as setting, target, resource, and agent), in the blueprint approach the community is primarily *the setting* for an outside design; in the explosion approach the community is primarily *the target*; in the additive, it is primarily *the resource*; and in the biological, it is primarily *the agent*.[6]

To start with, it is important to realize that the term *scaling up* has multiple meanings. These do not conflict one with each other, but rather operate simultaneously in different directions. Commonly, scaling up is erroneously viewed as simply linear growth from small to large. The view is erroneous because how is it possible to go from small to large in the socio-econo-biosphere without acknowledging the defining impact of its complexities. The complexities inside the system rule. Thus to usefully clarify the complexity, SEED-SCALE uses the SCALE acronym to distinguish multiple processes, carrying the acronym through multiple "powers." The words that define the acronym change as different aspects of scaling up are engaged. SCALE as applied to the whole process is an acronym for Systems for Communities to Adapt Learning and Expand. When only quantitative growth is being referred to, it is SCALE One (Stimulating Community Awareness, Learning, and Energy). When describing the rising quality of life, it is SCALE Squared (Self-help Centers for Action, Learning, and Experimentation). When portraying the context required for SCALE One and Squared, the acronym is SCALE Cubed (Synthesis of Collaboration, Adaptive Learning, and Extension). In the acronym-loving world of development, an acronym was intentionally developed to encapsulate this complexity. Despite the apparent opacity of these multiple meanings, this notation emphasizes that "going to scale" occurs in multiple dimensions all the time (hence the mathematical language which adds each meaning of SCALE as a new "dimension"), and that actions playing out in one dimension influence the others. Scaling up happens in a complex world and that fundamental reality must be reflected in order to utilize the process.

The first acronym, SCALE, is the umbrella: Systems for Communities to Adapt Learning and Expand. This clarifies that *systems* scale up, not a one-dimensional result from resource inputs. What this umbrella acronym describes is that systems are *adapting* to achieve *expansion among communities*. Scaling up is the adjusting of relationships where the components are *learning* to relate more effectively. Scaling up is making the sum of the parts more effective in their interaction and learning to use these dynamics. As a result, quality of life may rise, or numbers may increase.

As noted, the common meaning of *scale* is growth in numbers (what UNICEF Executive Director Jim Grant initially had in mind), but to view scaling up just as numerical growth is like viewing humanity as a mass of bodies and forgetting that they can interrelate one to another and it is from their interaction that the truly important dynamics evolve. There is a parallel aspect, therefore, qualitative growth, which, when it interacts with increasing numbers, causes scaling-up. Societies when they "develop" do not just expand in numbers or geographical coverage. Fundamental dynamics change: new ideas are born, and life gets better. Qualitative improvement gives birth to more life, and that causes numbers to increase. Increase in the quality of life brings in more numbers. Moreover, for this to happen, such quantitative and qualitative growth occurs within a larger enabling environment of policies, financing, knowledge, and value systems, either in partnership with or in reaction to this environment. Consider how this unfolded with the expansion of nature conservation in the Tibet Autonomous Region of China.

TAKING CONSERVATION TO SCALE IN THE TIBET AUTONOMOUS REGION[7]

The expansion of conservation in Tibet summarized above may be surprising to those unfamiliar with this recent conservation success, a "I can't believe it happened" to people who view the modern-day Tibet as a place where only bad things happen. In a context of undoubted firm authoritarian control, how was it possible that 40 percent of land area could be protected so that deforestation decreased by 80 percent, and endangered species populations began increasing? And if such protections had taken place, surely they must have occurred through a rigorous command-and-control approach and not as suggested through Bottom-up, partnership-based action? How could partnership with the people occur in a context exclusively viewed as a place of oppression? And yet, not only did conservation go to scale with remarkable effect, it did so in partnership with local populations, engaging people to prevent deforestation and poaching, growing from one park to a Tibet-wide strategy.

The idea of large-scale, people-based conservation in Tibet was initiated in 1985, an instance in which impetus came from outsiders, namely Daniel and a remarkable colleague, Chun-Wuei Su Chien. The Communist government in Beijing did not have conservation as a priority, and at the time, the Tibet Autonomous Region was closed to foreign partners; moreover, the Tibetan people had no idea what was being proposed, nor were they at first consulted. Nonetheless, from an outside initiation, a seed was planted and people's active participation began in one nature preserve (then the largest in Asia) and kept growing so that fourteen nature preserves developed across Tibet, a region the size of France, Germany, and Italy combined, expanding to cover 40 percent of Tibet's land area.

This expansion grew with modest external resources, at a cost for its first decade of one million dollars a year, and for its second decade, approximately four million dollars a year, sums that included investments by both national and international sources, though as the third decade begins, funding from the Chinese government has risen substantially, with new government priorities on both Tibet and conservation. One million or even four million dollars a year may sound expensive, but when the scale of protected impact is taken into account (a protected area roughly the size of Germany), it is evident that the scale of achievement for the price paid is a bargain. The bargain is especially evident when one considers that costs usually dramatically increase when operating at high-altitude.

Conservation (or any other developmental initiative) does not grow without resources. Social change requires resources for systems of communities to adapt learning and expand. Money needs to be spent; the choice is whether the scaling up is externally driving the process, hence costing more, or the scaling is from internal growth, hence using significant internal resources. However, as a rule of thumb, the internally driven process costs about one-fifth to one-quarter that of the external.

By mid-2005, more than a hundred million acres of land was preserved across the Tibet Autonomous Region. Outside those protected areas, a massive tree-planting effort was underway across the whole region, as well as an effective Tibet-wide ban initiated by this effort on killing wild animals and the sale of pelts and other animal products. This growth occurred because the external conservation agenda was advanced in conjunction with local priorities. Had a traditional approach been used, grounded in global priorities (protect the gene pool of biodiversity, save rare endangered animals or plants, or rescue a world treasure from destruction), a few preserves would have been created, each much smaller in size, and at much higher levels of external funding. There would be ongoing expectations of continuing external support for

Figure 8.1. The highest place on Earth (Qomolangma/Everest National Nature Preserve—the mountain and its pastures) and the highest priority before humanity—learning to live in balance with natural systems. *(Photo credit: Daniel Taylor)*

the external agendas, and one of the greatest challenges would have been to figure out how to enforce those agendas on the local population.

THE CONSERVATION AND DEVELOPMENT BALANCE

In 1985, the Chinese government's priorities were to strengthen its relations with communities and to improve its image internationally. Providing schools, health clinics, and physical infrastructure of roads and communications, the traditional ways governments engage their people, was difficult to establish. This was a time when China lacked funds and when Tibet was one of the most isolated of regions. The government, especially Hu Jintao, then Party Secretary of Tibet and later China's president, was looking for innovative ways to engage the population. From the other direction, two and a half million people, who lived at the world's highest elevations and frequently in desert conditions, wanted access to the world outside their valleys, energy sources, and health care.[8] A nature-preserve design was put forward that addressed these goals, using ideas presented in this book about breaking down the isolation of knowledge rather than emphasizing physical infrastructure and transportation, and improving health care. Nature conservation of the Mount Everest ecosystem was our "Outside-in" priority. This we candidly presented to both government and people. It went forward because it was coupled to advancing the priorities of each partner; in the government's case, partnership with the people; and in the people's case, with the two priorities of access and health. A three-way-win partnership was advanced.

The Tibet Autonomous Region was in a state of environmental crisis. Mountainsides of forests were being clear-cut to support economic growth in inland China. The timber demand was huge. Hundreds of trucks every day were carrying timber into China.[9] Until 1996, when this project's partnership ban was put in place, wildlife was being wantonly killed, at times ruthlessly with automatic weapons. One self-defeating rationale given by poachers and their government patrons was that they made more money, the rarer these animals became. At the same time, proposals were being advanced to drain lakes and start high-pressure sluice mining for gold—all allegedly to jump-start economic development in this poorest region of China. Furthermore, centuries of feudal and theocratic rule had left the Tibetan people impoverished, illiterate, and in poor health. Tibet was a society in the mid-1980s of centuries-long endurance, not prosperity. Almost all societies exploit their environments, and ancient Tibet was no exception. Environmental exploitation had been underway in Tibet with deforestation and overgrazing for centuries, now exacerbated by the appetites of modernizing China.

In May of 1985, we formally proposed to the governments in Lhasa and Beijing a massive new preserve surrounding Qomolangma (Mount Everest). The 8.4-million-acre area, encompassing four counties, was larger than the island of Taiwan or the country of Denmark. The idea was not to remove people from the area, but to include them through management partnerships with town, county, and regional governments. After two years of discussions— a period during which teams also documented the livelihoods of the 65,000 people who lived inside, mapped the ecological resources through seven heavily forested valley systems and the arid desert behind Everest and her sister mountains, and in addition the work had planned the restoration for four monasteries and three hermitages—the preserve was approved. Surveys revealed that it contained the highest agricultural fields on earth, plants previously unknown in the area, and totally unexpected surprises such as fossils of a three-toed horse.

In 1987, the preserve was designated Qomolangma Nature Preserve (QNP). Actions to improve people's lives started quickly in child health, using approaches already described for Palin and Bameng. More than health, though, was the aforementioned point that the people wanted access to the outside world. These villages had, across the centuries, received essentially no outside assistance, and with the exception of a few traders who led yak caravans into Nepal and India, had had little contact with outsiders. Their desired connectivity was achieved by giving to these long-isolated villages connectivity to county government, regional government in Lhasa, national government in Beijing, and the outside world. Village leaders were taken to Lhasa to see new ideas to bring home. Regional leaders were taken to Beijing, Bangladesh, Canada, and the United States for parallel study trips. Leaders and experts came the other way, and with them began a flow of government services.

To the villagers themselves, access that would reach every village to the outside was achieved by nominating individuals in each village to link the village to outside ideas. Whereas normally government tried to link to its people through services, this program showed it is easier and less expensive to get communities to link to government through establishing a designated position for certain community members to provide such linkages. The program is termed *Pendeba* (Tibetan for "worker who benefits the village") and is described in detail later. With this program a *quid pro quo* was created: You get health care and links to the outside world; the world gets conservation in return. Conservation was not their priority, but a deal was made so they embraced it, and even more importantly conservation was redefined under the rubric of "long-term development" so in time they came to see it as making their lives sustainable.

Conservation is often presented as taking resources away, but here it was presented as improving local livelihoods because it was coupled to services the people wanted *and also* it was shown as to how it would make their developmental momentum last. By 1994 enough evidence had grown that it was clear that this management approach was achieving its objectives, both as a nature preserve and as development. The QNP was elevated to Chinese National Treasure status and became Qomolangma National Nature Preserve (QNNP). Using this conservation approach over the next decade, a dozen more preserves were established across Tibet.

In 1987, when the QNP was authorized at the regional level, uncontrolled harvesting was denuding forests in the seven pristine valleys. Commonly 90 percent of a tree was left on the ground and only heartwood taken out over mountain passes by yak. Mount Everest's slopes were littered with garbage, abandoned equipment, empty oxygen bottles, and even the bodies of dead climbers. Sixty-five thousand people lived in the preserve, at elevations from 7,000 to 17,000 feet in the harsh high desert. Literacy was two percent, and roughly five out of every eight pregnancies did not survive into adulthood. This was among the most difficult of lands to live on in the world, but by 1987, people had started moving into the area, for there was a sense that progress was underway. The feedback loop had begun between growth in quality of life and rising quantitative participation by people.

While preserves were being designated for 40 percent of the land area, regulations were put in place in 1996 that banned the sale of wild animal skins and body parts throughout the entirety of the Tibet Autonomous Region.

Figure 8.2. One of many open-air stalls in the Lhasa market before the ban on selling wild animal pelts and body parts. *(Photo credit: Daniel Taylor)*

However, a provision in this was made to respect the needs of people: they could continue to kill animals, even endangered species, for personal reasons, to eat or to protect their crops, but they could not profit economically from this killing. Demand for skins and body parts of endangered animals had been coming from markets outside Tibet: snow leopard pelts for fur coats, musk deer pods for perfume, the world's softest under-fur from the Tibetan antelope, bear gall bladders. To protect the forests across Tibet, regulations were established on forest management in 1998, controlling tree-cutting on steep slopes and in fragile ecosystems. In almost every respect, conservation action went to scale in Tibet. This represented a major shift.

IMPACT

When the preserve started, it had one bank, but by the time it became the QNNP, there were five, and by 2009, seven. Initially, not one of the 320 villages had a protected water supply, but by 2009, seventy-four villages did. The number of primary schools increased from five to fifty-eight. Human population swelled to 85,000, partly because of in-migration for trade to the border towns with Nepal, but also because dramatic improvement in child survival meant that children were no longer dying as before. (China's one family/one-child national policy does not apply to minority populations.) Family-planning use, essential if land is to be protected, had increased significantly, as people became more confident their children would now survive. From 1988 to 2009, wildlife populations of every species increased, in many cases more than doubling. Surveys by the county QNNP offices show snow leopard population increased fourfold; the majestic argali bighorn sheep began a recovery; musk deer and black bears, two species that were almost extirpated, returned with solid populations. Timber-cutting, initially the most pressing conservation challenge that was destroying the habitat on which all else depended, was reduced by more than 80 percent with the remaining 20 percent of cutting being licensed.

News passed from community to community and built confidence for more action. An example is the garbage left by climbers on Mount Everest. To solve this problem, people were given jobs going high on the mountain to bring down litter. To pay them, climbers were charged a trash-disposal fee when entering the preserve (so much per person and another amount per vehicle). The China and Tibetan Mountaineering Associations and agencies bringing expeditions at first refused to pay the trash-collection fee. A guard gate was installed. One day an expedition showed up, refused to pay, and tried to drive though the gate. However, the population was aware that the QNNP was not getting the fees that would be used to pay them, and an extra group of villagers was poised behind the guardhouse. A modest roughing up of the guide by the villagers was followed by a lecture to the bewildered foreign mountaineers about how the associations were not paying the cleanup fees. The behavior of the imperious mountaineering associations soon changed. Over the next decade, the base station of Mount Everest was transformed from a mess where high-altitude winds blew all kinds of litter around, to a place where in 2010 shopkeepers in four-dozen stalls are neatly aligned selling their wares and keeping the Rongbuk Valley tidy. With the county administrations involved, the cleanup extends to towns that were once were broken-bottle scrap heaps, and includes widespread latrine use.

EXPLANATION OF THE NEW MANAGEMENT MODEL

Until the QNP showed an alternative, community-based model, groups wanting to partner with people in various parts of the world to protect areas typically sought to win cooperation, typically by giving schools, clinics, or direct financial subsidies (or all three), so the people would no longer harm the land. It was a "buy-them-off" approach. The management model that evolved in what was to become the QNNP (as the regional preserve changed to national-treasure status) got them to buy-in by building their capacities in communities to grow all the abovementioned services.

Efforts to build community-based capacity were led by the *Pendeba*, the "person who benefits the village." Pendebas taught people health strategies such as how to give oral rehydration therapy, boiling drinking water to kill germs, and childbirth care, similar to the activities described earlier. They also helped connect villagers to the outside, linking the community to government services, and bringing new innovations like solar cookers, tree-planting initiatives for fuel and animal fodder, and so on. Through the Pendebas, the people learned how to have healthier families and lives, new agricultural techniques, strategies for how to make money from tourists who were coming into their area, and how to connect to governing and support systems. This village-to-outside connection, where the connections being promoted focus on changes inside the village, emphasizes a different kind of connectivity than the usual bringing in of roads and communications, though these are also needed. The goal is not to "reach in" to the people, but to enable them to reach out, which is less expensive, more rapid, and empowers them to take ownership of the action.

One of the most striking features of the QNNP is that it has never had a separate conservation administration or warden force. From the beginning, conservation management has been implemented using the levels of government (township, county, region, nation), and the staff of the four counties. Preserve boundaries were intentionally drawn to be the same as the four county boundaries to take advantage of the extant county personnel with their connections to township and region and the state. This allowed the conservation program to use staff and offices without spending money to set up governing structures. The costs avoided of building conservation administration could then be invested in services for the people. Conservation was presented, not as a priority in conflict with development, but as the basis of long-term social development, to be integrated into all other areas of life and governance.

Another feature of this model was its landscape-level vision. Prior to the QNNP, conservation in the Himalaya focused on pockets of precious biology. While seemingly simple, this protect-the-pocket approach was in fact more complicated, because each pocket had to be linked through corridors to other pockets to achieve adequate scale to protect adequate gene pools. Furthermore, each of these structures had to be supported through separate financing and management. This new build-within-existing-administrative-units model changed how conservation was planned. A zonal mosaic of land-use strategies was set up: eight core areas were demarcated for strict protection, buffer zones allowed use of land as long as natural balances were not disrupted, a third zone was for sustainable agriculture, and towns constituted a fourth zone for intensive human use where disruptive activities were permitted under town-limited environmental management.

As this model moved into implementation during the late 1980s, sitting among village groups on the Tibetan Plateau, we would unroll satellite images of their valleys and talk with them about how to protect the land they knew so well. We explored how an idea would work in a certain valley and why it would not in the adjoining one. Behind us as we talked would unfold the splendid sunsets that occur particularly vividly at the world's highest altitudes on crystalline snowy summits. Sights of majestic wild rams on skyline ridges, or of tracks in the snow of their leopard predators, or the thrill of Tibetan wild asses running alongside our vehicles blended with the usual park planning work of cataloguing rare animal and plant species. Science, government priorities, funding, and people opening to the outside world, all adapted to the others' priorities. Working across a landscape level gave room for flexibility and compromises between conservation and human priorities.

This overall picture of balance and adaptation should not obscure the fact that effective conservation involves difficult, and delicate, choices and negotiations. Some ecosystems are particularly vulnerable and need special protection. In these instances where the land was stressed and needed people off, it was possible to move the people who lived there to other, less fragile or ecologically important areas. Moving people from one valley to another can meet with fiery resistance if they are told (or forced) to go. Experiments as to what would work in the Tibetan context showed that by providing incentives (such as plowing the fields with QNNP tractors for them in the new areas for several years and carving out substantial irrigation ditches, or even building them

Figure 8.3. Blue sheep ram on the skyline in Qomolangma/Everest National Nature Preserve after the conservation initiative established by communities. *(Photo credit: Daniel Taylor)*

free houses) enticed them to move of their own free will. Even if only half the people moved, that improved conditions substantially in the area where preservation was wanted, and then over a decade or so as quality of life improved in the new area, and supplemental services were reduced on a preannounced schedule so as to give an incentive to act now, many of the once-recalcitrant decided follow their neighbors.

THE ROLE OF THE FOUR SEED-SCALE PRINCIPLES

Tibet under the Communist Party is not a place were Bottom-up participation is expected, and full people-based empowerment is indeed not present. But it is worth keeping in mind that the Chinese Communist Party was founded on empowerment—in health action through the barefoot doctors, in education through peasant scholars, and in the 1980s in surging economic growth through Deng Xiaoping's liberalizations. (However, the emphasis on centralized planning seen in most communist governments does certainly run counter to the emphasis on complexity that we advocate throughout this book, and most certainly the Communist Party of China has always been a group intent upon control.) What is important to realize is that empowerment is not a concept aligned only with democracy, or even less so, capitalism. Mobilization of people's energies into a shared direction can occur in any political or economic system. Empowerment, as a community growth process, is mobilizing human energies to work *within your given system*. Tibet led in that process, applying it through nature conservation, but as shown in the next chapter, people-based environmental action is also growing across China, with university students leading the way.

Conservation can be managed using wardens to enforce rules (as in American national parks) or behaviors implemented through partnerships with the institutions in society. Communities have, after all, evolved various relationships with nature across the ages, many of them at least reasonably sustainable, or the communities would not have survived. The warden approach requires setting up and paying for whole management structures. The partnership approach engages the range of existing institutions so that the most important input is raising awareness. In Tibet, growing awareness was achieved by building on success, not lectures about all the things people must stop doing. The objective was for officials and communities to come to the idea, rather than to take concepts and practices to them through instruction. In such a context, it was crucial to publicize successes, even when just one village had achieved the success. People were congratulated; officials recognized. Opposition was brought on board. People get a sense of worth and power in such moments. In 1998, the United Nations named the QNNP as one of fifty outstanding examples of sustainable development, and a decade later, though the rest of the world has forgotten this moment, around the preserve that recognition still is spoken of with pride.[10]

Another approach used from the first was taking leaders to see successes in other countries. Not only did these people learn transferable ideas on these trips, but the affirmation they received visiting these sites for protecting the global treasure of Mount Everest also energized their work. Educational travel from Tibet to see microcredit schemes in Bangladesh or Glacier National Park in the United States may seem expensive, but when participants are carefully selected and real education is done with classes and discussions rather than simple observation tours, such travel is actually highly cost-effective. When the leaders returned, there was then in-place the connecting link for transferring learning to the village level through the Pendeba worker in every village. While various international study tours were organized, and some individuals earned international master's degrees, travel does not need to be international or undertaken as formal study. For community members, travel to places like Lhasa, regional cities, or other villages serves a similar purpose. It gets them away from daily distractions and into a structured learning context. In 2009, a Pendeba Society was created in the QNNP to bring these community-supported leaders into a forum for both recognition and the sharing of ideas and techniques. (This was only the second nongovernmental organization ever permitted in rural Tibet.) Though recent, this formalized structure appears to be a watershed event because it provides a continuing mechanism for mobilization in organized Bottom-up action in addition to ongoing learning and experimentation.

The principle of evidence-based decisionmaking has proven vital to this process. The late 1980s were early years for Geographic Informational Systems (GIS), a useful tool in synthesizing information and presenting tangible evidence. Using this technology opened community participation and multisectoral analysis in ways that before GIS would have been impossible. Combining GIS technology with satellite mapping allowed large, complex issues to be presented on maps so that villagers and politicians could comprehend how people-use connected to wilderness. For outsiders, mapping Mount Everest is exciting; so is finding ancient fossil beds and planning the reconstruction of destroyed monasteries. What interested the people, though, was to have the outside innovations such as satellite pictures that they could use, running their fingers over ancient trade routes whose climbs and descents they knew well, or to get aggregated reports from scientific surveys of crop yields that neighboring valleys were getting.

Behavior change that causes forests and snow leopard populations to return is an aggregation of what one person does with actions of others. The complex system is adapting, and the relationships in it are being refocused. The QNNP's successes came because new behaviors made sense to whole populations. While building on success and accentuating the positive was a fundamental principle, success does not always come from incentives. Regulations must also be used. This is where most parks would rely on the warden force, which takes years to train and millions of dollars to finance. The other approach, of working through partnerships and community pride, also takes years, but it costs much less. What was surprising in the QNNP was how quickly the partnership approach moved. Certainly one reason was the Communist Party control that is embedded in every township and institution. But a reason with larger relevance was the manner in which conservation discussions connected to life-improvement rather than placing limitations on it. One day in a meeting a villager said, "As the technology of pictures allowed us to see our valleys from the sky, so also we can use our minds to cover large visions. Starting today, let us consider all plans for their hundred-year consequences, asking: What is the consequence of ideas we suggest today one hundred years from now?"[11]

This community-based model grew, driving the growth from a local human-energy base from 1994 to 2009. Then, in 2009, China gave a housing subsidy to 200,000 families in Tibet (roughly $1,500 per household—enough to build nice houses), as part of a stimulus package in response to the global economic crisis. (And, perhaps, also to win the hearts of the Tibetan people following a year of unrest sparked by Tibet-related protests internationally relating to the 2008 Beijing Olympics.) By 2009, China had become a wealthy nation, so in addition to the direct subsidies in Tibet, also underway were massive construction of superhighways, a railroad, telephone communications, primary schools, clinics, and three new airports. Whether this new money-driven approach undermines the human-energy base and creates passive recipient behaviors in Tibet, or whether this massive stimulus accelerates Bottom-up engagement, is an outcome yet to be determined. But, scaling up momentum initially driven by the people is now changing to a scenario in which action is led by government, and driven by money, technology, and force across this once very isolated region. Had the Bottom-up capacity building not been initiated, then the result would much more likely turn Tibet and Tibetans into a dependency-grounded population such as the U.S. Government has been doing with its Native American population in seeking their welfare.

THE CONCEPT OF GOING TO SCALE: QUANTITATIVE AND QUALITATIVE GROWTH

With SEED-SCALE, when procedures are implemented as a package, going to scale seems to self-assemble. One change (for example, in health) prompts other changes (for example, income generation), and all the while new communities are entering the process, and thus and more people are experiencing changes in both areas. This understanding of going to scale differs from the more common one where a single aspect of change (immunizations, a microcredit program, or girls' education) grows in scope through numerical expansion.

Malcolm Gladwell argues that in going to scale a "tipping point" is reached, and adoption expands exponentially.[12] He points to how an idea is adopted by attitude leaders, then grows with something qualitatively happening that raises the energy level; as a result, the idea starts to feed off itself. People excited about the idea connect to larger networks, and nodes of growth occur with the rate of adoption continuing to expand. Gladwell's description is descriptively helpful, but it does not tell us how to make such transformative change happen.

To drive this feedback loop, many tools are available: advertising, incentives, education, or coercion. Whatever the driver, growth occurs incrementally. One place or one person adopts a behavior, then others. Improvements occur, and that prompts other adaptations. From the outside, massive change is apparent, but inside, it is people changing one by one. In this process a feedback loop nurtures synergistic cross-pollination between quantitative and qualitative expansion. It is a process driven by people's expectations for ever-rising quality of life and their willingness to work to achieve it. Whether termed the "dialectic of desire" by philosophers or the "revolution of rising aspirations" as we use the term, the concept is much the same—one satisfied desire leads to another. Ultimate satisfaction is impossible, but a never-ending quest is underway. See Figure 8.4 below. People have aspirations that: their children will live, or for more money, or for peace and security, or better food. It does not matter what these aspirations might be, what matters is that an aspiration causes people to work, and through applying their energies the aspiration becomes fulfilled. Then people get new aspirations, they work for these; that produces further aspirations. This repeating aspiring, action, re-aspiring cycle drives the human endeavor. It is at the core of human prosperity. Yes, this process also drives up consumption with its consequences for climate change and resource depletion The need is to channel this feedback loop to produce a more just and lasting lifestyle for all. Furthermore, it is only through such a process that action to address resource-depletion can hope to go to global scale quickly enough to address the mounting climate change crisis.

It is important to focus on the dynamic of growth, rather than on targeted initiatives that give medicines for illnesses, advantageous interest rates for business expansion, genetic manipulations for food crops, and so on. The fundamental, relationship-reorganizing force is the application of human energy in a complex socio-econo-biosphere (not application of funds and consumption of goods), doing so widens options as the synergistic process of rising numbers and rising quality cross-stimulates each other to grow.

This model of going to scale is amplified by using SCALE as a series of acronyms. The first meaning, as mentioned previously, applies to the whole process of scaling up: Systems for Communities to Adapt Learning and Expand: *Systems* cause *communities* to change in the dual aspects of *adaptive learning* (qualitative change)

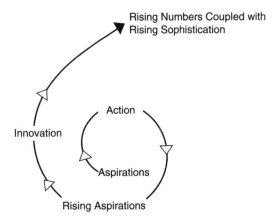

Positive Feedback Loop
Revolution of Rising Aspirations

Figure 8.4. Revolution of Rising Aspirations.

and *expansion* (quantitative growth). Three dynamics within it break apart this process: SCALE One, SCALE Squared, and SCALE Cubed. Each is also an acronym, and, as noted earlier, the acronym is intentionally SCALE with different meanings to accentuate that this is a process with interactive dimensions in a constantly changing manner.

SCALE One is expansion in numbers across a region. SCALE Squared is growth in the quality of life. SCALE Cubed is the support provided by policies, financing, information, and values that enable SCALE One and SCALE Squared to grow. *Going to scale means different things depending on what is being emphasized.* Any given situation looks different depending on whether it is viewed from the perspective of communities, government, and or experts (to name just three). For example, a community sees inconvenience when months are taken to repair a road, while the government sees an improving situation, and the contractor sees juggling jobs to maximize income. There has been a tendency to overlook these multiple facets, and for each group to insist on its view. But to use what each can provide, each perspective needs to be distinguished and named. SCALE does this in functional terms.

SCALE ONE (STIMULATING COMMUNITY AWARENESS, LEARNING, AND ENERGY): CHANGE IN COMMUNITIES OCCURS AS PEOPLE PARTICIPATE

SCALE One is expansion in numbers of people involved.[13] An intervention is introduced in one or more places and more people adopt it. The more enabling are policies, financing, and access to information (SCALE Cubed), the greater

Going to SCALE

Systems for Communities to Adapt Learning & Expand

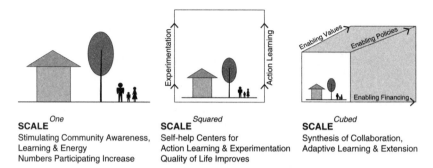

SCALE One
Stimulating Community Awareness,
Learning & Energy
Numbers Participating Increase

SCALE Squared
Self-help Centers for
Action Learning & Experimentation
Quality of Life Improves

SCALE Cubed
Synthesis of Collaboration,
Adaptive Learning & Extension

Figure 8.5. SCALE One, Numbers of people growing. SCALE Squared, the quality of life growing; SCALE Cubed, an enabling environment that grows both people numbers and quality of life.

the probability more people will become involved. Expansion can occur either additively, community to community (1, 2, 3... 12, 13, 14...), or it can explode exponentially (2, 4, 8... 64, 128, 256...). The concept of SCALE One is not confined to an empowerment-based driver. SEED-SCALE emphasizes exponential growth through empowerment, but other methods, from coercion to incentives, can certainly also increase numbers of participants.

In Tibet, the Pendebas mentioned above led extension at the village level, but to do so, they needed to be trained. When we began to train Pendebas in 1994, a class of two dozen had gathered, individuals selected by their villages because of a vague promise that they would learn how to help their village. Several of the Pendebas were still in their teens, and most had never been away from their villages. A few were in their forties, former "barefoot doctors" from the commune days who had been diligently providing medical care for decades in some of the remotest villages of the world. Because there were far fewer literate women then in Tibet, only about a quarter of that first group were women. Some students were so timid that when we spoke to them, they literally crouched behind their desks.

The Pendebas needed to deliver real results when they returned home. As noted earlier, primary health care can produce quick results with small amounts of money, and it is something in which everyone has an interest, thus opening the way to other changes. To anchor the process in local evidence, we asked the former barefoot doctors to tell about the illnesses they cared for, then explored with them alternative ways of caring for these problems. In addition, findings were introduced from the health survey that we had done in rural Tibet two years earlier.[14] Ten days later, the twenty-five students went to Tsakor Township, where that earlier survey had been done.

It had taken two weeks to cover three villages using the international professionals. The Pendeba trainees surveyed the three villages in one day and covered nine villages in three days. Back in the classroom, the groups totaled their data and found the primary illnesses were pneumonia, diarrhea, and malnutrition—the same ones and at the same levels as identified by the international team—and also corresponded to the anecdotal reports that their classmates, the former barefoot doctors, had reported from nearby villages.

The class enthusiastically turned to learning what they could do for these problems. They learned how to determine whether a young child had pneumonia that required antibiotic treatment, but since they lacked watches, practiced measuring breathing rates by making a string pendulum with a rock weighted on its end.[15] For the diarrhea the formula for home-based oral rehydration was adapted to be two matchboxes of roasted barley flour and half a beer-bottle cap of salt into one beer bottle of boiled water. Two years later, during the annual repeat training, these same Pendebas were surveyed to discover what conditions were now in their villages. It was discovered that the number of babies who died from diarrhea averaged two per village rather than the earlier five; and there were fewer (though this was hard to quantify) deaths from pneumonia. Because of political restrictions, systematic and adequate sample size assessments were not attempted. But even this level of evidence was convincing, for cutting death rates by more than one-half is a result that can be seen in a village. When the Pendebas pointed out the changed numbers for their villages, trust in them grew, and their advice on subjects such as conservation was more readily adopted.

In 1998, a different problem arose during the Pendeba training. Officials from the four counties walked into the training class saying there was a problem: we assumed that we had overstepped some political boundary and were about to be invited to leave Tibet. However, it turned out that the problem was the eighty-seven Pendebas who had by then been trained. News of their contributions had traveled village-to-village, and now a hundred villages across the QNNP wanted Pendebas of their own. The officials mandated that the program expand to all 230 villages in the park that summer. An abrupt program revision was put into place with this mandate from the Top-down. Each county was to set up a training program using the best of the trained Pendebas. Two years later, almost all the villages had a Pendeba, but as often occurs with going to scale, expansion in numbers had outstripped quality control.

The spurt in numbers of Pendebas is SCALE One growth. An idea was introduced and spread. Villagers voiced demand, officials took action—it was grassroots mobilization, Tibet-style. SCALE One growth followed. Then, as the training quality went down, that prompted a new debate among villagers. Pendebas were supposed to "benefit the village," and the definition of "benefit" was rapidly rising with new expectations. Health was no longer the top priority. The speed at which aspirations rise is fast—that is why people must view change as a process they do themselves not something outsiders are obligated to give to them. If development is viewed as the product of services given, it will never be able to keep pace with expectations. (The revolution of rising expectations will be underway rather than the empowering revolution of rising aspirations.) In the QNNP by the late 1990s, it was expectations that had taken off. It was time to introduce the SCALE Squared dynamic.

SCALE SQUARED (SELF-HELP CENTERS FOR ACTION LEARNING AND EXPERIMENTATION): QUALITY OF LIFE CHANGES THROUGH OUTSIDE-IN LEARNING AND EXPERIMENTATION

SCALE Squared promotes increase in the quality of life. There are two aspects: the educational role of action learning and the evolutionary role of experimentation.[16] Advancing the quality of their lives is a topic people seem to learn best by doing (who really likes being told what to do?), and the process moves by evidence-based refinement.

In the QNNP, when rising quality of life stalled because of numerical expansion, people's aspirations, which were now rising rapidly, caused them to start taking actions in other ways to improve their lives: planting trees, marketing medicinal plants, promoting the health of sheep and yaks, installing window glass in homes, plastic pipes for water systems and solar cookers. It is unlikely that if the Pendeba program had been strong community aspirations would have naturally turned in these ways so quickly. The switch in focus is important: with the central support capacity of the Pendeba program weak and expectations rising, action moved promptly to these other areas because the people realized that change was their responsibility. Expanded Pendeba training was important here. Pendebas did not know the new subjects. They were under community pressure, and many were also a bit resentful because they wanted more central support and training (which ideally should have been provided). However, since they viewed themselves as workers to benefit the village (and were responsible to the village not to central paychecks), the best of them started making their own connections to agriculture or other services. Workers paid for by government in a particular sector would have said, "That type of work is not my job." But the Pendebas are villagers first. As such they realize that all elements of village life are interconnected, and as the best of the Pendebas started connecting to other sectors, news of what they were doing spread to others.

Self-help Centers for Action Learning and Experimentation are places where people can go, see options, and take home ideas that they are going to try. Being real places, they make ideas visible. A SCALE Squared Center is usually not a building but a cluster of communities. As with SCALE One, SCALE Squared does not need to be driven by empowerment (though the process tends especially to generate empowerment). Many externally funded blue-print models use a SCALE Squared format to adjust the blueprint for local effectiveness (for example, during the high-promotion period of the Green Revolution in the 1960s when demonstration farms were set up that were simply action-learning showcases and local experimentation labs). Ideally, a SCALE Squared Center will have classrooms and organize its experiments, but one can be effective without physical structure or organized curriculum. What is important is that after visits, people go home with ideas, and then adapt these to further fit their locale. This will be much more effective if the SCALE Squared Center status is formalized, with a budget to support people coming to see, and community members trained to teach.

Except in a very informal way, communities cannot be expected to support learning for other communities from local resources. It is best if Top-down or Outside-in partner(s) formalize and finance these centers. For the QNNP, a large SCALE Squared Center (an actual building) was constructed with out-side funding. After it opened, we realized that while the building had tradi-tional Tibetan design with updated modern comforts (and hence was appealing to us outsiders), it was uncomfortable for the villagers. It was too big, and made them feel out of place. So, despite the half million dollars invested, a simpler building was built, and the first facility was converted into offices and a hotel.

There is a major need to identify global SCALE Squared Centers. A well-documented, up-to-date, Internet clearinghouse of high-stature places would be an important reference tool and valuable resource. Around the world, many sites are doing superb action learning to extend methodologies. Fewer are doing rigorous field-based experimentation, where trials (sometimes bril-liant, scientifically controlled studies such as at the Society for Education Action and Research in Community Health in Gadchiroli, India)[17] are under-way advancing practical solutions. The Millennium Development Villages pre-sume to be such places, and certainly many of their specific demonstrations can be used. However, as whole models the millennium villages overlook the function of rigorous experimental monitoring. Plus, they offer solutions that require extensive external financing, meaning that attempts at replication would require similar external (and probably ongoing) support.

Over time, a particular SCALE Squared Center may decline in effectiveness. Centers lead only as long as their members want to, and, as is typical with innovation, the front always moves on. Other communities may become more suited to lead as they develop new innovations. The point is not to establish centers on the model of educational institutions built for that purpose, but rather to call attention to the necessary *function* performed by such sites of experimentation and learning. As with most aspects of the process, there are nested features, raising the possibility of nested elements akin to fractals, where SCALE Squared Centers operate within SCALE Squared Centers. For example, Tibet as a whole could be viewed as a demonstration for the world of synergistic nature conservation and development. In the QNNP, the training center in the town of Shegar serves this function for Tibet-wide extension. And at the micro-level, each village looks to the Pendeba for new ideas to extend to the villages.

SCALE CUBED (SYNTHESIS OF COLLABORATION, ADAPTIVE LEARNING, AND EXTENSION): POLICIES, FINANCING, VALUES; SUPPORTING COMMUNITY ACTION

SCALE Cubed creates the enabling environment in which SCALE One (numerical expansion) and SCALE Squared (change in the quality of life) grow.[18] The more enabling the SCALE Cubed environment, the more synergistic the interaction between SCALE One and SCALE Squared. A colleague, Traci Hickson, offers a simple framework (Table 8.1) to distinguish the foci of SCALE One and Squared that is being grown (though, these being social phenomena, there is considerable overlap among the functions).

SCALE Cubed is the arena in which development professionals usually work. They pass laws; distribute and allocate budgets; implement services in health, education, and infrastructure creation; and influence financing mechanisms, governments, and religious systems. The individuals are employed in big business, organized religion, multinational nonprofits, academia, United Nations agencies, major media, and international think tanks.

An essential observation needs to be made concerning these agencies: their scarcity. While plentiful in the capital cities, it is hard to find them at community level: if seen making "a site visit," they quickly disappear in a cloud of settling dust as their vehicles speed off to the next community. It is hard to be generous about them, given their coziness in locating themselves close to the power and money and not to the people. Such professionals usually served at the community level in their youth for several years, and they remember those years as transformative, but by the time they are driving away in their speeding vehicles, obligations to their funding streams keep their attention (and residence) distant from their target areas. Comparable to the scarcity of

Table 8.1 POLICIES, FINANCING, VALUES (THE SCALE CUBED DYNAMICS) ENABLE GOING TO SCALE

SCALE One Changes:	SCALE Squared Changes:
Quantity	Quality of life
Size	Substance
Extension of an Idea	Local Adaptation
Outward Growth	Internal Transformation

the agencies themselves is that of the resources with which these agencies operate. Money is almost by definition scarce. Moreover, the agencies are competing among themselves for it, so small amounts remain for the communities in whose names and needs the money was raised. But even scarcer, surprisingly, than the agencies and their money is administrative capacity among the local agencies as well as the support capacity of outside-in expert agencies. Robert Chambers observes: "The literature of development is well seasoned with references to public administration as a bottleneck. Delays, inefficiencies, shortages of properly prepared projects, inadequate or inaccurate information, failures to draw down funds allocated for public-sector expenditure."[19] The administrative bottleneck is so tight that very seldom is it enabling, taking real time to work with communities. Almost always the only way that space can be opened is to squirt in modest resources and let people determine locally how to use them.

Betsy Taylor describes this administrative skill–scarcity at the community level as a "grass floor" of fractured civic ability.[20] Grassroots workers often possess technical skills, whether formally or experientially acquired, but generally lack administrative experience and with it the specific knowledge of how to bring forward capacities in the grassroots. In subsequent work, especially building on community mobilization in Arunachal Pradesh, she goes on to elaborate how the absence of formalized professionalized accreditation creates a "grass ceiling" where workers, despite expert ability to effect grassroots change, did not get promoted to positions commensurate with their expertise to lead larger extensions. There is also a "grass floor" which is the level of the truly poor, illiterate, too-sick-to-come-to services, and other outliers to whom services will never penetrate because those less disadvantaged in their community grab the services headed that direction. Grass ceilings and grass floors are real and major barriers around the world, from wealthy countries to poor, creating invisible but real barriers to scaling up. It is the grass floors and the grass ceilings that make the give-assistance model of development unable to ever probably reach the bottom quintile of a population. The only means we believe (after nearly a century of trial ourselves and observation of others) is to build community capacity to reach to the services rather than trying to reach "the last mile" to those most in need.

Robert Chambers argues that, meanwhile, since administrative capacity is so limited, communities should treat all aspects of the Top-down as a scarce resource, and not rely on this as the main channel to create social change, and certainly not as one that will reach Top-down to those most in need. Most Top-down capacities in the current global financial climate are now fully extended, if not being cut back. Limited administrative resource combined with limited funding encumbers capacity Top-down capacity to support scaling up; its optimal use is to provide sparingly for capacity building, husbanding what it offers in policies, financing, knowledge, and values.

The fact of their scarcity, however, does not mean that Top-down resources are not vital. They need to be wisely used, rather than being viewed as determinative. Like rain that comes down on fields in arid areas, one must take advantage of every drop. The work to make fields grow, the only factor that can be controlled, is with the local farmer, but without at least a little bit of rain, that work is for naught. While the Top-down likes to present itself as the "food" for the process, instead of treating it like the meat and potatoes, consider it the butter, salt, and pepper that flavor the calories the farmer provides (which, it should be noted, are inputs unhealthy in large quantities).

For the more effective human energies to go to scale across a population, three functions of SCALE Cubed are needed: collaboration, adaptive learning, and extension:

The function of collaboration. In keeping with the Second Law of Thermodynamics (energy spontaneously flows from being concentrated to being diffuse), the normally scattering energies in a community need structure to prevent them from going in their respective self-serving directions. Factions need to be bridged, not only internally between community interest groups, but also between NGOs and government services. Promoting collaboration is essential for empowerment to grow.

Particularly challenging is persuading officials and change agents to adjust their self-perceptions of professionalism. Recognizing this, we sometimes describe the SCALE Cubed acronym as "Stimulating Change of Attitudes in Leaders and Experts," or if less cynical about their self-serving behaviors, "Strengthening Capacity Among Leaders and Experts." Chambers has advanced a helpful range of ideas about how to promote the attitude change among experts.[21]

Incentives coupled to disincentives are effective. The Gama Valley of QNNP was brought to the world's attention by the first British expedition to visit Mount Everest in 1921: "little did we realize at the time that we were about to find one of the most beautiful valleys in the world."[22] The Gama Valley is certainly spectacular: three of the world's five highest mountains circle the valley, and throughout are lush forests with alpine meadows populated by herds of wild blue sheep, and along ridge crests, the scrape markings of snow leopards. When the preserve was created, this valley was set apart for strict protection, but in 1990 it was found villagers from Karta were sneaking in and taking the timbers out for sale. An incentive was offered. The villagers wanted electricity, and in return they promised not to cut the trees. The bargain stipulated a disincentive: that if cutting started again, electricity to all homes would be cut. Three years later trees were being cut, but after a month of dark nights, the villagers brought the lumberjacks into line.

Incentives when offered should benefit everyone. For scaling up of either quality or quantity they are counterproductive if presented as part of the scarce currency resource pool and create competition. Incentives mobilize community energy only if they foster collaboration not competition. When the electricity was brought in, it went to all the homes so that the whole community became invested. (Doing anything else would simply have provided an incentive for the excluded to go cut trees.) When the entire community is included, the entire community can be called on to help regulate. All too often, incentives are available only to the leaders or to the entrepreneurial, either because resources are limited or as an explicit attempt to stimulate the entrepreneurial spirit. (Or, in post-conflict situations, are denied to members of an opposing group that is wise to include, such as the Taliban in Afghanistan.) Every community has pioneers, and they are incredibly valuable, but they are likely to take innovative action with or without the incentives. To go to scale in a manner that lifts the whole community, support is usually more needed for the followers than for the trailblazers. Pilot projects are pilots, not by their design or even when set up as such, but only when others follow.[23]

Donor prescriptions ("so much for the poor, so much for gender parity") are an option to promote collaboration, but their use requires care. Prescriptions may achieve short-term priorities, but they become counterproductive when they depress community energy by creating senses of discrimination or when they change focus to external priorities. Telling people what to do seldom makes them want to act. When prescriptions are used (as was true in providing electricity to the village in return for protecting the forests), they tend to be most effective when there are no false efforts to camouflage outside priorities. *State deals in clear, contractual forms*, so people know what they have to do, what they get out of the deal, and what the possible consequences of noncompliance will be.

Well-proven tools of collaboration are many: common spaces for gathering, festivals, sports competitions, concerts, and workshops. Events are especially effective when repeated annually and linked to each other, as this helps build community momentum and cohesion. Their visibility causes people to move into communities. Such events can be expanded from entertainment and relaxation into platforms for social action and education where people learn new options. If grassroots leaders are given showcase moments, these can be platforms to lift them up through the grass ceiling and into greater leadership. When projects are showcased, they can help penetrate the grass floors and get to the people (bringing Pendebas to some villages made more villagers demand the same). Politicians and officials enjoy attending such public events for the recognition. This gives a benefit beyond collaboration, since these leaders may then reciprocate for that exposure by announcing an expansion of the Topdown through expanding government services and connecting to the grassroots leaders, either with recognition or by networking.

The function of adaptive learning. Adaptive learning grows from the interaction of the two SEED components (Self-Evaluation and Effective Decision Making, both actions in the Seven Tasks) that combine community needs and resources with agreed-upon and achievable action. Adaptive learning gives communities a way to replicate options that were successful, adapting them for greater effectiveness. Outside-in change agents working in partnership with communities usually lead adaptive learning, but it works better when it occurs with Top-down support of policies and financing.

Fostering collaboration in Tibet was easy since the government could simply tell groups to work together, and the government was strong enough that people so ordered would collaborate. Adaptive learning, however, was more difficult to achieve. Tibet has lower-than-normal education, health, transportation, and economic bases on which to build. Added to this was its isolation, first for centuries under the Dalai Lamas, and then under the Communist regime. In addition there were huge barriers to promote learning because of the mountains, extreme cold, one-third less oxygen than sea level, and a largely desert environment. Mandating village-to-village adaptive learning was impossible. This is where the SCALE Squared Center is important, and where leadership capacity is needed among the Bottom-up, in this case the Pendebas. Indeed, it is hard to imagine the Bottom-up mobilization that occurred in the QNNP without the Pendebas.

Transformation in international perceptions concerning Tibet's environment was noticeable. In the 1980s and early 1990s, the tens of thousands of tourists who came each year to see the highest mountain in the world commented on the garbage, but by 2010 these visitors were commenting on the

Figure 8.6. Pendeba teaching community members how to improve their lives with what they possess, starting with what they have and connecting to available services. *(Photo credit: Daniel Taylor)*

unbelievable modernization, with solar lighting, paved roads, telephone service, and a wide variety of food. Indeed, the modernity seemed to be disturbing to the visitors who appeared to want the Tibetans to be still following the ancient ways. Other aspects that were new, however, such as the blue sheep now seen on the approach to Everest Base Camp and the lush forests along the drive through the Nyalam Gorge, they assumed had always been there, not realizing that a robust environment in Tibet is a sign of modernization. When tourists got sick, they sometimes went to the local Pendeba, believing in some cases that they were being cared for by traditional Tibetan practitioners rather than a person trained in modern methods adapted to the locale.

The function of extension. So far, extension of nature conservation in the Tibet Autonomous Region has been discussed mainly as it occurred in QNNP, but by the late 1980s, conservation extension was growing across this area (the size of France, Germany, and Italy combined), and as noted in the epigraph, 40 percent of the land area is now protected. Populations of wildlife species have increased, including endangered species such as the snow leopard, Tibetan antelope, and wild yak. Deforestation was now controlled all over Tibet, and over three million acres of new trees were planted. Domestic energy bases were shifting from diesel electrical generators and burning brush and yak dung to renewable energy with solar, geothermal, and water power.

To protect a total area of 100 million acres, the concept of protecting nature through county administration was modified as each new preserve was started: NamTso, Mankham, Changtang, Lhalu Wetlands, the Tsangpo Crane Preserve—fourteen protected areas in all. Adaptation in each preserve did not follow a central plan but grew from dynamics within Tibet. Regional government provided the basic structure; local governments adjusted the design. Junior officials appreciated the approach because it gave them greater control, and their superiors followed it because it delegated action down the line. As mentioned earlier, Hu Jintao was one of the first to see the value of this approach as Party Secretary of Tibet in the late 1980s, and he advised in its creation and facilitated it in its first years of implementation.

In northern Tibet, the Changtang National Nature Preserve is 74 million acres, a land of rolling high savanna and mountain tundra ranging in altitude from 15,000 to 20,000 feet, with half the oxygen density found at sea level. In terms of its life-support systems, this land is halfway to outer space. Each step made at that altitude sucks on empty air, and the thin air makes the colors vivid and the scenery sparkle. The great herds of animals are hard to believe: wild yaks, an animal once on the verge of extinction, are in substantial herds now, as well as other animals which a few years ago had populations sharply declining: Tibetan antelopes, blue bears, snow leopards, argali sheep, wolves, gazelles, wild asses. The massive Changtang preserve evolved through a three-way partnership between officials, international assistance, and the people who each day watch the steppe as part of their well being.

In addition, a second mega-landscape-level protection challenge existed in southeastern Tibet. Across an area larger than England and Wales, four fast-flowing rivers off the Tibetan Plateau carve down the most rumpled geography on Earth, with the gargantuan gorges of the upper Yangtze, Mekong, Salween, and Tsangpo/Brahmaputra rivers. With an altitude difference of 25,000 feet from top to bottom, the Tsangpo/Brahmaputra Gorge is four times deeper than the Grand Canyon in the United States. Roads began to penetrate the once off-limits steep slopes of these valleys that contain one-seventh of the timber in China. In the forests is a wealth of unique animal species, including clouded leopards, high-altitude tigers, takins, both red and gray ghorals, serows, snub-nosed monkeys, and red pandas. The area is like a living museum of Asia's mega-biodiversity. Natural systems in these valleys are compacted, bringing together ecological zones caused by differentials of precipitation from less than ten inches per year to over 200, combined with the ecological zones span of the gorges whose valley bottoms are subtropical, and as slopes ascend, biology moves through temperate, alpine, and arctic habitats. A ten-year effort tried to make this region into a unified conservation project, but the great challenges of the area pushed decision makers to another solution.[24] A mosaic of eight smaller preserves was created: Great Canyon of Yarlung Zangbo, Mangkam Cada, Nyingchi Pagq, Riwoqe, Chamoling, Bome Gang, Nyingchi Dongjug, Rdzayul, and a larger forest-management policy connecting these preserved areas.

As conservation action grew across the Tibet Autonomous Region, so did the Pendeba momentum. The QNNP Pendebas have been described, with their focus initially on home health action. In the Changtang National Nature Preserve, Pendebas focused on veterinary skills to protect their sheep and

Figure 8.7. Satellite view showing the boundaries of the fourteen community-based nature preserves that now comprise 40 percent of the land area of the Tibet Autonomous Region. *(Photo Credit: WorldSat International Inc.)*

goats, and in the preserves of the Four Rivers area, they focused on promoting income-generation. As government began to see the merits of this approach to communities and to conservation, it started training similar workers by the thousands, and these are now stationed in every prefecture in Tibet. But there is a crucial difference: whereas each home village supports its Pendeba, these latter workers are on the government payroll and are called "development envoys," not "workers who benefit the village." Job descriptions are similar, but the envoys report to the government; Pendebas report to their respective villages. This transition is emblematic of a larger pattern.

Thus, when effective, (like the Pendebas) community-based projects are prime targets to be co-opted by donors or government. The co-option usually occurs through offers of money, putting volunteers onto salaries, and so on, and is usually motivated by genuine enthusiasm for the projects' successes. Government wants to help. The problem is that the community loses ownership. Donors and governments have trouble seeing that often the absence of their engagement (when it results in taking control from the community) is the greatest help. The objective for true scaling up of quantity and quality is support that moves the locus of control ever closer to that of human energy mobilization.

Across the Tibet Autonomous Region, conservation success occurred because the concept was presented as development. Conservation was presented as a way to improve people's lives—not as taking natural resources away but as building from the work of people's actions and aspirations. This was achieved by shifting the time horizon for development from immediate returns (how budgets usually function) to sustainable returns to the people (where their aspirations are). By connecting with sectors of development such as health and education, there were immediate returns at the level that mattered most to the communities. And, because a little bit of progress is better than big, empty promises, those actions could be small at the outset. To defend conservation from the perception that it is locking off resources that could have benefited the people, it helped greatly to promote conservation at a macro-landscape level. Zoned out in those large territories, certain areas could be indeed locked off as pristine pockets, and around them buffer areas established that allowed careful developmental activities. The economic development zones are just that, places where development is actively promoted, but now under a larger aegis of conservation. As Tibet showed, and as two examples in the next chapter show, it is possible to take environmental action to greater levels by coupling it with social and economic development.

Just like the women of Palin who accelerated out in front and thereby dramatically altered community momentum and direction toward greater gender equity, so, too, conservation in Tibet got out in front of the economic momentum and altered its direction toward sustainability. Complex systems provide such options because the dynamics are based on interactions among relationships.

Figure 8.8. Domestic yaks and their herders engaged in sustainable income-generating activities inside a core zone of the Qomolangma/Everest National Nature Preserve. *(Photo credit: Daniel and Jesse Taylor)*

Thus, action in one arena having effects in another is not simply possible, but inevitable. Finding these actions sometimes happens spontaneously, but with the SCALE Squared process they can be intentionally grown. First one iteration, then another with improvement; another follows, then through several applications the paradigm shifts, and acceleration is under way. Momentum and mass are self-assembling in a new order. The key is the iterative cycles, partnerships with people, government, and change agents—all of these channel the gathering energies. A second key is action at the level of the whole system. When the old idea of setting the pristine area apart and protecting nature in pockets is relinquished, and the new insight is embraced that conservation is part of the complex system of life, then it is possible to expand beyond even the heights of Himalaya.

CHAPTER 9

The Global Imperative of Going to Scale

Examples of Environmental Action in New York City and China

The Chinese Red Army's Long March in 1934 is legendary. Soldiers marched over 10,000 kilometers and stepped into a new chapter of China's history. Today, a 'Green Long March' campaign is underway across China. . . . University students march across the country in summer holidays to document conservation efforts at the grass-roots level . . . the largest youth conservation movement in China. Last year, 2,000 students from 43 universities formed relay teams and traveled by train and foot along ten routes.

China Daily, June 23, 2008

Going to scale: an elusive goal, seemingly miraculous when it occurs. When social change sweeps through a population it can appear unstoppable, even inevitable. But large-scale, transformative change is neither. Nor does it rest on large-scale, transformative action. Instead, going to scale is the result of myriad individual actions feeding off of one another until they reach a "tipping point" where they become fundamentally different from the sum of their parts. In foresight, it can be difficult to see how those disparate actions might fit together.

What causes such growth in numbers and improving quality of life? Transformative leadership? critical mass? learning? gathering knowledge? planning? collective action? refining earlier action? The answer is all of the above, which are the seven SEED-SCALE tasks by other names. When scale-level shifts occur, what has coalesced is a massive readjustment in interaction among the parts, readjusting relationships throughout the system. As Ilya Prigogine observed in his work on non-equilibrium systems, the whole system shifts in relation to itself, the classical letting go and a new interactive framework creating internal realignment.[1] This is what makes the result so different from the sum of the parts. William Easterly describes such moments as "a complicated tangle of political, social, historical, institutional, and technological factors." In this context, "A Searcher hopes to find answers to problems by trial and error experimentation. . . . only insiders have enough knowledge and most solutions must be homegrown."[2] Easterly's argument is not encouraging, particularly in the larger context of a book in which he skewers formal development assistance. For Easterly, what appears to be essential is a particular type of person—the aforementioned "Searcher," who looks for answers at the grassroots, as opposed to "Planners" who think they have all the answers. Paul Hawken sees the answer in a Bottom-up comprised not of individuals but of nongovernmental organizations: "By any conventional definition, this vast collection . . . is dispersed, inchoate, and fiercely independent. . . . One of its distinctive features is that it is tentatively emerging as a global humanitarian movement arising from the bottom up."[3] Hawken estimates at least a million, maybe two million organizations are evolving a scale-level impact in the systems around the world, here, there, piecing together a base of global hope. Even more optimistically, Michael Hardt and Antonio Negri posit a "multitude" against the amorphous sovereignty of global empire, in an attempt to recapture utopian communism for the twenty-first century.[4]

These diverse arguments respond, rightly, to repressive aspects of development planned and financed from the Top-down, as well as its inadequacies in dealing with complexity.[5] However, such juxtapositions of the Top-down and the Bottom-up, while they might present as heroic postures to write about, oversimplify, indeed misrepresent, the dynamics in play in ways that are particularly crippling when one begins to talk about taking initiatives to scale. A pitched social battle is not a forward-moving experience. When such are over, there is no obvious next step. As we argued earlier, energy-growing social change occurs in a three-way nexus of the Top-down, Bottom-up, *and* Outside-in, which unseats the oppositions created by a binary structure, brings in new ideas and innovations, facilitates communication and exchange, *and points the way forward*. Scale-level Bottom-up action is needed, it provides the energy, but it will not come from dynamic individuals taking the lead (there are simply not enough Gandhis around to get the job done), nor will it come from the now struggling Bottom-up organizations alone. When Top-down and Outside-in dynamics are utilized the whole societal context changes. Cultural, demographic, and economic plates adapt in tectonic shifts.

The coming destabilizations of climate, demography, rising fear among people, threatening pandemics, and uncertain economics will be some of the greatest challenges humanity has ever encountered, not only because of their specific impacts and their potential for negative synergisms, but also because addressing these material issues raise fundamental yet-to-be-answered ethical questions. What are the rights of other species? Has a nation that loses territory to rising seas caused by another country's consumption suffered an "act of war"? Are plagues in one country that send out infection valid reasons for other countries to intervene? The coming changes promise more than one kind of terror, and in the face of such, people can be frightened into giving up their number-one resource: collective, proactive engagement. But proactive engagement is the only way these challenges will be solved at the large-scale level. For instance, the looming threat of terrorism cannot be solved by military action; it must engage people. There is no physical enemy to fight; the terrorist's conquest is the mind. The ever-present possibility of a global pandemic requires public action by governments and experts, and, above all, by individuals. The dangers of an unfettered market have been made painfully clear. The fragile worldwide economic systems are the product of scattered over-extension that demands the resources of stable, large organizations to redress. While inspiring, examples of people-based positive scaling-up in remote areas like those presented in the previous chapter from Tibet are frankly distant in more ways than geography from the rest of the world. Examples are also needed that show the engagement at the heart of global modernity rather than its margins.[6]

Let us take the particularly urgent challenge of changing global environmental practice through human energies. The World National Parks Congress in Bali, Indonesia, in 1982 was a watershed moment, the moment when the management model for protected areas began to go beyond the earlier "Yellowstone model" of fencing off the area. The Bali Conference recommended that people be included in preserves. A surge of experiments followed in the 1980s, of which the QNNP was the first example in Asia to show how a partnership with people could be implemented through existing administrative systems. Other demonstrations, like that of the United Kingdom, whose parks similarly incorporate humans into the management scheme, are also advancing a people-based conservation.[7] As the challenge of climate change grows and as natural resources on land, atmosphere, and oceans become more damaged, other examples will evolve. Our future depends on these, both for the protection they give to their own sites and as SCALE Squared sites from which others can learn.

The practice of excluding people from nature is as old as conservation action itself. The premise that people must be excluded to conserve nature occurred from Stuart England to Mogul India, a practice continued from 1872 on, with the national parks in the United States taking form in Yellowstone and Yosemite.[8] It was advocated as the ideal into the 1990s, even after the Bali Conference, but is now virtually discarded. Conservation that engages people—as the QNNP example shows—is more effective and less expensive.[9] With the global Great Recession beginning in 2008–2009 and an evident limiting of funds against the rising expectations of people, the economic rationale makes a lower cost approach pragmatically the only option. Interestingly, the history of conservation amidst one of the densest human settlements on Earth is a powerful and essentially unknown example.

The story of New York City conservation has grown across three and a half centuries. This city, one of the world's great concentrations of people and economic growth, was built partially atop wetlands. Yet today, despite three and a half centuries of commerce, industry, culture, and growing population pressure, the five boroughs also remain a vibrant crossroads of nature and the human-built environment.[10] New York contains nearly 57,000 acres of city, state, and national parks.[11] The city is in the forefront of pioneering urban environmental action by residents.[12] Furthermore, the New York example grows increasingly relevant because we are becoming an urban species. In 2008, the majority of the world population was urban for the first time in history. By the middle of the current century, two-thirds of humanity will live in urban areas. Thus, for humanity's collective future, environmentally engaged living in cities must evolve.[13]

New York's environmental action is not just that of maintaining clean city streets and pleasant park benches. It represents a directive to shape the whole city so as many of its systems as possible are positive in the larger landscape. As Steven Johnson has argued, "If we're going to survive as a planet with more than six billion people without destroying the complex balance of our natural

Figure 9.1. Maxwell Place Cove along the Hudson River in Hoboken, New Jersey. The fact that one-sixth of New York City's land is now in safe, clean parklands has created not only recreational opportunities, but also stronger communities. *(Photo courtesy of the Hoboken Cove Community Boathouse)*[14]

ecosystems, the best way to do it is to crowd as many of those humans as possible into metropolitan spaces and return the rest to Mother Nature."[15] The imperative grows more pressing as human population numbers rise past seven billion to at least nine billion. Cities enable efficiencies of scale, particularly in the all-important arenas of energy use and waste management that will lower the environmental impact of a planet whose new defining feature is people. To achieve the potential of cities, mindsets and directions must change in how cities are managed. Furthermore, what urban celebrants like Johnson often overlook is the need to evolve mechanisms for equitable interaction between the country and the city, lest urban efficiencies be purchased at the expense of sacrifice zones filled with industrial agriculture and strip mines to fuel the appetites of the metropolis.

Cities represent a created environment, a human-constructed world seemingly apart from the natural, where people are brought together in extraordinary proximity, creating a human-centered habitat where people happily live stacked one on top of another up to one hundred floors high. Cities are a new type of natural habitat for humans, one in which the majority of humanity now lives. In it they must create a new type of shared natural world, shared with themselves and shared with the old nature outside. Part of this act of creation involves what Herbert Reid and Betsy Taylor amplify under the term "recovering the commons," showing how, in recovering common space, then values, actions, and collective ownership of the future come together.[16] Parks are one of the oldest of human inventions to achieve this end.

The oldest parks in New York City date to 1686, when what are now known as Battery Park, Bowling Green, and City Hall Park were first set aside by charter from the colonial governor (though they were not formally designated as parks until the 1730s).[17] But after that beginning, the 1811 plan for the city included almost no land for parks, and between 1830 and 1850, when there were still forests and farm fields across most of today's five boroughs, only forty acres of additional land was reserved for parks. Four of the parks established in this period—Bryant Park, Washington Square, Union Square, and Madison Square—were built on former potter's fields and graveyards for the indigent and unknown.

Serious greening of New York City began in 1850 as leaders woke up to the "swarmingness of population" (Walt Whitman's phrase). The city then was a maze of people-packed streets where nature was disappearing.[18] Population had increased from fewer than 100,000 in 1811 to nearly half a million. Mayors and public-minded citizens called for a large park in the center of Manhattan, and by 1856, the land for Central Park had been acquired, 853 acres. It was not set apart to capture the pristine habitat, but re-landscaped and engineered by Frederick Law Olmstead and Calvert Vaux, who altered the curves of the land and introduced exotic plant species, all with the purpose of enriching the lives of the people, not protecting nature.[19]

But an even more farsighted plan involved acquiring land for parks in *antic-ipation* of New York City's growth, land that did not require the significant and artificial design of Central Park. In 1881, a citizen's movement created a Bronx parks system that added nearly 4,000 acres to the New York park system before the Bronx was even part of New York City.[20] Unlike Central Park, the Bronx parks were set apart as parks recognizing the presence of natural fea-tures such as waterfalls, forests, lakes, and marshes. "It was desirable that the tracts should be natural parks, *requiring the least expenditure possible to adapt them for public use* [italics in original], not like the Central, a mere waste ground, the improvement of every acre of which cost thrice the original price of the land."[21] This people-centered recognition is remarkable.

Like the commons of England, the New York parks were places for people to share collective space. Some, notably including the seven designed by Olmstead and Vaux, did not seek to mimic the wild, but rather to create a domesticated "Nature." Others, like the parks acquired in 1888, were left in a more natural state, and to this day, large portions of two of them, Van Cortlandt Park and Pelham Bay Park, are managed as natural areas.

In 1898, modern New York City was formed by consolidating what was then called New York (Manhattan and the western part of the Bronx), with the rest of the Bronx, Brooklyn, Queens, and Staten Island. This added existing parks in these areas to the new city's total park acreage. By 1900, New York was the second-largest city in the world, with three and a half million people, and already a global commercial center. But it had also expanded its parkland from fewer than fifty acres to 7,000, a 140-fold growth. Furthermore, this parkland expansion did not slow with continued economic and population growth. From 1930 to the 1960s, under the heavy hand of Robert Moses (with plenty of controversy over his forceful Top-down leadership) parkland acreage of the five boroughs doubled again, with outdoor places for the people's use, amusement parks such as Coney Island, expansive public beaches, and "park-ways" with green spaces along highway edges.[22] As the city grew, so did the sense that people needed to be connected to nature. (Curitiba, Brazil, offers an example of a greening city in a rising economy using similar human-centric conservation approaches.[23])

Awareness of the need to couple economic growth to environmental pro-tection went beyond the city's geographic boundaries. In the early 1800s, it had become clear the city's prosperity depended on using the Hudson River to reach Midwestern cropland, so New Yorkers promoted the Erie Canal. As the canal grew, continued economic growth in the city made it clear that the canal needed an abundant water source, so the Adirondack plateau, where the state's last remnant of largely uncut timber provided a protected watershed, became designated as a state park in 1885. (The Adirondack State Park was and is the largest protected area in America's lower forty-eight states.) Once protected, the Adirondack State Park began adding other human-benefiting-from-nature

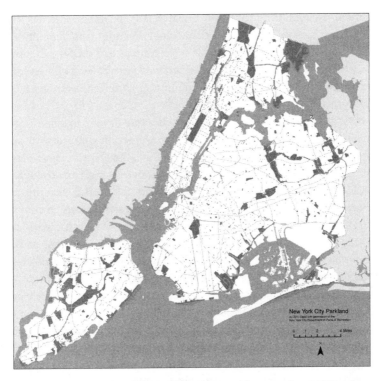

Figure 9.2. The five boroughs of New York City: showing the more than 1,700 parks encompassing nearly 29,000 acres. *(Photo credit: New York City Parks and Recreation Department)*

actions for New York City: health promotion with tuberculosis sanatoriums (tuberculosis was then America's second-most-prevalent malady), soul-rejuvenating wilderness trips, and vacation getaways, and it was twice the site of the winter Olympic Games, in 1932 and 1980.

With the Adirondack State Park, a different way of city planning was evolving, one that not only connected urban needs with nature conservation, but extended these connections beyond the city itself, recognizing that the city exists as a hub within a broader network. Such actions were reinforced by setting aside the Croton Reservoir in the mid-1880s as the drinking-water source for New York City.[24] Nature was being used, but through that use it was also being protected. While preservationist factions argued that the nature in places like the Adirondack Park should be totally locked away, the use-the-wilderness contingent prevailed. People owned half the land, and on this half, use plus protection strictures were set. This private land then connected with "forever wild" state land on the other half. The idea was to find a balance between nature and people so they could support each other. Central in this understanding was protecting as large an area as possible, then dividing that into human use zones, the same approach used by QNNP. As an increasing diversity of uses grows in the park (research labs, businesses, mines, hydro-electric dams, prisons, even controlled timber cutting), the diversity of the wilderness also grows as wild animals once gone return (beaver, moose, and maybe even wolves and cougars).[25] The park with its growing effectiveness in conservation has become a center of economic growth for the struggling economy of upstate New York.

In order to achieve planetary-level protection, we need to extend this model to a global scale. We need landscape-level conservation coupled with people-benefiting action that takes into account the relationships between city and country, coal mine and light switch, exhaust pipe and iceberg. Fortunately SCALE Squared demonstrations are appearing around the world, experiments at significant scales, with action-learning extending their lessons to new areas. New York City and the Adirondacks are examples. But more broadly, so too, are larger transnational projects around the world such as "Yellowstone to Yukon" between the United States and Canada, South Africa's Kgalagadi National Park connecting to Botswana and Kruger National Park linking South Africa, Zimbabwe, and Mozambique. The QNNP is part of an eight-park *de facto* linkage (though yet to be reinforced by formal cross-border cooperation) linking China with Nepal; Sikkim, and Arunachal in India; and Bhutan. These are some of the world's macro-examples that provide core zones and varied human-use zones for pan-regional conservation on three continents: North America, southern Africa, and Asia. They are part of the beginnings for a planetary low-carbon development solution. At the forefront of such action, New York City is an unexpected player.

It may be counterintuitive, but conservation turns out to be more effective the more that people are included. The larger the area being protected, the more important (and inevitable) it is to include people.[26] In New York, conservationists pressed for protectionist regulations to meet a range of threats to nature that had emerged in the Adirondacks (rampant tourism, second-home construction, and mines and manufacturing). Governor Nelson Rockefeller did not acquiesce, instead creating a forum in which people, governments, and commercial interests had to battle out compromises. What resulted was an evolution in understanding how factions could balance their priorities, a system in dynamic tension where all forces must adapt. As a result, today in the Adirondacks there is no Top-down superintendent. The absence of a central executive has proven to be a brilliant management decision because it forces dialogue. Two state agencies, 105 townships, numerous nonprofit groups, and hundreds of businesses must reach compromises, constantly reevaluating priorities.[27] Many conservationists argue relentlessly that a boss is needed.[28] And indeed, absent such authority, negotiations are often rancorous with all interests included, but a balance has resulted over time.[29] The more people are included, the more effective the conservation.[30]

A similar progression occurred in New York City itself. By 1970, the economic growth that had once catapulted the city had slowed, leaving budget woes in its wake. By then, the Top-down approach driven by Robert Moses had protected ten percent of the land area, but with a crumbling city economy the expensive park budget was one place the city cut to save basic governing infrastructure. In a matter of two years, Central Park (which is a police precinct unto itself) had become the second-most-dangerous part of the city. Madison Square Park and Bryant Park became drug-selling havens. The populace demanded more police and better conservation, but there was no money for either. The financial crisis threatened the city with bankruptcy. It was the passionate loyalty of the people that prompted a rebirth of the major parks. Wealthy residents living around Central Park started the process in 1980 by creating the Central Park Conservancy with the mission to restore Central Park. Hundreds of people joined as volunteers. By 2008, 85 percent of Central Park's budget came from such contributions, combined with 33,000 annual hours of volunteer labor.

The people-based model spread through the five boroughs with an array of contracts between people and park officials creating public–private partnerships. Citizens raised money, picked up litter, repaired facilities, and kept their eyes open for crime. Business partnerships expanded. Human energy was the common-to-all feature. Services previously performed by the government were taken over by professional operators as fee-paying concessions. For example, the golf courses, which lost two million dollars in 1978 under city management, turned a nine-million-dollar profit in 2007. With parklands providing income, a new problem arises: who gets the money, the city or the parks? Not surprisingly, the city. The city is getting the money, and the human energy is picking up the slack—and the overall process is working better.

But with the city taking the major income, a conundrum of equity has grown. The flagship parks in wealthy neighborhoods have fared quite well, both from citizen gifts and from special events, but the small neighborhood parks struggle. While many of the parks have a citizens' "Friends Of" committee, they lack wealthy residents and revenue-generating special-event venues. Yet care of the more modest parks goes forward, chafing under their "have not" status. When the city budget shrinks in economic downturns, staff in these parks are cut even more, swimming pools closed, and sports facilities not kept up, but in Manhattan (especially north of 59th Street) and wealthy parts of the city, private contributions step in. In less-flush neighborhoods, park facilities are more vulnerable to decline. The New York model is growing in its ability to engage the criterion of equity; providing another glimpse into why the criterion of equity is of vital importance.

Building community through conservation is a benefit as important as the conservation action itself. From the 1970s onward, arguably no part of the five boroughs was more traumatized than the South Bronx, home to lawlessness, race riots, drug activity, and deteriorating housing. But in 1997, the Bronx River Working Group formed. Under youth leadership, an alliance was

Figure 9.3. Members of the Bronx River Alliance Conservation Crew removing tires and other debris dumped along the Bronx River at what would become the Concrete Plant Park. *(Photo courtesy of the Bronx River Alliance)*

created with the Army Corps of Engineers, which hauled sunken cars, boats, and all manner of junk out of the river and then transformed the length of shoreline into public space and parklands.[31]

In 1984, monitoring across the five boroughs tracked, not just park management, but also environmental status, and by 2007, thousands of assessments were being conducted annually using sixteen criteria. Some are done by the Parks Department. Report cards on parks and beaches are done by New Yorkers for Parks. A Partnership for Parks program has grown to 250 Friends of the Parks groups, each with its specific park. To augment city funding, in 1989 the Department of Parks and Recreation created the City Parks Foundation, an independent nonprofit organization to raise private funds for city parks by obtaining gifts that would never be given to the city itself ($13 million was raised in 2009). People give money, time, and labor for the simple reason that the parks make their lives better.

It goes without saying that the New York City park system is not an application of SEED-SCALE, but in this experience it shows all four principles are at work. That the New York City example is not an intentional application of SEED-SCALE is obvious. However, it is very important to bring forward such examples, for they illustrate the point made earlier that when we have observed scale-level societal change, consistently SEED-SCALE principles are found operating. It was from an examination of past experience, looking at over a hundred global examples, beginning with the UNICEF task forces in the early 1990s and continuing over the years since, that these principles were seen to be at work. SEED-SCALE provides an explanation of what has been occurring among successful communities for a very long time.

In the New York City experience, while various elements have been stronger or more active at various times, a three-way partnership seems to be always engaged between government, private sector, and civil society. Decisions are being made from increasingly strong evidence bases with the argumentation New Yorkers love. A citywide change in behaviors grows as more people go for exercise and relaxation in the parks, take their children, or sit and read with little concern about safety, as most who pass through the parks now, like the residents of the QNNP, act as wardens in varying ways.[32] People-government-nonprofits build on successes as one park experiments, ideas that work are tried by others, although there is a tendency for the better-funded and staffed flagship parks to first drive innovations and the smaller neighborhood parks to then adapt them. Parks are one of the few places where homeless people mingle with wealthy elite, bringing people together like the city's subways do.

Most important, however, is the fact that conservation action jumped out of the parks and onto the streets. It is in this regard where New York is a useful model in terms of planetary impact, because it shows change in people's thinking. Citizens pay for public benches, gather in workforces to plant parks and highway borders with flowers, dig up concrete sidewalks to plant trees, and start youth environment programs.[33] Schoolchildren go out and learn about the city's environment. One hundred thousand trees were planted from 1998 to 2007. Momentum burgeoned to planting 20,000 trees on April 12, 2008, alone, and it continues with a target to plant a million trees.[34] A green rooftops initiative has started, and gardens are literally climbing the walls. The home of Wall Street, the island of Manhattan is perhaps the epitome of a human-made environment, and yet yearly it shows more jungle amidst the concrete.

Momentum for conservation action is everyone's responsibility, and action is being driven from all three directions: Bottom-up community demand, vigorous Outside-in advocacy, and recently with pro-active Top-down policies in an initiative begun in 2007 called PlaNYC (Plan + NYC).[35] In its first three years, PlaNYC created 200 miles of bicycle lanes and doubled the number of commuters who bike to work. PlaNYC has a greenhouse gas reduction target of 30 percent by 2017, and by 2010 had achieved a nine-percent reduction, also causing per capita electrical use to decline. One of the city's many excited leaders of this environmental engagement described how this three-way participatory process works:

> I was at the Bronx community workshop on the waterfront plan. About eighty
> people were there from every corner of the Bronx. The City Planning Commission

had divided our waterfront into four "reaches." The professional planners had identified three to six "opportunity areas" in each reach for development of the watershed in the next ten years. We split into groups according to where we lived (and what we knew) and over about two hours prioritized the opportunity areas, and gave suggestions, critiques, completely insider information—things that professionals could never know, but people who walked, biked, or lived by the waterfront could and did know. One striking piece of local knowledge in my group concerned the High Bridge, the bridge that originally carried the water from the Croton Aqueduct across the river to Manhattan . . . we locals knew that it was of huge historic significance, that the mayor and governor and parks commissioner had already started plans for its restoration, and that it should be considered as low-hanging fruit for the watershed plan. In EVERY reach there turned out to be local knowledge that significantly added to the possibilities and ideas concerning waterfront development.[36]

By 2007, total city-protected lands in the five boroughs encompassed nearly 30,000 acres in more than 1,700 official parks, some as small as a few square yards, up to Pelham Bay Park with 2,700 acres.[37] If lands protected by all the partners are included, the figure is 57,000 acres. One of the most intensely settled places on Earth protects nearly 15 percent of its land, and the percentage is rising. That is the critical point: the ongoing direction of change, the conservation percentage and diversity of activities rises as the city continues its economic growth. Green space is expanding, not being cut back by the rising aspirations of the people. Greening goes into the wholeness of life. During Wildflower Week in May 2010, New York documented 778 native plants and held forty-five public events (botanical walks and talks, youth education sessions, and restoration events) to celebrate and connect New Yorkers to their native wildflowers. Young people have led the way in reclaiming industrial sites as green space.[38] The Metropolitan Waterfront Alliance, formed in 2000 by the venerable Municipal Arts Society, and spun off as an independent organization in 2006, now has over 400 civic, labor, and corporate organizations committed to wise planning and development of New York City's 500 miles of waterfront.

This the most densely populated part of the United States grows as a migration center for birds as they move up and down the crowded East Coast. Two hundred seventy-five migratory species are now seen in Central Park and 325 in the Jamaica Wildlife Refuge. In 2007, a beaver (a key indicator of pristine wilderness) swam down the Bronx River and built a dam in one of these protected nooks.[39] A second beaver showed up in the summer of 2010. The native alewife herring was reintroduced into the Bronx River in 2006 and 2007; in 2009 and 2010 it migrated home from the ocean for breeding.[40]

The first lesson from New York City is that if conservation is viewed as a service provided by government, it is vulnerable: flourishing in times of prosperity, precarious in times of financial hardship. A second lesson is that protection of natural heritage can be spectacularly achieved at sustainable costs when people are engaged. A third lesson is that when nature is brought to people, other benefits also come forward. A fourth lesson is that what builds a city worth living in is people's engagement. Recovering the sense of the commons in New York has been important in recovering the city ("city" in Latin *civitas*: community of citizens). The choice is not one of voluntarism versus services, but both. The choice is not public or private funding and management, but creative use of both. Too frequently, when it comes to funding and management of public spaces, people have viewed paid-for services as better than voluntarism, but a balance is best. This is also true of drives to "privatize," which is often limited to handing something from governmental to corporate management with little engagement of the people.

New York City shows how essential Top-down engagement is for going to scale. Examples were given earlier from Arunachal Pradesh and the city of Kabul where seeds of human energy made an impressive impact. But in those examples the seeds did not grow beyond neighborhood scale. Grounded in human energy, they had sustainable impact but did not attain self-sustaining larger levels. In those contexts, sufficient Top-down enabling environments did not exist—just as they did not exist in Nepal despite massive money infusions from the top. By contrast, in the Tibet Autonomous Region an enabling Top-down environment was in place (as it is in New York City) and the radiating rise in growth expands to regional limits. *Policies are more important than money in creating an enabling environment, and creating enabling policies need not cost much money.* Tibet and New York City—on one side the policies of a communist government, on the other the policies of a democracy. For scaling up, it is not the type of government that matters so much as the way the policies restructure relationships to transform the whole into more than the sum of the parts. Any government can probably create policies to enable scaling up, provided it relinquishes the ideas of control and exclusive service delivery in favor of the principles of nurturing partnership with community and Outside-in innovation. China relinquished control to local participation in environmental management in Tibet (though assuredly not in political activity). New York City relinquished the Robert Moses Top-down control. When that occurred in both instances environmental actions flourished.

The agencies that can provide the enabling policy, financing, and knowledge environment vary. Today in New York City, the Top-down is government, but when the city was near bankruptcy, wealthy citizens stepped into the Top-down role. In Afghanistan, such scaling up must include the religious institutions. In New York it must include the financial sector. The Top-down can even be international donor agencies, though seldom is this source able to enable sustainable scaling-up, in part because they are visitors and thus not directly invested in the burgeoning self-sufficiency of the process. However, for scaling up to occur, there must be a Top-down component from some sector(s), be this government, religion, or business.

SCALE AS A TOOL TO MONITOR CHANGE

SEED-SCALE can also be used as an analytical framework (as we have implicitly done above in our account of New York's parks). Returning to the importance of monitoring, the SCALE acronyms highlight the distinctive views from the Bottom-up, Outside-in, and Top-down. Each gives a valid perspective. But SCALE does more than give a nomenclature for differing views. It also enables assessment of community change to track shifting dynamics across time.

Until now, measurement of social change was almost universally conducted sector by sector. Economic growth, education, or health surveys were conducted by different bodies using different methods, with little connection to one another. The first problem is that it is very easy to over-interpret the accuracy of a number such as gross national product or child mortality, where each is a moment in one aspect of society subject to all sorts of measurement error. Yet, social change needs a way to track its complex progress. Hard measurement of the kind demanded of scientific experiment is impossible. But going forward without adequate external references for direction and progress is like passengers in the back of the airplane sending 'I think messages' up to the cockpit to fly the plane. To transition from today to the desired tomorrow will be more effective (and more safely done) with data that monitors performance. Experiments are underway to bring options in assessment synthesis.[42] While it is extremely important to recognize the limits to accuracy, SCALE can bring together the perspectives of Top, Bottom, and Outside so as to allow the following of social change's aggregate impact over time. The key function of this approach is not measurement of a state at any point of time, but developing a concrete way to understand the direction and character of change. What SEED-SCALE can do is to offer a multidimensional, quasi-formulaic way to quantify the change through the complex socio-econo-biosphere.

SCALE One, Squared, and Cubed can be used as three dimensions on a graph. Assigning a value to each gives a perspective on how many people in a community have what quality of life in relation to the enabling conditions provided by their society. With a first set of points noted, three new values can be added as the iterations of the process move forward, showing how the earlier three have changed and creating a map of a community's journey. It is a crude map, the actual numbers should be considered very crude approximations, where the value of the product is that of depicting direction rather than stating position, but use of such graphic representations helps systematize community dialogue, allowing people to grasp complexity. Furthermore, such numbers can be publically posted, and having a visual indicator of progress creates a sense of accomplishment that feeds back into continued momentum.

SCALE One is the y-axis that indicates the number of people involved. The number here can be either the population participating or the percentage of people involved as part of the larger population.[43] SCALE Squared is the x-axis, and it records the quality of life. The common indicator (Gross Domestic Product) looks only at economic activity, and that is too narrow a perspective of quality of life. Experiments are underway using the Grameen Bank's Progress out of Poverty Indicator (PPI) with applications in more than twenty countries.[44] The Human Development Index (HDI) is being used at national level and combines life expectancy, ability to utilize information, and standard of living, and experimental modifications for community level use are underway.[45]

SCALE Cubed is the z-axis showing how policies, financing, and information systems create the enabling environment of social change. Unlike SCALE One and SCALE Squared, which are calculated for each locale, SCALE Cubed can be standardized across regional and national contexts. To assess policies, the Worldwide Governance Indicators (WGI) of the World Bank combine six variables: voice and accountability, political stability and lack of violence, government effectiveness, regulatory quality, rule of law, and control of corruption.[46] This number is available from the World Bank and can be used directly. A tool to assess financing at the community level has not yet evolved, though work is underway by the World Bank's Household Financial Access.[47] In the interim, a proxy may be the Gini Coefficient, which calculates financial disparities between rich and poor, a number that is publicly available.[48] Assessing information systems has challenges, but a variable of growing validity is Internet access using UNESCO's Digital Opportunity Index (DOI), also available for many countries.[49] To find an aggregate among these for the z-axis on a zero-to-one scale as the others have, we propose that the WGI be weighted at one-half, the Gini Coefficient at one-quarter, and the DOI at one-quarter.

Collectively, these approximations provide coordinates for a community's socioeconomic sphere. A useful analogue here is to the latitude, longitude, and altitude position locating numbers that mark physical location on the geosphere. Any place from the center of the Earth outward can be located using latitude, longitude, and altitude. If something's physical location then moves, three different numbers locate the new position. Similarly, a community can use changes in its approximate percentage of people engaged (relative to the overall population), quality of life, and larger enabling environment to track movement through the socioeconomic sphere (this metric does not engage biosphere assessments). Movement is multidimensional, rather than lying along one line, as in tracking GNP, and it thus more accurately reflects the multidimensionality of human aspiration. As one goal is achieved, that influences the next, with such goals often changing in kind rather than degree: for example, from health, to money, to security, to leisure. Such transformations are now only revealed in language and aesthetics, which reflect cultural changes in a manner infinitely more complex than even the most intricate measurement systems. But to describe aesthetics as "measurement tools" is to reduce them beyond recognition. SCALE gives a graphic way for communities to see approximations of their progress and compare these with earlier progress and with other communities.

LESSONS FROM THE ROOF OF THE WORLD

The conservation achievements we helped start in Tibet prompted the hope that these ideas could extend across China to promote synergistic prosperity and environmental action in a population presently single-mindedly pursuing economic growth. To open dialogue on this challenge, we developed the idea of the Green Long March, which has been run for four years, from 2007 to 2010. (The Green Long March was intentionally ended in 2010 at the height of national extension with 80 participating universities because the pace of national change and four years of accomplishments brought forward next stage opportunities for environmental engagement.)

The original Long March was the event when China accepted Communism, and went "red." In October of 1934, the Communists had been nearly annihilated. The Kuomintang Army had Mao's army surrounded in Jiangxi Province, when the Communists broke out and, lacking reserves and equipment, fled. The Long March started—Communists running, Kuomintang chasing: leaving the fields of southern China, escaping into the rugged mountains of western Sichuan, and two years later they arrived in the mountains and caves of the isolated northwest Shangxi Province. During the Long March, beleaguered and hungry, Mao's armies learned the process of partnership with the people. As they fled they helped the people plant, tend, and harvest fields. By the time they were locked away in the Yenan caves, with the Kuomintang believing their enemy was beaten, the energy of peasants had begun to mobilize behind Mao's troops, with the energy that would make Communism truly a movement of the people spreading through the complex systems of China.[50]

The Long March allowed Mao's scaling up by giving him insights on people–government partnership. After Mao consolidated control in 1949, he pushed his people-based agenda with programs based on peasants (shifting away from the Soviet premise of factory laborers), adapting lessons from many places but perhaps the most important the Ding Xian Experiment that had pioneered in the 1930s the health and education models of the Barefoot Doctors and peasant scholars.[51] Some of Mao's other peasant-based ideas were not grounded in scholarship, perhaps most notably the attempt to industrialize the peasantry through the Great Leap Forward, and these were unmitigated disasters.[52] However, we must also not lose sight of the fact that Bottom-up mobilization during the next three decades gave a foundation of education and health for China's present prosperity. Before the revolution, China's poverty was such that the Long March went through villages in which people did not even have clothing, and illness rates were so high that in some counties each person carried fifteen pounds of worms in their gut.[53] Thus, despite the multitude of its sins, Communist action did create a platform for the economic growth that took off in the 1980s by building a foundation in health and education.

China's breakout with rapid and large-scale social and economic advancement was the result of experimentation and action learning. From 1984 to 1986, Carl had the opportunity to work at high levels of the Chinese government when he served as UNICEF Representative to China, a period when Deng Xiaoping was actively shaping a new direction to evolve maximally effective solutions. The Model Counties Project evolved a new financing structure for Chinese health care, directly extending to 160 million people in 400 counties across the country. The former Barefoot Doctor program had collapsed, and the Model Counties solution set in place a process that evolved county-specific solutions.[54] A similar process set up innovation across China that advanced agricultural production, which in the late 1970s and 1980s was still the basis of Chinese life. The sequence was then applied in manufacturing in the 1980s and 1990s, as Dani Rodrik notes: "China owes a great deal of its success to a willingness to experiment pragmatically with heterodox solutions."[55] In none of these instances did China take internationally recommended practice, but the country evolved internally fitted models, which, once perfected, were extended (experimentation and action learning).

The Green Long March was designed to influence popular understanding using people-based action. Instead of focusing on China's environmental problems, as global discourse continues to do, the March would highlight China's environmental successes: "the transformation of China initiated through turning red, now must add to that momentum the color green."[56] The message-carriers would be the youth of China. On July 7, 2007, as summer vacation began, students from thirty-two universities started by bus, train, and foot following ten routes across the country: the Gold Coast, Inner Mongolian Grasslands, National Treasures Route, Northwestern Deserts, Rainforest Exploration, Snowlands and the Tibetan Plateau, the Yangtze River, and the Yellow River. "We march in ten directions toward the same objective," they said as they went from community to community. That objective was to identify environmental successes, and put these forward as green seeds for national growth.

In 2007, along the Grand Canal route (the commerce corridor on which Chinese civilization had grown for a thousand years) marchers stopped in eighty villages, recording how each community with an average population each of 3,500 people was spread out across an average 1.8 kilometers, with thirteen sub-communities. The successes identified through their surveys were

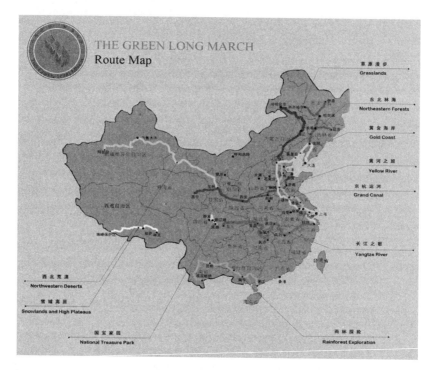

Figure 9.4. Routes of the Green Long March across China.

featured in national and local media, in hundreds of newspaper, television, and radio stories. Along the Northeastern Forest route, the students engaged with forty-nine communities that were much more spread out, covering five kilometers on average and typically having only five village subcommittees.

As the March passed through communities, the students probed for what was working. One item identified was that crews on road repair duty were often planting trees beside the roads; others were planting trees on marginal agricultural lands as a source of income or as "green Great Walls" around towns to protect them from sand storms. Other locals undertook beautification with flowers and bushes in community open areas. The March also revealed an expanding focus on irrigation to conserve water and a focus on reusing waste in garbage disposal. Across the country, students found rapid increases in local energy generation using solar, wind, and geothermal energy, as well as new utilization of dung to generate gas for cooking. An increasing number of factories were generating electricity from surplus heat. Sixty-six percent of the 333 communities the students surveyed said that because of these successes, their communities were environmentally better off in 2007 than they had been before, and the surveys identified 2,578 individual cases of community-based environmental successes.

Targeting China-wide change requires partnerships. The Green Long March did not start environmental action in China, but rather added spark to the Chinese environmental movement already underway. The SEED-SCALE idea was redefined into the Chinese language by a colleague, L. J. Jia, adapting one of Mao's phrases, as *xing hou liao yuan*, "sparks that set the land on fire." Seven ministries and government organizations put their red stamp of support on the papers, along with the fifty universities. The March evolved so that, by 2010, a national movement was underway with a year-round, five-part program. In 2009, it received the Mother River Award, China's supreme environmental award.

The Green Long March is an attempt to change behaviors through non-confrontational mobilization. In many countries, youth movements are common, as the young are mobile and easily energized. In China, examples of youth movements shaping historical events can be seen in such diverse instances as the Red Guards in the Cultural Revolution and students at Tiananmen Square. Both of these were examples of human energy rising in confrontation with the established society, and both led to bloodshed. We raise these comparisons not to point to either as models, but to highlight the tremendous energy latent in organized youth. How can such energy be turned to positive momentum? Latent, waiting, energy cannot be denied. One feature the Green Long March demonstrates is that it can be turned

Figure 9.5. Ten thousand students attending the opening ceremony of the 2007 Green Long March at Beijing Forestry University. *(Photo credit: L. J. Jia)*

positively. In this case, the call of the young adults focused on bringing people together: "Let's do better with the best of what we are already doing." The image used to create engagement was ten large mirrors moving across the country so China could see its environmental posture changing. Engaging the youth positively is terribly important, because their considerable energy can quickly turn to terror if it is frustrated.

A demonstration students conducted to get the message across was: "hop on one leg" (the student would hop), "this was like doing economic development alone" (and those watching could see how quickly it used up energy). "Now hop on the other leg" (the student tires more quickly because this is the weaker leg); "this is like doing conservation alone." Finally with both legs (and visible relief) the student says, "This is conservation and development working together," and marches across the room. Combining economic development and conservation allows a society to march a very long way.

THE SCALING-UP IMPERATIVE

In the past, as earlier noted, conservation of nature has tended to be presented as a Top-down activity where people were kept out, with a less-visible countermovement celebrating an idealized version of indigenous land management that never likely existed at any scale level. Conservation can now reach across this imagined divide into partnership. A new, more sustainable model will not come quickly. We do not yet know how to improve livelihoods at acceptable environmental costs. This fact alone should illustrate the imperative of bringing as many partners, ideas, and philosophies to the task as possible because for our collective human and planetary future we must evolve a more accommodating path for human and natural world coexistence. Features of the coming solution are obvious, but the process and schedule to get there are not yet known.

What we do know is that such answers are not going to emerge whole cloth, but will instead be reached through a function-driven process of iterative adapting and tailoring within systems of the socio-econo-biosphere. Procedures will drive the evolutionary moves, not prescribed solutions. That these procedures will be precisely the principles, tasks, and criteria (values, actions, and analytical frames) of SEED-SCALE is unlikely, but they will be a functional framework that enables adaptive self-learning to mature with experience. The complex systems of the planet are in flux, changing as direction and momentum are changing, agents acting and readapting in parallel, with control dispersed. Order will emerge, but it cannot be predicted. It will emerge through simple, evolving procedures. Communication and cooperation will rise, and necessary specializations will develop. Learning will be growing because the process senses progress, seeks it out, and builds direction from it.

False starts are simply left by the wayside, like a river finding its way through a mountain range, gradually cutting a canyon. Progress accumulates with iterative sophistication; the unimaginable becomes inevitable through layered generation of iterative cycles.

The process will surely be participatory, growing site-specific seeds fitted to each locale. In defining this model, Tibet offers one vantage point, from the true fringes of the habitable world, where existence is a success in itself. New York City shows movement in the same direction in the midst of commerce and human modernity. The Green Long March shows a beginning made by students with the support of a control-oriented political system among the largest population on Earth, surging into the future. Today, somewhat more than ten percent of Earth's land area is protected in nature preserves: the journey has begun. We are one-tenth of the way there. There is a long way to go. A variety of people-based approaches, the only kind the global economy can afford long-term, are experimenting with options and advancing methodologies.[57] Nature-protection is no longer only a matter of protecting nature's special places but is a matter of creating the foundation of life *for all*.

Movement toward a sustainable future is underway, but it will scale up in quantity and quality only if it also enables people to achieve the lives they aspire to, and works from a resource base that is available to all. Such a base must be that of human energy and mobilized through empowerment. Furthermore, it can only succeed insofar as it recognizes, and indeed thrives on, the complexity of global systems. No other base is universally available, nor flexible enough to globally adapt. In Chapter 2 a table (Table 2.1) was shown that contrasted the choices. Choices such as whether:

- Planning process will go from community agenda, to plan, to budget; or begin with the money and go from budget, to agenda, to plan;
- Ultimate accountability will be to community or to donor;
- The planning mindset will be one of iterative growth or get-it-right construction engineering;
- Desired outcomes will be behavior change or measurable results;
- And, the commitment horizon, will it look to utility to the community or to the donor's budget cycle?

Here toward the end of this book, it helps to draw such stark distinctions. The traditional approach to social change and that of SEED-SCALE are fundamentally different, but they are not mutually exclusive. In reality, the contrasts are complementarities. Development is a process constantly folding back over itself. The two approaches can work together, creating a synergy that gives self-assembling direction. When the human-energy approach leads, it can bring in financial opportunities and economic growth, which will in turn lead to an expanding array of options. The potential of human energy usually gets overlooked when the monetary approach leads, as emphasis focuses on competition for scarce monetary resources, but often it is human energy that makes new opportunities for wealth creation possible, as revealed repeatedly in history.

In that larger context, an iterative process creates a feedback loop between the two approaches. Opportunity will increase more than either could produce on its own. Ilya Prigogine and Isabelle Stengers have shown how such feedback loops functionally operate in the dynamics of non-equilibria.[58] Transferred to social change, their interpretation reveals why the dynamics of empowerment need not succumb to the inexorable tendency for energies to dissipate (the Second Law of Thermodynamics). A small advantage generated by one set of successes feeds into generating a further small advantage in the next cycle, like the acceleration of a flywheel. Running the cycle again magnifies the impact.

Applying the positive feedback loop in economics, Brian Arthur of the Santa Fe Institute has demonstrated how the principle of diminishing returns usually operates in economics. Give a man earning ten dollars an hour a ten-dollar raise and you double his income, but a second ten-dollar raise only is an increase of one-half, and returns diminish even further with the next. In the real world, people do not let diminishing returns operate. People see the inefficiency when they have the breadth of options of life and are not confined just to economics. They change what the next ten dollars is invested in to an investment worth ten dollars to them. This starts a process of increasing rather than diminishing returns.[59] The tendency toward diversification is key, much like new stores and restaurants opening in a neighborhood actually expand each other's opportunities for business. As Stephen Johnson argues, "Like any emergent system, a city is a pattern in time."[60] That pattern encourages certain businesses to flourish in certain places—"silk weavers clustered along Florence's Por Santa Maria, the Venetian glassblowers on Murano, the Parisian traders gathered in Les Halles"—because of the feedback loops that enable them to feed off of one another.[61] Positive feedback loops of increasing returns operate in economics, but they engage more dramatically when the feedback loops connect energy-based returns to monetary ones, opening many more options.

This point is of utmost importance for our planetary future: the feedback loop of increasing returns can drive massive scaling up, but such feedback loops can also work in the opposite direction, with global climate destabilization being perhaps the most obvious example (and increasing sectarian violence being another). Positive feedback loops must be started. This is the only way that climatic adjustments that are so huge can turn into solutions. Beginning with the resource available to all, people can come together. Once moving, then money and natural resources can be directed. Applying all its resources, humanity has created the world in which we live, both its marvels and its crises. The need now is to direct those energies using an adaptive process that iteratively grows solutions within the complex challenges.

IN RECAPITULATION

The idea that human energy is the foundation of social change is not new. It has been the basis of religious movements and revolutions throughout history. Marx described the exploitation of human energy as the core of injustice, and revolt as the way to break that injustice. As will be discussed in the next chapter, Gandhi offered the path of truth-energy to recoup ownership in moving toward independence. Native Americans speak of larger life forces as "medicine" that needs to be grown. Hindus talk of this force as *Brahma* from which comes the fulfillment of life, while the Chinese speak of *Qi* that connects us with larger life. And, the American Revolution identified life, liberty, and the pursuit of happiness as the core of the new order they sought to build. (It is noteworthy that economic prosperity is not mentioned in this foundation statement for the American experience).

Today, seven billion people search for ways to create the lives they wish to lead—including the more than two billion who have been excluded from the benefits of modernity. By 2040, the United Nations estimates that that number will rise to nine billion. Where will we find food, shelter, and satisfying livelihoods for two billion more people? Such questions are especially urgent given that the two billion will primarily be born to the poor, and so will only have the resource of their energy to work with. While much about the future is impossible to know, it is unlikely that one-third more natural resources will be discovered in the planet. Furthermore, any new resources will, if history holds true, be taken by the rich. In a context of ever-rising competition for wealth it is difficult to imagine that significant monetary gains will be shared with the poor. The trends are clear, and human behaviors are well established. We are entering a world of greater human desperation. While the planet has become more interconnected, the connections have not grown between the haves and have-nots. On the contrary, the divide has rigidified.[62]

Thus, by a process of elimination, the options for the coming two billion are reduced to what can be done with the one resource base the have-nots have. It is not just the disadvantage's last and only option—it is also ours as well. The seven billion now living and two billion coming will need an expanding resource base if they are to live up to their aspirations. In the past, the have-nots who moved into prosperity did so primarily through hard work. Today they continue to work hard (and that is of course human energy). However, because the world has become so interconnected through the deregulation and liberalization of the last decades, the context of applying that resource base is both more competitive and easier to exploit by corporate interests.

Hard work in Bangladesh competes against hard work in China, and that competes against hard work in America. Fathers and mothers sacrifice for their children, believing that their labor, love, and hope can provide. Sometimes benefits fall in place, but more commonly, when all is done, such families find themselves in situations that have changed little despite their labors. Hard work is no longer enough (and increasingly vulnerable to exploitation). The specifics of the future cannot be predicted, but certain tendencies are clear: the danger may be violence, as those who strived so valiantly despair because they invested all and have little left to lose. We may indeed see pandemics spawned by crowded living conditions. A shrinking landmass with rising ocean levels may cause massive migrations. These are the kinds of details that we cannot know about the future—most likely it will be some combination of these and more. Rising pressure on an unstable planet is certain.

The required action of response is to integrate with the natural resource that was given to us three million years ago when we became *Homo sapiens*, wise humans. While the specifics ahead are not clear, the immediate next steps are. Locally specific answers that use available, not scarce, resources, that fit to each aspect of the local socio-econo-biosphere must evolve in this complex global system: create coordinating committees, identify the successes we have had and build on them, learn about successes others have had and adapt them, gather relevant evidence about our situation (not opinions or ideology) with which to plan, make plans that include all, and then revise with each step more informed than the last.

The pace of change is unlikely on its own to slingshot us onto a sustainable path, which means that painful and even devastating changes are almost inevitable. But it can start walking us toward such a path as our human species goes through an adaptation it does not want to do (and which the longer it is put off, the greater the ultimate pain). The alternative is one where change's rate and direction totally escape our control. The examples of greening New York City and China's Green Long March give widely divergent points of hope—and there are hundreds, even thousands, of others. These can be global SCALE Squared Centers to extend action learning and experimentation. Social action no longer needs to be a random Brownian movement of ideas and grasping attempts in the socio-econo-biosphere. We now have a methodology to systematically take seeds of empowerment to scale.

CHAPTER 10

Confronting Empire

Become the change you wish to see.
                    Mohandas K. Gandhi

Discussion thus far has focused on how the Bottom-up can use the Top-down environment in collaborative partnership. But sometimes the Top-down is hostile to community mobilization. How can the processes described in this book be applied when the larger system does not want social mobilization to grow? How do communities grow their energies when their government does not want that—and in such hostility how are energies grown without a bloody revolution?

Around the world, a variety of forces impinge on communities' ability to determine their futures. Some of these forces will not compromise, blatantly seeking to plunder resources, exploit people, and rely on obfuscating paperwork or even brutality to advance their self-serving agendas. They intend to take advantage of communities, and have no intention to change. Continuing with the functional nomenclature of SEED-SCALE, these forces can be grouped under the concept of "empire." Michael Hardt and Antonio Negri have argued that such forces include not only military or political infringement by governments in the manner of classical imperialism, but also encroachment by corporations and international bodies, and also *development agencies* that allegedly avow community empowerment.[1] Communities are often rendered complicit in their exploitation, going along because of a variety of compensations. In situations of complicity, little can be done. But at other times communities want to break away, they want to confront. How can they?

While SEED-SCALE is primarily a means of seeking social evolution rather than revolution, its principles, and more generally the larger idea of growing empowerment, can be used to confront the oppression and malfeasance of empires. In this context, the example of Mahatma Gandhi continues to be relevant.[2] Gandhi's lesson is often viewed only as an achievement of politi-cal independence, but we want to focus not on the end he achieved but the method he used to get there: empowerment. Unlike the freedom movements before him, such as the American, French, Haitian, and Soviet revolutions, Gandhi did not fight the Top-down, but in his use of nonviolence he most certainly used force—the force of human energy. Gandhi used philosophical values that enabled people to take ownership of their future, a process that began with the smallest of actions in people's own lives. Instead of discarding the Outside-in of British media and religion, he was selective, turning a seg-ment of Britain's media and religion to his purpose. Building from the energy of individual action, he drew together the collective energies of India to over-throw the imperial yoke. In all, his purpose was *swaraj*—self-rule.

Our family was privileged to be in India during much of the time Gandhi was developing his movement, and to have direct contact with him. As the years have passed since, we keep going back to lessons learned from his move-ment. The innovations he brought forward become only more timely. And, his innovations of process represent the best means for confronting the new empire that is upon us.

Mahatma Gandhi coined the word *swaraj* (literally "self-rule," but he trans-lated it as "self-control," and sometimes "a morality based in truth") to describe ownership by people in determining their future. To understand the term *swaraj* in a purely political context impoverishes the concept. Gandhi was in South Africa at the time, and the idea of people rising up for independence through nonviolent action that would later become synonymous with his name was not his initial purpose. His idea was that a small group of people could control their destiny by taking control of the basic functions of life. Colonialism was a condition of loss of control for the Indian community; so, too, were racism, poverty, illiteracy, and illness. It was these issues of holistic advancement that concerned him above and beyond political independence. He wanted to reconfigure an idealized village. Idealized village life became his life organizing social frame, for at the village level colonialism could be confronted, but so could many more oppressions. Later in India as his inde-pendence movement started to mature, he held to the belief that political freedom means little when broader well-being does not follow (a point that recent history as borne out in Pyrrhic elections and anticolonial revolutionar-ies turned repressive autocrats). Good governance begins in (and must be held accountable to) practices that improve lives at the local level.

In the beginning, Gandhi simply wanted to improve lives on a marginal piece of land in South Africa. What would grow into a freedom movement for one-fifth of humanity, and inspire many other freedom movements of the twenti-eth century, began as an intentional community for a few. Years later, in India, when the movement had begun to expand from a community of intellectuals and activists to national scale, Gandhi added a term, *gram swaraj*: community self-rule (or community-based freedom).[3] *Gram swaraj* generates internal, community-wide, sustaining energy; it remains village focused and promotes a village based on idealized principles. It contains self-correcting direction because it is inspired and regulated by what Gandhi termed "experimenting with truth." He argued that what brings change to people's lives comes not from the marketplace or armies, nor from religion or political process, but from the knowledge of reality: truth. For Gandhi, truth must be internalized and adhered to so that it continually corrects action.[4] Growing understanding from experimentation thus redefines society from the small to all. (This is much the same process we term Self-Evaluation for Effective Decision Making, SEED.) As revealed in the title of his autobiography, *The Story of My Experiments with Truth*[5] freedom grown in this manner is never totally achieved but is always made greater by the truth-centered quest. As John Chathanatt notes, "Like Plato, Gandhi considered the search for Truth to be more important than Truth as such."[6] Gandhi was a thinker of process.

The spinning wheel visibly conveyed this message: freedom through the work of village hands. Each individual turning his or her wheel gave evidence

Figure 10.1. Gandhi constantly experimented and searched for truth—and his methods often caught his associates off-guard. Here it is assumed he is looking at the leprosy bacillus, a disease primarily characterized by the exclusion of the sufferers. *(Photo used by permission of the M. K. Gandhi Centre)*

of self-potential. The act of spinning used resources grown in that place (*swadeshi*, self-sufficiency), locally grown cotton, locally grown wood that made the wheels. What is important is not the practicality of spinning, but the *practice* of it, as an emblematic action with direct consequences in people's lives. When people wore *khadi* (homespun) cloth, they embodied proof that they could take the fabric of life into their own hands (in his words, "become the change you wish to see"). As Gandhi said to news reporters who puzzled over why this man leading a national freedom movement spoke to them from behind a spinning wheel and why he wore homespun clothes, "The song of our spinning wheels is the song of freedom—the freedoms we are making in our own lives."[7]

The British Raj relied heavily on pageantry and spectacle to dramatize its power, from crisply ironed whites and pith helmets to the grade parades of Victoria's Diamond Jubilee, from elephant-back tiger hunts modeled on their Moghul predecessors to Gothic architecture modeled on their own imperial capitol.[8] Gandhi was a master of counter-spectacles: from the Salt March, to his numerous hunger strikes, and always back to the spinning wheel—homespun, home-woven, how stark the difference with the pagents of empire. Gandhi was perhaps the first great practitioner of today's political "photo-op." Indeed it was arguably the *spectacle* of nonviolence that made it such an effective political force as is palpable in contemporary media accounts:

> In eighteen years of reporting in twenty two countries, during which I have witnessed innumerable civil disturbances, riots, street fights, and rebellions, I have never witnessed such a harrowing scenes as at Dharsana ... the sight of men advancing coldly and deliberately and submitting to beating without attempting defense. Sometimes the scenes were so painful that I had to turn away momentarily ... they were so thoroughly imbued with Gandhi's non-violence creed, and the leaders constantly stood in front of the ranks imploring them to remember that Gandhi's soul was with them. . . . hundreds of blows inflicted by the police, but saw not a single blow returned by the volunteers ... [or] even raise his arm to deflect the blows from lathis. There were no outcries from beaten swarajist, only groans after they had submitted to their beating.[9]

This is power, visible human power, which commands the gaze precisely through being nearly unwatchable. In the above account part of what is so unsettling is how the *swarajis* subvert the pomp and circumstance of military parades, with their flags, banners, and aestheticization of weaponry as a means to forget the realities of violence.[10] Nothing renders the painful reality of violence more starkly than this spectacle of its deliberate refusal. Gandhi well understood the importance of such scenes. For instance, he encouraged people to wear clean white clothes so the dirt and blood of beatings would show on photographs all over the world, mobilizing widespread support though his appeal to the gazes of those distant from the struggle.

None of these examples are *only* symbols or purely aesthetic, however. Instead, Gandhi's actions present a seamless fusion of the symbolic and the literal so that attempting to disentangle those dynamics becomes an exercise in futility, much the way that Gandhi argued for the inextricability of the body and ethics or political and personal freedom. Nowhere is this more evident than in the product of the villagers' spinning: *khadi*.

Done collectively, the production of homespun *khadi* showed that India could weave the warp and woof of a new life, threads of local resources from one direction, massive energy of the people from the other. *Khadi* was their flag long before it was woven into the official banner of the independent nation.[11] Wearing this flag of self-reliance as they marched in clothes harvested from their lands and created by their hands, the people were pointing toward a future of their own making. They were marching against empire. Britain had established itself in India first as an economic force, a charter by Queen Elizabeth I in 1600 for the East India Company. It was only when rebellion rose in 1857 that the Crown took explicit political and military governing control. Where the British Empire's purpose was to feed the growth of the world's first industrial economy., Gandhi's purpose was to feed the growth of his country's capacity.

The industrial age factory was a powerful symbol of modernity 100 years ago. In manifest contrast to the power emblemized in belching factories in which human beings become hands attending to vast machines, nonviolent protestors wearing *khadi* gave proof of the homegrown strength of a turning wheel on a mud floor, evidence of new processes of production from millions of people and tens of thousands of villages. *Swaraj* of communal making strengthened India with tightly wound new fiber that Gandhi hoped would lead beyond deep forces of oppression: caste, poverty, ignorance, fear of leprosy, and gender discrimination.

Today, as military powers send soldiers to distant lands and call them "liberators," as corporations are freed to plunder the Earth for raw materials and circle the globe for cheap labor, the question must be asked (even if it cannot be answered): what freedom is this? While unseating oppressive regimes and providing jobs do enable freedoms, targeting freedom in the manner pursued by peacemaking forces and corporations misses the central tenet that guided Gandhi: truth is in the never-ending journey, and it grows from fealty to principles.

Freedom is not given.[12] The genuine freedom opened by empowerment grows when people come together to rule themselves, working for mutual benefit. However it is approached, freedom is made by people. Gandhi often reminded his followers that people often find themselves in bondage because they have allowed it to be imposed upon them. This is not to blame the victims for their own oppression, but rather to emphasize that people always have the option to stand up as individuals and join together as communities. Doing so not only liberates those who do, but also creates a momentum that can reach all. It is the way of universal freedom: "If we are to make progress, we must not repeat history but make new history. We must add to the inheritance left by our ancestors."[13]

Nothing better illustrates Gandhi's method of working as an individual within the environment at hand to enable the strength of many than his use of fasting. Self-denial to the point of death for the well-being of others created untenable resonance within British Christian ethics, implicitly evoking to the model of Jesus dying for sinners. It appealed also to the British notion of self-less honor in willingness to die for one's country, especially in the two decades following the carnage of World War I where the populace hungered for some justification for purposeless death and had begun to question the mythology of empire. And for the people of India, fasting was an act they could relate to, tied as it was to a condition skirted by many every day. Fasting is anchored deep in the Hindu religion: an act of purification, and purification of India was Gandhi's ultimate objective. In India, announcement of a Gandhian fast was like a bomb, news of which flew across the land even when telegraph lines were denied, communicating a simple message that brought people together: our "great soul" risks his life for us; we must join in solidarity with him.[14]

Sadly, the momentum Gandhi had started retreated to distant *ashrams* (study centers) when he was assassinated on January 30, 1948. That week the Mahatma had stepped out in solidarity with the Muslims with whom Hindus and Sikhs had been fighting in the Partition riots. In his talk at evening prayers he had asked others to share their thoughts for how to advance *gram swaraj* for the poor, the sick, and the marginalized. It was already then obvious to him that what was coming was a new empire, a new Indian elite in control of the levers of production. What was coming was a planned, Top-down economy allegedly in the interests of the people, but, as the next forty years of economic failures would show (the economic model changed in the 1990s), it used economic centralization to augment central political control.[15]

In Gandhi's view, the journey for real freedom only began with political independence. His quest was for a freedom that transcended politics, a quest that remains to be achieved. After independence the government that unfolded adopted forms and processes that mirrored the British model, but identification with the people remained symbolic: leaders might wear *khadi*, but they did not actually spin the thread to make it. They had mistaken *khadi* for cloth.[16] The will of the people was solicited every five years at elections; for the rest of the time, bureaucracy ran the country in the name of the people.

Important questions lie here unanswered. How much can a leader achieve against deep social defects, for example Gandhi's failure to adequately address the caste system? Gandhi is today frequently blamed because he did not "solve" the caste problem. Undeniably he could have done more, but such blaming of earlier leadership also implicates the followers for not carrying on the quest. Continuing social reform comes from on-going action. One generation's unsuccessful attempt does not relieve the next from trying again. Those who are oppressed by millennia-old discrimination (as the outcastes, *dalits*, "those who are Untouchable," continue to be) are apt to blame attempts that do not reach them.[17] Gandhi while leading a freedom movement was also holding it together (he failed to hold the Muslims inside it). Could he have held the higher castes in if he had worked harder to lift up the lower castes? The answer is not known. But what is known is that today the opportunity exists to push on.

Today, the reality of India is that a new empire is in place, one of continued oppression for the poor, lower castes, women, and tribals. While India now has a surging economy that has transformed life for the upper and middle classes and achieved world-class status in medicine and technology, the country remains home to the diseases of pneumonia, malaria, tuberculosis, dysentery, and leprosy that Gandhi so worried about. The first disease killed his wife; the last afflicted a man living in a hut close to his. Seven hundred million in India are indeed better off, but 300 million still live on the margins, and for them conditions get worse.[18] This entrenched exclusion would bother Gandhi. A movement in which enough prosper to lift the overall average, while the abyss of inequity separating 300 million grows ever wider, and is held in place by the violence of political leaders and the police, is a world of empire and legitimized violence. Words of equity go forward, selective statistics that describe progress mount, but persistent inequity rots the foundation of India's alleged progress; it creates a state not of civilization but of empire. And this rot is endorsed by the international agencies whose mission is to alleviate poverty, illness, and discrimination. How much does the Washington Consensus of today (implemented by people who visit the villages in the day only to return to five-star hotels at night) differ from the crowning of Queen Victoria Empress of India (she never set foot on the subcontinent), or the days when Gandhi saw the mills of England denying the potential for productive labor in India. Decisions made in air-conditioned boardrooms have life-or-death consequences in villages the deciders will never see. The promises of aid agencies fade like the dust behind a Land Cruiser speeding back to the capital. Gandhi had his faults, but he put the emphasis on the resource that the people had: their energy. As Amartya Sen, whose early research described the potential of equity, argues in his book *Development as Freedom*, the energy of people has the potential to set them free, expanding capabilities, and giving them the way to choose how to live.

Our family went to India a century ago. John and Beth Taylor (Carl's parents) lived a traveling life through what was then jungle, as medical missionaries. In those days, the family would spend a week in one village, administering medical care, then camp was broken, oxcarts loaded, and off they would go to another cluster of villages. Six to eight weeks later, the oxcarts trundled back to the earlier villages. As the years passed, the mode of transport changed as the oxcart was discarded for Model-T Ford, then a World War II surplus Jeep, but the mode of giving services did not. As John and Beth returned to villages, they brought healing, yet the maladies they treated remained. The deeper realization began to grow that helping people does not help them change the circumstances of their lives. On contrary, it can cause people to wait in villages becoming dependent on such assistance, continuing much as they had been, and taking away their empowerment.

In 1947, John and Beth were with Gandhi following the Panipat massacre. After that terrible bloodshed, looking across the crowd in which Hindus had surrounded the Muslims, massacring the fringe and terrifying the rest, Gandhi turned to John and asked if he should start a fast. John's answer was, "They have suffered enough. Let the Muslims (and Hindus) go their separate ways." Gandhi did not go on a fast. He had already decided half a year earlier that, in the larger context of creating peace, he must let India and Pakistan, Hindus and Muslims, go their separate ways. What was instructive about this exchange for John was that he could see Gandhi searching, not to relieve the suffering in front of him (as John and Beth, the doctors, had been trying to do), but to find a way by which people who had just been killing each other would reach out to each other, strengthening their relationships in order to create a larger collective context. "We who seek justice will have to do justice for others," Gandhi had once said, recognizing that the larger context that must replace empire is one of justice.

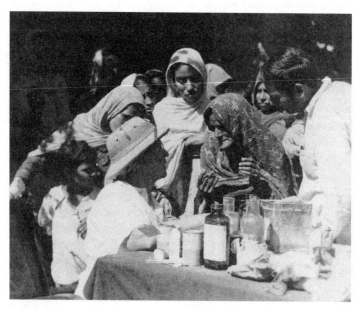

Figure 10.2. Dr. Beth Taylor caring for refugee patients during the 1947 riots that accompanied the Partition of India and Pakistan. *(Photo credit: Henry Ferger)*

Today in India, the process has advanced of engaging the marginalized. It advanced because people who were marginalized kept pushing for justice. Opportunity for all is codified in the constitution; Babasahib Ambedkar, the leader of the *dalits* during Gandhi's time, saw to that. But after the constitution was written, implementation did not follow. High castes and the wealthy remain in power, hiding behind the words, still discriminating in their actions against *dalits*, women, and those of tribal heritage. But across the half-century, using their toe-hold in the constitution and using the ethical framework Gandhi inspired that undergirds modern India, those on the margins kept confronting the new empire, in communities displaced by large dam projects, forcible slum-clearance initiatives, or the struggle for justice such as in Bhopal mentioned in Chapter One.[19] In this context, the Gandhian movement of empowerment grew. In 1992 the 73rd amendment to India's Constitution came into being: *panchayati raj* (rule by community).[20] One-third of representation in elected bodies is now guaranteed to women, low castes, and tribal peoples. Local governance can now control twenty-three different aspects of budget management. States that have sincerely implemented this amendment (for example, Andhra, Kerala, and Rajasthan) are showing progress. Getting there took four decades after Gandhi's death and the sympathy generated by the assassination of Rajiv Gandhi, Nehru's grandson, to generate the political pressure to pass the 73rd amendment, but it passed—and that pressure would not have grown if people had not kept pushing.[21]

A fact omitted in most histories of Gandhi is that after independence he did not want the Congress Party to continue as a political party. He wanted Congress to keep pushing toward *sarvodaya* (literally translates as "the rise of all," development of the whole individual as well as community), with political parties being separate. His hope was that the Congress Party would depart politics to focus on the higher goal of social mobilization, and would become a check on government and turn its advocacy for freedom from poverty, caste, ignorance, and discrimination in the new India.[22] But Nehru and the others did not go along; they argued if one party stayed in control, there would be constancy in leadership, fitting with their vision of a centrally planned modern state.

Whether or not Gandhi's solutions as he envisioned them are practical for today's world is not the point. (Indeed, some of them hardly seemed practical in his day.) We bring his mode of social change forward to show that effective solutions against empire come out of never-ending process on evolving priorities: people gathering together, fashioning lives in communities, and growing change to scale across a subcontinent. Effective process comes from using procedures as guides for what to do next. A constantly adapting plan defined by time and circumstance enabled Gandhi to stay ahead of the British, who wanted to make their engagement with him into a life-and-death confrontation, a force that he defied by advocating life for all and that there is "no wealth but life"—a philosophy drawn directly from John Ruskin.[23]

Gandhi's complex world was as entangled as any today: confrontations of Hindu and Muslim, caste and outcaste, possible seceding states like Hyderabad and Kashmir, intractable diseases whose true remedies lie not in infections cured with medicines but in social dynamics such as poverty and ignorance. In the years before August 15, 1947, *Pax Britannica* kept rioters off the streets with the threat of repressive military force. In that era, when Gandhi had needed to find the next step, he retired to his ashram. But as Partition exploded, with the spiraling rise of deaths of three million and the relocation of twenty million people underway, Gandhi had been able to mitigate the violence in Bengal, in part through his fast. His principle-based method had a problem, though. Nonviolent resistance, like violence, requires a foe. With the British quitting India, that principle became almost useless. What was there to non-violently push against? The industries of India were not the foe. Nonviolent action could not be turned against leaders who had just inspired them. As a stand-alone principle, nonviolence was incomplete; like all principles in a complex system it requires other, balancing principles so the process is continually refined so as to be always advancing.

There was potential in *sarvodaya*, but it was not brought forward. Indeed it was undermined, for in the India of 1948 already the socialist-leaning modernization policies of the Nehru government were referring to the people of India as "poor, ill, uneducated, needing services," a diminishing approach that does not build empowerment. The people of India were no longer being viewed as strong, despite the fact that they had just thrown out the greatest empire the world had then seen. Instead of building from that and coupling it to "experiments for truth" and emphasizing behavior changes (like spinning *khadi*) that could be engaged by all, India focused on building its change on scarcities and technologies. The country started down an aid-receiving path that would make the country for the next half-century the largest aid recipient in world history (combining multilateral, bilateral, and nongovernmental loans and grants). A platform that was in-place of self-reliance was ignored. Dependency was begun. India in 1948 had an alternative base; here it is stated in the context of SEED-SCALE's four principles.

- Build from success. Gandhi had built such a capacity, making sure every protest was successful, thinking through whether he had enough people to make a showing, understanding the temperament of each British commandant, and identifying the leaders possessing values that would chafe when confronted with nonviolence. Gandhi (or Nehru) could have built on that base; it would have meant an economy based on the industries of the people, not central economic planning.
- Three-way partnerships. Top-down Gandhi got a minor segment of liberal British on his side to create public pressure in Britain so strong it prevented massacres as some British wanted (as at Amritsar on April 14, 1919).

Gandhi divided the political Top-down by making allies in the progressive community influenced by Ruskin. And he engaged the Top-down of religion: Hindus through their religious texts, Christians by quoting the Beatitudes, Buddhists by emphasizing nonviolence. Outside-in, he brought in the media by giving them vivid stories to carry his actions to the world. And Bottom-up, 300 million people, the largest voluntary mobilization ever achieved. Collectively, these three forces changed relationships in a large and complex adaptive system.

- Evidence-based decisionmaking. Independence Day on August 15 was evidence of one type of freedom for all, a precursor to possible further freedoms to the Indian people. Identity could have been grounded in the nation's evident growing *gram swaraj*, not in evidence of poverty, illness, and illiteracy. The energies of one-fifth of the world's people would have then spread, pointing toward deeper freedoms that could be achieved.

- Behavior change. The most important behavior was in place: self-reliance. Across the whole subcontinent, this behavior had endured millennia of hard living and had grown new behaviors in manufacturing self-made cloth and salt that forced out the British. Gandhi had already taught them that victimization came from acquiescing behavior. Had the new leaders who had modern orientation appreciated the connection of behavior changes gone beyond Gandhi, behavior changes that created health, mobilized community-based financial growth, evolved appropriate technologies, could have catapulted the nation forward. Gandhi, captivated by idealism, did not have truly effective behavior changes, but he had presented the foundation of behavior change by all.

We need an understanding of independence that frees people to determine ways in which they want to live, finding opportunities that fit their aspirations and allow them to act. Furthermore, new networks of communication allow communities to connect with others. Around the world consciousness grows that such holistic freedom is possible.

To grow a nation, locally appropriate solutions must be always evolving. These will come not just by mobilizing the energies of people. In an interlinked socio-econo-biosphere we must also mobilize the economy. In India today, economic growth without engagement of the people, while it produces great wealth, continues to primarily benefit those who already have money and leaves 300 million in absolute poverty and creates a new empire only a level of abstraction removed from colonial empires that saw as legitimate the exploitation of Africa, Asia, and the Americas so long as wealth was growing in the home country. Where the empire Gandhi confronted legitimized racism, this new empire legitimizes poverty, perpetuating a population segment in absolute poverty of the same numerical size as it was a half century ago.

Just as America believed for two-thirds of a century that by legitimizing slavery in its constitution it could deny justice, India perpetuates the myth, also for two-thirds of a century, that it has combined Gandhian values with economic growth, a point shown when one hears of the "Gandhian solution." This cruel joke, or its parallels, is heard often when giving a bribe, for the Mahatma's image is printed on all rupee notes: "just give a few Gandhis." Those who placed Gandhi's picture on the rupee notes may have thought they were honoring the man, but they clearly had forgotten his understanding, emblazoned in a quote hanging on the wall of his simple *ashram* room: "There is no wealth but life."

Gandhi's mode of leadership stood in stark contrast to others on the world stage. He was actively working from 1893 to 1948, a time when other major world leaders included Tsar Nicholas II, Vladimir Lenin, Joseph Stalin, Theodore Roosevelt, Woodrow Wilson, Franklin Roosevelt, Kaiser Wilhelm, Adolf Hitler, Chiang Kai-Shek, Mao Zedong, Queen Victoria, and Winston Churchill. Each came to leadership with some version of the premise that the leaders held their positions by strength, and that it was through the exercise of that strength that they could be effective. What sets Gandhi apart is not simply his espousal of nonviolence, but his understanding that power lies in aggregating the individual act. The others above all mobilized their forces and sent them to war. Gandhi mobilized perhaps even more powerful forces and sent them to define a new way forward: as he so wonderfully said, "There go my followers, I'd better hurry and catch up."

What he had to catch up to was one of strongest positive feedback loops of all time. The money he used was modest and the technology minimal. (The wooden spinning wheel could easily have been made more efficient with bearings and better design, but then it could not be made in the villages.) The feedback loop gathered people from all castes, religions, and walks of life, building a tornado that spiraled across the Indian subcontinent, rising in spin-drifts of human energy from the villages. Hundreds of *satyagrahis* (those who followed Gandhi's path of nonviolence) added their energies, and soon they became tens of thousands. As the whirlwind swept from Gandhi's Sevagram *ashram* headquarters, across the Deccan plateau and the Rajasthan desert, tens of millions soon were spinning across the Punjab plains, then the Bengal delta. Against global pressures, both economic and military, seeking to break the principles and instigate even one of these groups into violence, against efforts to bribe or entice away sectors, against daily realities of poverty and starvation pressing on people to attend to immediate needs, against a host of forces of energy-dissipation, Gandhi grew the whirlwind, teaching it how to grow itself. He drew in the energy of others. He led by example.

This was a self-learning, self-assembling system, and that feature allowed it to unravel the complex systems of British politics, economics, and power. Gandhi did not have the plan at the beginning; he evolved it along the way, and the hundreds of millions who would come to participate did so along with him. Growing this force was possible because the means were the end; then through the means the end came. Could an organized command-and-control model have brought together such force? A command-control mode would have splintered, or it would have succeeded through a bloodbath.[24]

Ultimately, Gandhi lost the movement's focus. Even if he had not been assassinated, he would likely have been marginalized from the political process in a year or two, probably returning to his ashram. But, as a continuing message, the achievements of this man prove it is possible to grow a system of adaptive change using little more than the energies of people applied to grow using process.

Rima's movement of women and men on the Bameng Ridge is tiny, the example in Palin that was ten times larger, are also clusters of such energies that move toward the holistic rise of all (*sarvodaya*). People's energies and economics now work together, and while people in these examples too often act selfishly, theirs is a process of learning by people, not one of giving to them. A similar lesson comes from the rough-and-tumble settlement of Kabul; they do not know where they are going, but they are learning how as they go. The same is true for the communities at the base of Mount Everest, and they do so within the confines of Communist Party rule. Collectively, what the examples in this book present is an opportunity for all to join. The political framework is not what is important, nor the starting levels of poverty or strife. The question that starts the process is whether we are going to be controlled by empire or whether we are going to mobilize to meet the challenges of our unstable planet.

It is not really a choice. The feedback loop of growing human energies must integrate with the feedback loop of economic growth that has dominated development thinking for so long. The latter we cannot (and do not want to) wish away with, but we must recognize that economic growth is an approximation of the real dynamics underway, rather than an end it itself The graphic below (Figure 10.3) points to the balances needed: accelerating technologies with traditional skills; local resources with donor resources; indigenous knowledge with new knowledge in the Information Age; and old social norms with the new policy, values, and globalization environment. A constructive dialectic among these nurtures the balance and grows *gram swaraj*, or community empowerment.

"Empire" and "Empowerment" are not either/or states to choose between. It is more accurate to present them as ends along a continuum, where a variety of dynamics tug and pull communities toward these ends. The concern should not be location on the continuum but where the whole continuum is going: toward empire or toward empowerment. In this tug and pull, as local control, response sophistication, locale sensitivity, and people's participation increase, the energy within the system, empowerment, rises. Higher empowerment has

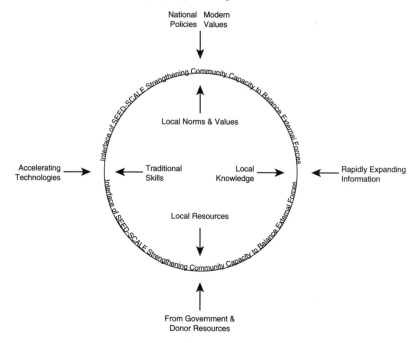

Figure 10.3. External and internal forces.

higher human energy. For empowerment to rise, each new achievement is assessed in relation to past performance and collective experience, there by feeding the feedback loop. Communities set the standards for themselves. The process being measured differs from those in an empire, where human energy is constrained because the measures of change are of products that by their nature are available to only a few. When measures of change are exclusionary, the society takes on those characteristics as well. The following pairings (Figure 10.4) outline the tug and pull:

A spinning wheel going around suggests same-cycle repetition, but in fact the wheel pulls out a constantly changing cluster of strands, ordering what had been a confused clump. Each handful straightens a complex tangle; as fingers feed in fibers in the circling process, and from that adapting of earlier confusion grows a thread entwined with other that forms the clothes of life. The iterative process does not repeat but reshapes new life off the wheel of change. In his teaching at evening prayers, Gandhi was explicit in saying how learning to spin was at first clumsy, but with iteration upon iteration, the threads would grow long and strong.

It is important to realize that the continuum for one society does not transfer to others. Societies are not ahead or behind one another, for they do not

Empire		Empowerment
less community control	⟷	more community control
less sophisticated response	⟷	more sophisticated response
less sensitivity to situation	⟷	more sensitivity to situation
less local participation	⟷	greater local participation

Figure 10.4. Empowerment and Empire.

develop along a single line called "development." Each society moves on its own continuing line, having achieved its place at any particular time by doing the best it could, sometimes against nearly insurmountable obstacles. Through the particularities of each of our lives, as Gandhi said when explaining how the way forward was found, perhaps remembering an African proverb he may have heard decades before, "We make our path by walking it."[25]

How to walk forward together? (The White Mountain Apache, when we were teaching them SEED-SCALE, translated the idea "as our community walking forward together.") No community is "developed," all are developing; and the cohesion comes through walking forward together on separate journeys along mutually supportive paths running in myriad directions. It is here that the arrow of time in not allowing movement backward, moves us always forward, but are we going forward with constantly improving process? Effective, progress is evaluated against itself, then movement retargeted. As aspirations evolve, so must actions. This adaptation, as it builds capacity within local context, is what drives that community's direction from the "empire" side of control to empowered local energies.

Einstein's equation $E = MC^2$ offers an apt means to describe the powerful growth of these energies: human energy equals what matters taken to an exponential scale. While the socio-econo-biosphere may be complicated, what matters is not complicated: to people it is whether their lives are getting better, and that matters a lot. Massive energy can be generated when people produce a little that matters to them. Other people then rush to join in. It is the direction unfolding that matters, and whether that matters to the larger whole. When people see direction as going their way, they press on. The communities in Arunachal Pradesh, Afghanistan, Tibet/China, and New York City, are each in very different conditions, but all are gathering their energies, investing what they possess. What they share is that process.

To guide action into the future, it is useful to return to an injunction from Gandhi, *lokniti*, "people-centered polity." (*Lok* means "people," *niti* means "ethics/policy guideline.") *Lokniti* offered participatory governance based on ethics. The Outside-in and Top-down were partners to serve the people. While Gandhi's insight on this was great, his specifics were impractical. *Khadi* cloth is comfortable in the hot Indian climate, but it is not particularly durable. His health ideas, grounded in philosophical traditions rather than science, were not a reliable way to wellness. Nonetheless, despite a near absence of utility, *lokniti* and *satyagraha* ("truth force") brought control into people's hands, and that is the starting point. A spinning wheel, the great Salt March to the Sea, people sitting down before the police: collectively these actions grounded in ethics changed their conditions of their lives.

In *lokniti* applied at national scale, the answer is not deregulation. Going local does not mean letting go, in the manner of Ronald Reagan or Margaret Thatcher, by taking away the appropriate role for the Top-down in creating an enabling environment and structures to protect equity. Government regulations are one of the comparatively few ways the will of the people can challenge empire that without such checking will happily run roughshod over communities. The great insight of Gandhi (and of Deng Xiaoping, as described in the previous chapter with promoting local economic experimentation in the special zones) was to move the locus of action to the people, allowing them to grow solutions that take advantage of their specific position within the constantly changing socio-econo-biosphere. Moving the focus to process rather than politics will be hard for many to absorb, but actually this recognition opens a wonderful range of opportunities in a world of rising dogma.

We live now on an interconnected planet where every community connects to global systems. As communities use the potential to learn from one another, capacity and options advance; the learning occurs through feedback loops. This is a larger frame of the community growth process of increasing returns described by economist Brian Arthur, drawing on complexity theory.[26] Positive feedback loops are like investing money and getting interest that continues to compound. Moreover, since nested beside and inside one process are multiple feedback loops, returns not only come to the individual worker but accrue to all.

As the spinning wheel is emblematic of Gandhi's process, so the computer might be for today's social change. But unlike the spinning wheel that served as a symbol for simple village life, the modern machine reflects the multitasking complex modern world. Before computers, machines worked separately: the adding machine, typewriter, slide projector, mailbox, appointment book, clock, and reference library. But when a shared operating system was provided, one machine could engage many functions simultaneously, and each in much more complex ways: spreadsheet analysis, word processing, PowerPoint, email, scheduling, and information access through search engines. Furthermore, a multitasking machine enabled the great, interconnected hive-mind that is the Internet. Through this metaphor we can conceive the needed simultaneous multiple functions at community level. Where before it was believed that community processes had to be separated (health, education, income generation, food production, and security through separated services), using an integrated system that works upwards from the bottom (as the examples in this book indicate), communities can gather all functions into synergy and more effectively engage the Top-down services. This is not a revolution of the community taking over, but growing of partnership through engaging the base of community resources. The currency used in this social operating system is human energy, and directing output is the workplan. And if workplans are written with open code, others can rewrite them to fit their needs. Additionally, as with cloud computing where the operating system moves outside the machine to a shared but nebulous global service even greater integration becomes possible while retaining local specificity and keeping effective interdependent globalization.

Similarly, Gandhi's understanding of spectacle and the power of communication networks is relevant for the new era. As the revolutions of the "Arab Spring" showed, new technologies provide a way for communities to coalesce in cyberspace only to burst forth with material force into the streets as images are uploaded to distribute evidence of action or atrocities. Pacé Naomi Klein, logos and brands are not merely tools of corporate power but also avenues for resistance because a brand is something that a company must defend, and thus becomes something to which they may be held accountable.[27] Greenwashing (and related issues pertaining to social justice) is a genuine problem, but it is also evidence of companies' need to protect their public image. Just as Gandhi appealed to the eyes of the world to witness *lathis* (sticks) bloodying bodies in white *khadi*, today's communities can appeal to a global gaze starting through billions of screens to assert their presence on the world stage.

In today's age of information overload, pummeling people with falsehoods, facts, and trivia, experiments with truth are perhaps even more needed than in Gandhi's time. Equally essential is to recognize that there are different truths and they must live together. Truth, as used by Gandhi in his iterative experimental searching, was not usually black or white, truth or falsehood, but a process to work out nuance amid the flood of facts. In this quest for discernment, a distinguishing line needs to be drawn between zeal and the mobilization achieved by empowerment. Zeal zeros in from fundamentalisms to exclusiveness. Empowerment opens up space to engage the energies of all.

In such searching, insights from Gandhi's lifetime of prayer, fasting, jail sentences, speeches, unending spinning, and odd dietary practices do not represent the logical method. But at the center of this process, amid swirls of compromise and expediency, was his compulsion to avoid violence. Nonviolence could easily be misunderstood as passive, but it was anything but inaction. However within his use of nonviolence can be seen an important behavioral feature often overlooked: the imperative of listening (whereas in violence it is hard to listen). There was something about the openness created by his espousal of nonviolence that led people to talk to Gandhi: British colonials, rajas, tycoons, reporters, and most important, the destitute. In listening to their confusion he gave back principles, with the result that relationships were strengthened. Nonviolence, while zealous in its application also created openness to the positions of others.

Many people have tried to return to Gandhi's vision of nonviolence. This great man used that tool and achieved a success from it that is so captivating it is easy to become focused on him and the tool and to miss the meaning of the process he was walking toward. He was a *Mahatma* (great soul), but, like every human who lacks infallible divine insight, what he saw (and what we all must learn) is the preeminence of process: learning from experimenting with truth. The integrity of experimenting with truth is today particularly valid, and we now know more clearly how to engage that. It allows us to constantly update process to the new age, the resulting evidence (not the past) becomes determinative; it portrays what is true in what context, a dynamic of balance, where when one principle acts, others are also acting, correcting potential errors produced by the first.

Human Energy: The Currency of Change

⇒ The Resource that Everyone Has
⇒ The More Used, the More It Grows
⇒ Can be Passed Community to Community
⇒ As Energies Aggregate, Synergy Grows Among Them
⇒ More Just and Lasting Change is Possible

Figure 10.5. Our unstable planet, and the resource everyone has.

In that journey, Gandhi brought one further important trait: perseverance. Going forward together, experimenting, learning how to learn in complex systems, we gather further understanding about process. The knowledge we have now of the process is more than enough to work with, a process vastly more sophisticated than what Gandhi brought from South Africa that set one-fifth of humanity free. It worked then at a moment of history when humanity waited on the cusp of economic growth. Process is what social development is, and it allows seeds of human energy to achieve global change. The process of people getting to work toward all their aspirations creates the wealth of life. It is time to gather our energies collectively and get to work. Here again comes that phrase of Bapu's:[28] "There go my followers. I'd better hurry and catch up."

NOTES

INTRODUCTION: A PROCESS FOR CHANGE AVAILABLE TO ALL

1. John Ruskin, *Unto This Last and Other Writings* (New York: Penguin, 1997), 222.
2. As will be developed later in the book, advancing only a part of society in an age of globalization, even if it is the vast majority, increases the burden on the advancing sector, with potential pandemics, civil strife, and population migration that threaten all. Societies that are equitable have numerous social benefits (lower crime, better health, happier populations): Richard Wilkinson and Kate Pickett, *The Spirit Level: Why Greater Equality Makes Societies Stronger* (New York: Bloomsbury Press, 2009).
3. Many superb books and websites are published on the coming global challenges (and also many inflammatory and poorly supported ones). A troublingly characteristic of almost all of these macro engagements is that they call for unlikely macro action. The well-meaning United Nations publications offer an example, consistently framing the questions as though global interventions are the only answer. While it, too, suffers from this tendency, some of the best analysis is found in Tim Jackson's *Prosperity Without Growth: Economics for a Finite Planet* (London: Earthscan, 2009). The need is for practical action that people can take today with what they have. An example with a solution arising from individual actions is McKibben's *Deep Economy*.
4. William Easterly, *The White Man's Burden: Why the West's Efforts to Aid the Rest Have Done So Much Ill and So Little Good* (New York: Penguin, 2007).
5. Population figures used are based on the United Nations Population Division's; estimates used here are for 2011. See http://www.un.org/popin/wdtrends.htm.
6. "Absolute poverty," "the poverty trap," and "the unreached," are varying ways of characterizing this group. How many are involved (from one billion to three) depends on where defining lines are drawn. For the purposes of this book, the line used is the $2 per day per person subsistence figure. United Nations estimates in 2011 were that 2.3 billion people live at this level out of a world population of seven billion. The World Bank standard measure of poverty is based on income alone, defining anyone who earns less than $1.25 per day to be "poor" (making 1.44 billion poor). However, the UNDP and Oxford University in July 2010 advanced a multi-factor index that defines poverty by considering living standards, child mortality, years of schooling, and access to drinking water—the Multidimensional Poverty Index that estimates 1.71 billion as poor. Issues of measurement are important, for they give the targets toward which

action is directed. All such numbers are estimates, there is no uniformity in various countries' census methods.

7. As a sustainable solution the path of economic growth carries a conundrum that even its celebrants have been forced to acknowledge: to date, no country has been able to grow its economy without a corresponding rise in carbon emissions. See Benjamin Friedman's *The Moral Consequences of Economic Growth* (New York: Alfred A. Knopf, 2005) and the critique mounted in Bill McKibben's *Deep Economy: The Wealth of Communities and the Durable Future* (New York: Henry Holt, 2007).

8. Michel Serres, *The Natural Contract*, translated by Elizabeth MacArthur and William Paulson (Ann Arbor: University of Michigan Press, 1995), 43.

9. The idea that Britain, as the first country to industrialize, serves as a paradigm for the spread of industrial modernity around the globe is an historically problematic one and has been the subject of much debate, given that industrialization in other countries did not (and does not) *replicate* the British model. Furthermore, recent scholarship on the industrial revolution in Britain has emphasized the extent to which it was dependent on global dynamics rather than emerging in isolation. See, for instance, Robert C. Allen, *The British Industrial Revolution in Global Perspective* (Cambridge, U.K.: Cambridge University Press, 2009); Joseph E. Inikori, *Africa and the Industrial Revolution in England: A Study in International Trade* (Cambridge, U.K.: Cambridge University Press, 2002). For discussion of Britain as "paradigm" for global development, see Raymond Williams, *The Country and the City* (Oxford, U.K.: Oxford University Press, 1973), and the critique in Jed Esty's *A Shrinking Island: Modernism and National Culture in England* (Princeton, N.J.: Princeton University Press, 2004), 192–195.

10. John Ruskin, *Unto This Last and Other Writings* (New York: Penguin, 1997), 168.

11. Ruskin, *Unto This Last*, 180.

12. Amartya Sen, *Development as Freedom* (Oxford, U.K.: Oxford University Press, 1999).

13. Stephen Marglin, *The Dismal Science: How Thinking Like an Economist Undermines Community* (Cambridge, Mass.: Harvard University Press, 2008), 3.

14. Also drawing on Ruskin, Herbert Reid and Betsy Taylor have recently shown how this collective sensibility concerned with the idea of the commons (as opposed to the individual celebrated within liberalism) is in fact fundamental to the emergence of democracy, from the Magna Carta to the contemporary global justice movement. See Reid and Taylor's *Recovering the Commons: Democracy, Place, and Global Justice* (Urbana and Chicago: University of Illinois Press, 2010).

15. It is hardly surprising, in this respect, that Benedict Anderson would describe nations as "imagined communities." *Imagined Communities: Reflections on the Origins and Spread of Nationalism* (New York: Verso, 1991).

16. Paul Collier, *The Bottom Billion: Why the Poorest Countries Are Failing and What Can Be Done About It* (Oxford, U.K.: Oxford University Press, 2007).

17. See Walter Rodney's influential *How Europe Underdeveloped Africa*, rev. ed. (Washington, D.C.: Howard University Press, 1981); also Stephen G. Bunker, *Underdeveloping the Amazon: Extraction, Unequal Exchange, and the Failure of the Modern State* (Chicago: University of Chicago Press, 1990).

18. Daniel Taylor-Ide and Carl E. Taylor, *Community-Based Sustainable Human Development—Going to Scale with Self-Reliant Social Development* (New York: UNICEF, 1995); Carl E. Taylor, Aditi Desai, and Daniel Taylor-Ide, *Partnership for Social Development—A Casebook*, The Independent Task Force on Community

Action for Social Development (Franklin, W.V.: Future Generations, and Johns Hopkins University, Department of International Health, 1995).

19. Daniel Taylor-Ide and Carl E. Taylor, *Just and Lasting Change: When Communities Own Their Futures* (Baltimore, MD.: Johns Hopkins University Press, 2002).

CHAPTER 1. WHAT WE CAN DO WITH WHAT WE HAVE, HERE, TODAY

1. Indra Sinha, *Animal's People* (London and New York: Simon and Schuster, 2007), 106.

2. The evidence reported in this chapter is drawn from fieldwork in January 2007 that compiled the Bameng Valley experience from 1999 to 2007, and has been supplemented by subsequent reports filed by Dr. Tage Kanno, executive director, Future Generations Arunachal, submitted in 2009.

3. We are aware that sample sizes are too small to create reliable mortality statistics and that such self-reporting holds bias, but what is underway here is *local evidence-gathering*. This is a departure from the traditional basis of decision making: storytelling. Rima set in place a feedback loop: one of information guiding actions, monitoring progress. This created community confidence to keep pressing forward.

4. One principle of the SEED-SCALE approach is "evidence-based decision making." For that, what is important is on-time evidence to guide decisions as they are being discussed, not coming at the end. To guide such discussions, "quick and clean"—in contrast with "quick and dirty"—information gathering is useful, an emphasis Robert Chambers terms "appropriate imprecision" (see *Whose Reality Counts? Putting the Last First* [London: Intermediate Technology Development Group Publishing, 2000], 157 and elsewhere). Rima had actual evidence by the end of her first day, not just impressions gathered as she climbed the hill. These were not statistically significant, but they were numbers based on an assessment of reality. They showed that children were more likely to die than live—and that provided a base on which to build action. See Chapter 7 for more on the process of self-evaluation.

5. John Holland, *Emergence: From Chaos to Order* (New York: Basic Books, 1998), 7, 225-226.

6. John H. Holland, *Emergence: From Chaos to Order* (New York: Basic Books, 1998), 225–226.

7. See Claude Lévi-Strauss *The Savage Mind* (Chicago: University of Chicago Press, 1966). For discussion of *bricolage* in the context of modernist aesthetics see Frano Moretti *Modern Epic: The World-System from Goethe to Garcia Marquez* translated by Quintin Hoare (London & New York: Verso, 1996).

8. United Nations Habitat, *State of the World's Cities 2006/7: The Millennium Development Goals and Urban Sustainability* (London: Earthscan, 2006), 16.

9. This is the argument mounted by Jane Jacobs in her classic *Death and Life of Great American Cities*, in which she challenged the slum-clearing projects popular in urban planning of the mid–twentieth century. Jacobs argued that slums had valuable "social capital" to build from, and that was obliterated when the slums were demolished (New York: Vintage, 1961), 138.

10. See Mike Davis, *Planet of Slums* (London and New York: Verso, 2006). Davis emphasizes the dire conditions in slums and argues against the notions that people there can simply "pull themselves up by their bootstraps." It is not our contention that the suffering of slum life should be ignored or minimized in any way; rather, we emphasize the remarkable testament of the power of

human energy and the will to live that those in such marginalized conditions exhibit. It is worth noting in this context that Davis suggests the outcast slum residents have "the gods of chaos on their side" (206). In keeping with the broader argument of this book, such a phrase might be revisited within the rubric of emergence, as the means by which sophisticated order arises out of the complexity of apparent chaos.

11. Sinha, *Animal's People*, 106.

12. Similar "local currencies" have been introduced in other communities around the world with considerable success. See Michael Shuman's *Going Local: Creating Self-Reliant Communities in a Global Age* (New York: Free Press, 1998), esp. 191–192.

13. Rogerio Arns Neumann, Alison Mathie, and Joanne Linsey, "God Created the World and We Created Conjunto Palmeira: Four Decades of Forging Community and Building a Local Economy in Brazil," in Alison Mathie and Gordon Cunningham, editors, *From Clients to Citizens: Communities Changing the Course of Their Own Development* (Warwickshire, U.K.: Intermediate Technology Publications, 2008), 39–62.

14. In Chapter 6 we offer an example of SEED-SCALE put to use by a struggling urban community of 85,000 in Afghanistan.

15. Harlan Cleveland and Garry Jacobs, "Human Choice: The Genetic Code for Social Development," *Futures*, 39, no. 9 (November 1999), 959–970. It should be noted that the useful idea here lies in taking "genetic code" metaphorically, in the sense that effective development might be encoded in social practices, not in the literal sense of a genetic code "hardwiring" development into certain populations.

16. Robert Laughlin, *A Different Universe: Reinventing Physics from the Bottom Down* (New York: Basic Books, 2005).

17. Planning, followed by the subsequent attempt to force the reality's complexities to conform to the simplifications of the plan, is at the heart of the "high-modernist ideology" that James C. Scott blames for why attempts to improve the human condition often end in authoritarian repression. Scott, *Seeing Like a State* (New Haven: Yale University Press, 1998).

18. John H. Holland, *Hidden Order: How Adaptation Builds Complexity* (New York: Basic Books, 1996), 4–6.

19. See Jacobs's *The Death and Life of Great American Cities*, and Steven Johnson, *Emergence: The Connected Lives of Ants, Brains, Cities and Software* (New York: Simon and Schuster, 2002).

20. Benoit B. Mandelbrot, *The Fractal Geometry of Nature* (New York: W.H. Freeman, 1992), 133.

21. Yaneer Bar Yam, *Making Things Work: Solving Complex Problems in a Complex World* (Brookline, Mass.: Knowledge Press, 2005).

22. Peter A. Corning, "The Re-Emergence of Emergence: A Venerable Concept in Search of a Theory," *Complexity*, 7, no. 6 (2002), 18–30.

23. Holland, *Hidden Order*, 5–10.

24. Yaneer Bar Yam, *Making Things Work*, esp. 119–216.

25. M. Mitchell Waldrop, *Complexity: The Emerging Science at the Edge of Order and Chaos* (New York: Touchstone/Simon and Schuster, 1992), 145–198.

26. In this book we will regularly create a distinction between complex adaptive systems and the command line of control systems; we do so for clarity knowing we overstate what is more a duality than a polarity. For example, even the military operates through command-and-control systems only

up to a point. When command-control is not possible, the military has complex adaptive system decision rules for troops on the ground to cope with the chaos. This book draws distinctions more sharply than perhaps real—for there are very real differences—because we are trying to be clear about the choices.

27. David Ekbladh, *The Great American Mission: Modernization and the Construction of an American World Order* (Princeton and Oxford: Princeton University Press, 2010), 3–4.

28. David C. Korten, *The Great Turning: From Empire to Earth Community* (San Francisco: Berritt-Koehler and Kumarian Press, 2006), 10.

29. The exception is a probing review done by Ben Ramalingam and Harry Jones, with Toussaint Reba and John Young, *Exploring the Science of Complexity: Ideas and Implications for Development and Humanitarian Efforts* (London: Overseas Development Institute, October 2008).

30. There is a strong correlation here with Arjun Appadurai's idea of the "capacity to aspire"—the means not only to hope for the future, but to imagine the means of realizing that hope. Poverty, in Appadurai's account, entails an existence not only diminished of material means, but also such aspiration. Getting beyond such a cycle of impoverishment becomes both the means and the goal of effective development: "...in strengthening the capacity to aspire, conceived as a cultural capacity, especially among the poor, the future-oriented logic of development could find a natural ally, and the poor could find the resources required to contest and alter the conditions of their own poverty" (59). Among other things, this idea fits with the idea expounded throughout this book of culture as the means to adapt to the future, rather than simply an artifact of the pre-modern past. Arjun Appardurai, "The Capacity to Aspire: Culture and the Terms of Recognition" in Vijayendra Rao and Michael Walton, editors. *Culture and Public Action* (Stanford, CA: Stanford University Press, 2004), 59-84.

31. Donella H. Meadows, Dennis L. Meadows, and Jorgen Randers, *The Limits to Growth: The 30-Year Update* (White River Junction, Vt.: Chelsea Green Books, 2004).

CHAPTER 2. CONNECTING TO THE LARGER FIELD OF DEVELOPMENT & SOCIAL CHANGE

1. John Maynard Keynes, *The Collected Writings of John Maynard Keynes, Volume 9* (London: St. Martin's Press, 1972), xviii.

2. See the UN Millennium Project, available at http://www.unmillenniumproject. org/documents/overviewEngi-1LowRes.pdf, Overview, page xvii.

3. See the UN Millennium Development Goals at http://www.un.org/ millenniumgoals/pdf/MDG%20Report%202009%20ENG.pdf, p. 4. The one major country consistently ahead in reaching its MDGs is China, and the magnitude of its progress with one-fifth of the world's people is having a beneficial impact on global totals. The reason for China's progress is worth noting: the country is focusing not on specific targets, but on overall national growth, getting the complex adaptive systems of China working so quality-of-life improvements reach across the population. And this national growth, calibrated as it is now in economic terms, was made possible because prior to its takeoff in the 1980s there were decades of much social action in health and education that transformed the human capital (albeit with the major social trauma of the Cultural Revolution in the middle). Dani Rodrik

argues that countries (such as China) that learn from what is working in their situation, and then adapt and extend that, do better; moreover, he argues that the countries that follow UN, IMF, or WB prescriptions in fact do worse. In *One Economics, Many Recipes: Globalization, Institutions, and Economic Growth* (Princeton, N.J.: Princeton University Press, 2007).

4. Paul Collier, *The Bottom Billion*, 189–192.

5. Millennium Development Goals, at http://www.un.org/millenniumgoals/pdf/ MDG%20Report%202009%20ENG.pdf, p. 3.

6. People at the implementation level are able to give major insights. An example is from the search for a cure to the number-two killer of children worldwide, childhood pneumonia. Differential diagnosis from a simple childhood cold to pneumonia used to require chest X-rays or at least a doctor with a stethoscope. But following insights from mothers who said "watch the baby's breath," an accurate diagnostic method evolved of counting the rate of respirations and comparing that to the age of the child. A partnership between people and practitioners is arguably the world's strongest research team for social change. See Taylor-Ide and Taylor, *Just and Lasting Change*, 126–143.

7. Personal communication to Daniel Taylor, Geneva, July 2009.

8. The "Shirky Principle" after Clay Shirky, instructor of new media at New York University: "Institutions will try to preserve the problem to which they are the solution." Though it may sound cynical, the history of international development is an apt illustration of the point. It is worth emphasizing, though, the institutional facet.

9. Easterly, *The White Man's Burden* (quotation made in dozens of places throughout the book).

10. The Millennium Villages on the surface appear to be parallel to SCALE Squared Centers promoted by SEED-SCALE. There is a key difference, however. Millennium Villages are bringing in ideas from the outside and are funded by the outside; as a result they are hard to sustain and hard to scale up without continuing outside support. SCALE Squared Centers are places where external help has identified local experiences that are working (in much the same manner that Positive Deviance projects also operate) and these local successes are advanced as places for regional learning, with primarily external support only being given to the educational role they are performing.

11. Sachs made many efforts to address poverty through macroeconomic analysis, with a particular focus on South Africa, the fracturing parts of the Soviet Union, and Bolivia. His approach is summarized in Warwick J. McKibben and Jeffrey D. Sachs, *Global Linkages, Macroeconomic Interdependence and Cooperation in the World Economy* (Washington, D.C.: Brookings Institution, 1991).

12. Jeffrey D. Sachs, *The End of Poverty, Economic Possibilities for Our Time* (New York: Penguin, 2005).

13. Scott, *Seeing Like a State*, 4.

14. Even in the sterilized world of the laboratory, the realities of research are often much messier than the standard accounts of such inquiries will let on, as the work of Bruno Latour and others has illustrated. See *Science in Action: How to Follow Scientists and Engineers Through Society* (Cambridge, Mass.: Harvard University Press, 1988). As will be discussed further, in Chapter 7, Latour's work is often mischaracterized as an argument against scientific truth, but the real insight of his work is that it does *not* throw out the "reality" of science, but rather gives us an under-the-hood glimpse of how science produces facts.

Latour takes up the "reality" argument in *Pandora's Hope: Essays on the Reality of Science Studies* (Cambridge, Mass.: Harvard University Press, 1999).

15. Sachs, *Commonwealth*, 295–296.
16. Easterly, *The White Man's Burden*.
17. Dambisa Moyo, *Dead Aid: Why Aid Is Not Working and How There Is a Better Way for Africa* (New York: Farrar, Straus & Giroux, 2009).
18. Rodrik, *One Economics, Many Recipes*.
19. Gregory Clark, *A Farewell to Alms: A Brief Economic History of the World* (Princeton, N.J.: Princeton University Press, 2007). Clark's argument also shares with ours the sense that social change is comprised of individual behaviors. However, we do not share his idea that these behaviors may in fact be biologically inherited (which he raises as a possibility rather than a fact), rather than simply learned. However, it is not necessary to go along with this element of his argument to accept the insight that certain patterns of individual behavior are key to massive historical shifts such as those witnessed in Britain during the Industrial Revolution.
20. Thomas W. Dichter, *Despite Good Intentions: Why Development Assistance to the Third World Has Failed* (Amherst: University of Massachusetts Press, 2003). Paul Polak, *Out of Poverty: What Works When Traditional Approaches Fail* (San Francisco: Berrett-Koehler Publishers, 2008).
21. John Perkins, *Confessions of an Economic Hit Man* (San Francisco: Berrett-Koehler Publishers, 2004).
22. Majid Rahema and Victoria Bawtree, editors, *The Post-Development Reader* (London: Zed Books, 1998), 381.
23. Collier, *The Bottom Billion*, xi.
24. W. W. Rostow, *The Stages of Economic Growth: A Non-Communist Manifesto* (Cambridge, U.K.: Cambridge University Press, 1960).
25. W. Arthur Lewis, *The Theory of Economic Growth* (London: Taylor and Francis, 2003).
26. Theodore W. Shultz, *Investing in People* (Berkeley: University of California Press, 1981).
27. Francis Fukuyama, *The End of History and the Last Man* (New York: Free Press, 1992).
28. The World Bank, *Economic Growth in the 1990s: Learning from a Decade of Reform* (Washington: World Bank, 2005), xiii.
29. Amartya Sen, *Development as Freedom*, and *Resources, Values, and Development* (Oxford, U.K.: Basil Blackwell, 1984).
30. Friedman, *The Moral Consequences of Economic Growth*.
31. Vijayendra Rao and Michael Walton, editors, *Culture and Public Action* (Stanford, Calif.: Stanford University Press, 2004), 4.
32. World Commission on Environment and Development, *Our Common Future* (Oxford, U.K.: Oxford University Press, 1987), 1, 43.
33. Bill McKibben, *The End of Nature*, 2nd ed. (New York: Anchor Books, 1999). Intergovernmental Panel on Climate Change, *Climate Change 2007* (New York: United Nations, 2007) available at http://www.ipcc.ch/publications_and_data/publications_and_data_reports.htm#1.
34. Report of the South Commission, *The Challenge to the South* (New York: Oxford University Press, 1999).
35. Paulo Freire, *Pedagogy of the Oppressed* (New York: Continuum, 2007), 14.
36. Personal communication to Daniel Taylor, Harvard University, winter of 1969.

37. Peter Evans, *Embedded Autonomy: States and Industrial Transformation* (Princeton, N.J.: Princeton University Press, 1995); Fernando Henrique Cardoso, *Charting a New Course: The Politics of Globalization and Social Transformation*, edited and introduced by Mauricio A. Font (Lanham, Md.: Rowman & Littlefield Publishers, 2001); Rothko Chapel Colloquium, *Toward a New Strategy for Development* (New York: Pergamon Press, 1979).

38. Ruth Alsop, Mette Bertlesen, and Jeremy Holland, *Empowerment in Practice: From Analysis to Implementation* (Washington, D.C.: The World Bank, 2006). Deepa Narayan, editor, *Empowerment and Poverty Reduction: A Sourcebook* (Washington, D.C.: The World Bank, 2002).

39. Deepa Narayan and Patti Petesch, editors, *Moving Out of Poverty: Cross-Disciplinary Perspectives on Mobility* (Washington, D.C.; Houndsmills, England: The World Bank and Palgrave/Macmillan, 2007).

40. Moses Coady, *Masters of Their Own Destiny* (New York: Harper & Row, 1939), 163.

41. Robert Fisher, *Let the People Decide: Neighborhood Organizing in America* (New York: Twayne Publishers, 1994).

42. D. H. Bates, *Lincoln in the Telegraph Office* (New York: Century, 1907).

43. Taylor-Ide and Taylor, *Just and Lasting Change*, 24–26.

44. Yangchu C. James Yen, *Y. C. James Yen's Thoughts on Mass Education and Rural Reconstruction—China and Beyond*, Martha M. Keehn, editor (New York: International Institute of Rural Reconstruction, 1993), i.

45. Robert Chambers, *Whose Reality Counts?* xvii.

46. The formal processes of community participation found early articulation in 1968 in Rothman's remarkably complete *Strategies of Community Intervention*, outlining the interplay of locality-based development, social action, and planning with policy engagement, with a splendid menu of options; Jack Rothman, John L. Erlich, and John E. Tropman, *Strategies of Community Intervention*, 7th ed. (Peosta, Iowa: Eddie Bowers Publishing, 2008); For more recent overviews, see Somesh Kumar, *Methods for Community Participation: A Complete Guide for Practitioners* (Warwickshire, England: Intermediate Technology Publications, 2008); and Lyra Srinivasan, *Tools for Community Participation: A Manual for Training Trainers in Participatory Techniques* (New York: PROWESS/UNDP, 1990).

47. Gary Paul Green and Anna Haines, *Asset Building and Community Development*, 2nd ed. (Thousand Oaks, Calif.: Sage Publications, 2008).

48. John P. Kretzman and John L. McKnight, *Building Communities From the Inside Out: A Path Toward Finding and Mobilizing a Community's Assets* (Skokie, Ill.: ACTA Publications, 1993); Alison Mathie and Gordon Cunningham, *From Clients to Citizens: Communities Changing the Course of Their Own Development* (Warwickshire, England: Intermediate Technology Publications, 2008).

49. Richard Pascale, Jerry Sternin, and Monique Sternin, *The Power of Positive Deviance: How Unlikely Innovators Solve the World's Toughest Problems* (Boston, Mass.: Harvard Business Press, 2010). See also Thomas Bertels and Jerry Sternin, "Replicating Results and Managing Knowledge," in Rath and Strong's *Six Sigma Leadership Handbook* (Hoboken, N.J.: John Wiley & Sons, 2003), 450–458.

50. The World Bank, *World Development Report 2000–2001* (Washington, D.C.: World Bank Publications, 2001).

51. Narayan, *Empowerment and Poverty Reduction*, xvii. A number of excellent publications have been produced on empowerment; as an overview of the field

bringing together especially the work of a wide variety of scholars, we recommend Cecilia Luttrell and Sitna Quiroz, *Understanding and Operationalizing Empowerment*, Swiss Agency for Development and Cooperation, 17 July 2007; available from www.poverty-wellbeing.net. See also Ruth Alsop, Mette Bertlesen, and Jeremy Holland, *Empowerment in Practice: From Analysis to Implementation* (Washington, D.C.: The World Bank, 2006); and Deborah Eade, *Capacity Building: An Approach to People-Centered Development* (Oxford: Oxfam UK, 1997).

52. Narayan, *Empowerment and Poverty Reduction*, xix, xx.

53. Deepa Narayan, editor, *Measuring Empowerment: Cross-Disciplinary Perspectives* (Oxford, U.K.: Oxford University Press, 2005).

54. Ruth Alsop and Nina Henderson, *Measuring Empowerment in Practice: Structuring Analysis and Framing Indicators*, World Bank Policy Working Paper 3510 (Washington, D.C.: World Bank, 2005). Alsop, Bertlesen, and Holland, *Empowerment in Practice*.

55. Barbara Ward, *The Lopsided World* (New York: W.W. Norton, 1968).

56. Robert Chambers, "Participatory Rural Appraisal (PRA): Challenges, Potentials and Paradigm," *World Development*, 22, no. 10 (1994), 1437–1454.

57. Paul Hawken, *The Blessed Unrest: How the Largest Social Movement in the History Is Restoring Grace, Justice, and Beauty to the World* (New York: Penguin Books, 2008), 2.

CHAPTER 3. IF TRADITIONAL DEVELOPMENT PRACTICES WERE EFFECTIVE

1. Report to His Majesty King Birendra Bir Bikram Shah Dev, presented by Daniel Taylor, following the fifty-year follow-up survey on health conditions, repeating a south–north transect of the country and health survey conducted in 1949. Kathmandu, Nepal: The Royal Palace, May 2000.

2. John Friedman, *Empowerment: The Politics of Alternative Development* (Oxford, U.K.: Blackwell, 1992).

3. Central Bureau of Statistics, *Nepal Statistical Pocket Book* (Kathmandu: Government of Nepal, 2002).

4. The U.S. government had a remarkable and lavish source of funding for India and Nepal from the late 1950s through the 1970s with the rupee-based payments for purchasing American wheat. Disbursement of these funds was directly under the control of the AID mission director, mostly unshackled from Washington politics, and generous in its support for agriculture, education, family planning, malaria eradication, communications infrastructure, and similar projects. These were often nicely coordinated with Peace Corps volunteers for local technical support.

5. Carl E. Taylor, "Medical Survey of the Kali Gandaki Valley," *The American Geographical Review* (American Geographical Society, 1953). This 1949 expedition, whose focus combined both ornithological and health surveys, was the first visit by non-Nepalis through the now often-traveled Kali Gandaki Valley. The expedition walked across the breadth of Nepal, from India to Tibet, from what were then pristine jungles to 18,000 feet in the Himalayas, being the first group to visit and make scientific observations of places like Pokhara, Tansen, Baglung, and Jomsom. Carl described the changes in "The Last Home of Mystery" in *Harvard Medical Alumni Bulletin*, Spring 2001, 36–43.

6. Clark, *A Farewell to Alms*, Chap. 3 and elsewhere.

7. A look behind the façade of the Gurkha of legend is revealing: the first Gurkhas joined the British Army in defiance of their rulers, an offense punishable by death, in hopes of escaping the grinding hardship of their lives. See Heather

Streets, *Martial Races: The Military, Race and Masculinity in British Imperial Culture, 1857—1914* (Manchester, U.K.: Manchester University Press, 2004).

8. During their time at Harvard, Birendra and Daniel began a lifelong friendship (until 2001, when Birendra was assassinated), a relationship that provided many of the facts privately communicated in this chapter. Moreover, the fact that it was common knowledge among Nepalis and internationals that Daniel had this special and frequent relationship caused others to confide in him with their perspectives on the unfolding national situation.

9. An extraordinary three-decade-long tracking of caste and gender implications in the development of Nepal has been led by Lynn Bennett with a series of Nepali partners. Multiple sites across Nepal were studied, and a consistent pattern of embedded caste and gender discrimination has been identified as possibly the major barrier to social change (a point also made by the Maoists in starting their rebellion). One recent statement from this three-decade series: Lynn Bennett and Kishor Gajurel "Negotiating Social Change: Gender, Caste, and Ethnic Dimensions of Empowerment and Social Inclusion in Rural Nepal," in Ruth Alsop, Mette Bertlesen, & Jeremy Holland, editors, *Empowerment in Practice: From Analysis to Implementation* (Washington, D.C.: The World Bank, 2006), 193–217.

10. One baffling question for those outside positions of national or even community leadership is "Why doesn't the leader just change the system?" To almost any participant, obvious steps are apparent. Daniel had long discussions with King Birendra, and the response to proposals for change was always, "You don't understand how constrained I am." Those with power (if they are observant) feel the weak points along their line of control, realizing that exercising their power compromises other powers. When leaders understand how to change the dynamics of function in complex systems, creating synergy among components (rather than exercising power), then massive change is possible. Such facilitation is not leadership to which they are typically conditioned.

11. The young lady had inherited a double curse: her paternal great-grandfather had been the last Rana prime minister, who, when forced from power in 1950, had predicted that an heir would reclaim the throne. On the maternal side five generations earlier, an illegitimate Rana son had been banished from Nepal, then had married into the royal family of Gwalior, and now this tainted bloodline threatened to return.

12. We have confirmed the instance about the afternoon argument with his parents over abdication by interviews with two different individuals who personally knew of the altercation.

13. Omkar's solution is evidence of his creativity. That the Planning Commission forwarded his request, and the Finance Ministry approved it, are evidence of their creativity. This case, however, remained isolated because no group took this as an "action learning and experimentation" example (see Chapter 8) and used it as a SCALE Squared experience to point to a national change of course. Doing so would have threatened the control systems of both government and donors—expanding impact was an end that both wanted—but the systems have to change for that to occur, and that is done by turning examples such as Omkar's into action, learning, and experimentation centers (not just proud points in politicians' speeches).

14. The history of change in Sherpa communities over the past half-century is a powerful testimony of social change through human energy maximizing the

potential of the resources at hand—in this case, the spectacular summits and the Sherpas' facility in climbing them. See Sherry Ortner's *Life and Death on Mount Everest: Sherpas and Himalayan Mountaineering* (Princeton, N.J.: Princeton University Press, 2001).

15. The impact cannot be overstated of the Kathmandu Guest House as the leading creative edge of Nepali ecotourism. A nice summation is from founder, Karna Sakya: "It took six or seven years for Thamel to develop into a centre of tourism, and today it is an internationally renowned tourist destination, boasting of hotels, restaurants and shops at par with the best tourist destinations in the world. From the son of the late American president John F. Kennedy to Jimmy Carter, from the Beatles to Ricky Martin. On the occasion of the thirtieth anniversary of *Lonely Planet*, the founder of the publication, Tony Wheeler, listed Kathmandu Guest House on top of his thirty favorite travel highlights of the world." Karna Sakya, *Paradise in Our Own Backyard* (New Delhi, India: Penguin Press, 2009), 81.

16. This is the central argument of Steven Johnson's *Emergence*.

17. In this very useful categorization of the four roles of community, we are indebted to development of the concept by: Kenneth McLeroy, Barbara L. Norton, Michelle Kegler, James Burdine, Ciro Sumaya, "Community-Based Interventions," an editorial in *American Journal of Public Health* (April 2003, vol. 93, no. 4).

18. Personal communication, Captain Sabin Basnet to Daniel and Jesse Taylor, following two helicopter flights across Nepal in June 2010. (Tragically, Captain Basnet was killed by an avalanche falling onto his helicopter three months after this communication; he had landed high on a peak to try to rescue two international climbers who had recklessly exceeded their climbing abilities.)

19. Rural Roads Forum of Nepal, "Minutes of Annual Meeting," 27 November 2009, Summit Hotel, Kathmandu.

20. Nawang Singh Gurung, Future Generations Study Report, January 2011. Report available at http://www.future.org/publications/Governance.

CHAPTER 4. THE OPTION AVAILABLE TO EVERYONE: MOBILIZING HUMAN CAPACITY

1. Holland, *Emergence*, 1.

2. Ilya Prigogine, *The End of Certainty, Time, Chaos and the New Laws of Nature* (New York: Simon & Schuster, 1996).

3. Alsop, Bertlesen, and Holland, *Empowerment in Practice*, Appendices 1–6, 220–340.

4. The Rostam and Saya Dara fieldwork referred to here was conducted during 2005–2006 by Carl E. Taylor and Hassan Shukria; follow-up fieldwork was conducted during 2008–2009 by Carl Taylor, Luke Taylor-Ide, Sakhizada Besmillah, and Mullah Azzizi.

5. To access the simple but full survey used: www.seed-scale.org.

6. A. Edward, P. Ernst, C. E. Taylor, S. Becker, E Mazive, and H. Perry, "Examining the Evidence of Under-Five Mortality Reduction from Community-Based Vital Registration Systems in Gaza Province, Mozambique," in *Transactions of the Royal Society of Tropical Medicine and Hygiene*, 101 (August 2007), 814–822.

7. For more on the inadequacies of a purely physical, mechanistic approach to human energy see Anson Rabinbach's *The Human Motor: Energy, Fatigue, and the Origins of Modernity* (Berkeley, CA: University of California Press, 1992).

8. The double-sided question of whether to pay people for development work or to expect them to work as volunteers cannot be clearly answered, for the answer is "both." But one conclusion is clear: it is easy to pay people too much. Then the people work for the pay rather than the results; they are protecting jobs rather than seeking ends. This challenge has been nicely summed up by Clay Shirkey in what is widely called the Shirkey Principle: "Service institutions will try to preserve the problem to which they are the solution." See Clay Shirkey, *Here Comes Everybody: Revolution Doesn't Just Happen When Society Adopts New Technology, It Happens When Society Adopts New Behaviors* (New York: Penguin Books, 2008).

9. Ashraf Ghani, Overseas Development Institute Report, 2002. Sadly, the numbers have not improved in the years since, as revealed by a conference on the topic in Kabul in July, 2010.

10. William Wordsworth, *The Prelude*, Book VI, line 340. See Rebecca Solnit's discussion of both the euphoria and the opportunity that follow disaster in *A Paradise Built in Hell: The Extraordinary Communities that Arise in Disaster* (New York: Viking, 2009).

11. See Holland's *Emergence* and Bar Yam's *Making Things Work*.

12. The bonds in social energy are not as easy to define as in physics. First, there is the unpredictable element of free will at play in human energy. And second, there is the fact that in social mobilization, rather than bonds being *broken* as in generating physical energy, bonds are *formed*, not only among people but also among multiple "energy forms" of people (labor, passion, and intellect, for instance).

13. A point of clarification is needed: We are using "positive" versus "negative" feedback loops here in both a technical and a non-technical sense. In the technical sense, a positive feedback loop is generated with the inputs are accentuated by the dynamics of the system, whereas a negative feedback loop is generated when the dynamics of the serve to nullify the inputs. Thus, a "positive feedback loop" in the technical sense can lead to decidedly "negative," even disastrous, consequences. Global climate change is the most obvious example: warming caused by atmospheric gases causes ice caps melt, exposing more ocean (which is dark, and thus absorbs heat much more than the reflective surface of snow and ice). It also causes permafrost to thaw, releasing large quantities of methane, a potent greenhouse gas, which in turn leads to further heat-trapping and warmer temperatures. Both of these are examples of "positive feedback loops" that, in the colloquial sense, are anything but. In the example of Afghan aid, the feedback loops are negative insofar as infusions of money are not leading to dynamics that accentuate the initial infusions (thus they are negative in the technical sense), leading instead to worsening situation on the ground (and thus they are negative in the non-technical, colloquial sense as well).

14. See Johnson's *Emergence*.

15. Waldrop, *Complexity*, 145–147.

16. P. Glansdorf and Ira Prigonine, "Thermodynamics, Nonequilibrium" in *The Encyclopedia of Physics*, 2nd ed., edited by Rita Lerner and George Trig (New York: VCH Publishers, 1991), 1256–1262.

17. An argument for social energy as the formative dynamic has been advanced by many individuals, the most significant of whom was Mahatma Gandhi and his use of *satyagraha* (truth energy) to free India from the British Empire and initiate community-based change. More recent advocates include Robert

Putnam, *Making Democracy Work: Civic Traditions in Modern Italy* (Princeton, N.J.: Princeton University Press, 1993); Norman Uphoff, *Learning from Gal Oya: Possibilities for Participatory Development in Post-Newtonian Social Science* (Ithaca, N.Y.: Cornell University Press, 1992); Albert Hirshman, *Getting Ahead Collectively: Grassroots Experiences in Latin America* (New York: Pergamon Press 1984); and Ilya Pyrogene and Isabelle Stengers, *Order Out of Chaos: Man's New Dialogue with Nature* (New York: Bantam Books, 1988). Leslie A. White uses the idea of energy and its application to develop a theory of culture and social change. However, White relies on an evolutionary paradigm that is similar in many respects to the discourse of "developed" and "developing" that we do not intend to emulate. White, *The Science of Culture: A Study of Man and Civilization* (New York: Grove Press, 1958).

18. To understand the basis for this assertion, one helpful way to think of it is to look at physical energy through its bond structures. Einstein's landmark equation $E = MC^2$ is usually thought of in its dramatic form, *nuclear* energy. Rupturing the atomic bond creates the atomic bomb, with a specific amount of matter liberating C^2 (lightspeed) energy. But mass holds energy also through another bond, the chemical bond (although not at the same concentration as specified by Einstein's equation). The chemical bond releases energy by burning (oxidation) or through biological processes such as the Krebs cycle. Thus, a glucose molecule releases heat, electricity, or light, when it fractures into carbon dioxide, water, and an energy-carrying unit of adenosine triphosphate (ATP; which can be thought of as a tiny battery). In people, if the resulting energy is muscular, it can be measured in calories. Mental energy can be measured in electrical neuron transmissions. And while humans do not produce light, in lightning bugs the ATP unit is transformed into light energy. The important point to note is that our presentations of human energy (whether mental, music, muscle, or heat) are all real energy forms.

19. Benedict Anderson's famous definition of nations as "imagined communities" is crucial here when considered in relation to our discussion of "community." If nations are communities, and communities are groups of people with something in common and the potential to act together, then it is the potential to take collective action that makes a people a nation.

20. A simple summary of laser mechanics is that it amplifies the power of light through a couple of mirrors; as the light bounces back and forth between them, it gains power through being pumped up by stimulated power. Key in this is the tight focusing of the energy so that light waves ride on other waves, using all their energy not only to go in the same direction but also to help each other do so.

21. Marglin, *Dismal Science*, 3–7 and elsewhere.

22. Gary S. Becker, Kevin M. Murphy, Robert Tamura, "Human Capital, Fertility, and Economic Growth," in *Journal of Political Economy*, 98, no. 3, (1990), pt. 2.

23. Cleveland and Jacobs, "Human Choice," *Futures*, 959–970.

24. "Water with Sugar and Salt," editorial in *Lancet* (1978): 300–301.

CHAPTER 5. TO GROW EMPOWERMENT: FOUR NECESSARY PRINCIPLES

1. Johnson, *Emergence*, 20.

2. Initial fieldwork—specifically, setting the baseline experienced with the cholera epidemic referred to in this chapter in the community of Palin— was conducted by Carl E. Taylor and Betsy Taylor during the spring of 1998. Subsequent monitoring of the evolution of the Arunachal experience, from

1999 to 2010, was by Tage Kanno, Luke Taylor-Ide, Audrey Apang, Omak Apang, Betsy Taylor, Manjunath Shankar, Daniel Taylor, and the community groups in Palin, Ziro, Sille, Sangram, and Bameng.

3. Story recounted at Palin women's action group meeting, Arunachal Pradesh, India, March 2004.

4. The role of women leading social change is arguably the most underutilized intervention in the proactivity repertoire, a point that Kristoff (and many others) makes repeatedly. The women's action group concept utilizes this. The error for subsequent action that these accounts make, however, is that typically the story is cast as a male/female confrontation or one of female/policies liberation. See Nicholas D. Kristoff and Sheryl WuDunn, *Half the Sky: Turning Oppression into Opportunity for Women Worldwide* (New York: Random House, 2009). But as this Palin example illustrates (in the face of major physical threats), what women are expert at is building relationships among relationships to move the whole community forward.

5. Chandra Mohanty, "Under Western Eyes: Feminist Scholarship and Colonial Discourses," *Feminist Review*, 30 (Autumn 1988), 61–88.

6. See Sen's *Development as Freedom*.

7. Many citations have been given already of the money-hungery side of development assistance. The case against aid, once made, frankly gets tedious. To look deeper into the dynamics driving the business of development and aid, see Carol Lancaster, *Foreign Aid: Diplomacy, Development, Domestic Politics* (Chicago: University of Chicago Press, 2007).

8. See Verrier Elwin, *A Philosophy for NEFA*, 2nd ed. (Shillong, India: Government of Arunachal, 1959). And on the former, see Ramachandra Guha, *Savaging the Civilized: Verrier Elwin, His Tribals, and India* (Chicago: University of Chicago Press, 1999).

9. A fourth location was also initially included, but almost immediately closed due to being in the middle of a local tribal insurgency. Our experience suggests it is usually best to begin in four to five locales as one or two frequently do not take off without outside incentives; more than five is harder to deeply engage with at the beginning when it is beneficial to optimize a localized mix of trainings.

10. The SEED-SCALE work plan is described in Chapter 6. One distinctive feature about this plan is that it is one page. It lists community objectives, and then all the W's—who is going to do what, where, with what, and when. It is a public document; this means that the people know who is to take responsibility for each aspect of the work.

11. The Panchayat system formalized (by the 73rd amendment to India's Constitution) the ancient practice of village councils. Specifically, it gave local leaders control over a range of developmental services, and it mandated representation from the disenfranchised, both women and also tribal members. Citizens elect several types of local bodies (*panchayats*) that are then able to get government funds and administer services such as health, education, local forests, and the like.

12. For a more complete description of the Comprehensive Rural Health Project, see www.jumkhed.org. Also see Chapter 12 of Taylor-Ide and Taylor, *Just and Lasting Change*.

13. In our earlier writing, SEED-SCALE proposed that the foundation for social change was "accenting the positive," and for that there were three necessary principles: three-way partnership, evidence-based decision making, and

behavior change. As understanding grew from field applications plus critiques from colleagues, dynamics became clearer. We now believe that "building on success" should be deemed an operative principle, rather than simply being an intangible philosophy of "accenting the positive."

14. Of the many dehumanizing tropes of development discourse, few have been as vigorously debated as those about population. Among the most pernicious aspects is a persistent racist tinge that links "the population problem" to an overabundance of poor people in the Third World. But, very practically, family planning is embraced more readily when parents expect their children to survive, and similarly by those who see that with fewer children they have access to employment.

15. Michael Hardt and Antonio Negri identify a tripartite structure in their definition of Empire that is similar in some respects to what we are describing here, which they dub three "tiers" of imperial sovereignty: monarchic, aristocratic, and democratic. They identify versions of these operating from Rome to the United States, where they appear not only in the three branches of government, but also in the diverse workings of power, which they characterize as military, monetary, and ether (i.e., "cultural capital" etc.). Hardt and Negri, *Empire* (Cambridge: Harvard University Press, 2001), 345–347. The reason this line of convergence is useful for our purposes is that it highlights the extent to which these three dynamics are always in play, with the goal being to move them toward the effective partnership that generates empowerment, rather than the repression of Empire.

16. Our Afghan colleague Hamidullah Natiq, whose work focuses on fostering peace, finds it more helpful to describe the three-way partnership in terms of a plant. The environment brings from the outside nutrients of oxygen, sunshine, carbon dioxide; branches and leaves on top produce the sugars and wood, the wealth of the plant; the roots, working unnoticed, not only ground the plant to its place, but also bring a second, usually unseen set of nutrients from soil and water. Helpful about this description is that it addresses a critical aspect of the three-way partnership: the focus on interdependence. It is easy for people from the bottom to be not noticed. The top, meanwhile (government, big business, or organized religion) see themselves as the substance of the tree (trunk, branches, and leaves)—but the tree would neither stand up nor get nourished without the hidden roots. And this view gives an interesting perspective to the outside—its resources of oxygen, sunshine, and carbon come from all over the world. The plant becomes a complex system only because all three are working together. Each of the three partners is transformed by that process, and in so doing is made into a new reality.

17. This summary of the features of complex adaptive systems comes from one of the pioneers of Emergence, John H. Holland, and was the core of a lecture he gave in 1987 at the Santa Fe Institute. Summary presented in Waldrop, *Complexity*, 145–147.

18. It is tempting in such a situation for experts to step in and give the answers. After all, mapping the spread of cholera onto a bad water supply literally replays the famous episode of John Snow's mapping of cholera cases in London in 1854, a moment often considered the invention of modern epidemiology. However, in a recent retelling of the Broad Street story, Steven Johnson replaces the image of the lone scientific genius laboring in his laboratory

with a much more Palin-esque reality: "It is not an accident that of the dozens and dozens of cholera outbreaks that he analyzed in his career, the one for which he is most famous erupted six blocks from his residence. . . . Snow brought genuine local knowledge to the Broad Street case." *The Ghost Map: The Story of London's Most Terrifying Epidemic and How It Changed Science, Cities, and the Modern World* (New York: Riverhead, 2006), 147.

19. Robert Chambers, *Rural Appraisal: Rapid, Relaxed, and Participatory* (Sussex, U.K.: Institute of Development Studies, Discussion Paper 311, 1992).

20. F. Barrett and R. Fry, *Appreciative Inquiry: A Positive Approach to Building Cooperative Capacity* (Chagrin Falls, Ohio: Taos Institute Publications, 2005).

21. W. Edwards Deming, *Out of the Crisis* (Cambridge, Mass.: MIT University Press, 1986).

22. See cases in Taylor-Ide and Taylor, *Just and Lasting Change*.

23. Dee W. Hock, *The Birth of the Chaordic Age* (San Francisco: Berrett-Koehler, 1999).

CHAPTER 6. MAINTAINING MOMENTUM: SEVEN TASKS

1. The quotations of Heraclitus (535–474 BCE) no longer exist in an organized form. All are now fragments. The particular quotation used here has been cited many times by different later Greek philosophers; another, more cryptic wording being, "On those stepping into rivers the same, other and other waters flow."

2. The non-linearity is crucial to the ways social change as described here is an "emergent" phenomenon, working in accordance with the principles of emergence laid out in Holland, *Emergence*, 225–226.

3. The case of DehKudaidad, Kabul, Afghanistan, was initially studied by Abdullah Barat, Daniel Taylor, and Carl Taylor during 2005–2006. Subsequent monitoring of the continuation of their experience was led by Luke Taylor-Ide, Ajmal Shirzai, and Aziz Hakimi during the years 2008–2011.

4. The figure of the powerless Third World woman is a common one in development discourse and media coverage. For critiques, see Mohanty, "Under Western Eyes," 61–88; and Arturo Escobar, *Encountering Development: The Making and Unmaking of the Third World* (Princeton, N.J.: Princeton University Press, 1995).

5. As James C. Scott argues, such projects to render haphazard, chaotic urban spaces "legible" have been a central project of modern state power, reaching back to Baron Housmann's redesign of Paris under Napoleon (*Seeing Like a State*, 103–146). The difference in this instance is that, while such schemes have often been dictated by authorities as a means of controlling urban populations (and have been ardently resisted as such by the populace), here the community members were taking such tasks upon themselves. This is both empowering *and* helps to render the area legible to outsiders, enabling effective engagement with authorities. Rather than simply celebrating the life of the slum, in other words, the initiative shows people taking ownership of the processes of modernity.

6. Expanding to subcommittees was a brilliant move. Not only did it not alienate those who had contributed early on, it also brought in new recruits, set up a more direct means of engaging with the substantial population of 85,000, and with ten sites of expansion, there was now healthy competition among sites, plus a structure to try experiments as one ward initiated an idea while others watched to see whether it would work. One of the essential needs to cause empowerment to grow is to make room for all—but also to make the work hard; change is not just coming to meetings, but in hard collective work there is opportunity for all.

7. The "cycle of seven tasks" grew originally from a UNICEF methodology termed Triple A (assessment, analysis, action), which, like the positive-deviance methodology mentioned earlier, was also developed for nutrition programs. It is not happenstance that nutrition programs regularly produce innovations in promoting behavior changes. Although some programs continue to hand out supplemental food, in nutrition long-term answers will come only through changing behavior. To do so requires tasks that people can do.

8. The Jamkhed demonstration is a twenty-five-year community-based experience that helped evolve many of the ideas that would later coalesce in the SEED-SCALE process. See Raj and Mabelle Arole, *Jamkhed: A Comprehensive Rural Health Project* (London: Macmillan, 1992). Also the Jamkhed case study in Taylor-Ide and Taylor, *Just and Lasting Change*, 150–160.

9. One method of causal analysis has community members list the most urgent problems. One priority may be babies dying, another poverty, another poor transportation access, and a fourth government indifference to local needs. Each should be talked about, and people are asked to itemize the causes of each. Movement to deeper understanding comes when underlying causes are linked to several problems. One action that can solve several problems is especially cost-effective: Participants tabulate their explanations. Discussion continues. Only two or three priorities should be finally selected to be in any given work plan.

10. A method helpful in circumstances characterized by entrenched disputes is termed *searching*. It brings together twenty to thirty community members, gathering the most divergent representation possible, to create inside the meeting situations as similar as possible to those outside. With the full group broken into subgroups of six, each struggles for an hour and a half to seek agreement on tasks to do. That is followed by another hour and half seeking a *group objective* for steps to make progress toward the tasks. Subgroup membership is shuffled (each new subgroup has one member from each prior subgroup): for an hour and a half people share their different conclusions. The process becomes more effective as it is done several times.

11. One method of doing a functional analysis asks people to list (in discussion groups) interventions that can correct specific problems. How many people will be needed for each task from inside and outside the community? Can actions be simplified or brought closer to the home? Can solutions be combined so that simple problems are dealt with locally and complex problems referred to the outside? Functional analysis keeps the focus on desired results and seeks alternatives. It classifies activities according to the technical and human resources required to figure out how to address the causes of the problem.

12. A classic example is the deaths from dehydration with childhood diarrhea—which has for centuries killed more people each year than any other cause. First, hospitals installed wards to give IVs, but they were not able to lower death rates outside their hospitals (although the hospitals were making a lot of money). Then oral rehydration salts (ORS) made by drug companies moved treatment to mothers, and diarrhea mortality dropped. But millions of babies still died. Continuing research evolved a more effective and economical alternative: cereal-based oral rehydration therapy, which mothers could make at home for negligible cost. But international agencies and WHO continue to promote ORS because they had massive investments in producing ORS packets. It is striking that even when the cure for the commonest cause of death can be

given to mothers for free, the UN and drug companies continue to work against such solutions.

13. A critical distinction is separating these four types of "community-based work, community as *setting*, community as *target*, community as a source of *free labor*, and community as the *agent of change*." McLeroy, Norton, Kegler, Burdine, and Sumaya, "Community-Based Interventions." an editorial in *American Journal of Public Health* (April 2003, vol. 93, no. 4).

CHAPTER 7. STAYING ON COURSE: THE FIVE CRITERIA OF EVIDENCE-BASED DECISION MAKING

1. Scott, *Seeing Like a State*, 309.
2. As James C. Scott argues, such monitoring techniques are at the heart of modern statecraft, and have informed initiatives ranging from the metric system, to official languages, to the establishment of surnames. See *Seeing Like a State*, especially pp. 24–32 and 64–73.
3. Carl V. Patton, "Being Roughly Right Rather than Precisely Wrong: Teaching Quick Analysis in Planning Curricula," in Jack Rothman, John L. Erlich, John E. Tropman, editors, *Strategies of Community Intervention; Macro Practice*, 5ᵗʰ ed. (Itasca, Illinois: F.E. Peacock Publishers, 1995), 297–307.
4. Shahidur R. Khandker, Gayatri B. Koolwal, Hussain A. Samad, *Handbook on Impact Evaluation: Quantitative Methods and Practices* (Washington: The World Bank, 2010).
5. Kumar, *Methods for Community Participation*.
6. Beyond the citations given above in the paragraph, the following are alternative avenues into relevant research methodologies: the recently republished Eugene J. Webb, Donald T. Campbell, Richard D. Schwartz, and Lee Sechrest, *Unobtrusive Measures*, rev. ed. (Thousand Oaks, Calif.: Sage, 2000). A useful one-volume collection of the approaches that have evolved is presented in Norman K. Denzin and Yvonna S. Lincoln, *Sage Handbook of Qualitative Research*, 3rd ed. (Thousand Oaks, Calif.: Sage, 2005); H. S. Becker, *Tricks of the Trade: How to Think About Your Research While You're Doing It* (Chicago: University of Chicago Press, 1998); S. J. Taylor and R. Bogdan, *Introduction to Qualitative Research Methods: A Guidebook and Resource*, 3rd ed. (New York: John Wiley, 1998); and Deepa Narayan, *Participatory Evaluation: Tools for Managing Change in Water and Sanitation*, World Bank Paper 207 (Washington DC: World Bank Publications, 1993).
7. Kwame Anthony Appiah, *Cosmopolitanism: Ethics in a World of Strangers* (New York: W.W. Norton, 2006), 29.
8. See Bruno Latour, *We Have Never Been Modern*, Catherine Porter, translator (Cambridge, Mass.: Harvard University Press, 1993), 18. Latour's work has often been misunderstood, by both his critics and his fans, to suggest that the products of science are not "real." However, this misses both the importance and the complexity of his thinking, which instead seeks to call attention to the dynamics of the *processes* through which scientific facts are produced. Latour calls attention to the ways in which facts do not simply *exist*, but are produced and maintained through processes and procedures, which cannot be disassociated from their broader contexts. It is precisely for this reason that *participatory* research methods like those described in this chapter are so crucial to the SEED-SCALE process. For more on Latour responding to the "unreality" question, see Latour, *Pandora's Hope*.

9. Drawing on the work of Michel Foucault, James Ferguson critiques the idea of objectivity in development and attempts to bypass politics based on it in *The Anti-Politics Machine: Development, Depoliticization, and Bureaucratic Power in Lesotho* (Minneapolis: University of Minnesota Press, 1994).

10. For more on the background of the Self-Evaluation methodology, see Taylor-Ide and Taylor, *Just and Lasting Change*, 261–263.

11. The Talle Valley fieldwork in Arunachal Pradesh, India, discussed in this chapter was led by Jesse Taylor-Ide, Nani Sha, Pekyom Ringu, Omak Apang, Robert Fleming, Jr., and Daniel Taylor during 1997–1998. Monitoring in the Talle Valley and other places across Arunachal is ongoing by community members, and a formal follow-up of the initial survey organized by Tage Kano of Future Generations Arunachal is currently underway using updated equipment and the same participatory methods.

12. On conservation colonialism and its legacies, see William M. Adams and Martin Mulligan, *Decolonizing Nature: Strategies for Conservation in a Postcolonial Era* (London and Sterling, Va.: Earthscan Publications, 2006); and Ramachandra Guha and Juan Martienez-Alier, *Varieties of Environmentalism: Essays North and South* (London and Sterling, Va.: Earthscan Publications, 1997). Community-based conservation is discussed at greater length in the following chapter.

13. Severine Deneulin with Lila Shahani, editors, *An Introduction to the Human Development and Capacity Approach: Freedom and Agency* (London: Earthscan/International Development Research Centre, 2009), 4–5.

14. In earlier applications in Nepal and other countries, we tested the Self-Evaluation concept in otherwise equal comparisons between local people and professional researchers. Was it more accurate to use local people or trained outside surveyors? In those experiments, local participation led to higher enthusiasm and lower costs and achieved nearly 100 percent coverage, while the professional teams were typically satisfied with 90 percent coverage and sometimes as little as 70 percent. Locals knew where to find the outlier respondents that the professionals missed, the outliers being the respondents who are frequently the most critical to know about. Moreover, community enthusiasm engendered by their engagement produced rapid responses, which allowed surveys to be completed more rapidly. Additionally, the involvement of local people made it dramatically likelier that the community would later believe the findings, and thus be poised to act in accord with their discoveries. Again, it is crucial to recognize the importance of monitoring as a process, and the potential for empowerment (or disempowerment) within it.

15. The literature on PRAs is vast; in it there is some confusion about what the acronym represents (Participatory Rural Appraisals, Participatory Research Appraisals, or Participatory Rapid Appraisals). We earlier have commented on particular aspects of this powerful and widespread tool. A more complete summary of the references than that provided earlier is: Srinivasan, *Tools for Community Participation*; and Robert Chambers, *Rural Development: Putting the Last First* (Essex, U.K.: Addison-Wesley Longman, 1983); Chambers, *Whose Reality Counts?*; Chambers, "Participatory Rural Appraisal (PRA): Challenges, Potentials and Paradigm," *World Development*, vol. 22, no. 10 (1994), 1437–1454; and Chambers, *Ideas for Development* (London: Earthscan, 2007). Also see Kumar, *Methods for Community Participation*.

16. "Key indicator," as used in SEED-SCALE, is an adaptation of "key performance indicators" as used in business and management. In business, the key

performance indicator provides a means of measuring an activity; specifically, how successful it is. Tracking one indicator (or sometimes several, for complex systems) allows monitoring a whole process. For more, see David Parmenter, *Key Performance Indicators* (Hoboken, N.J.: John Wiley & Sons, 2007).

17. This approach is an adaptation for social change of a larger research methodology known as "operations research," a methodology well established in manufacturing, business, and the military. Classical operations research has four steps (plan, do, study, act) that create a feedback loop between analysis and action; that is, research and operations. A system is set up that is self-contained, measuring with great accuracy, but against itself, not an outside standard. The four operations research steps can be seen in the Seven Tasks, discussed in Chapter 5.

18. The people for whom this is most likely to be a problem are outside researchers whose research agendas (and the demands of peer-review, promotion, tenure, and funding, etc.) depend on precisely the ability to render more specialized data and compare them across contexts. Such concerns cannot be dismissed, because the researchers' ongoing participation as productive partners depends on these factors. However, researchers should not assume that data that meet their needs also serve the community. Instead, it is better to be upfront and clear about how research agendas correspond with community needs and where they differ, recognizing that multiple sets of data, with multiple uses, will be produced. For the purposes of the present argument, we focus on how to produce evidence useful for the community, on the assumption that the researchers will figure out how to look after themselves.

19. Related terms and concepts are "keystone species" and "flagship species." More broadly, "indicator species" refers to any species that can be taken to signal broader dynamics within an ecosystem, often due to their sensitivity to change.

20. Worldwide, three animals are called "leopards": the spotted leopard (found in Asia and Africa), the snow leopard (found in the Himalaya and mountains of Central Asia), and the clouded leopard (found in cloud forests from the Eastern Himalaya to Indonesia), although the jaguar of South America, mountain lion of North America, and cheetah of Africa might also be included in this group. Among these, the clouded leopard is the least known. Recent study has revealed that the clouded leopard found in Indonesian jungles is actually a separate subspecies from the one found on mainland Asia.

21. The number of five perspectives is arbitrary; what is important is the idea of multiple perspectives' balancing multiple values. In earlier writing we proposed six perspectives. See Taylor-Ide and Taylor, *Just and Lasting Change*, 249–260.

22. It is, in this respect, telling that Stephen Marglin argues that the market, which thrives on the inequalities it creates, undermines community. See *Dismal Science*, 3–10.

23. See Kwame Anthony Appiah, *The Honor Code: How Moral Revolutions Happen* (New York: W.W. Norton, 2010). It is striking to note that Appiah's examples of once-standard practices are no longer considered ethically tenable in the societies that practiced them, from aristocratic dueling in Europe, to Chinese foot-binding, to the slave trade: all involve inequities formerly taken to be acceptable. His notion of "honor," then, is bound up with an awareness of, and even embarrassment over, the inequities in place in a given cultural context.

24. The countries are, in order of highest income-based equality: Japan, Finland, Norway, Sweden, Denmark, Belgium, Austria, Germany, the Netherlands, Spain, France, Canada, Switzerland, Ireland, Greece, Italy, New Zealand, Australia, the United Kingdom, Portugal, and the United States. Jackson, *Prosperity Without Growth*, 55–60.

25. The countries are, in order of stable mental health: Japan, Belgium, Germany, the Netherlands, Spain, France, Canada, Italy, New Zealand, Australia, the United Kingdom, the United States. Wilkenson and Pickett, *Spirit Level*, 7, 21, 63–72.

26. Regardless of genetics, this measurement remains roughly the same in children between the ages of one and three, because at those ages, growth is primarily longitudinal and not in muscle mass, so measuring upper-arm circumference provides relatively accurate evidence of community nutrition.

27. Personal communication from Rita Thapa, formerly Director of Maternal and Child Health, Government of Nepal, to Daniel Taylor, Kathmandu, November 15, 2009.

28. For more on this concept, see Carl E. Taylor, "Surveillance for Equity in Primary Health Care: Policy Implications from International Experience," *International Journal of Epidemiology*, 21 (1992), 1045–1049.

29. See *2010 World Development Report* (Washington: The World Bank, 2010). An online version of the report is available from: http://go.worldbank.org. United Nations Development Program, *2009 Human Development Report* (New York: UNDP and Oxford University Press, 2009).

30. Amartya Sen presents expanding capabilities and development as aspects of freedom. See Sen, *Resources, Values, and Development* (Oxford, U.K.: Basil Blackwell, 1984); and Sen, *Development as Freedom*.

31. United Nations Development Program, *The 1999 Human Development Report* (New York: UNDP and Oxford University Press, 1999).

32. Narayan, *Measuring Empowerment*.

33. Alsop, Bertelsen, and Holland, *Empowerment in Practice*, 243–340.

CHAPTER 8. THE PROCESS OF GOING TO SCALE: INTERACTION AMONG THREE DYNAMICS

1. Robert L. Fleming, Jr., Liu Wulin, and Dorje Tsering, *Across the Tibetan Plateau: Ecosystems, Wildlife, and Conservation* (New York: W.W. Norton, 2007), 6.

2. Taylor-Ide and Taylor, *Community-Based Sustainable Human Development*, 9.

3. Marge Koblinsky, Zoe Matthews, Julia Hussein, et al., "Going to Scale with Professional Skilled Care," *The Lancet*, 368, no. 9544 (14 Oct. 2006), 1377.

4. Gavin Yamey, "Scaling Up Global Health Interventions: A Proposed Framework for Success" in *PLoS Medicine* 8(6): e1001049, June 28, 2011

5. Taylor-Ide and Taylor, *Just and Lasting Change*, 50–58.

6. C. Merzel and J. D'Afflitti, "Reconsidering Community-Based Health Promotion: Promise, Performance and Potential" in *American Journal of Public Health*, 93, no. 4 (2003), 557–574. Such neat definitions are, of course, complicated by inevitable overlap between the categories.

7. The fieldwork for creating the Qomolangma (Mount Everest) National Nature Preserve and the related expansion of this conservation work was led by Daniel Taylor from 1985 onward. He was joined in field leadership of this work by Chun-Wuei Su Chien, Robert Fleming, Sarah Werner, Jesse Taylor, Puchong, Tsering Drolga, Carl Taylor, A'bu, Tsering Norbu, and many others.

8. From 1986 to 1989, a survey across the four counties of Dingri, Nyalam, Kyrong, and Dingie (the four counties encompassing the north slope of the central Himalaya, two of which were the poorest in all China) revealed that the three priority desires of the 65,000 people living in this region were transportation access, fuel for fire, and health care. Absent were both literacy and poverty alleviation, factors that surely would have been at the top of any external agenda. Absent also was mention of restoration of their religious institutions, many of which had been destroyed; the reason for not mentioning this item could be political sensitivities as well as simply a lower priority. Isolation, cold, and ill-health, when these conditions are acute, are demanding life priorities.

9. The rate of deforestation grew rapidly from the early 1980s until 1998, at which point it peaked at 350 trucks per day carrying timbers. The forest management controls established in 1998 were achieved by proactive publicity by conservation activists linking deforestation to river flooding on the Yangtze River.

10. The environmental movement worldwide has a tendency to publicize problems. Unfortunately, while this approach may help fundraising and legal action, it creates the sense of a battle to defend the planet from humans—and that, naturally, alienates the humans who most need to be convinced. What the movement did in Tibet, at the beginning when the situation was dire, was to create a positive outlook, and to engage people as partners by using positive publicity, showing what was possible, not what was being threatened.

11. Public statement at a village planning meeting, by Peku Lake, Kyirong County, Qomolangma National Nature Preserve, May of 1995.

12. Malcolm Gladwell, *The Tipping Point: How Little Things Can Make a Big Difference* (New York: Back Bay/Little, Brown, 2002).

13. In our earlier writing, the acronym SCALE One stood for "Selecting Communities As Learning Examples." This acronym, which emphasized the learning that was occurring in community extension, caused some confusion, as it suggested that SCALE One is a process of "each community teaching another community." The SCALE One dimension does involve community-based extension, but the acronym is more descriptive if it emphasizes the expansion of awareness, learning, and energy in this extension.

14. Carl E. Taylor et al., "Health Survey of Tibetan Villages North of Mount Everest," *National Geographic Research and Exploration* 8 (1992): 372–377. This was the first externally led health survey ever conducted in the Tibet Autonomous Region, an effort involving fourteen international health professionals that examined three villages of Dingri County, Tibet, seeking out health evidence from every household.

15. A rock on a 25-cm string will swing 60 times a minute, right for babies under two months; a 35-cm string swings 50 times a minute, the rate to identify pneumonia in babies under 12 months, while 55-cm swings at 40 cycles per minute is right for young children.

16. SEED-SCALE use of experimentation is often termed *impact evaluation* in the literature where the objective is to test if the intervention is working and see how to improve its impact.

17. See: http://www.searchgadchiroli.org.

18. In our earlier writing, the SCALE Cubed acronym stood for "Systems for Collaboration, Adaptive Learning, and Extension," suggesting that these were separate actions. SCALE Cubed should more accurately suggest the synthesis of these functions.

19. Chambers, *Ideas for Development*, 30.

20. Betsy Taylor, "Place as Prepolitical Grounds of Democracy: An Appalachian Case Study in Class Conflict, Forest Politics, and Civic Networks," in *American Behavioral Scientist*, 52, no. 6 (Feb. 2009), 834.

21. Robert Chambers suggests that eight elements may have the potential to transform practice among development practitioners: "To address ego and power attitudes, behavior change; To transfer knowledge more effectively, move from self-perception as teachers to that of facilitator; To open leaders' awareness of the potential of people, show them examples; To let the awareness of potential sink in, allow time for reflection, do not rush the attitude change; To give real understanding, provide immersion experiences for the leaders of experiences, this is not something they learn by being told". Chambers, *Ideas for Development*,165–178.

22. C. K. Howard-Bury, *Mount Everest: The Reconnaissance, 1921* (London: Edward Arnold & Co, 1922; republished in Varanasi, India: Pilgrim's Book House), 112.

23. On the issue of promoting entrepreneurship, much can be learned from examining the experience of Bangladesh. While the microcredit programs of Grameen Bank and Bangladesh Rural Advancement Committee (BRAC) are large and well known, other, smaller adaptations of these models are also evolving. Particularly interesting are the evaluations of the impacts. The findings seem to agree that microcredit most successfully transforms poverty when linked to promoting collective behavior changes, not when focusing on advancing the entrepreneurial individuals who use the help to leave the community. Entrepreneurship is most effective when the entrepreneurial concepts are encouraged to remain in the community, sparking widening change.

24. Complicating the challenge were the human demands of the region with 800,000 people jammed in towns and fields along the deep gorges, and the economic potential from massive possible hydroelectric projects and mining possibilities; all this against the backdrop of pressures from the surging economic growth of China.

CHAPTER 9. THE GLOBAL IMPERATIVE OF GOING TO SCALE: EXAMPLES OF ENVIRONMENTAL ACTION IN NEW YORK CITY AND CHINA

1. Prigogine and Stengers, *Order Out of Chaos*, 2–4, 311–312.

2. Easterly, *The White Man's Burden*, 6.

3. Hawken, *Blessed Unrest*, 2–3. The key point on which we differ from Hawken is in the role of the "Outside-in." Nongovernmental organizations may, as he describes, participate in the "Bottom-up," but if they do so exclusively, they minimize their impact and preclude the key role they have to play in unsettling oppositions between the Top-down and the Bottom-up, bringing new ideas, technologies, and innovations to the table, and forging connections among disparate groups.

4. Michael Hardt and Antonio Negri, *Multitude: War and Democracy in the Age of Empire* (New York: Penguin, 2005).

5. This is essentially the argument mounted in Scott's *Seeing Like a State*. However well intentioned, Top-down development relies on simplification of complexity and enforced conformity, often through violence and repression. Indeed, at times it can appear that better the intentions, the greater the violence waged in their implementation.

6. Fikret Berkes, "Community-Based Conservation in a Globalized World," *Proceedings of the National Academy of Sciences*, 104, no. 39 (Sept. 25, 2007), 15188–15193.

7. Community-integrated parks were formalized at the national level in the United Kingdom following World War II, but the history of people pressing their claims against the enclosure of the commons reaches back centuries. Wordsworth's Lake District, for instance, is and was an almost entirely inhabited "Nature." Legal contained engagement is also evident throughout the United Kingdom, whether through right-of-ways, forest use allowances, or grazing rights such as those allowed through the Crofter Acts of 1886 in Scotland. This experience with conservation–community partnerships is nuanced has not been adequately incorporated into global discourse on the subject.

8. The Yellowstone model, while it has preserved treasures (Wallace Stegner called it "America's Best Idea,") views the management of nature to be through setting the land apart and giving its management over to government professionals. What Stegner really saw as the best idea in the national parks concept was that the great natural treasures were being given to the public.

9. Two of us were among the authors of a global review of community-based conservation effectiveness. Michael A. Rechlin, Daniel C. Taylor, Jim Lichatowich, Parakh Hoon, Beberly de Leon, Jesse Oak Taylor, *Community Based Conservation: Is It More Effective, Efficient and Sustainable?* Gordon & Betty Moore Foundation Report, March 2008. Available at: http://www.future.org/publications/community-based-conservation-it-more-effective-efficient-and-sustainable.

10. See Michael R. Bloomberg's "Introduction" to Phillip Lopate and Joel Meyerowitz's *Lecacy: The Preservation of Wilderness in New York City Parks*, (New York: Aperture,2009).

11. New York City Department of Parks and Recreation (29,000 acres); National Parks of New York Harbor (27,000 acres), see http://www.nps.gov/npnh/index.htm; New York State Parks (344 acres), and Hudson River Park, which is a combined city-state park (550 acres).

12. See, for instance, Ben Jervey's *The Big Green Apple: Your Guide to Eco-Friendly Living in New York City* (Guilford, Conn.: Globe Pequot Press, 2006). PlaNYC, the city's sustainability plan, focuses on land, air, water, energy, transportation and a 30 percent reduction in carbon emissions.

13. One constantly updated site on these examples of people-based conservation action in cities and elsewhere is at www.localconservation.com.

14. For more information about "Hoboken Free Kayaking Day," sponsored by the Hoboken Cove Community Boathouse, please visit www.hobokencoveboathouse.org or www.ioby.org.

15. Johnson, *Ghost Map*, 233.

16. Reid and Taylor, *Recovering the Commons*.

17. A brief history of New York City Parks is available as an online tour of the NYC Department of Parks and Recreation: http://www.nycgovparks.org/sub_about/parks_history/historic_tour/history_oldest_parks.html.

18. *National Geographic* magazine, September 2009, describes the environmental change of New York City over the four hundred years from 1609 to 2009. Primary source is: Eric W. Sanderson, *Mannahatta: A Natural History of New York City*, illustrated by Markley Boyer (New York: Abrams, 2009). Also see this terrific website at: http://themannahattaproject.org/

19. The park took 16 years and five million cubic yards of stone, earth, and topsoil to build.

20. Two of the city's largest parks, Van Cortlandt Park (1,140 acres), and Pelham Bay Park (2,700 acres) were acquired in 1888, along with Bronx Park, which now

houses the New York Botanical Garden and the Wildlife Conservation Society's Bronx Zoo, Crotona Park, Claremont Park, and St. Mary's Park.

21. John Mullaly, *The New Parks Beyond the Harlem*, 131. Originally published in 1887 by the Record and Guide (New York), and republished by the Bronx County Historical Society in 2008.

22. Robert Moses is firmly within what Scott calls the "high-modernist ideology" of improvement schemes enacted via plans and power, often at the expense of anyone who got in the way (Scott, *Seeing Like a State*, 88). This ideology is in many respects directly counter to the participatory methods advocated throughout this book. However, the key in this context is how Moses' actions fit within the broader history of the city's parks. For more on Moses, see Robert Caro, *The Power Broker: Robert Moses and the Fall of New York*. (New York: Vintage Books, 1975). Also see Andrew Ross, *The Chicago Gangster Theory of Life: Nature's Debt to Society* (New York & London: Verso, 1995).

23. See Bill McKibben, *Hope, Human and Wild: True Stories of Living Lightly on the Earth* (New York: Little, Brown & Company, 1995); and Taylor-Ide and Taylor, *Just and Lasting Change*, 143–149.

24. A very interesting summary of the history of New York City's drinking water is available at: http://www.nyc.gov/html/dep/html/drinking_water/history.shtml

25. Bill McKibben, *Hope, Human and Wild*.

26. Rechlin et al., *Community-Based Conservation*.

27. Taylor-Ide and Taylor, *Just and Lasting Change*, 113–125.

28. Barbara McMartin, "The Adirondacks: It's Not a Model; It's a Mess," *Adirondacks Journal of Environmental Studies*, Spring/Summer 1999.

29. Philip G. Terrie, *Contested Terrain: A New History of Nature and People in the Adirondacks* (Syracuse, N.Y.: Adirondack Museum/Syracuse University Press, 1997).

30. Bill McKibben, *Hope, Human and Wild*.

31. Lee Stuart, "The South Bronx Restoring Civil Society to Restore a Community," in *Hoffnungstrager Zivilgesellschaft? Governance, Nonprofits, und Stadtentwicklung in den Metropolenregionen der USA* (Berlin: Reihe Planungsrundschau, 2007), 174–175. For more on the Bronx River Alliance, see their website: www.bronxriver.org.

32. Such surveillance by "eyes on the street" is one of the key dynamics identified by Jane Jacobs in successful cities. What Jacobs referred to as "sidewalk culture," in which residents know each other just enough to pay attention, to note patterns and irregularities and step in when something goes wrong, is a far surer path to safety than reliance solely on the police. Jacobs, *Death and Life of Great American Cities*, 31–33. Also discussed in Scott, *Seeing Like a State*, 133–139.

33. New Yorkers for Parks, in partnership with the NYC Dept. of Parks and Recreation and Hans van Waldenberg, a Dutch bulb supplier, annually mobilizes over 20,000 citizen volunteers to plant daffodils. Originally conceived as a living memorial to the September 11th victims, over 4 million daffodils have been planted since 2001.

34. All data used in this summary come from official statistics of the New York City Parks Department.

35. PlaNYC is available at http://www.nyc.gov/html/planyc2030/html/home/home.shtml. This is the Mayor Bloomberg's sustainability plan for New York City and includes things like a partnership with the New York Restoration

Project for the Million Trees Project. Another project of PlaNYC, in partnership with the Trust for Public Land, is to restore 151 schoolyards and community parks.

36. Lee Stuart, executive director, New Yorkers for Parks: letter to Daniel Taylor, May 5, 2010.

37. Total protected area includes 29,900 acres in city parks, 900 acres in state parks, and 27,000 acres as part of the national park system.

38. Amy Frykholm, "Justice for the South Bronx," *Christian Century*, July 28, 2009. 10–11.

39. Peter Miller, "Before New York," *National Geographic Magazine*, 216, no. 3 (Sept. 2009), 126.

40. See http://www.bronxriver.org/?pg=content&p=calendarandnews&m1=53#ev136.

42. A number of metrics have been advanced: Gross National Product, Gross Domestic Product, the Human Development Index, Genuine Progress Indicator, and the like. While useful at the macro-level, these indicators are not useful at the community level. In addition, they omit the important component of assessing the societal enabling environment. (In this discussion we use *assessment* for such monitoring rather than *measurement* because the features are still a long way from being measurable.)

43. To get an estimate, SEED-SCALE projects typically conduct a household survey (part of Self-Evaluation in the Seven Tasks). Another option is to get data from municipal records, or surveys that are regularly repeated that show how many are participating in the change.

44. For current details, see the Grameen Foundation's website: www. grameenfoundation.org/what_we_do/microfinance_support/social_ performance/the_ppi_tool/.

45. Life expectancy can crudely be approximated by a question on the household survey, where ages of the people who died in the prior twelve months are obtained. The ages of all the dead are summed, then divided by the number of people in the survey. Ability to utilize information in the HDI is calculated by giving a two-thirds weight to literacy and a one-third weight to school enrolment. The literacy rate can be approximated by implementing UNESCO's definition: "literacy is the ability to identify, understand, interpret using printed materials" simplified to a question on the household survey (from the data-gathering of the Seven Tasks) about the number in the household who can read, understand, and take action on material in a local newspaper. School enrollment can be calculated by adding up the numbers of children enrolled in primary and secondary school and dividing that number by the total number of school-age children. Standard of living in the HDI is a logarithm of the Gross Domestic Product and the Purchasing Power Parity. Getting that information at the community level is impossibly difficult. Until such a method evolves, we are using the national average GDP index. Aside from the regrettable use of a national average at the community level, the GDP also is not measuring key variables such as voluntarism, environmental damage, or prevalence of leisure time amid social change. This is the weakest part of this assessment, and we are following experiments to find accurate assessments of community-level economic activity.

46. To find the WGI for a particular country, consult the World Bank's data at http://info.worldbank.org/governance/wgi2007/sc_country.asp.

47. See http://go.worldbank.org/ARGZ333710.

48. In using this index, the assumption being made is that countries low in their Gini Coefficient probably have restricted access to financial opportunities for their non-wealthy members.

49. To assess that, UNESCO's Digital Opportunity Index (DOI) balances information utilization/usage and quality, infrastructure/network and device, and opportunity/affordability and accessibility, for the 180 major global economies (http://www.itu.int/osg/spu/publications/worldinformationsociety/2006/).

50. Harrison Salisbury, *The Long March: The Untold Story* (New York: Harper & Row, 1985).

51. Taylor-Ide and Taylor, *Just and Lasting Change*, 93–101.

52. A recent study of the scope of the disaster brought on by the Great Leap Forward is Frank Dikötter, *Mao's Great Famine: The History of China's Most Devastating Catastrophe, 1958–1962* (New York: Walker, 2010).

53. Salisbury, *Long March*; Gerald F. Winfield, *China—The Land and the People* (New York: W. Sloane Associates, 1948), 437.

54. See "China's Model Counties: Going to Scale with Health Care," in Taylor-Ide and Taylor, *Just and Lasting Change*, 224–238.

55. Understanding of the socioeconomic growth of China as a model in contradistinction to the conventional economic development understanding has been perhaps best presented by Dani Rodrik, "Diagnostics Before Prescription" *Journal of Economic Perspectives*, 24, no. 3 (Summer 2010), 33–44, 37. For a further discussion of the economic growth of China (as well as connecting the parallels there to the recent economic growth in modern India), see Rodrik, *One Economics, Many Recipes.*

56. Daniel Taylor, speech at the opening ceremonies of the 2007 Green Long March before an estimated 10,000 students, Beijing Forestry University, April 1, 2007.

57. Jules Pretty and Hugh Ward, "Social Capital and the Environment," *World Development*, 29, no. 2 (2001), 209–227.

58. Prigogine and Stengers, *Order Out of Chaos.*

59. Brian Arthur, *Increasing Returns and Path Dependence in the Economy* (Ann Arbor: University of Michigan Press, 1994).

60. Johnson, *Emergence*, 104.

61. Johnson, *Emergence*, 105.

62. The World Bank 2000, contributors Vinod Thomas, Mansoor Dailami, Ashok Dhareshwar, et al., *The Quality of Growth* (Oxford, U.K.: Oxford University Press, 2000).

CHAPTER 10. CONFRONTING EMPIRE

1. Hardt and Negri, *Empire*. While parsing the intricacies of this massive volume becomes cumbersome, the core of Hardt and Negri's argument, that amorphous forms of global sovereignty that are mobile, disparate, and yet capable of crushing force, seems difficult to refute in today's world. Flashes of old-school imperialism, such as the muscular American foreign policy of the Bush years, hardly erase this broader trend.

2. Deane Curtin also suggests Gandhi as a model for both international development and practical, ethical action in environmental justice in *Environmental Ethics for a Postcolonial World* (Lanham, Md.: Rowman & Littlefield, 2005).

3. The India of Gandhi's day was a subcontinent of British effective suzerainty that included India (which then included was is now Pakistan), Sri Lanka, Bangladesh, Burma, Bhutan, and Nepal.

4. Gandhi saw three types of *swaraj* nested inside each other: at the individual level, where one learns to control oneself in nonviolent life; in control of the collective, where the individual lives (*gram swaraj*); and in the nation, which practices nonviolent policies and fosters the dignity of all.

5. The book, written halfway through Gandhi's professional life, is cumbersome, but its key message is one of iterative reflection and action in testing ideas. Readers who come to this work seeking clear insights, indications that Gandhi knew his way early on by the illuminations of genius, are inevitably disappointed. He hammered away on the anvil of truth, testing ideas, examining results, performing experiments—or, what SEED-SCALE would term "evidence-based decision making and adaptive learning."

6. John Chathanatt examines Gandhi as a theoretician and practitioner of liberation in *Gandhi and Gutierrez: Two Paradigms of Liberative Transformation* (New Delhi: Decent Books, 2004), 230.

7. Gandhi's widely quoted phrases seldom come from his writings, which suffer from a style that is typically poorly organized and obscure. The vast collection of his now oft-quoted phrases comes from his speeches and interviews. Journalists pounced on these phrases to capture his message. Regrettably, there has yet to be collected an authoritative compilation of these sayings. Across India today, there is an enormous lexicon of attributed discourse. When we give a quotation that lacks a source citation, it is from this large body of attributed sayings.

8. Nehru's fascination with creating a spectacle of modernity in independent India, with grand projects such as big dams or the planned city of Chandigarh (discussed below) can be understood as similar (if in other respects diametrically opposed) to Gandhi's response. The role of spectacle and symbol in British India (and empire more broadly) permeating nearly all facets of life has been extensively discussed. See, for instance, Ian Baucom, *Out of Place: Englishness, Empire and the Locations of Identity* (Princeton, N.J.: Princeton University Press, 1999); Bernard Cohn, *Colonialism and Its Forms of Knowledge: The British in India* (Princeton, N.J.: Princeton University Press, 1996); Anne McClintock, *Imperial Leather: Race, Gender and Sexuality in the Colonial Contest* (New York: Routledge, 1995); and Edward Said, *Culture and Imperialism* (New York: Vintage Books, 1993).

9. Richard B. Gregg, *The Power of Non-Violence* (New York: Fellowship Publications, 1944), 25–28; quoted in Chathanatt, *Gandhi and Gutierrez*, 158.

10. In this respect, more recent parades, in which India's nuclear warheads have been put on display draped in marigold garlands and lauded almost exclusively as *symbols* of national power, rather than literal technologies of destruction, offer an ominous counterpoint.

11. Later, once India was an independent nation, the new national constitution would mandate that the national flag always be made from *khadi* cloth.

12. It is for this reason that another great anticolonial thinker, Frantz Fanon, advocated the use of violence in overcoming oppression: "The violence which ruled over the colonial world, which has ceaselessly drummed the rhythm for destruction of native social forms and broken up without reserve the systems of reference of the economy, the customs of dress and external life, that same violence will be claimed and taken over by the native at the moment when, deciding to embody history in his own person, he surges into the forbidden quarters." Fanon, *The Wretched of the Earth*, translated by Constance Farrington (New York: Grove Press, 1963), 37. In other words, Fanon held that

"giving" freedom to people only perpetuated their disempowerment, as the real power still lay with the colonial rulers and their choice to relinquish control. In violent uprising, on the other hand, the colonized *proved* their power through force. His emphasis on reciprocity bespeaks the "physics" of human energy, in which energy can be neither created nor destroyed, and every action begets an equal and opposite reaction. In this context, Gandhi's genius lies not in advancing an ethics of nonviolence, but in showing a means to nonviolent empowerment.

13. Mahatma Gandhi, "Young India," May 6, 1926. Collected in *All Men Are Brothers: Autobiographical Reflections* (New York: Continuum International, 2004), 157.

14. One intriguing, unsolved mystery of Gandhi's management system was how he organized what appears to be a totally confidential communications system. A freedom movement is not achieved without secure, encrypted communications. Denied use of the British telegraph, although sending out sometimes a hundred letters a day with the two scribes he simultaneously dictated to (letters that were opened by the British), how did he send secure messages across the span of the Indian subcontinent?

15. Jawaharlal Nehru is a prime example of a leader in the sway of the "high-modernist ideology" decried by Scott in *Seeing Like a State*, esp. 130–132.

16. Carl and Daniel recall driving as father and nine-year-old son across the Punjab in the fall of 1955 to attend the ribbon-cutting of the state's new capital, Chandigarh, which Nehru proclaimed to be "unfettered by the traditions of the past, a symbol of the nation's faith in the future." Nehru had wanted the grand opening of the city, designed by the Franco-Swiss architect Le Corbusier standing by his side, to be a great movement of people toward the new future of a new India. He had instructed that hundreds of thousands be mobilized to attend, and the numbers dutifully responded (including ourselves). We stood in a packed crowd waiting for the prime minister, who was simultaneously waiting for a proper truck to be prepared on which he, the symbol of the people, would ride with the architect, into the symbol of the future. The first truck broke down. The second, allegedly, did not look right. Nehru took the stage two hours late. The energy of the people had withered. The people had had delivered unto them a city, but it was one that lacked productive industries, was totally one of planned new services; what they had not done was build this new city themselves.

17. The issue of caste, which Gandhi dubbed "the most pernicious prison in India," was something he was able to do little to correct. Babasahib Ambedkar, leader of the *dalits* (Untouchables), the man who later drafted the Indian Constitution and used that platform to make the document a social contract in which abolishment of caste was structurally addressed, became frustrated with Gandhi as political freedom became more evident, but not actions for freedom from this most pernicious of prisons. Gandhi, whose wife nearly left him over caste acceptance, who repeatedly risked his life because of caste, argued that he could not push harder. But the *dalits* saw Gandhi letting the caste system remain intact so as to hold his movement intact, accommodating caste discrimination by beautiful words (such as calling the Untouchablesm *harjan*, children of God) and symbolic deeds. The accusation is valid; Gandhi advanced a priority for rapprochement with the Muslims ahead of that with the *dalits*.

18. As noted in the Introduction, where the discussion was at the global level using the statistic of two billion in absolute poverty in today's world of seven billion, the number in absolute poverty seems to be an intractable constant

when the processes being used for change are those that presuppose economic growth, a process that in order to start growing requires capital, a currency that the absolute poor lack, either in actual money or its natural resource surrogate. Economic growth seems to accommodate the increasingly wealthy segment, but it seems incapable of accommodating those who truly are without financial means.

19. See Rob Nixon, *Slow Violence and the Environmentalism of the Poor* (Cambridge, Mass: Harvard University Press, 2011).

20. One of the dramatic stories is of the work of a simple village worker, from the Comprehensive Rural Health Project in Jamkhed India, Parubai (from the discriminated-against shepherd caste). She so energized her community that the Collector of Ahmednagar supported her in making it a village, and then that community grew so successfully that the Collector took the example to Rajiv Gandhi. A planned short photo opportunity with the prime minister turned into an hour's presentation, where she outlined to him what would result if women were given one-third representation in elected bodies. Parubai had gone into her meeting with the prime minister concealing a small burning lamp inside her apparel; then, when the prime minister greeted her, she pulled out the burning lamp and said, "I am just one fire. Your job is to bring forward the flames of millions across India!"

21. Thousands of Gandhian and similar groups, activists and ashrams, have carried on over the decades pressing for change. Arguably the most famous group is that of Vinoba Bhave. But political action is not enough—practical solutions are needed for how people in a modern way can lead the empowerment of India. In the Gandhian tradition, arguably the most outstanding institutional example is community-based research by the Society for Education Action and Research in Community Health (SEARCH). SEARCH has evolved methods (and backed these up with high-quality data) outlining affordable, implementable ways how communities can address fundamental issues that improve their lives. To point to just the SEARCH innovations in neonatal mortality: Abhay T. Bang, Rani A. Bang, and Hanimi M. Reddy published a series of a dozen articles that composed a whole edition of the *Journal of Perinatology* (vol. 25, March 18, 2005).

22. One of the few recent authors to discuss in depth Gandhi's vision of the Congress Party as a social movement is Sunil Khilnani, *The Idea of India* (New York: Farrar, Straus, & Giroux, 1997), 34–35.

23. There can be no question that Gandhi revered Ruskin—but his choice of Ruskin (as opposed to Tolstoy, whom he also admired, for example, and whose name he used in his second intentional community in South Africa) was also astute, for a significant segment of Britain's intelligentsia revered Ruskin because of his pioneering social ideals. This community became a Britain-based advocacy group on Gandhi's behalf, supporting his cause as the colonialist side persisted with repression. Each time Gandhi quoted Ruskin, he received affirmation in Britain.

24. There is a further lesson of process here—the political and tactical angles. Had Gandhi tried direct counterattack, the casualties of bodies would have numbered in large populations. Many in the British military (and including Winston Churchill) felt that at the first chance their troops should be ruthless, but Gandhi was careful to not give the British the excuse. Gandhi kept adjusting to each event, and ultimately what set India free also benefited the

British Empire. The hidden violence inherent in imperialism was rendered so blatant by his action that it caused the British themselves to self-correct. From understanding the strength in interdependence comes strengthened interdependence.

25. As we noted earlier, in modern India, absent an authoritative compendium of Gandhi's sayings, and where many of the now-attributed sayings were given in news interviews and public speeches, a vast number of quotations are ascribed to Gandhi, and "We make our path by walking it" is one such. This particular phrase, however, is generally credited to Africa, and as noted in the text we suggest Gandhi may have brought it with him when he returned to India.

26. See Arthur, *Increasing Returns and Path Dependence*.

27. See Naomi Klein, *No Logo: Taking Aim at the Brand Bullies* (New York: Picador, 1999).

28. The people of India alternated between calling Gandhi "Mahatma" (great soul) and "Bapu" (grandfather)—what more appropriate nominal split for one who walked with them and also sought to empower them to continue on.

ABOUT THE AUTHORS

This book gathers lessons that span a century-long dialogue, in which the authors include many more than the three generations of father, son, and grandson who crafted this narrative. We each learned the lessons here from teachers steeped in life experience, and wisdom often fertilized by economic scarcity. Our teachers shared an understanding that the fullness of life comes from community bonds. If this book can be simplified to a sentence, it is this: we improve our lives from strengthening the bonds in which we live, and when we do so profound life growth is available to all. From the jungles of India to the mountains of Appalachia, we were first taught this lesson by those marginalized by the world's systems, their evidence base was the fact that they had done so in their lives.

Carl Taylor was born in India, and began his life traveling by oxcart from village to village with his parents, who were running mobile health clinics. His great love was the jungle, where he spent days upon days learning its sounds and signs and quieting his own, mastering the art of listening. As he grew up, he moved out of the jungle and was listening to villagers, connecting their insights to his own scientific training and research.

After medical school at Harvard and serving in Panama during World War II, Carl returned to India with his wife, Mary, and infant son, Daniel. During the partition of India and Pakistan in 1947, Carl led a team that provided the only formal health services on both sides of the border. Though suturing sword wounds and quelling three cholera outbreaks provided health care on one level, it became clear to him that real health resulted from behavior changes rather than the technologies of medicine. Carl returned to Harvard to complete a doctorate in public health. His dissertation was the first to assert the correlation between malnutrition and infection, framing patterns of his life's work—interdisciplinary connections and a profound commitment to equity.

In 1961, Carl became the founding chair of Department of International Health at Johns Hopkins University, a position that enabled him to lead in international forums and to conduct field research (often in the company of current or former students) in more than seventy countries. He taught his last class in February of 2010, ten days before his death, as this book was in its final stages of review. Carl has over 200 peer-reviewed scientific publications and numerous honorary degrees and public service awards.

In 1992, after sharing twenty years of collaborative Himalayan research, Daniel joined Carl in chairing a three-year-long UNICEF task force examining the global evidence base on how to lead social change "to scale," or scaling up. From these task forces came the SEED-SCALE conclusions. Daniel, who had also completed his doctoral work at Harvard, was cofounder of the Mountain Institute, and focused first on running programs in experiential education, and then on mobilizing community-led large-scale nature conservation. Daniel was instrumental in creating major national parks encompassing the Mount Everest ecosystem in Nepal and China. These parks were the first examples in Asia of a people-managed framework for nature protection that also advanced socioeconomic well being (see Chapter 8).

At the encouragement of Jim Grant, then Executive Director of UNICEF, Daniel founded Future Generations to apply the task forces' insights. As field demonstrations of SEED-SCALE grew dramatically in China, India, Peru, Afghanistan, and other countries, he initiated Future Generations Graduate School, which now offers an accredited master's degree in applied community change and conservation. For his work, Daniel was knighted by the king of Nepal with Gorkha Dakshin Bau III, made the first honorary professor of quantitative ecology by the Chinese Academy of Sciences, and received the Order of the Golden Arc from Prince Bernhard of the Netherlands.

Jesse Oak began learning about the resilience of life from creative farmers and hunters in the mountains of West Virginia, and then, he too connected these to fieldwork in the Himalaya. These experiences led to his interest in how narrative frames cross-cultural encounters and human interactions with animals and the natural world. A graduate of Middlebury College, Jesse Oak earned his doctorate at the University of Wisconsin-Madison, and has published scholarly articles on a range of topics dealing with environmentalism, empire, and the production of knowledge. He has also written for the *National Geographic*. Currently a visiting assistant professor and ACLS New Faculty Fellow at the University of Maryland, he is at work on a book examining representations of the London fog to trace the relationship between conceptual emergence, climate change, and the metropolis in the late-nineteenth and early-twentieth centuries. Jesse Oak has also taught at Georgetown University and has been a research fellow at the University of Warwick in the United Kingdom.

THE SEED-SCALE PROCESS: A GLOSSARY

While it attempts to offer simple procedures to build solutions of great complexity, the various acronyms, principles, tasks, and criteria that make up SEED-SCALE can be confusing; therefore the definitions and key elements are laid out here for easy reference.

SEED-SCALE:

> SEED: Self Evaluation for Effective Decisionmaking
> SCALE: Systems for Communities to Adapt Learning and Expand.

Four Principles:

1. Build from success
2. Form a three-way partnership between the Bottom-up, the Top-down, and the Outside-in
3. Make decisions based on tangible evidence and data rather than opinions
4. Focus on behavior change rather than on providing services.

Seven Tasks:

- Organize a local coordinating committee
- Identify successes already occurring
- Learn from the experiences of others
- Gather data about local results
- Make a work plan
- Hold partners accountable
- Make midcourse corrections to strengthen the Four Principles.

Five Criteria for Self- Evaluation:

- Equity
- Sustainability (environmental, economic, and cultural)

- Holism
- Interdependence
- Iteration

Dimensions of SCALE:

SCALE One: Stimulating Community Awareness, Learning, and Energy
(Numerical expansion)
SCALE Cubed: Self-Help Centers for Action, Learning, and Experimentation
(Rising sophistication and quality of life)
SCALE Squared: Synthesis of Collaboration, Adaptive Learning, and
Extension
(Expanding enabling environment).

INDEX

Adirondack State Park (New York)
192–194
aesthetics 13, 83, 101, 119, 202,
214–215, 231 n. 7
Afghanistan 66–85, 113–136
Barat, Abdullah 115–118, 123,
127, 135
DehKudaidad 120–123, 135, 151,
157
Hazzan, Shukria 67, 128
Islam 79, 81, 119
Jhagori, Mahmood 124–127, 134
Kabul 72, 84, 115–121, 135, 144,
199, 223
mosque-based schools 78, 82, 118,
124–126
Natiq, Hamidullah 243 n. 16
poppies 70–71, 74, 82
Rostam and Saya Dara Valleys 66–69,
82, 84, 115
Taliban 70–71, 74, 81–82, 98, 116,
122, 126, 181
Alma-Ata, Kazakhstan (International
Conference on Primary Health
Care) 28–29
Al-Qaeda 70–71, 74, 122
Ambedkar, Bahasahib 219, 257 n. 17
analysis (see also *assessment*)
causal 130, 245 n. 9
needs 8
functional 130–131, 245 n. 11
Anderson, Benedict 230 n. 15, 241 n. 19
Apache, White Mountain 225
Appadurai, Arjun 233 n. 30
Appiah, Kwame Anthony 138, 248 n. 23
appreciative inquiry 110, 127
Arab Spring, the 227

Arthur, Brian 208, 226
Arunachal Pradesh (India) 5–24, 87–112,
137–156
Amko 90–96
Bameng 5–23, 27, 39, 46, 66, 69–70,
83, 84, 89–90, 93–94, 103, 106,
108–109, 128, 130, 138, 151,
157, 163, 223
history 6, 93,
jungle 140–145, 148, 153
Langbia, Rima 5, 7–12, 16–18, 28,
39, 65–66, 69, 74, 83, 89, 93,
102, 223
Palin 87–112, 124, 128–130, 138,
144, 147, 151–153, 157, 163,
185, 223,
Rocket 95, 112
Sha, Nani 144
Talle Valley 142, 151
tribes 6, 12, 93, 96, 144, 219,
Asian Development Bank 61–62
assessment (see also *monitoring*) 40, 68,
104, 128, 137–148, 151–156, 254
n. 42 & n. 46
needs assessment 8, 12, 126
vulnerability assessment 126
Asset Based Community Development
(ABCD) 40, 98, 110,

Barefoot Doctors see *China*
Bawtree, Victoria 33
Becker, Gary 83
Becker, Stan 68
Bennett, Lynn 238 n. 9
Bergrren, Gretchen 40
Bhopal (India) 4, 219
bricolage 13

bridges 12–13, 56–57
British East India Company 215
Bronx River Alliance 196
Bronx River Working Group 195
Bruntland Commission, the 36

camera traps 139–145, 151–154
carbon emissions 230 n. 7
Cardoso, Fernando 37
Carnegie, Andrew 39
Central Park Conservancy (New York) 195
Chambers, Robert 40, 44, 132, 154,
    179–180, 251 n. 21
chaordic 112
Chathanatt, John 213
Chien, Chun-Wuei Su 161
child mortality 7, 67–68, 82–83, 85, 128,
    135, 200, 245 n. 12
    childhood pneumonia (diagnosis) 234
        n. 6, 250 n. 15
child nutrition 26, 147, 244 n. 7,
    249 n. 26
China xii, xv, xxi, 29, 35, 39, 49, 52–53,
    55, 61, 93, 106, 109, 157–186,
    187, 202–210
    Barefoot Doctors 174, 202–203
    Great Leap Forward 202
    Green Long March xxi, 187, 202–210
    MDGs in 233 n. 2
    Model Counties Project 203
    Long March 201–202
    Tibet Autonomous Region of,
        see Tibet
cholera 87–89, 93–94, 99, 110, 151, 153,
    243 n. 18
cities 14–15, 22, 30, 44,58, 80, 113–114,
    190–191, 199, 208, 231 n. 9, 244
    n. 5, 253 n. 32 see also New York
    City; Afghanistan – Kabul; and
    slums
climate change xi–xii, 27, 36, 148, 172
    188–189, 208, 210, 240 n. 13
    Copenhagen Conference 148
    United Nations Panel on 36
clouded leopard 139–140, 142–145, 148,
    151–153, 184, 248 n. 20
Coady, Moses 38
Cold War, the 34–35
Collier, Paul 33
community (defined) xvi–xvii, 79, 100,
    243 (participation) 236 n. 46

community as target, resource, location,
    or agent 61, 132, 159, 239 n. 17,
    246 n. 13
complex adaptive systems xx, 9–10,
    16–21, 31, 34, 37, 41–43, 53, 76,
    85, 103–104, 107–111, 159, 172,
    206, 228
    contrasted with command-and-
        control systems 232 n. 26
Congress Party (India) 219
Conjunto Palmeira (Brazil) 15
conservation xvii, xxi, 60, 109, 111, 139,
    143, 157, 160–186, 187, 189, 190,
    192–198, 202–207
    history 247 n. 12, 252 n. 7–8
    see also wildlife and Qomolangma
        National Nature Preserve
        (QNNP)
Clark, Gregory 32, 47, 235 n. 19
Cleveland, Harlan 15
Green Long March see China
cultural capital 11
currency, local 232 n. 12

Dalai Lama 52
dalits 217, 219
Davis, Mike 231 n. 10
dialectic 102, 172
Dichter, Thomas 32
digital divide 36
Digital Opportunity Index (DOI) 201

Easterly, William 29, 31, 188
ecotourism 46, 57–61, 64, 101, 151
education xv, 7, 12, 16, 21–22, 26, 39, 41,
    46, 48–50, 66–69, 82–83, 94, 96,
    104, 111, 116, 122, 124, 128, 132,
    134, 150–151, 169–170, 176–178,
    181–182, 185, 200, 202–203
Einstein, Albert xiv, 82, 85, 225
Ekbladh, David 19
emergence xx, 10, 17–21, 57–58, 65–67,
    76–78, 80–81, 87, 92, 107, 122,
    208, 242 n. 2
Empire xiii–xv, xvii, 48, 70, 110, 124,
    188, 211–225, 243 n. 15
empowerment xiv–xxi, 4, 8, 23, 27,
    37–44, 76, 82–83, 95, 108,
    144–147, 155, 169, 174, 208,
    211–212, 215, 223–225, 236 n. 51
Evans, Peter 37

Everest, Mt. xv, xxi, 58, 60, 163–168,
170, 183, 186
mountaineering on 164, 166, 180
see also *Qomolangma National Nature
Preserve (QNNP)*
Evidence-based decisionmaking 21, 61,
90, 103–105, 109, 115, 130, 137,
170, 221, 231 n. 4
equity xxi, 137, 145–148, 152–153, 156,
195, 217, 265, 229 n. 2
surveillance for 148
experimentation xvi, 95, 123, 127, 139,
159, 170, 173, 176–177, 188, 203,
210, 226

Fanon, Frantz 256 n. 12
feedback loops (defined) 240 n. 13
Ford Foundation 40
fractals 18, 54, 177
Freire, Paulo 37
Friedman, Benjamin 36
Future Generations 87, 94
Future Generations Afghanistan
68, 116
Future Generations Arunachal 96,
107, 111

Gandhi, Indira 49
Gandhi, Mohandas K. xiv–xv, xvii, 53,
92, 110, 115, 123, 188, 209,
211–229
Gandhi, Rajiv 219
Ghani, Ashraf 72
Gini Coefficient 35–36, 201
going to scale xviii, 23, 90, 157–160,
171–186, 187–189
Google Earth 144
Gladwell, Malcom 172
Grant, James xiv, 157, 160
Grameen Bank 201, 251 n. 23
grassroots xvii, 4, 8, 30, 41, 95, 179,
181, 188
great divergence, the 47,
Great Leap Forward see *China*
gross domestic product (GDP) 26, 201
gross national product (GNP) 14, 34–35,
137, 200

Hardt, Michael 188, 211, 243 n. 15,
255 n. 1
Hawken, Paul 44, 188, 251 n. 3

Heraclitus 114
Hoboken Community Boathouse 190
Holism xxi, 145–146, 150–153, 156
Holland, John 9–10, 65, 243 n. 17
human capital 34
Human Development Index 35, 201
human energy xi–xiv, xvi, xx, 5, 14–15,
23, 31, 42, 60–66, 70, 76–84, 97,
110, 113, 116, 121, 155, 172, 185,
195, 199, 205, 207–209, 212, 222,
224–229, 239 n. 7, 240 n. 12 & n.
17, 241 n. 18, 256–57 n. 12

Industrial Revolution, the 47, 230 n. 9,
235 n. 19
interdependence xxi, 63,83, 106,
145–146, 149–150, 152–153, 156
International Development Research
Centre (Canada) 141
iteration xxi, 32, 74, 77–78, 131–135,
145–146, 151–154, 156, 186, 200,
208, 224

Jacobs, Garry 15
Jacobs, Jane 231 n. 9, 253 n. 32
Jackson, Tim 147
Jamkhed (India), Comprehensive Rural
Health Project 95, 245 n. 8
Jia, L.J. 205
Jintao, Hu 162, 183
Johnson, Stephen 87, 190–191, 208

key indicators 141–156, 247 n. 16
Keynes, John Maynard 25, 34, 141
Keynes, John Neville 141
khadi xv, 214–216, 220, 225, 227,
256 n. 11
Khandker, Shahidur 137
Korten, David 19–20,
Kretzmann, Jody 40
Kristoff, Nick 91
Kruger National Park (South Africa,
Mozambique, Zimbabwe) 194
Kumar, Somesh 138

Lancet, The 83, 158
Lao Tzu 120
Latour, Bruno 234 n. 14, 246 n. 8
Lévi-Strauss, Claude 13
Lewis, W. Arthur 34
Lincoln, Abraham 38–39

Local Coordinating Committee xxi,
117–123, 130–131, 133–134
lokniti 225–226
Lot Quality Assurance Sampling (LQAS)
68, 84

Mahler, Halfdan 28–29
Marglin, Stephen xvi
Marx, Karl 209
McKnight, John 40
measurement *see monitoring*
Metropolitan Waterfront Alliance
(New York) 198
Millennium Development Goals (MDGs)
25–31, 54 92, 152, 158, 233 n. 3
Millennium Development Villages 177,
234 n. 10
modernism
aesthetic 13
high-modernist ideology 30, 232 n.
17, 253 n. 22, 257 n. 15
Mohanty, Chandra 91
monitoring 33, 66–70, 84–85, 104, 131,
137–156, 177, 196, 200
see also *self-evaluation*; key *indicators*;
assessment; and *evidence*
Moses, Robert 192, 195, 199, 253 n. 22
Moya, Dambisa 32

Nankani, Gobin 35
Narayan, Deepa 41
National Geographic Magazine
143–144, 151
needs-analysis,see *assessment*
Negri, Antonio 188, 211, 243 n. 15,
255 n. 1
Nehru, Jawaharlal 30, 219–220, 256 n.
8, 257 n. 15–16
Nepal xx, 32, 45–64, 66, 70, 74, 76, 101,
105, 112, 147–148, 163, 166, 194,
199
Kathmandu Guest House 58, 239 n. 15
Gautam, Omkar Prasad 56, 238 n. 13
Gurkhas 48, 57, 237 n. 7
Maoists 50, 54–55
Rana (family) 48–49, 238 n. 11
regicide 55–56,
Shah, Birendra (king) 45, 49, 54–55,
62, 238 n. 8, 238 n. 10
Shah, Dipendra (crown prince)
55–56, 238 n. 12

Shah, Gyanendra (king) 55–56, 60,
Shah, Mahendra (king) 48
Sherpas 238 n. 14
trekking (see *ecotourism*)
Tribhuvan (king) 48
New York Times 91
New York City xii, xxi, 25,109–110, 187,
190–200, 207, 210, 225
Parks Department 196
PlaNYC 197, 252 n. 12, 253 n. 35
New Yorkers for Parks 196
Newton, Isaac 66, 80–82
Nonaligned Nations 49
North East Frontier Agency (NEFA) see
Arunachal Pradesh, history

Olmstead, Frederick Law 191–192
operations research 248 n. 17
oral rehydration therapy 83, 87–88, 107,
138, 167, 175, 245 n. 12

Panchayati Raj (73rd Amendment to
Indian Constitution) 53, 94, 102,
127, 219, 242 n. 11
Participatory Research and Action (PRA)
see *Participatory Rural Appraisals*
Participatory Rural Appraisals (PRA) 40,
110, 128, 138, 141, 247 n. 15
Partition (India and Pakistan) 218, 220
Patton, Carl 137
Peace Corps 48
Pendeba 164, 167–170, 174–175,
183–185
Perkins, John 32
pilot projects 19, 181
Polak, Paul 32
population growth 31, 36, 190–192,
229 n. 2, 5 & 6, 242 n. 14
Positive Deviance 40, 98, 127, 130
poverty xii, xv, 6, 12, 20, 22, 26, 29, 32,
45–46, 91, 94, 99, 109–110, 139,
141, 150, 154, 201, 203, 212, 215,
217, 219–223, 257 n. 18
absolute poverty 229 n. 6
pregnancy 67–69, 84, 107, 128
Prigogine, Ilya 187, 208
Progress out of Poverty Indicator
(PPI) 201

Qomolangma National Nature Preserve
(QNNP) 162–186, 194

Rahema, Majid 33
Rao, Vijayendra 36
Rapid Assessment Procedures (RAP) 40
Rapid Rural Appraisals (RRA) 40
Reagan, Ronald 226
Reid, Herbert 191, 230 n. 14
revolution of rising aspirations xvi,
    22–23, 70, 101, 159, 172–173,
    233 n. 30
revolution of rising expectations 22
roads 61–64
Rodrik, Dani 32, 202
Rostow, W. W. 34
Ruskin, John xi, xiii–xiv, xvii, 15, 17,219,
    221, 258 n. 23

Sachs, Jeffrey 29–31, 234 n. 11
sarvodaya 219–220, 223
satyagraha 226
Scott, James C. 30, 137, 232 n. 17, 244
    n. 5, 246 n. 2, 251 n. 5, 253 n. 22
SEED-SCALE (defined) xviii, 265
    Dimensions of SCALE 159–160,
        172–180
        SCALE One 174–176
        SCALE Squared 176–178
        SCALE Cubed 178–180
    Five Criteria 137, 145
    Four Principles 20, 90, 97–112
    Seven Tasks 113, 117–119, 121–136
    SCALE as analytical framework
        200–202
self-evaluation xxi, xviii, 105, 127, 130,
    134, 137–156, 181, 213,
    247 n. 14
Sen, Amartya xv, 36, 92, 217
Serres, Michel xiii,
Shirky, Clay 234 n. 8, 240 n. 8
Shultz, Theodore 34
Sinha, Indra 4
    Animal's People (novel) 4, 15
slums 3, 14–15, 76–77, 99, 113–114,
    121, 231 n. 9–10
Snow, John 243 n. 18
Society for Education Action and
    Research in Community Health
    (SEARCH), Gadchiiroli (India) 177,
    258 n. 21
Stengers, Isabelle 208
South Commission, the 37
Surveillance for Success 127

sustainability xxi, 26, 65, 98, 145–146,
    148–149, 152–153, 156, 185
    sustainable development 36,
        148–149, 169
swadeshi 214
swaraj 212–213, 215–216, 221, 223,
    256 n. 4

Taylor, Betsy 179, 191, 230 n. 14
Thapa, Rita 147–148
Thatcher, Margaret 226
Tibet Autonomous Region (China) viii, 6,
    25, 46, 52, 59–60, 108–109, 157,
    160–186, 189,194, 199, 202–203,
    207, 225 see also Qomolangma
    National Nature Preserve and
    Pendeba
Tocqueville, Alexis de 38
total quality management 110

umbrella species, see key indicators
underdevelopment xvii
United Nations xix, 26, 36, 48, 55,
    149–150, 169, 178, 209
    Human Development Report 149
    UNESCO 201
    UNICEF xiv, 157–158, 160, 197, 203
United States of America 48, 52, 54–55,
    61, 75, 93, 108–109, 147, 164,
    170, 184, 198, 222
    Agency for International
        Development (USAID) 46, 49,
        54–55, 237 n. 4
    Army Corps of Engineers 196
    National Parks 189, 194

Vaux, Calvert 191–192

Walton, Michael 36
Ward, Barbara 43–44
Washington Consensus 35, 217
Whitman, Walt 191
wildlife 52, 60, 139, 164–165, 183, 198
    see alsoconservation; clouded
    leopard; and key indicators
Women's Action Groups (or "Women's
    Workshops") 7, 66–67, 69, 82,
    84–85, 94–96, 242 n. 4
Wordsworth, William 75, 252 n. 7
workplans 94–95, 118–119, 128–133,
    138, 151–152, 227

World Bank 27, 30, 33, 35, 37, 40–41, 61–62, 66, 101, 137, 150, 155, 201

World Health Organization (WHO) 28–29, 107

World National Parks Congress (Bali, Indonesia) 189

Worldwide Governance Indicators (WGI) 201

Xiaoping, Deng 169, 203, 226

Yellowstone to Yukon (U.S. and Canada) 194

Yen, Jimmy 39

Zedong, Mao 49, 54, 202, 205, 222